Confederate Finance and Purchasing in Great Britain

Confederate Finance and Purchasing in Great Britain

Richard I. Lester

University Press of Virginia
Charlottesville

THE UNIVERSITY PRESS OF VIRGINIA

First Published 1975

Library of Congress Cataloging in Publication Data

Lester, Richard I 1930–
Confederate finance and purchasing in Great Britain.

Bibliography: p.
1. Finance, Public—Confederate States of America. 2. United States—History—Civil War, 1861–1865—Finance, commerce, confiscations, etc.—Confederate. 3. Confederate States of America—Foreign economic relations—Great Britain. 4. Great Britain—Foreign economic relations—Confederate States of America.
I. Title.
HJ254.L47 973.7′1 74–13916 ISBN 0–8139–0513–3

Printed in the United States of America

To

Christel, Christine, Stephen,

Rachel, and Mother

PREFACE

THE ORIGINAL MANUSCRIPT of this book was written in England between 1958 and 1961. However, due to administrative responsibilities, the work lay dormant until only recently, when some effort was made to revise it. Despite the impressive amount and high quality of literature written about the American Civil War before and since the centennial, the original manuscript was resurrected with the hope that it could in some small measure add yet another chapter to that ever fascinating story of Confederate operations abroad.

Previously published works dealing with the finance and purchase operations of the Confederacy in Europe have usually concentrated on only one or two aspects of this subject. Some have centered their story on the workings of "King Cotton," or on the financial experiments of the South in relation to the flotation of loans; others have considered the Confederate purchasing agents and their trials and conflicts both with agents of the United States and among themselves, or the mechanics of importation and the romance of blockade-running.

However, to understand more fully the significance and impact of Confederate finance and purchasing particularly in Great Britain and its importance to the war at large, it is helpful to relate financial policy directly to purchasing operations and also to consider the actual material imported, its quantity and quality, and the extent to which it met the military needs of the Confederacy.

Thus the primary objective of this work is to present, insofar as possible, while making maximum use of British sources, an analysis of Confederate finance and purchasing operations in Great Britain and to show how these negotiations and transactions and their accompanying legal ramifications affected the course of the Civil War. A good proportion of these operations concerns finance. As some very astute modern students of the Confederacy have demonstrated, this subject cannot be avoided. It touches the entire Confederate experience; limitations of money severely restricted the overall Southern war effort both overseas and at home. The basic weakness of Confederate finance is clearly shown in the reduced purchasing power of Confederate money in Great Britain at various periods of the war.

In the opinion of this writer, most students of the war have tended to underestimate the importance of Confederate financial and procurement operations in Great Britain. In 1861 the wealth of the South consisted chiefly of land and slaves; it was an agricultural community, poor in industrial and manufacturing resources. Its means of transport were far behind those of the North, and its cities, with the exception of Charleston and New Orleans, were of comparatively slight importance as trade centers. The states against which the Confederates waged war comprised roughly two-thirds of the country's population. The resources of the North were far superior to those of the South, and this superiority finally prevailed. To a significant degree, then, the South was able to sustain a war lasting four years largely because of the energetic activities of a small band of men in Europe, who labored continuously to supply the needs of the Southern military machine. This study emphasizes that Confederate finance and purchasing agents in Great Britain played an important, if relatively inconspicuous, role in the struggle for Southern independence. Southern troops were valiant fighters and, in the main, were well led, but they could not fight without arms or supplies, and Southern arsenals and manufacturers could not possibly meet all their demands. This book points up the chronic and acute scarcity of all types of Southern war material and the pressing need to import as much equipment as possible, including ships. The Confederate government, rapidly organized, was quick to appreciate the situation; early in the war it had dispatched its finance and procurement agents to Europe, and especially to Great Britain.

From the outset the Confederate representatives were faced with a delicate task. Great Britain, then the leading industrial power in the world, was obviously the most likely source of supplies and finance; it was also the champion of free trade. But the majority of English people were opposed to slavery, so that it was necessary to avoid the slavery issue and concentrate on free trade. Of all the European powers the Confederates looked to Great Britain for sympathy and assistance. Thus the primary need was to establish good public relations between Great Britain and the Confederate states. In this the South succeeded, quickly laying the foundations of an entente which, although subject to fluctuations, served admirably as a basis for four years of trade and financial cooperation.

An analysis of Anglo-Confederate commercial relations such as this book attempts leads to an appreciation of the Civil War, not just as a localized conflict between opposing states, but in its world setting. The Civil War may be considered as the last of the old wars and the first of the new. Operations in the field were in the main conventional, but the strategy of the Confederates in seeking aid abroad represented, in the persistent manner in which it was applied, a new chapter in international affairs. Naturally the Confederates hoped for official recognition of their government by Great Britain and even for armed intervention; in these objectives they failed. But it is a tribute to their perserverance that, although unrecognized, the Confederate agents in Great Britain helped to sustain the Confederate forces for as long as they did. In effect they were able to do so much with so little.

The "global" impact of the Civil War may be judged by the effect it had on the people of Great Britain: it divided the nation and its classes as no previous foreign conflict had done. In the main the upper classes tended to be pro-Southern; the middle and working classes, pro-Northern. The English aristocracy saw in the uprising of the South a possible chance to divide the United States, whose democratic practices they questioned; the middle and working classes viewed the struggle as an opportunity to overthrow slavery. The British government was in a quandary: should it allow the upper class to dictate their policy? Would the federal blockade of cotton supplies necessitate intervention as a defensive measure? This book attempts to touch upon some of these questions.

It might be said that the American Civil War was the first great conflict begotten of the Industrial Revolution, and as I shall show, it sprang in large measure from economic causes and was supported in part by Great Britain's need as a great power to trade freely and widely. British dependence on cotton supplies and the South's poverty of industrial resources gave the Civil War economic stresses absent from most previous conflicts of similar magnitude.

A study of Confederate purchasing in Great Britain throws into relief other aspects of this first of the new wars. Before the 1850s the design and manufacture of armaments had been static for many years. Cannon, for example, had changed little since the previous century. Then the advent of the Industrial Revolution and the evolution of steam power made it possible to manufacture weapons of much greater power and precision. The rifled barrel, the invention of breech-loading instead of muzzle-loading cannon, and many other improvements followed in close succession. Rifling, for example, was in its infancy at the outbreak of the Crimean War, where rifled guns were used in action with a varying degree of success. Ten years later British armament manufacturers, having profited by the experience gained in the Crimea, were able to supply North and South with ordnance more accurate and deadly than the world had ever seen. Thus the American Civil War was the first major conflict in which modern weapons were used to any extent, and these new weapons clearly indicated the flaws in traditional strategy. For many years after the last echo of the last gun had died away, military strategists were pondering the lessons to be learned from the Civil War and were devising the new tactics necessitated by the great advances in technology and naval power. In this connection I have attempted to bring new respect for technical matters relating to military hardware of the nineteenth century. Although there have been exceptions, historians rarely have had a sufficient grasp of technical matters to win the respect of military analysts. This book, within limits, also considers the technical features of the military equipment procured in Great Britain by the Confederate purchasing agents.

To sum up, it is difficult to reach a complete understanding of the Civil War without a thorough study of Confederate finance and purchasing in Great Britain. The war was not only fought on the battle fields of the North and South; it was also waged in the streets of London, Liverpool, Manchester, and Glasgow by men who may never have heard a shot fired but who made it possible for the South to sustain its cause for years instead of months. It is difficult to overestimate the importance of Confederate commercial activities in Great Britain, and it is possible that if the war had been fought merely as an American conflict, it would have ended within a year to eighteen months.

I hope that this study and future efforts of this nature will contribute to a more comprehensive account of the larger overseas Confederate experience.

This book could not have been written without the special guidance of Marcus Cunliffe, Dr. M. A. Jones, and Harry Allen. For information, help, and advice I am indebted to a great many people and institutions. Among them: James Ainsley, secretary, Manchester Chamber of Commerce, Sir Lindon Andrews, editor, *Yorkshire Post,* Leeds; C. R. Ball, publicity manager, Royal Insurance Company Ltd., Liverpool; Madame Colletee Barichou, Valleguif, Paris; Captain Jack Bauer, U.S.N., Washington, D.C.; C. W. Black, city librarian, the Mitchell Library, Glasgow; Frederick G. Blair, F.S.A., librarian, The Athenaeum, Liverpool; Eric G. Braelsford, Leeds, Yorkshire; Peter A. Brannon, director, State of Alabama, Department of Archives and History, Montgomery, Ala.; A. E. Bristen, Home Office, London; Clara Mae Brown, reference librarian, Joint University Libraries, Nashville, Tenn.; H. D. Brown, John Brown & Co., Ltd., Clydebank; A. S. E. Browning, curator of technology, Glasgow Museums & Art Galleries, Glasgow; B. H. Campbell, Glasgow University; T. M. Cass, Liverpool Orphanage, Liverpool; Rear Adm. Robert W. Cavenagh, U.S.N., naval attaché, U.S. embassy, London; G. Chandler, F.L.A., F. R. Hist. S., F.R.S.A., city librarian, City of Liverpool Public Libraries; Professor S. G. Checkland, professor of economic history, Glasgow University; R. Clutton, manager, Toby Caulfield, managing director, and R. Weisweiller, chief dealer, Foreign Exchange Department, Henry Schroder & Co., Ltd., London; R. M. Corlis, B. F. Stevens and Brown Ltd., American library and fine art agents, London; Dr. B. R. Crick, British Association for American Studies, London; Charles A. Davis, former dean of the faculties, Florida State University, Tallahassee, Fla.; J. E. Deyes, secretary, Martins Bank Ltd., Liverpool; George Dickinson, editor, *Sea Breezes,* Liverpool; William A. Dunn, editor, press section, U.S. Information Service, London; Rear Adm. E. M. Eller, U.S.N., naval historian, Washington, D.C.; C. H. Faulkner, agent, Cotton Exchange, Liverpool; J. Firmin, managing director, Firmin & Sons Ltd., London; John F. Ford, Jr., numismatist, Rockville Center, Long Island, N.Y.; C. G. Gascoin, Records Branch, Companies Registration Office, Bush House, London; Douglas Gilliat, director, Gilliat & Co., London; Baron de Gerlache de Gomery, ambassade de Beligique, London; Victor Gondos, Jr., archivist in charge Civil War branch, Francis J. Heppner, Civil War branch, and Legare H. B. Obean, chief of Loan Division, Library of Congress, Washington, D.C.; Professor A. Goodwin, Dr. W. O. Henderson, and Dr. W. H. Chaloner, University of Manchester; the late T. W. Green, research secretary, Confederate Research Club, Southampton; A. H. Hall, managing director, Corbett & Dixon Ltd., London; C. B. Hall, manager, Barclays Bank Ltd., Liverpool; D. Howard Halliday, F.L.A., chief librarian, County Borough of Northampton; Higley Halliday, M.R.I.N.A., M.I.A.E., M.I. Mech. E., F.R.G.S., engineer, London; W. G. Hanlon, chief agent, Liverpool Conservative Association; Brigadier O. F. G. Hogg, C.B.E., F.S.A., Greenwich; Hope K. Holdeamper, fiscal branch, General Records Division, National Archives and Records Service, Washington, D.C.; Professor F. E. Hyde, Department of Economics, University of Liverpool; J. H. Iliffe, O.B.E., director, City of Liverpool Public Museums; Rupert C. Jarvis, F.S.A.F.R., librarian, H. M. Customs & Excise, King's Bream House, London; E. Jeffcott, reference librarian, Metropolitan Borough of Saint Pancras Public Libraries, London; Robert W. Johnson, managing director, Cammell Laird & Co. (Shipbuilders and Engineers), Ltd., Birkenhead; George P. Kaye, late lieutenant R.N., F.R.G.S., Gillingham, Dorsetshire; D. W. King, librarian, the War Office, London; D. Laird, Herefordshire; Robert H. Land, acting chief, Manuscript Division, and David C. Mearns, chief, Manuscript Division, Library of Congress, Washington, D.C.; J. B. Leather, Liverpool; J. C. Maclagan, managing director, Greenwood and Batley Ltd., Albion Works, Leeds; H. S. Magnoy, director of education, College of Technology, Liverpool; Hilda M. McGill, librarian, Great Hall, Manchester Public Libraries; Taylor Milne, secretary and librarian, and William Kellaway, assistant librarian, Institute of Historical Research, University of London; Rear Adm. Samuel E. Morison, U.S.N.; the Countess Mountbatten of Burma, C.I., G.B.E., D.C.V.O., London; Sir John S. Muirhead, Glasgow; Matthew Neil, secretary, Glasgow Chamber of Commerce; Allan Novick, USAFI, Madison, Wis.; Harriet C. Owsley (Mrs. Frank L.), senior archivist, Manuscript Division, Tennessee State Library and Archives, Nashville; Susan Parisi, USAFI, Madison, Wis.; Milton F. Perry, curator, Harry S. Truman Library, Independence, Mo.; J.H.P. Pifford, Goldsmith's Librarian, University of London; A. J. Quiggin, Liverpool; D. S. Ramsay, cashier, Erlangers Ltd., London; Howard C. Rice, Jr., chief, Rare Books and Special Collections, Princeton University Library, R. Riley, deputy editor, Share & Loan Department, the Stock Exchange, London; Mrs. T. D. Robinson, Mowhawk, N.Y.; Lilian de Ros, secretary, J. D. Scott Vickers Ltd., London; W. G. Sanders, G. B. Gaunt & Son Ltd., Birmingham; L. H. Sawyer and G. L. Newman, Thomas De La Rue & Company Ltd., London; Professor Louis M. Sears, Washington, D.C.; V. H. Simms, London; C. Songster, publicity officer, Fawcett, Preston & Company Ltd., Bromborough, Cheshire; Robert E. Stocking, assistant in manuscripts, University of Virginia Library, Charlottesville; H. Taylor, archivist, Liverpool Record Office, Liverpool; C. K. Thompson, director, Attree & Kent Ltd., Brighton; Professor Frank E. Vandiver, the Rice Institute, Houston, Tex.; A. H. Waite, deputy curator of models and relics, National Maritime Museum, London; Arnold Wilson, Henry Young & Sons, Liverpool; Leslie Wilson, London; H. Wright, director, Smith and Wright Ltd., Birmingham; K. Young, district registrar, High Court of Justice, Liverpool.

CONTENTS

Part I

HOW THE CONFEDERATES FINANCED THEIR PURCHASES

CHAPTER I

THE CONFEDERACY USES COTTON AS A BASIS FOR CREDIT

THE ECONOMIC RELATIONSHIP between the North and the South in the 1850s, which resulted in an uncompromising and uncontrolled egocentric Southern sectionalism, was one of the principal reasons for the outbreak of the American Civil War.[1] It has been suggested frequently that the South was compelled to secede from the Union because of the election of Lincoln in 1860. However, a significant incentive to secession was the slow erosion of the Southern economy and its growing reliance upon the economic power of the North. In effect, the South was in revolt against a financial system upon which it relied to buy and sell its produce, but which in times of stress created an artificial and degrading depression amid the abundance of nature.[2] At the beginning of the war Southern indebtedness to the North amounted to $400 million, and it was the Northern banks that were financing the cotton crop each year. It might be said, not unfairly, that before the war the North took ample profits from Southern wealth, and it might also be argued that the South was subject to the power of Northern banks.[3] As Jefferson Davis contended, the war was not brought on by a single cause but was the result of a long series of irritations between two sections of a population with directly opposed economic and social systems.[4] In

[1] Paul M. Angle, *The American Story* (Great Neck, N.Y.: Channel Press, 1956), p. 193; *Times* (London), 24 Dec. 1862; Frank E. Vandiver, "Some Problems Involved in Writing Confederate History," *Journal of Southern History* 36, no. 3 (1970): 401, 405; *The South, Old and New Frontiers: Selected Essays of Frank Lawrence Owsley*, ed. Harriet Chappell Owsley (Athens: University of Georgia Press, 1969).

[2] *Bankers' Magazine: Journal of the Money Market and Commercial Digest* (London), 1861, pp. 17–18. For the withdrawal of Southern bank balances from Northern banks, see James B. Walker, *The Epic of American Industry* (New York: Harper & Brothers, 1949), p. 151; *Georgia Messenger*, 22 Nov. 1862.

[3] John C. Schwab, *The Confederate States of America, 1861–1865: A Financial and Industrial History of the South during the Civil War* (New York: Scribner's, 1901), pp. 3, 249.

[4] Harold U. Faulkner and Tyler Kepner, *America, Its History and People* (New York: McGraw-Hill, 1947), pp. 256–57. Historians still debate the reasons for the war. Said James Ford Rhodes, "It may be safely asserted that

secession the South sought economic freedom, a chance to exploit its wealth in the form of the cotton crop, which was in great demand in the industrialized countries.[5] By the 1850s British textile machinery had become so efficient that it produced cloth cheaply enough to be sold profitably to the poverty-stricken millions of Asia and Africa. The resulting demand for raw cotton brought prosperity to the Deep South. Not until the middle of the twentieth century did the South again reach the prosperity it enjoyed in the 1850s. The production of cotton during this period broke all previous records. As new plantations were cleared in Mississippi, Louisiana, Arkansas, and Texas, the yield rose from under 2 million bales in 1849 to 4,540,000 bales in 1859. Seven-eighths of the world's supply of cotton came from the United States, and raw cotton comprised three-fifths of American exports.[6] The South felt, with some justice, that the North had fastened on its wealth and was exploiting it to the South's detriment.

But the very reason for its desire for economic freedom, for an escape from what the South believed to be unjust exploitation of its resources, meant that the Confederate States necessarily lacked any basic financial structure that could support them as an independent nation; their deficiency also meant that they had to wage war against an enemy incomparably better endowed with industrial resources.

The South was not a society of bankers or industrialists but an agricultural area whose principal source of wealth was cotton exports.[7] Its diplomatic and financial policy both before and during the early years of the war was based on the dependence of Great Britain, France, and the Northern states of the Union on an uninter-

---

there was a single cause, slavery." Another interpretation was made popular by Charles Beard, who said that the war resulted from the conflict between the interests of "northern capitalists and free farmers" and those of the planting aristocracy of the South. A more recent interpretation, widely supported, is that it was a needless war, caused less by rival economic interests or disputes over the rights of slaveowners than by popular hysteria whipped by "irresponsible leadership."

[5] It can, of course, be argued that most historical work indeed cannot help being relevant to economic development. James L. Sellers, "The Economic Incidence of the Civil War in the South," *Mississippi Valley Historical Review* 14 (1928):179–91.

[6] Henry W. Bragdon and Samuel P. McCutchen, *History of a Free People* (New York: Macmillan, 1954), p. 294.

[7] Frank L. Owsley, *King Cotton Diplomacy*, 2d ed. rev. by Harriet Chappell Owsley (Chicago: University of Chicago Press, 1959), p. 1. See also Henry Ashworth, "Cotton: Its Cultivation, Manufacture and Use," a paper read before the Society of Arts, London, 10 Mar. 1858.

rupted supply of cotton.[8] In seceding from the Union, the South looked to the power of cotton to coerce Great Britain and France to support its cause.[9]

It was true that Great Britain, then the leading industrial power of the world, looked to American cotton to the extent of three-quarters to five-sixths of its total supply: in 1840 Great Britain had imported 487,856,504 pounds of cotton from the Southern states; by 1858 this figure had grown to 732,403,840 pounds.[10] Thus, reasoned the South, "Cotton is king," and this slogan, coined by David Christy and the title of the famous book to which he contributed, colored all Southern thinking.[11] It led Southerners to anticipate a war likely to last less than four months, instead of more than four years.[12] It led them also, in the early stages, at any rate, to embark upon the disastrous policy of withholding cotton in an attempt to secure the support of Great Britain and France against the North, instead of seeking to sell all they possibly could to bolster their shaky finances. This was the policy instituted by Jefferson Davis and supported by the majority of the Confederate States, although according to Mrs. Davis many opposed it from the first. That the opposition was not without significance is shown by the fact that the capable Alexander H. Stephens, the vice president, was a strong supporter of the policy of shipping cotton to Europe, where it could be stored with greater safety and provide funds to finance the war. Such a policy was also endorsed by Robert Toombs, first Confederate secretary of state.[13] It is probably true that the shipment of 200,000 bales of cot-

[8] *Bankers' Magazine* (1861, pp. 72–73) hoped that there would be peace in America yet recognized that war would give England a better balance of trade because England was importing twice as much as it was exporting to America.

[9] John Chapman, *The Cotton and Commerce of India Considered in Relation to the Interests of Great Britain* (London: G. Chapman, 1851), pp. 1–3; *Bankers' Magazine*, 1862, p. 705; John M. Blum et al., *The National Experience* (New York: Harcourt, Brace, 1968), p. 343.

[10] In 1860 England obtained 2,580,700 bales or about 80% of her total cotton supplies from the Southern states (W. O. Henderson, *The Lancashire Cotton Famine 1861–1865* [Manchester: Manchester University Press, 1934]), p. 35.

[11] *Cotton Is King and Pro-Slavery Arguments* . . . , ed. E. N. Elliott (Augusta, Ga.: Pritchard, Abbott, and Loomis, 1960).

[12] It is Frank Owsley's thesis that the year 1860 was an unpropitious one to choose for the final act of secession; that the South should have chosen a time when a cotton famine made their staple industry indispensable.

[13] *Bankers' Magazine*, 1862, p. 690. Alexander H. Stephens considered France and England jealous of the growth of the United States; therefore, they would be of little financial help (Henry Cleveland, *Alexander H. Stephens in Public and Private* [Philadelphia: National Publishing Co., 1866], p. 761). Confederate naval personnel maintained there were not enough vessels to carry out the cotton. The government also had no funds with which to make purchases

ton to Liverpool during the first year of the war would have strengthened Confederate finances immeasurably.

But the majority prevailed, and thus the Confederacy, in its very beginnings, was founded on a grave financial misconception of the true needs of the situation—a misconception not aided by the fact that the whole of the surplus had been taken by Europe, thus making an immediate famine impossible.

It is, however, easy to be wise after the event. In the late 1850s the South had excellent reasons for treating cotton as a major instrument of commercial negotiation. British reliance on American cotton has already been noted. Much of the financial and industrial prosperity of Great Britain depended on this import. In the twenty years preceding the war, strenuous efforts to escape from growing dependence on American cotton had been made, to no avail. The amount of Indian cotton available was limited, and it was far inferior to American cotton.[14] In taking up its position at the outbreak of the war, the Confederacy could look to a score of reports, hearings, and books, all emanating from Great Britain and all stressing British dependence on American cotton.[15] In 1851, out of a total export of £54 million, nearly £29 million was cotton fabric; in the same year it was estimated that five hundred thousand operatives were employed in the Lancashire cotton mills, while a further four hundred thousand were employed in subsidiary industries, and another one hundred fifty thousand depended for their livelihood on the prosperity of the cotton mills. It was thought that there were three dependents to every worker, thus giving a total of about four million people dependent upon the cotton industry out of a total population of approximately twenty-one million for the whole of Great Britain and Ireland.[16]

At the time few fully realized that the Confederate States were engaged in a struggle for their very existence; poor in the natural

(James M. Callahan, *Diplomatic History of the Southern Confederacy* [Baltimore: Johns Hopkins Press, 1901], pp. 88–90). Varena Howell Davis, *Memoirs of Jefferson Davis,* (New York: Appleton, 1881), 1:89; *Bankers' Magazine,* 1862, pp. 784, 90.

[14] *Times,* 20 June 1861; *Economist* (London), 19 July 1862.

[15] *Index* (London), 10 July 1862. "There is no article of commerce that passes through so many hands as cotton" (ibid., 31 July 1862).

[16] Chapman, pp. 1–3; Ashworth, pp. 6–7; Henry Hamilton, *The Industrial Revolution in Scotland* (Oxford: Clarendon Press, 1932), p. 10. On the question of the Lancashire cotton operatives' attitude toward the war, see Joseph M. Hernon, Jr., "British Sympathies in the American Civil War: A Reconsideration," *Journal of Southern History* 33, no. 3 (1967):363.

resources of war, they had to create a treasury and establish a revenue so that they could buy from Europe the armament and munitions they themselves could not produce.[17] Great Britain and France, although admittedly dependent on cotton, were strong and immensely wealthy, so that any crisis was bound to hit the South sooner and harder than it could affect Europe. Time was not on the side of the Confederates. Europe certainly needed cotton, but the Confederate need of foreign war supplies was even more urgent and vital.

On Christopher G. Memminger, first Confederate secretary of the treasury, fell the heavy responsibility of financing a nation at home and overseas—a nation without bullion or credit.[18] The situation was desperate indeed: in the beginning, the Treasury Department could not even issue its own bank notes, for it had neither bank notepaper nor an engraver. The first cash was obtained through the seizure of $718,294.08 in the federal customs houses and in branch mints at New Orleans and Charlotte.[19]

A year before the beginning of the war, on 13 January 1860, the *London Times* had reported that there was a sudden and severe stringency in the London money market and that Southern bankers were busily searching for finance, making inquiries among discount brokers "for money at any price." English banks were already calling in loans because of the unsettled situation in America;[20] later in the same month the Bank of England raised the bank rate from 2.5 percent to 3 percent.[21] During the whole of 1860 the danger of civil war had operated unfavorably against the South;

[17] Richard Cecil Todd, *Confederate Finance* (Athens: University of Georgia Press, 1954), p. 2; Henry D. Capers, *Life and Times of C. C. Memminger* (Richmond: Everett Waddey Co., 1893), p. 335; James D. Bulloch, *The Secret Service of the Confederate States in Europe*, 2 vols. (New York: Putnam, 1883), 1:100–101, 152–53.

[18] Of Memminger, Schwab says that "he had displayed no peculiar fitness for the position of organiser and head of the Confederate finances" (p. 4). Not only did Memminger display no peculiar fitness for his position, but he was not the president's first choice. The president would have preferred Toombs.

[19] Clement Eaton, *A History of the Southern Confederacy* (New York: Macmillan, 1954), p. 233.

[20] The movement was due chiefly to the calling in of a large number of loans by parties who had dividends or interest coupons to pay. The demand for money by the Southern banks caused a general though slight decline in stocks. Southern investment stock was higher on the sellers' option than for cash. The calling in of loans by English banks was the cause of this decline.

[21] Ibid., 20 Jan. 1860.

foreign investment was understandably wary.[22] On 14 December 1860 the *Economist* noted that the South "hopes to maintain the value of its notes in whatever quantity they can be issued by making them exchangeable on demand for an 8% stock" and went on to ask, "But who is to maintain the value of the stock?" This was a pertinent question that the Confederate Congress might well have pondered in view of its policy in relation to cotton, its only source of real wealth. In December 1860 the Southern cause was further hampered by the suspension of payments by several American banks and the refusal of credit by many Northern merchants.[23]

So the prime question that faced the men who organized the Confederacy at Montgomery on 8 February 1861 was, How can we finance our nation? The very urgency of need led Memminger to place first emphasis on loans.[24] On 28 February 1861 the Confederate Congress approved "an Act to raise money for the support of the Government and to provide for the defense of the Confederate States of America." [25] This act authorized the president of the Confederate States to borrow on their credit a sum not exceeding $15 million, bearing 8 percent interest, payable semiannually. Bonds were issued for ten years but could be redeemed by the government any time after five years upon giving three months' public notice.

[22] Ibid., 2 Feb. 1860. However, the *Times* (31 Jan.) declared that the American discount market had become much more easy and the rate of exchange had advanced to 108¾ to 109. A well-written pamphlet, *American Securities*, by Mann Cornhill, purported to guide and warn British investors with respect to Southern investments (ibid., 2 Feb. 1860). The South Carolina legislature considered a bill which proposed that the government issue bonds to the amount of $400,000 bearing interest at 6% payable annually on the pledge of the state. On the basis of this information Georgia and South Carolina bank notes were taken at 5% discount (ibid., 12 Nov., 13 Nov. 1860).

[23] *Times*, 7 Dec. 1860. Southern banks discounted to the amount of nearly $1 million, and the merchants were correspondingly relieved. The Boston banks proposed a discount to the extent of $5 million. In December the major suspensions took place in Washington, Richmond, Baltimore, Charleston, Norfolk, Portsmouth, Wheeling, Boston, Augusta, and Trenton (ibid. See also ibid., 29 Dec. 1860).

[24] Todd, p. 24. In January, the *Economist* reported, "The bearings on the English economy resulting from American dissension would affect the Liverpool Cotton Market" (21 Jan., 29 Jan. 1861). The Confederates hoped to secure loans in Liverpool and other English cities. Long before the war Liverpool firms financed the export of Southern agricultural produce (F. E. Hyde, School of Social Science and Administration, Department of Economics, University of Liverpool, to Richard Lester, 21 Feb. 1958).

[25] *The War of the Rebellion: A Compilation of the Official Records of the Union and Confederate Armies*, 130 vols. (Washington, D.C.: Government Printing Office, 1880–1901), ser. 4, 1:116–17 (cited hereafter as *O.R.*). See also ibid. pp. 147, 148–49, 164 for other acts.

The loan was to be supported by an export duty levied on cotton at the rate of one-eighth of 1 percent on all cotton in the raw state exported from the Confederacy, to be collected from 1 August 1861. The secretary of the treasury was authorized and required to establish a sinking fund to carry into effect this provision of the loan. It was also stipulated that the interest coupons, when due, should be received in payment of the export duty on cotton.

Memminger immediately began preparations for the sale of stocks and bonds, which were printed in denominations of $50, $100, $500, and $1,000. The loan was publicly announced on 16 March 1861. Books of subscription were opened in all the principal towns of the Confederacy.[26]

Meanwhile, the Constitution of the Confederate States became effective on 11 March. Article I, Section 8, gave Congress the power to levy and collect taxes, duties, imports, and excises for revenues necessary to maintain the government. The same section empowered it to borrow money on the credit of the Confederate States, to "regulate commerce with foreign nations, and among the several States and with the Indian tribes," and to raise and support an army and navy.[27]

In Great Britain, merchants, looking to the future, were concerned about the interruption of cotton supplies,[28] and on 5 April 1861 the *Times* reported that Lairds, the Birkenhead shipbuilders, and A. M. Weir, a London shipowner, had offered to raise in Great Britain half the sum necessary to secure the establishment of a direct line of steamships between Charleston and Liverpool, but nothing came of the proposal. It was also proposed that a joint-stock company should be formed in England under the British Limited Liability Act in which Southern shareholders would be placed on the same footing with all others. Another idea was to establish a weekly ferry line of steamships of 20,000 tons between Chesapeake Bay and Milford Haven, England. Supporters of the Southern cause in England believed that such an arrangement would ameliorate the commercial difficulties and strengthen the financial and political posture of the South. However, Northern supporters in England suspected such schemes to be a contemplated nucleus for a future Southern navy.[29]

Banks and commercial houses in the South subscribed liberally to the first Confederate loan.[30] In doing so, they lost much of their

[26] Gladstone Papers, box 6, 9 May 1861 (MSS Division, British Museum).

[27] *O.R.*, ser. 4, 1: 136–47. [28] *Bankers' Magazine*, 1862, p. 693.

[29] Herbert Wender, *Southern Commercial Conventions, 1837–59* (Baltimore: Johns Hopkins Press, 1930), pp. 183–84.

[30] *Times* (10 Apr. 1861).

specie within a few weeks of the beginning of the war. Most of this specie was shipped abroad to pay for purchases in Great Britain and on the Continent.[31] Although there was much enthusiasm and success for the loan in the Southern states,[32] it was received coolly in Europe. "It has nothing to recommend it to European consideration," stated the *Times* flatly.[33] There is some evidence in the Gladstone Papers (W. E. Gladstone was chancellor of the exchequer at this time. He became prime minister in 1868) to support the position taken by the *Times;* the credit of the Confederate government was defined or measured by its power to levy taxes and by the disposition of the people to pay them, "either of which in times of disturbance cannot be depended upon." [34]

In May 1861 the first purchasing agent of the War Department, the hardworking and successful Caleb Huse, arrived in Liverpool, and after reporting to Fraser, Trenholm and Company, the financial agent of the Confederacy, he began his investigations to secure the shipment of small arms.[35] By 30 September 1861 some $1.4 million had been sent to Huse to buy supplies. A few days after Huse's arrival in England, the Confederate Congress, aware that debts were already mounting heavily, authorized a loan of $50 million in bonds,

[31] Samuel B. Thompson, *Confederate Purchasing Operations Abroad* (Chapel Hill: University of North Carolina Press, 1935), pp. 49–50.

[32] The call was oversubscribed and not a single bid was made under par. *O.R.*, ser. 4, 1: 265.

[33] 10 Apr. 1861. Regarding the financial act of February 1861, the *Times* claimed: "There are some considerations that tend to destroy confidence in these bonds as investments. The Southern Confederacy is founded upon the right of disintegration. In theory there is no obligation in any member to continue a member of the Federation beyond its own pleasure. Who, then is to pay this debt when it matures, or who is to dissolve?" The *Times* concluded that the government of the United States was also in the market for a loan of $8 million and it could get what it wanted. See also the report of Chase's financial proposals that were compared with the Confederate proposals for securing funds in England (ibid., 17 Apr. 1861). By 20 April the *Times* reported that the cotton market was firm.

[34] Memorandum relative to the status of Confederate money in Great Britain. Gladstone Papers, box 6, 509: 67.

[35] Thompson, p. 14. Fraser, Trenholm & Company were the bankers or depositories of the Confederate government (*Official Records of the Union and Confederate Navies in the War of the Rebellion*, 31 vols. [Washington, D.C.: Government Printing Office, 1894–1927], ser. 3, 2:64 [cited hereafter as *O.R.N.*]).

The *Times* believed that the waste of material for modern warfare was such that America had to be supplied by importations. It suggested that England should trade with and finance America if need be—so long as the overall structure of such a policy would lead to advantage for England's economic strength (6 May 1861). For a general condition of the British money market in May 1861, see ibid., 15 May 1861.

payable at the expiration of twenty years from their date and bearing interest not exceeding 8 percent per annum, to be paid semiannually. These bonds, after public advertisement in three newspapers within the Confederate States, were to be sold for specie, military stores, or the proceeds of sales of raw produce or manufactured articles to be paid in the form of specie or with foreign exchange.[36] Memminger, having observed the scarcity of money in relation to the previous loan, also recommended, and Congress accepted, that treasury notes should be issued in anticipation of the revenue from the loan. At this point the need for funds was so great that Memminger was ready to cooperate in any measure designed to produce the desired result.[37]

A few days later, on 21 May, Congress authorized an act "to prohibit the exportation of cotton from the Confederate States except through sea-ports of the said States." [38] In the South many hoped that Great Britain and France, short of cotton, would put pressure on the North to come to terms.[39] The *Manchester Guardian* voiced the general opinion of the country when on 28 May it stated, "Of the various influences which are weighing upon the trade of the country, we believe that scarcely any has so much effect at the moment as the prevailing uncertainty respecting the future supplies of cotton." [40] Two months later the *Times* reported that the '61 cotton crop was being picked and in Georgia was very abundant.[41] But the

[36] *O.R.*, ser. 4, 1:328–29. [37] Ibid., p. 335.

[38] Ibid., pp. 338–39, 341–42.

[39] The mercantile letters from New York proved that although there had been little change in the political situation, there was a better feeling in the money market. The course of exchange in America on London for bills at sixty days' sight was 104½% to 105%, which, when compared with the par between the two countries, shows that the exchange was against England (*Times*, 22 May 1861; see also ibid., 27 May 1861).

[40] At this time cotton was still being shipped to Liverpool. T. C. Nelson, a member of the J. K. Gilliat firm (London) believed that the Civil War would not last long and that cotton would still be shipped through. This view was shared by many British businessmen (Nelson to George, 30 May 1861, Gilliat Papers [in possession of D. A. Gilliat, 10 Old Jewry, London]).

[41] 30 July 1861. Many planters of southwestern Georgia were engaged in picking, and the cotton crops of that section of the state were generally very abundant.

Statement of Receipts, Exports, and Stocks of Cotton

Year	*Receipts*	*Exports to Great Britain*
1860	3,636,701	2,174,331
1859	4,555,271	2,657,657

(William H. Russell, *My Diary North and South*, 2 vols. [London: Bradbury & Evans, 1863], 1:423.)

Confederate press was still vociferous for the economic coercion of Europe by a cotton embargo and believed that only a few months' pressure would be necessary to make Great Britain and France active allies of the Confederacy.[42]

The new loan, like its predecessor, was aimed at acquiring specie, but whereas the first one had been directed primarily toward bankers and commercial interests, the $50 million issue was more specifically offered to the attention of planters and farmers who could respond, not by money, which was scarce, but by produce—cotton, tobacco, and so on.[43]

By autumn of 1861 Great Britain's reserves of cotton were beginning to dwindle, in spite of the good crop the year before. Three months earlier Consul Bunch at Charleston had reported to Lord John Russell, the foreign secretary, that although the '61 crop would be around 4 million bales, the planters would part with none of their produce until the blockade was raised.[44] By October cotton prices in Great Britain ranged from fifteen to twenty-two cents per pound "with not enough to last, if the usual amount is consumed, till the middle of December. Manufacturers are working but little more than half time, and paying diminished wages to labourers." [45] On 18 October the *Manchester Guardian* reported a public meeting in Birmingham "for the purpose of considering the effects of the cotton famine on Manchester and Birmingham industries, the best method of procuring a supply of cotton, and the opportunity the crisis affords of annihilating the slave trade by establishing the cotton industry in Africa." [46] Six days later the *Manchester Guardian* quoted the *Times* as saying: "We have felt the beginning of the

[42] Owsley, *King Cotton Diplomacy*, p. 28.

[43] J. C. Schwab, "The Financier of the Confederate States," *Yale Review* 2 (1893): 288, 301. See also Capers, p. 604.

[44] Great Britain, Foreign Office Papers, vol. 781, 23 July 1861; *Times*, 22 Dec. 1862.

[45] James D. Richardson, ed., *Messages and Papers of Jefferson Davis and the Confederacy*, 2 vols. (Washington, D.C.: Washington Post Co., 1905), 2:99–102 (cited hereafter as Richardson). The *Manchester Guardian* (9 Oct. 1861) claimed that the demand for cloth and yarn was insufficient to take up even the lessened production and advised that if producers were wise they would continue to reduce their manufacture as cotton became dearer. The grain crop, too, although of admirable quality was not particularly large, and it was thought that considerable amounts would have to be bought. Lancashire was directly opposed to the purchase of what they termed "slave products" and preferred to allow cotton mills to close down rather than use American cotton (Professor Hyde to Richard Lester, 21 Feb. 1958).

[46] The market was so tight that clear gain of £6 per bale was involved in the resale of cotton (*Manchester Guardian*, 21 Oct. 1861).

pressure, and the results are undoubtedly serious—mills working short time, to be closed, perhaps in a few weeks altogether; cotton still rising in price, labour lacking employment, and manufacturers destitute of materials. These, with the winter before us, are signs of no common trouble." Further, the *Manchester Guardian* claimed that when America appeared in the market again, India should be her match, and if this could be accomplished England would be relieved of any risk of another cotton famine, while India would be enriched by a trade of many millions a year.[47]

In England it was commonly believed that the Confederate government had forbidden the export of cotton to neutral powers. In fact, this was not so; the embargo was extralegal, or even illegal, and was imposed by the will of the people: planters, merchants, and shipowners, loudly supported by the Southern press. A formal embargo was often mooted in Congress but no act was ever formulated or passed. However, the Confederate Congress did prohibit the exportation of cotton for the use of the enemy or through the enemy's territory.[48]

Early in November the *Economist* was hopefully reporting that the Southern states were "utterly defective in pecuniary resources" and that their total deposits in the banks only amounted to £15,000,000,[49] but the embargo held firm; meanwhile, the results of the "produce" loan had been gratifying and on 19 August Congress extended the second loan by authorizing the Hundred-Million Dollar Loan.[50] The act approved the funding of the loan by placing a war tax on property, payable in gold, silver, or treasury notes. Initial response was good, but as 1861 drew to a close, subscriptions tailed off.[51] In December the *Economist* saw trouble ahead for the Confederates. It characterized Southern monetary policy as convenient rather than correct and feared that they would soon issue paper money in excess of their real assets, thus risking an inflation of their whole economy.[52] The Confederates had not solved their real prob-

[47] See also Richardson, 2:110–11.

[48] Ibid.; Minute Book of the American Chamber of Commerce, Liverpool, 22 Nov. 1861, p. 453 (City of Liverpool Public Library).

[49] 16 Nov. 1861. This amount was little more than that of a single London joint-stock bank. Memminger suggested that planters ask aid from the banks. However, the banks did not have the money to lend.

[50] Todd, p. 34; *Journal of the Congress of the Confederate States of America, 1861–1865*, 7 vols. (Washington, D.C.: Government Printing Office, 1904), 1:367 (hereafter cited as *Journal of the Confederate Congress*).

[51] Todd, p. 35.

[52] Dec. 1861. The paper suggested that the sole safeguard against depreciation would be convertibility. Davis did not adopt this expedient. The Con-

lem: how to come by sufficient specie to finance their purchasing operations abroad. *Bankers' Magazine* commented weightily but accurately that while the South might temporarily be in funds because of the loans, these funds were acquired only by a sudden realization of its best assets; the South was compared to a spendthrift who loses sight of the fact that the receipts so obtained bear no relation to the real yearly course of either income or liabilities. The magazine further declared that if the war continued England would witness not merely a drain of specie to America but a suspension of cash payments.[53]

As the winter of 1861–62 proceeded, there was no sign that Great Britain and France would be moved to direct intervention, although it is certain that during the early months of the war intervention was considered by both governments.[54] Meanwhile, the purchasing operations in Europe necessitated further transfers of specie, and in the first three months of 1862, $1,261,600 were shipped to Fraser, Trenholm and Company, to be put at the disposal of purchasing agent Huse.[55] In January there were signs of a relaxation of the embargo. Judah P. Benjamin, the Confederate secretary of state, suggested to E. J. Forstal, a representative of a European banking house stationed in New Orleans, that cotton be placed in the hands of the bank's agent as collateral for a million-dollar loan to be deposited in England for the purpose of financing purchases.[56] Benjamin stipulated that the cotton was "to remain on this side until the blockade is raised," but it was a straw in the wind. Nothing immediate came of the proposal.

Nevertheless, the spring of 1862 saw a gradual removal of the cotton embargo. As the *Economist* said, the South was suffering and would suffer more; the bottom had fallen out of its currency, but at any rate it still had cotton.[57] In the South there was a grow-

federate president did not keep a reserve of real dollars in store to maintain the value of his paper. If he had those dollars, he would spend them in war, not retain them in a bank. The next best safeguard would have been a numerical maximum to his issues.

[53] 1861, p. 798.

[54] Bragdon and McCutchen, p. 329; *The Private Journal of Henry William Ravenel, 1859–1887*, ed. Arney R. Childs (Columbia: University of South Carolina Press, 1947), p. 59; *Times*, 12 Dec. 1862, 16 Jan. 1865.

[55] Richardson, 2:149; Minute Book of the American Chamber of Commerce, pp. 459–60; *O.R.*, ser. 4, 1:985.

[56] *O.R.*, ser. 4, 1:845–46. The cotton was to be stored and insured at the expense of the government at any convenient point designated, but not in a cotton port, during the existence of the blockade.

[57] 18 Jan. 1862; Richardson, 2:152. See also Minute Book of the American Chamber of Commerce, p. 458.

ing awareness of this fact; cotton was the only saleable commodity left to it, and American cotton held a position of relative superiority over the other cottons shipped into England.[58] It was also realized on both sides of the Atlantic that the Northern blockade was tightening and nothing could now prevent a cotton famine in Europe. In Manchester the prevalent opinion was that the Southern cotton crop would yield from 3.4 million to 3.6 million bales, the latter being the highest probable point it could reach in 1862. In the early part of the year the prospects were extremely good; but for various causes, including heavy rains, the crop did not yield as well as expected. On 1 February the *Manchester Guardian* reported that the Confederate government "with the assent of all the planters" had abandoned its resolution to prevent the export of cotton and that any vessel choosing to run the blockade could have supplies—for gold or goods. The paper confirmed that there was not a single port efficiently blockaded, and it mentioned the case of a ship that ran out of a blockaded port off which seven federal ships of war were stationed. The same issue provided a sidelight on the plight of the South in its shortage of just one essential commodity, shoes. Some twelve to thirteen million pairs were required per annum, but previously most of them had been bought in the North. Thus it was not merely a question of the South seeking armaments abroad. With secession and the outbreak of war, Southerners had to look toward Europe for the most ordinary necessities.

The policy "Cotton is king" was not quite dead, however. Early in 1862 curtailment of the coming crop, coupled with proposals for the burning of cotton in store lest it should fall into federal hands, was widely canvassed. During the spring and summer hundreds of thousands of bales were put to the torch—to the consternation of Great Britain and France.[59] It also became generally known that little cotton was being planted that spring.[60]

On 8 April the *Times* reported that the cotton market was dull and unsettled and that loans to Southern bankers and cotton brokers were less freely negotiated. Prime business continued to be scarce and was usually taken at 6 to 7 percent, mostly at the higher rate.[61]

[58] *Times*, 25 Jan. 1862; Minute Book of the American Chamber of Commerce, pp. 455–56.

[59] *Manchester Guardian*, 12 Feb. 1862; *Times*, 2 July 1862; Richardson, 2:288–89.

[60] *Index*, 15 May 1862.

[61] The estimated total stocks of cotton in Europe on 1 May 1862 were only 509,060 bales, while on the same date in 1861 the stocks were estimated at 1,433,500 bales (ibid., 8 May 1862). The *Times* (30 May 1861) declared that

The South certainly needed more money.[62] On 18 April Congress extended the amount of treasury notes, stocks, and bonds already issued to $250,000,000 and three days later accepted Memminger's recommendations to take articles in kind in exchange for the bonds. Memminger feared to sell cotton on account of possible political effects at home, stating that the federal government would make the blockade more effective if an attempt was made to take cotton out of Confederate ports and that there was little possibility that Europe would send vessels to get the product even if it was stored in seaports. He maintained that cotton stored by the government on plantations was the best basis for currency security and procurement of war supplies.[63] Under the 18 April act the efforts of the loan agents were directed almost entirely to the purchase of cotton with bonds, but many planters refused to sell their cotton and other produce to the government unless part of the transaction was paid in negotiable treasury notes rather than nonnegotiable instruments.[64] The South was now beginning to feel the realities of inflation.[65]

Meanwhile, the drain on specie for foreign payments continued; exchange rates were most unfavorable.[66] In January 1862 Henry

"the posture of Confederate financial affairs remains substantially the same," the money market was very easy, and there was every indication that rates would fall still lower.

[62] Richardson, 2:227–33; 224, 227; 235–39. In May 1862 Mason suggested the importance of a Confederate financial agency in Europe (Virginia Mason, *The Public Life and Diplomatic Correspondence of James M. Mason with Some Personal History* [Roanoke, Va.: Stone Printing and Manufacturing Company, 1903], no. 6, 19 July 1862 (cited hereafter as Mason).

[63] *Richmond Examiner*, 26 Feb. 1862.

[64] Treasury notes were not legal tender, except in payment of dues to the government, but the patriotism of the people was such that they passed from hand to hand as currency for all transactions. All Confederate notes were made payable six months after the treaty of peace with the United States, and were convertible at any time into coupon or inscribed bonds having twenty years to run, bearing 8% interest, but redeemable in ten years, at the option of the secretary of the treasury (*Economist*, 8 Aug. 1862).

[65] *Times*, 23 Apr. 1862. The *Index* (1 May 1862) declared that the transactions in cotton during April were on a large scale and that activity of demand had been met by firmness with a weekly advance of ¼d per pound. See also ibid., 8 May 1862.

[66] The *Index* (31 July 1862) claimed that when a new trade is opened to the enterprise of the business community, money becomes scarce in consequence of the additional quantity of bills created to carry on the fresh transaction. David Sandeman of the Glasgow Chamber of Commerce gave notice that he would bring forward the subject of the present state of affairs and suggest a speedy termination to the war (Minute Book of the Glasgow Chamber of Commerce, 12 Aug. 1862 [Glasgow Chamber of Commerce]; see also *Times*, 14 Aug. 1862).

Hotze, the Confederate commercial and propaganda agent and editor of the *Index,* writing to the secretary of state, pointed out that exchange on England was not obtainable in Richmond for less than twenty-five cents premium and, a few days later, that gold could not be bought in Mobile for less than thirty cents. In London gold went up to 23½ percent premium.[67] At this time the *Economist* claimed that the Civil War was being carried on a little by taxes, somewhat by loans, and mostly by an inconvertible currency. This analysis was quite correct. In the Confederacy it was not possible to levy heavy taxes: the country was poor and sparsely populated; because of the war its main industry, cotton, had been almost suspended. As the Confederates found, it was not possible to raise regular loans under such circumstances, for the floating capital required did not exist. Nor was it possible for an inchoate state like the South to borrow much money.[68]

By autumn of 1862 millions of dollars had been spent in Europe by the official Confederate purchasing agents and contractors; their resources had become so limited that their credit was endangered.[69] Huse had purchased about twice as much as he could pay for and was hard pressed; other agents were inactive for lack of funds.[70] Something had to be done quickly. Letters of credit and bills of exchange were no longer of any use. The supplies of gold and silver coin that could be shipped to Fraser, Trenholm and Company in England to cover these letters and bills were almost exhausted.[71] In the opinion of the *Economist* nothing in recent American history was more remarkable than the almost complete ignorance that prevailed in Great Britain with regard to the financial position of the Confederate States. It was realized that the Confederacy must have obtained a great deal of money, for such a war as it was waging could not be sustained without capital, but exactly how great its

[67] Richardson, 2:147–79; *Times,* 14 Oct. 1862.

[68] 18 Oct. 1862. In London gold went up to 29% premium (*Times,* 23 Oct. 1862; *Bankers' Magazine,* 1862, p. 749).

[69] Thompson, p. 50. In the North, paper currency was becoming so inflated that real distress threatened the working classes. Gold was being shipped from the country in millions, and the value of the paper currency was changing daily from extended issues and a ruinous inflation of all prices was taking place (*New York World,* 1 Nov. 1862). By October 1862, the war had cost the South $500 million (memorandum of Earl Russell regarding the Civil War, 25 Oct. 1862, Gladstone Papers, 510:86).

[70] Thompson, p. 50. Henry Cook of London intended to present to the Confederate government certain propositions for laying telegraphic cables at points on the coast of the Confederate States and establishing communications with Europe (Richardson, 2:329).

[71] Owsley, *King Cotton Diplomacy,* p. 385.

resources were nobody in Europe seemed to know.[72] It was generally felt that the South should be congratulated on having made war not only with considerable success but very cheaply.[73]

By now cotton was leaving the Southern states, but only in small quantities; it was the only source for obtaining exchange. It could not possibly meet a tenth of Confederate needs, and it was obvious that other means had to be found. The first means suggested was the sale of Confederate bonds in Europe. The authorities at Richmond were not sanguine about their likely success, and the secretary of the navy wrote to the extremely able J. D. Bulloch, the chief agent of the Confederate Navy Department in Great Britain: "Another suggestion occurs to me. You may possibly be able to obtain advances upon our agreement to repay the amount with 8% interest in cotton, the question of the price of cotton to be determined when the advances are made. You might offer another proposition, that the amount of all advances made by you shall be expended here by the Treasury Department in the purchase of cotton on account of the creditor, he being allowed the difference of exchange. Cotton thus purchased would be stored by the Treasury and all facilities for shipment would be afforded." [74]

By now the Confederacy had no alternative but to raise funds through the sale of its cotton. As a result of the produce loan, it now owned some 400,000 bales.[75] As autumn ripened, Benjamin's proposal of the previous January was examined with anxious attention as the only practical means—in the absence of any government fleet of blockade-runners—of gaining credit for cotton. The Navy Department, under Stephen R. Mallory, secretary of the navy, was the first to use cotton certificates. Mallory dispatched an agent, G. N. Sanders,[76] to Europe with authority to use certificates for the construction of ships. Mallory proposed that Sanders should contract for ships to be paid for in cotton delivered at any port of the Confederate States at the price current at the time of delivery.

[72] 29 Oct. 1862.

[73] *Economist*, 28 Oct. 1862. Sir G. R. Lewis estimated the cost of the Crimean War to Great Britain at £77,588,000 and argued that the Crimean War could not be compared in magnitude to the tremendous struggle in which the Confederate States were engaged, "that such a war as ours cost us; that nevertheless £76,708,000 covers the whole expenditure, military as well as civil, while £77,588,000 was requisite for only the military part of ours" (ibid).

[74] Bulloch, 2:221–22. For an analysis of various methods of fund raising by the Confederates in Europe, see Judith Anne Fenner, "Confederate Finances Abroad" (Ph.D. diss. Rice University, 1969).

[75] Thompson, p. 50; *Bankers' Magazine*, 1862, pp. 691–92.

[76] Sanders or Saunders. Spelled both ways by various correspondents.

Funds for these transactions were to be negotiated by the hypothecation of cotton for future delivery.[77] Sanders went to the banking house of William Lindsay and Company to raise money on the contract, but there he was advised that while the scheme was good, the bonds or certificates could not be negotiated unless a definite price was fixed for the cotton. Lindsay suggested that this price should be fourpence, or eight cents, a figure that would be immediately attractive, since at that time cotton was selling in England at four times that price. James Mason, the Confederate commissioner in London, and John Slidell, the commissioner in Paris, do not appear to have been instructed about this particular scheme for raising money, but because they were the recognized agents of the executive government, both the purchasing agents and English business houses came to them for advice and approval of engagements. In the case of Sanders, Mason was unwilling to assume the responsibility, and Sanders returned to Richmond to effect the change of the contract.[78]

Meanwhile, George T. Sinclair had arrived in England under orders to build a ship for the Navy Department and had been advised that Comdr. James D. Bulloch would provide him with funds.[79] But Bulloch's credit was exhausted,[80] and Sinclair appealed to Mason, who on this occasion took the responsibility of furnishing Sinclair with £62,000 of cotton bonds at eight cents per pound.[81] The Confederate government endorsed this issue, and thus the Sinclair bonds were the first to be issued in Europe.[82] These bonds were not put on the market but were privately placed by Lindsay and Company with two or three buyers for the entire sum, the transactions remaining secret.[83] Mason took the responsibility of fixing the price of cotton but asked for future instructions. He said, of what he had done regarding Sanders and Sinclair: "I am fully aware of the difficulties the Government must have in placing the funds in Europe necessary for its use. . . . I venture to suggest therefore that money may be commanded here by the Government

[77] Mason, no. 16, 18 Sept. 1862.

[78] Ibid. For a report on Southern cotton, see Gladstone Papers, 510:82.

[79] Ibid.

[80] The Confederate rate of exchange was 2 to 1, and it was next to impossible to secure money at all, "there being in fact nothing to draw upon" (ibid.; *Bankers' Magazine*, 1862, pp. 108–9, 477).

[81] The urgent necessity for transport ships led Mason to complete his engagement with Lindsay & Company.

[82] Mason, no. 24, 14 Jan. 1863.

[83] That both Mason and Slidell were suspicious of Sanders may help to account for the difference between the treatment accorded the two contracts.

on the terms and in the manner expressed. That is to say, that the delivery shall be made to any port in possession of the Confederate States when demanded by the holder of the bond, after reasonable notice or within three months or more after peace. . . . I believe that four or five millions sterling could be commanded in this form from this class alone." [84] Meanwhile, Memminger had been advised of Mason's representations, and he, in consultation with Benjamin, drew up a cotton certificate embodying the essential points of the Lindsay transaction.[85]

The scheme as developed at Richmond was to issue cotton certificates on the cotton thus purchased and by the sale of these certificates in England hypothecate the cotton.[86] Of these certificates Memminger proposed to send one thousand abroad.[87] Congress then authorized Mallory to make contracts for vessels to be paid for in certificates for cotton, and thereupon, to complicate matters, certificates were put directly into the hands of purchasing agents and contractors to be used for payment of goods and services. The difficulties that might arise from separate action in the market were, however, immediately perceived. Thus the cotton obligations were turned over to Fraser, Trenholm and Company, and the agents and Mason agreed to this course of action. A considerable number of Confederate money bonds were by this time in England, but in view of the arrival of the cotton certificates, it was agreed to withhold the bonds from the market, for the certificates were considered the better means of raising funds.[88] A short time later James Spence, an English financier and banker and a staunch friend of the South, was appointed financial agent for Europe with authority for the disposal of the bonds.[89]

The decision to put King Cotton to work had come not a moment too soon; on 23 October 1863 the *Times* reported considerable depression in Southern money values; gold had reached a premium of 29 percent. A few days later the *Economist* reported that up to 1 August 1862 the war had cost the Confederates £76,705,060 and that while it considered this inexpensive, detailed analysis of ex-

[84] Mason, no. 16, 18 Sept. 1862. [85] Callahan, p. 60.

[86] For a good analysis of the hypothecation of cotton see Ernest A. Smith, *The History of the Confederate Treasury* (Washington, D.C.: Southern History Association, 1901). By an act of 21 Apr. 1863, Congress passed a law allowing "produce" to be sold directly to the government for 8% bonds, $35 million being appropriated for the purpose.

[87] Mason, no. 22, 10 Dec. 1862. [88] *New York Times*, 18 Jan. 1863.

[89] Thompson, pp. 22–23.

penditure and receipts showed a deficit of nearly £4 million.[90]

The decision of the Confederacy to put cotton on the market was soon rumored among the banking houses of France and England. Coming at the moment when a cotton famine seemed unavoidable, it caused great interest. In particular, Isaac, Campbell and Company was delighted. Huse had used it almost exclusively as the agent for his purchases, and in November 1862 the Confederacy owed it about $2 million. Nevertheless, upon hearing of the cotton certificates, its representative in Nassau offered to supply equipment for a hundred thousand men, to be paid partly in cash and the remainder in bonds or certificates representing a certain number of bales. The company also offered to accept settlement of its outstanding debt in the same manner.[91]

Lindsay and Company, which had floated the Sinclair bonds, also offered to raise money for the Confederacy. Lindsay advised against a regular loan and believed that cotton bonds, which represented specified bales of cotton, would be more acceptable; the company offered to take £500,000 worth. The cotton certificates or bonds actually issued were of two types. In spite of Lindsay's recom-

[90] *Economist*, 28 Oct. 1862: "The mode in which this considerable though not excessive sum has been obtained is, we are informed, as follows:

Taxes	335,393	
Customs to the repeal of the Tariff	2,372,759	
		£ 2,708,152
Loans		
Loan Act of Feb. 28, 1861	3,500,000	
Loan Act of Aug. 19, 1861	5,743,114	
Call Deposits	8,753,546	
Balance of loan from Banks	2,459,312	
By Inconvertible Note		£ 20,455,972
Treasury Note Act, Mar 9, 1861	471,600	
Treasury Note Act, May 16, 1861	4,047,857	
Treasury Note Act, Aug 19, 1861	39,145,076	
Treasury Note Act, Apr 17, 1861	5,319,976	
Small Notes	197,400	
		£49,181,909
		460,779
		£72,806,812

Leaving a deficit on the 1st August of nearly £4,000,000." See also *Bankers' Magazine*, 1862, p. 748.

[91] *O.R.N.*, ser. 2, 3:605.

mendation, one type conveyed to the purchaser absolute ownership of a particular lot of cotton to be valued at "the expense of purchase plus the fees of agents, plus the amount cotton had appreciated since the date of purchase."[92] The other type, which found more general favor, stipulated a specific price per pound. Both types of certificates allowed the purchaser to run the blockade and collect his own cotton at the port designated on the certificate, should he so desire.[93]

The Treasury Department prepared 1,500 certificates of this type: 1,000 were for cotton to be delivered at New Orleans or Mobile and 500 for cotton to be delivered at Charleston or Savannah. Each certificate was valued at $1,000. The certificates were delivered by Capt. W. G. Crenshaw to Fraser, Trenholm and Company, and Spence was instructed to negotiate.[94]

The respite likely to be afforded by the cotton certificates and bonds was most opportune. In Manchester it was understood that the Confederate government was endeavoring to issue, privately or otherwise, bonds bearing interest at the rate of 8 percent per annum.[95] On 4 November 1862 the correspondent of the *Times* spoke of the continuing enthusiasm of the people of the South but went on to describe their extreme shortage of all supplies and the already ruinous state of the country—at war, "with an enemy three times as numerous as themselves and with complete command of the sea and an inexhaustible supply of every provision and munition of war."[96] Four days later the *Economist* stated that by 1 January 1863 the Confederates would require supplies to a total value of $209,550,487.

Meanwhile, unemployment in Lancashire was now widespread and relief funds were opened for the local victims of a war three thousand miles distant. For example, the minute book of the American Chamber of Commerce at Liverpool shows that on 27 November the chamber voted £1,000 for the "relief of the distressed operatives of Lancashire and Cheshire."[97] As the year waned the introduction of the cotton bonds and certificates tended to make business on the markets brisker and more cheerful. The report of

[92] Ibid., pp. 345–49.

[93] *Bankers' Magazine*, 1862, p. 691; *O.R.N.*, ser. 2, 3:345–49.

[94] Mason, no. 22, 10 Dec. 1862.

[95] *Manchester Guardian*, 11 Dec. 1862.

[96] See also *Bankers' Magazine*, 1862, p. 683.

[97] P. 465. This money was to be paid to the chairman of the Central Committee in Liverpool. "As a result of the American Civil War, England was undergoing privation unknown to the Island within the last forty years" (*Times*, 24 Dec. 1862).

the Liverpool cotton market showed a large business advance. The South at this point had cotton to borrow on.[98]

From the issue of cotton certificates and bonds came an offer from Emile Erlanger and Company, the famous German and French bankers.[99] The news of it is contained in a letter from Slidell to Benjamin, dated 28 October 1862:

> You will find herewith certain propositions for a loan made by Messrs. Erlanger & Company of Paris. In a previous dispatch I alluded to this matter. By that you will find that these gentlemen presented themselves to me without any suggestion on my part of a desire to borrow money for the Confederate States. I told them very frankly that I had no mission for that purpose, that my Government had agents in Europe for the purpose of arms and equipment for the Army and for the building and fitting out of ships of war—that if for those purposes they could make arrangements that appear to me, under all the circumstances, to be reasonable and fair, I would give the sanction of my approbation for whatever it might be worth.
>
> The first conversations did not contemplate anything further than the raising of such sums as might within a few months be required by the agents of the War and Navy Departments, say £600,000 or £700,000 sterling.
>
> Now, however, Messrs. Erlanger & Company proposed to embark in the speculation on a more extended scale. I have agreed to forward their proposition which, as you will perceive, binds no one until the agreement shall have been consummated in a manner stipulated.
>
> The propositions, of course, are subject to any modifications which the Secretary of the Treasury might suggest. The expediency of accepting them will be controlled or modified by the state of things which may exist when they may reach Richmond. The probability is that the agents of Messrs. Erlanger & Company will arrive there before this dispatch. All that I have to say is that they are one of the most extensive and responsible houses in Europe, and that they have been eminently successful in originating and carrying out many schemes of large loans. You will find herewith the evidence of this fact.

[98] *Times*, 6 Dec. 1862. The report of the Liverpool cotton market showed a large business advance. The South had cotton to borrow on (ibid., 22 Dec. 1862).

[99] Although German born, Emile Erlanger made his home and center of business in Paris. He had branch banks in practically every major city in Western Europe, including London. It is generally thought that Slidell's daughter Mathilde married Erlanger's son, but, rather, she married Emile Erlanger himself, and the couple had a very happy life together. Whenever Erlanger was forced to be away from home on business, they exchanged daily letters; some nine hundred of these letters are in existence, covering dates between 1862 and 1898.

I should not have gone as far as I have in recommending these propositions to the consideration of the Government had I not the best reason to believe that even in anticipation of its acceptance the very strongest influence will be enlisted in our favor.[100]

The negotiations for this loan were protracted and will be examined in the next chapter. Meanwhile, the purchasing agents were at a loss to meet their obligations and make new contracts. The cotton bonds and certificates had arrived, it is true, but Spence found that the bonds could not be used at better rates than fifty cents a dollar and withheld them.[101] The *Economist* said on 17 January 1863 that the rise in the rate of discount to 5 percent in England had come upon the country like "a clap of thunder" and remarked that if the Confederates were allowed to draw bullion out of the country through loans, they would discharge an unfavorable balance of trade and payments.

In any case it was deemed wise to hold the cotton certificates from the market until the result of the proposals for a direct loan was known. But Huse was desperate to secure funds and persuaded Mason to issue cotton warrants calling for the delivery of 7.3 million pounds of cotton at fivepence per pound as payment against indebtedness to Isaac, Campbell and Company and for new contracts.[102] About the same time Mason also endorsed for Maury, as a naval agent, 500 certificates for twenty bales of cotton of 500 pounds each, deliverable at New Orleans or Mobile, issued at the Treasury of the Confederate States under the date of 1 November 1862.[103] Thus, as an emergency measure 15.3 million pounds of cotton were pledged while awaiting the outcome of the transactions for the Erlanger loan.[104]

Before passing to a consideration of this loan, a review of the general situation as seen through the eyes of the British press at the end of 1862 may be useful. On 1 January 1863 the *Times* was reasonably confident:

The New Year commences with all the markets in a quiet state, and without a single symptom of prospective disturbance. Our stock of cotton too, is, in money value, more than equal to that of ordinary periods. In loans to foreign nations we have embarked about £15,000,000 sterling and we have likewise sent abroad an amount of probably £10,-

[100] Richardson, 2:339–40. [101] *New York Times*, 18 Jan. 1863.

[102] Mason, nos. 29 and 32, 5 Feb., 30 Mar. 1863.

[103] Ibid., no. 857, 18 Feb. 1863.

[104] Richardson, 2:361–63; Baroness Slidell Erlanger to Baron Emile Erlanger, 13 Mar. 1862, Erlanger Papers (Erlangers Ltd., London).

000,000 for Indian, Colonial and foreign railways and other commercial undertakings. The American war has created an enormous investment in England, so that it was a drain to America of all the bullion that can be attracted by high premiums from its hiding places. America needed English goods, because labour is every day becoming more scarce, to increase the amount of her productions, and, therefore, if materials of war and sustenance of armies are to be called for and consumed to the value of two or three hundred millions per annum, they must in part be procured from the labour of other countries. When the war commenced, the South held large stocks of goods of all kinds—coffee, sugar, tea, wines, hemp, wool, and these have since served her needs, but they are now for the most part exhausted, and henceforth she must return not merely to her old, but to a greatly increased scale of importations. We shall thus probably see that the large extra quantities of produce which have lately been sent from Brazil to find a market here which would otherwise have been obtained in New York will have to be bought from us by America at considerably enhanced prices; and the same result must be expected whether the war shall continue or terminate because if peace were announced, there would then be a speculative rush to regain as speedily as possible the stocks of merchandise now exhausted.

The fear that we may be drained of our specie by Indian cotton is groundless, because any further arrivals that may now take place will be distributed to foreign markets, and thus operate as if specie had been sent to us in return for that which we had sent away.

Loss of specie in England resulting in foreign investments amounted in 1862 to £20,000,000. A return of the rate of discount to five per cent would throw a majority of the schemes that are now floated to a heavy discount, and if additions are to be made to them during the early months of the new year at a pace similar to that which has lately been witnessed.

The *Economist*, on 3 January, was even triumphant:

The year 1862 will be memorable in the annals of English trade, for it has wholly dissipated a deep-seated and diffuse delusion, the notion of the Southern Americans that Cotton was King of England, and that England must do what was needful to obtain that material. The Economist showed at the very outset of the secession that Southern cotton was not essential to England, and that England could get on without it. The most convincing tests have been applied, and of any one the very best is the revenue. The nation at large cannot be suffering without the consumption of duty-paying articles being diminished, without the yield of the Customs and Excise being impaired.

It went on to show that the revenue of the Customs and Excise for the quarter ended 31 December 1862 was in fact nearly £280,000 higher than in the corresponding quarter of 1861.

It also published a variety of figures in relation to the cotton situation. These showed that a total of 72,369 bales of American cotton had reached British ports during 1862 (compared with 2,581,024 in 1860 and 1,841,643 in 1861) and, in 1862, in spite of short-term unemployment, Great Britain had used 1,195,450 bales. The stock of cotton in Great Britain at 31 December 1861 was given as 699,000 bales; weekly consumption in 1862 averaged less than half of that of 1861.[105] Reviewing the market for the year, the *Economist* stated:

> In April there was a decided improvement in Manchester; this led to an active demand for cotton, from which prices gradually hardened, the month closing with "middling" Orleans at 13 3/8d. In May the surrender of the City of New Orleans took place. In June of 1862 the unexpected intelligence of the Confederate victories over General Banks dispelled the idea of Southern submission; prices rapidly advanced and by the end of the month "middling" Orleans had risen to 16d. In August the market began to show indications of a strong upwards movement, and the month closed with "middling" Orleans at 27d. In October the demand was extremely limited and prices declined to 23d for "middling" Orleans. During November the business in Cotton was sold at 20d, a decline of 10d per pound in less than three months; this however was only temporary, and was followed by an immediate rally to the extent of 2d per pound. In December there was a favourable reaction; scarcity of goods in Manchester had at length been really felt, any spinners whose mills had been closed had resumed work, and the consumption of cotton during the last three weeks had materially increased. The year closed with "middling" Orleans at 24d. Sea Island—the value of Sea Islands had gradually advanced throughout the year, the price of "Fair cotton" on the 1st January was 24d, and it is now over 46d.

It was the considered opinion of the *Economist* that the war would last "for a year at least, perhaps two years more, till the next Presidential election," by which time "the substantial independence of the South" would be accepted by the Federals.

[105] According to the *Economist*, England received cotton from Brazil, Egypt, and the West and East Indies. England's weekly consumption of cotton in bales was as follows:

1862	22,990 bales
1861	42,265 bales
1860	48,700 bales
1859	44,121 bales
1858	41,818 bales

CHAPTER II

THE ERLANGER LOAN AND THE PLAN OF 1864

FROM THE DATE of their first meeting, John Slidell seemed to be captivated by the personality of Emile Erlanger. Erlanger was introduced to him as one of Europe's most important and influential bankers and a confidant of Napoleon's,[1] and it seemed to Slidell that the successful negotiation of Erlanger's audacious financial proposals was of prime political importance. He felt sure that if a satisfactory contract could be concluded, France would act most favorably on behalf of the Confederacy.[2] Erlanger and Company had inherited some interest in the previously French territory of Louisiana and had contracts with the Confederate government arising from this interest.[3]

Slidell and Huse, who was desperate to obtain funds for his purchases in England, drew up a tentative contract with Erlanger and sent it to Mason, the Confederate commissioner in London, for his signature.[4] This contract stipulated that Erlanger would underwrite bonds secured by cotton, put the proceeds of their sale to the credit of the Confederate procurement agents, and wait for the cotton until it could run the blockade or until peace was declared.[5] The agreement authorizing such bonds provided that the interest should be payable in coin or cotton at the option of the buyer; the cotton was to be valued at 8d sterling per pound.[6] Erlanger was to dispose of £5 million in Confederate cotton bonds, bearing 8%, but his profits were to be enormous. The original contract suggested that

[1] Robert D. Meade, *Judah P. Benjamin, Confederate Statesman* (New York: Oxford University Press, 1943), pp. 269–70. Emile Erlanger had influence with Lord Lyon's own secretary, Mr. Mallet (? name illegible). The banker also had a direct line to the Foreign Office (13 Aug. 1863, Erlanger Papers). For a chart of Erlanger banking history, see App. I.

[2] Meade, pp. 269–70. For a most comprehensive study of the history of the United States and France, especially as it relates to overall Confederate activity in France, including the Erlanger loan, see Lynn Case, *The United States and France* (Philadelphia: University of Pennsylvania Press, 1970).

[3] Confederate Cotton Loan, 1863, J. Henry Schroder Papers, file C, 1910, p. 11 (J. H. Schroder—Wagg & Co. London)

[4] *O.R.N.*, ser. 2, 3:568–72; *Bankers' Magazine*, 1862, p. 127.

[5] *O.R.N.*, ser. 2, 3:568–72.

[6] Capers, p. 360.

he should have all above 70% on the bonds, plus a 5% commission for disposing of the issue, 1% for handling the sinking funds and interest,[7] and a further 8% discount for anticipating any or all of the eleven installments. It was further stipulated that the Confederacy should redeem one-fortieth of the bonds semiannually, beginning 1 July 1863. Thus the Confederates would net only about £3.3 million out of £5 million, and even this sum would be rapidly reduced by the semiannual redemption and handling commission.[8]

Such a contract was hard, if not usurious, but Slidell was so impressed with Erlanger's importance and with the political favors he was sure would follow that he never seemed to realize just how exacting were the banker's conditions. In contrast to Slidell's enthusiasm, Mason was reserved about the whole project. Memminger was also more doubtful and recommended on 10 January 1863 that the rate of securities should be 6d per pound. Congress made the change, but also changed the option of coin or cotton payable from the holder to the government, which severely diminished their attractiveness to the foreign market.[9] "This converted the bond," says Memmenger, "into a simple 6% bond with the interest payable here." [10] Presumably, it was the objection stated by Memminger that prevented the sale of these bonds in autumn 1862. The negotiations arising over the Erlanger loan led to the withdrawal of the cotton warrants and cotton certificates from the market pending the fate of the offer of Erlanger to float a large loan secured by cotton, but the sale of these money bonds was not expected to be prejudicial to any cotton securities, and Spence made vain attempts to dispose of them in January 1863.[11]

In part, at any rate, Mason's attitude toward the Erlanger proposals was colored by the fact that Lindsay and Company had just made a similar proposal with less onerous commissions and rebates. Mason had been thoroughly gratified by the facility with which Lindsay had absorbed the £60,000 of the Sinclair contract, and with a view to presenting this matter more favorably to Memminger, he sounded Lindsay on the prospects of an extension of this operation, knowing the power and influence of the company. Lindsay encouraged Mason to believe that he could be successful on a large scale, provided that the price at which the government would "sell"

[7] Meade, pp. 269–70. [8] *O.R.N.*, ser. 2, 3:568–72.

[9] Capers, p. 360. These securities should not be confused with the Erlanger loan. Callahan has unknowingly caused such confusion. This was largely due to the fact that the Erlanger Papers were not available to him. (However, Callahan's work in this area is certainly worthy of note. See Callahan, p. 61.)

[10] Capers, p. 360. [11] Mason, no. 29, 5 Feb. 1862.

was low enough. Lindsay looked upon the venture as a speculation in "futures," pure and simple, and proposed that the government should offer, say, £100,000 (par value) of stock, quoting cotton at 4d per pound. Once the bonds were floated, they would certainly command a high premium if cotton were quoted at so low a price. Lindsay proposed that with this £100,000 of stock on the market, and a premium established, the government could float successive £100,000 blocks at will, taking advantage of the premium established by the first issue. Lindsay offered to market up to £500,000 of these bonds through his own house and connections alone.[12]

As an emergency measure the Lindsay plan indicates a lack of foresight. It failed to consider either the amount of money needed or the urgency of acting while the situation of the South could justify the confidence of an investing public. It disregarded the possibility of reverses, to say nothing of ultimate defeat. However, Mason, while questioning the low price at which cotton was nominated, recommended this scheme of finance in preference to that of Erlanger's.[13]

In the circumstances it is not surprising that Mason declined to sign the draft contract for Erlanger but passed it to Benjamin.[14] On 11 November 1862 Slidell wrote to Benjamin: "Messrs. Erlanger & Company have sent three special agents, who are now on their way to Richmond in relation to their proposals for a loan.[15] This fact proves, at least, that they are very much in earnest about the matter."[16]

The Erlanger proposals, forwarded by Mason, reached Benjamin on 31 December, before the agents[17] and the Confederate government looked on them with disfavor.[18] The government felt itself already committed to the cotton bond or certificate rather than to

[12] Ibid., no. 19, 4 Nov. 1862. Erlanger and Schroder were particularly friendly and worked well together in the management of financial affairs (Schroder Papers, p. 11).

[13] Of the two, Mason favored the Lindsay plan on the grounds that it could be adopted progressively as needed or discontinued, if found undesirable, without heavily committing the government. Richardson, 2:398–401.

[14] *O.R.N.*, ser. 2, 3:590–93.

[15] Schwab and Smith claim Erlanger actually went to Richmond. The Erlanger Papers reveal that Erlanger was in Paris at the time. Further, there is no evidence in his papers to confirm that Erlanger visited America during this period. See Allan Foreman, "A Bit of Secret Service History," *Magazine of American History* 12 (1884):323–31.

[16] Richardson, 2:361–63. [17] Ibid., 2:398, 401.

[18] *O.R.N.*, ser. 2, 3:648–51. Given Confederate sensitivity on the value of cotton, it is not so surprising that they hesitated before the proposal (Richardson, 2:398–401).

a definite loan, especially to a loan on Erlanger's onerous terms. Memminger and President Davis conferred over the letters from Mason and Slidell and objected specifically to the low price of cotton advanced by both the Lindsay and Erlanger propositions.[19] On 15 January 1863 Benjamin wrote to Slidell that "not withstanding our desire to ratify the outline of the contract drawn up in Paris," it would have been impossible to obtain the sanction of congress.[20] He went on to point out that after conference with Erlanger's agents, it seemed plain that the contract, nominally a loan, was really for the purchase of cotton "and that cotton would be demanded for the whole amount." [21] Benjamin set forth the ruinous terms to Slidell:

> A loan of 70%, with an allowance of 5% commission and a discount on the deferred payments at the rate of 8% per annum was found to leave a net result of about 61%. To pay the capital on demand at 6d per pound would therefore in reality have resulted in selling cotton at that rate with a deduction of 39%. In other words we would have obtained for each pound of cotton 61% of 6d or about three pence and two-thirds per pound, equal to less than thirty dollars per bale of 400 pounds. This was so much lower than other offers, and would have required such an enormous quantity of cotton to pay the $25,000,000 of nominal capital (say about 520,000 bales of cotton), that it was impossible to accept the proposals. Cotton is selling here now at from sixteen to twenty-two cents a pound, and will go higher. The crops of the three years, 1861, 1862, and 1863, when exported, will scarcely exceed one full crop in time of peace, and after the war the supply of cotton for some years must be less than in the past, owing to the diminished quantity of labor available.[22]

The secretary of state thus clearly indicated the fatal weakness of the financial policy of the Confederates and their absolute confidence, as yet, in the supreme importance of cotton to the world at large. The weakness of Confederate finance was its reliance on fiat money, with the futile funding operation by means of unsecured bonds. This was especially true in establishing a financial basis for the procurement of war supplies in Great Britain.

Finally, however, the Confederacy was impressed by Slidell's overweening belief in political advantages to be gained and agreed

[19] *Times*, 14 Feb. 1863. [20] Richardson, 2:405–8.

[21] Mason, pp. 350–53. The chief Erlanger representative was the Vicompte de Saint Roman (Richardson, 2:539).

[22] Richardson, 2:405–8.

to a modified form of the Erlanger proposal.[23] The government would take £3 million instead of £5 million; Erlanger was to be given more than 77% instead of 70% and the bonds were to bear 7% interest instead of 8% interest.[24] Even so, Benjamin was far from happy and wrote to Mason that the revised offer would never have been accepted if Richmond had not been swayed by Slidell's assurances of political favors to follow.[25]

The *Economist* did not like the loan. It claimed that if a Confederate loan were allowed to draw bullion out of the country, an unfavorable balance of trade and payments would be created since cotton did not have the substance of bullion transactions. It pointed out, as it had so often before, that bullion drawn out of the country in this manner would raise the rate of interest in England and make money tight. The *Economist* desired to bring money home and to balance the operation as nearly as possible.[26] However, it should be born in mind that most of the money was to be spent in England, and with the money so released by the loan many English merchants would be busy supplying the war needs of the Confederate government.[27] It is not unreasonable to suggest that the *Economist*, in this

[23] It was hoped that Emile Erlanger's name would not be connected with the loan because he might be adversely affected by it (Baroness Slidell Erlanger to Baron Emile Erlanger, 13 Feb. 1863, Erlanger Papers).

[24] Mason, pp. 350–53; Richardson, 2:412–13. The secretary of the treasury at this time informed Benjamin that he was actively at work purchasing cotton for European shipment. England was anxious to receive cotton, for it could see no end to the American conflict (*Economist*, 17 Jan. 1863). A certified original bond, in the possession of the author, shows the contract figures written in both pounds sterling and francs. The conversion rate was £1 = fr. 25 and £1 = $4.85. Thus, the Erlanger loan was equal to approximately $14,550,000 in Confederate money at the official exchange rate.

[25] *O.R.N.*, ser. 2, 3:648–51; Mason, pp. 350–53. Whether a large foreign loan could have been successfully floated on better terms is highly problematical. Richmond had great confidence in Slidell's judgment (Richardson, 2:398–401). Benjamin declared: "We have felt that it is to our unaided efforts that our independence is to be due, but we have a *right*, a clear, undoubted right, of recognition, and its continued refusal by Europe is disgraceful to neutral powers" (Benjamin to Edwin de Leon, 16 Jan. 1863, ibid., 2:412–13).

[26] The Bank of England and the Bank of France together held the principal reserve of bullion for the trade of Europe. The Bank of England held £14,102,169, the Bank of France £10,726,008—a total of £24,828,177 (*Economist*, 17 Jan. 1863).

[27] Ibid., 18 Jan. 1863. English banks were taking advantage of the cheaper rate of money in consequence of the absorption of stock for deposits by borrowing in the market on consols with a view to the strengthening of the reserve (ibid., 24 Jan., 21 Mar. 1863; J. K. Gilliat to William Gray, Richmond, 25 Apr. 1863, Gilliat Papers).

instance as in others, was prejudiced by its policy of nonrecognition of the South. For example, it stated that "recognition was opposed not only to sound precedent and good law, but likewise to common sense and evident discretion." [28]

While the negotiations for the loan were going forward, the purchasing agents were still in desperate straits for money. The War Department in particular was aware of the fact that Huse had incurred a large indebtedness that that department sought to provide for by remittances in Confederate bonds.[29] The first rumors that the Erlanger loan had been accomplished reached Europe in February 1863, but no definite details were known.[30] In the meantime the agents carried on as best they could. In February the English bank rate was raised from 7 to 8%; the effect was remarkable and immediate. Foreign capital was attracted to Great Britain and bullion ceased to leave the country. Before the increase it seemed that nothing would affect the money market, but as soon as the rate reached 8% the tide turned and there was a rush to send money to England for temporary investment.[31]

Before the first stories of the consummation of the Erlanger loan reached Europe, Mason, on 28 January 1863, informed Slidell that the Confederate agents could wait no more.[32] They must have £500,000 within a week or government interest and credit would flounder.[33] The money could be raised on cotton bonds, but Spence, financial agent to the Confederacy, had, as has been noted, held back further issues to avoid harm to the Erlanger proposals, although he viewed the projected contract with considerable misgivings.[34]

Early in February Mason in London gave way to Huse's steady pressure and approved payments and settlements of supply debts amounting to nearly £2 million by means of cotton certificates.

[28] *Economist*, 8 Aug. 1863. [29] Mason, pp. 381–84.

[30] *Times*, 7 Feb. 1863. The *Times* (20 Feb. 1863) reported that between £500,000 and £600,000 of a total advance of £3 million had been negotiated by Erlanger & Company. The amount was to be secured by cotton at 5d per pound and to be delivered on the cessation of the blockade.

[31] *Economist*, 7 Feb. 1863.

[32] The following day (29 Jan. 1863) an act of the C.S.A. Congress authorized an issue of a $15 million 7% "cotton loan" that was floated in Europe by Emile Erlanger & Company of Paris and Messrs. J. Henry Schroder & Company of London. Coupon bonds to the denominations of £100, £200, £500 and £1,000 were issued and extensively sold abroad. For years after the war these "Erlanger loan" bonds appeared, particularly upon the London market, their holders somewhat optimistic about the possibility of redemption. They were never redeemed, however (Cotton Loan, Schroder Papers, file C, p. 1).

[33] Mason, 12 Jan. 1863. [34] Ibid; *Times*, 14 Feb. 1863.

On 5 February Mason reported to Benjamin that Huse had contracted to deliver 2.3 million pounds of cotton for new purchases and 5 million pounds at 5d per pound as payment for supplies already purchased and shipped.[35] Mason went on to sum up the situation as it appeared in Europe: [36]

> In reference to the general subject of indebtedness here for account of the War and Navy Departments by their respective agents, I have felt it incumbent on me—though without express authority, under existing circumstances—to extend all aid in my power to those agents—to enable them to meet their engagements, and thus to preserve as of last importance the credit of the Government.
>
> As you are probably aware, large remittances have been recently made, as well by the Treasury as by the War and Navy Departments, to their respective agents in England, of Confederate bonds, as well as of cotton certificates, in the form adopted by the Treasury Department. After their arrival and after full consultation with the gentlemen to whom they were intrusted, it was deemed judicious not to put the cotton certificates, at least, upon the market until we could learn the result of the proposals for a direct loan which had been sent by special messenger to Richmond by a banking house on the Continent, lest by doing so (should the proposal be accepted) we might disturb the market on which those bankers relied to dispose of their loan. Thus, although at great inconvenience to existing engagements, no steps have been taken here in regard to disposing of cotton certificates sent from the Treasury.
>
> The same reason not applying to the Confederate money bonds, Mr. Spence, as financial agent, occupied himself in the proper form of inquiry as to disposing of them; but unfortunately, within the past two weeks, because of some disturbance of capital here, the rate of interest has been raised by the Bank of England from 3%, at which it had long stood, at first to 4 and afterwards to 5%; at which latter rate it now is, but with general expectations of a yet further advance. Mr. Spence's inquiries, therefore, were unsatisfactory and so far fruitless.[37]

Almost as Mason was writing, the Erlanger contract arrived in Europe and Spence considered his worst fears well founded.[38] Bickering broke out and was ended only by the appointment of Gen. C. J. McRae, of Alabama, as special agent for the loan. As Spence heard this painful news, he heard too that Erlanger would issue the bonds at 90%—much too high to be safe. At this point the

[35] *O.R.N.*, ser. 2, 3:675–77.

[36] While representing the Confederate government in London, Mason kept Benjamin well informed regarding Confederate finance and purchasing in Great Britain.

[37] *O.R.N.*, ser. 2, 3:675–77.

[38] Mason, pp. 381–84.

Bank of England lowered its rate of discount to 4%. This step was so generally expected that it produced no effect on funds, beyond confirming a previous tendency to steadiness.[39]

The secret act of Congress authorizing the loan was sealed on 29 January; the London papers had the story early in February.[40] On 15 March Erlanger, writing to Slidell from London, declared:

> I have been yesterday to Liverpool to arrange matters with Messrs. Fraser, Trenholm and Mr. Spence, and I am glad to say my trip has not been unsuccessful. Messrs. Fraser & Company will represent the loan at Liverpool. Here in London, Messrs. J. H. Schroder & Company will bring the loan out. They took it up very warmly and we have very fair prospects of great success. Of course we will open at the same time subscriptions in Paris, Frankfurt and Amsterdam. We are quite ready to start, the only thing wanting being the act of ratification. The solicitors here most seriously object coming before the public without this document in hand and we dare not expose ourselves to add to material difficulties and animosities a well-grounded legal objection which would expose the whole scheme to complete failure.

Erlanger could not understand why the official ratification documents had not arrived.[41] However, the official copy of the act finally reached England on 18 March.[42] On the nineteenth the bonds were put on the market at Liverpool, London, Paris, Frankfurt, and Amsterdam, as Erlanger had promised. They remained on sale until Saturday, 21 March, and nearly £16 million were subscribed.[43]

The following extracts from the prospectus set forth the terms or conditions of the issue of the bonds:

> The bonds to bear interest at the rate of 7% per annum in sterling, from 1st March, 1863, payable half-yearly in London, Paris, Amsterdam or Frankfurt.

[39] *Times*, 20 Feb. 1863. [40] Ibid., 7 Feb. 1863.

[41] Erlanger to John Slidell, 15 Mar. 1863, Erlanger Papers. See also Cotton Loan, Schroder Papers, file C, p. 9. During this period the cotton market showed an advance of ½d to 1d per pound in the Liverpool cotton market. This came at the same time as the Confederate loan was being introduced to the English money market (*Times*, 17 Mar. 1863; *Economist*, 21 Mar. 1863).

[42] *O.R.N.*, ser. 2, 3:712–16. The loan was expected to be introduced in London early the following week (*Times*, 14 Mar. 1863). An authenticated copy of the act of ratification of the contract could be inspected at the offices of Messrs. Freshfields & Newman, the solicitors to the agents of the contractors in London (*Economist*, 21 Mar. 1863). The solicitors of Fraser, Trenholm & Company were Stone, Fletcher & Hull (G. Chandler, City Librarian, Liverpool Public Libraries, to Richard Lester, 18 Sept. 1958).

[43] *O.R.N.*, ser. 2, 3:730–31; J. K. Gilliat to William Gray, Richmond, 25 Apr. 1863, Gilliat Papers.

The bonds exchangeable for cotton on application, at the option of the holder, or redeemable at par in sterling in twenty years, by half-yearly drawings, commencing 1st March, 1864.[44]

Article IV of the contract provided:

Each bond shall, at the option of the holder, be convertible at its nominal amount into cotton, at the rate of sixpence sterling for each pound of cotton—say 4,000 pounds of cotton for each bond of £100, or 2,500 francs; and this at any time not later than six months after the ratification of a treaty of peace between the present belligerents. Notice of the intention of converting bonds into cotton has to be given to the representatives of the Government in Paris or London and sixty days after such notice the cotton will be delivered—if peace, at the ports of Charleston, Savannah, Mobile, or New Orleans; if war, at points in the interior of the country within ten miles of a railroad or stream navigable to the ocean. The delivery will be made free of all charges and duties, excepting the existing export duty of one-eight of one cent per pound. This quality of the cotton to be on the standard of New Orleans middling. If any cotton is of superior or inferior quality, the difference in value shall be settled by two brokers, one to be appointed by the Government, the other by the bond holder; whenever these two brokers cannot agree on the value an umpire is to be chosen, whose decision shall be final. It is at the same time provided that holders that do not convert their bonds into cotton shall be entitled to retain the bonds, and receive interest at the rate of 7% per annum in sterling, payable half-yearly in London, Paris, Amsterdam or Frankfurt, at the option of the holder, until repayment of the principal at par. An annual sinking fund of 5% is provided for, whereby 2½% of the bonds unredeemed by cotton shall be drawn by lot half-yearly; the first drawing to take effect on 1 March, 1864, and to be continued on 1 September, following and on 1 March and 1 September in every succeeding year, so as to finally extinguish the loan in twenty years from the date of the first drawing.

The bonds to be issued at 90%, which is to be paid as follows: 5% on application, 10% on allotment, 10% 1 May, 10% 1 June, 10% 1 July, 15% 1 August, 15% 1 September, less dividend 3½%, 15% 1 October—£90. Subscribers will have the option of paying instalments in advance, on allotment, or on any of the above dates, under discount of

[44] Quoted in the *Times*, 26 Mar. 1863, Schroder Papers, pp. 6–9, 24. Apparently there were hundreds of different Confederate bonds (both coupon and registered): cotton, produce, stock, call, and nontaxable certificates were issued. Only two C.S.A. bonds examined by the author bear the phrase "Second Series." One, with coupons, in pale red and black, portrays the C.S.A. seal at the top with the equestrian statue of Washington. The other is for 4%, has no coupons, and shows the Confederate ironclad *Virginia*.

7% per annum on such pre-payments; but in default, all previous payments will be liable to forfeiture. (By payment under discount, the price of the cotton is reduced to about 5½d per pound).

After allotment scrip certificates will be issued to bearer. These certificates, after payment of the instalment, will be exchanged for bonds to "bearer," in sums of £100, £200, £500, £1,000 each, with coupons attached, payable 1 March, 1 September, as stated above. Arrangements have been made for the execution of the bonds in Paris. From the proceeds of the subscription the contractors and their agents are authorised to retain sufficient funds to pay the first two coupons. The drawings for the operation of the sinking fund will be duly advertised previous to the half-yearly redemption.[45]

On 18 March Erlanger, still in England, wrote to Slidell that he felt it his "duty to announce the probable great success of our loan." He went on, "You can scarcely imagine the excitement it had created in commercial circles and even in the political world and if no contretemps comes till Saturday the Confederate Government will have gained a moral battle with less bloodshed and perhaps as great an advantage as any of the gallant triumphs!"[46]

About this time a vessel arrived in Liverpool with 1,500 bales of cotton, the proceeds of which were to go toward the sinking fund for redeeming the bonds.[47] Although the market was dull, arrivals of cotton were quite considerable. The J. K. Gilliat firm of London had more cotton in 1863 than in 1862.[48]

Mason, writing to Benjamin on 19 March, was quite won over and filled with enthusiasm. He described the "decided and brilliant suc-

[45] *Times*, ibid.; Schroder Papers, p. 4. See also *Fifty-second Catalog of Choice U.S. Coins* (New York: New Netherlands Coin Co., 1958), pp. 8–9. Confederate cotton bonds marketed in England were nice in appearance, uncertain in promise, and based only on scriptural faith. In the loan an annual sinking fund of 5% was provided for, whereby 2½% of the bonds unredeemed by cotton would be drawn by lot half-yearly (*Economist*, 21 Mar. 1863).

[46] Erlanger to John Slidell, 18 Mar. 1863, Erlanger Papers; Schroder Papers, p. 26.

[47] For additional information concerning cotton imports, see Bourne to Fraser, Trenholm & Company, Liverpool, 22 Mar. 1863 (Bourne Letter Book, no. 2), in *Confederate Blockade-Running through Bermuda, 1861–1865: Letters and Cargo Manifests*, ed. Frank E. Vandiver (Austin: University of Texas Press, 1947), pp. 40–41 (cited hereafter as Vandiver, *Blockade-Running*). Much cotton was shipped to J. K. Gilliat & Co., London, in the blockade-runners *Annie Childs* and *Black Swan* (J. K. Gilliat to Liverpool [no name], 4 June 1863, Gilliat Papers).

[48] In 1863, 385,000 bales; in 1862, 289,000 bales (J. K. Gilliat to E. H. Green, Henderson, Tenn., 12 Aug. 1863, Gilliat Papers). Although the market was dull, prices were steady (Gilliat to J. P. Taylor, 15 June 1863, ibid.).

cess of the Confederate loan," and praised Erlanger as a man of "great diligence and tact." [49] The bonds were at a premium of 4½ to 5% on the first day. On 20 March the *Times* reported that they had "constituted the sole topic of attention today in the stock exchange and in every other department of business the transactions have been limited to flat prices." [50] Very little political feeling was manifested toward the floatation, and it seemed evident, that London viewed it as a cotton speculation, whose advantages or disadvantages would be determined by the people of Manchester and Liverpool.[51] There can be no doubt, however, that a majority of English merchants and capitalists would have preferred that the loan had not been introduced.[52] As to the money market, the *Times* suggested that it would lessen the drain of specie which might be expected on the announcement of the end of hostilities.[53]

On 21 March Slidell wrote to Benjamin: "You will, before this dispatch can reach you, have seen by the newspapers the brilliant success of Erlanger and Company's loan. The affair has been admirably managed by them, and cannot fail to exercise a most salutory influence on both sides of the atlantic. It is a financial recognition of our independence, emanating from a class proverbially cautious, and little given to be influenced by sentiment or sympathy." [54]

The *Economist* was fairly well pleased with the loan,[55] although it could scarcely imagine any combination of circumstances under which cotton would fall as low as 6d or even 7d per pound.[56] The paper went on to comment that it was somewhat startling that the Confederates should be able to borrow money in England so freely while the Federals "had been unable to obtain a shilling from that usually liberal and enterprising quarter." [57] It felt, however, that the loan was favorable to British investment, had an element of at-

[49] Richardson, 2:439–45; Mason, no. 31, 19 Mar. 1863.

[50] *Times*, 21 Mar., 20 Mar. 1863. The loan ranged between about 3 and 5% with very large and numerous transactions, the market being occasionally stimulated by quotations from Liverpool.

[51] Richardson, 2:541–43. [52] *Times*, 21 Mar. 1863. [53] Ibid.

[54] Richardson, 2:541–43.

[55] *Economist*, 21 Mar. 1863. The Confederate government was known to have in its possession 365,000 bales of cotton which at 6d per pound was more than sufficient to cover the entire loan. How to get the cotton out of the Confederate States was quite another matter.

[56] *Economist*, 21 Mar. 1863. It is interesting to note that subscriptions came direct from Russia (Mason, no. 32, 30 Mar. 1863).

[57] Writing to J. K. Gilliat on 6 Apr. 1863, M. H. Clark, of Clarksville, Tenn., claimed that when peace came Virginia would have perhaps 5 million bales of cotton to sell (Gilliat Papers).

tractive speculation in it, yet was well backed by cotton prices and Southern reserves of cotton.[58] The *Index* claimed that the transaction was an astonishing success and was by far the greatest triumph that the Confederates had yet achieved either in arms or by diplomacy.[59] The legality of the loan was questioned in some financial quarters but without reason. The *Index* maintained that during the Greek revolution the Corporation of London subscribed out of their municipal funds in aid of the Greek insurgents and was justified in its action by the British government.[60]

There were some who were not so pleased with the loan. On 31 March 1863 President Thomas Bayley Potter and other officers of the Union and Emancipation Society of Manchester issued an address to the chambers of commerce of Great Britain and Ireland protesting against the financial support of the Confederate war effort.[61] Gilliat and Company of London thought that there was the possibility of a war with the North. Gilliat was pleased with the loan but gave his opinion that "we are prepared for a violent burst of indignation and outcry against England because of the Confederate loan, and war with England would certainly *not* help them [the North] out of their present difficulties." [62]

The Erlanger agents noted that "bonds sold so well that some 154,728 were called back, followed by another 1,228." [63] In the Confederacy itself, conditions were serious, and the loan was a ray of hope, expected to sustain the war and remedy the ever-falling value of the currency. On 25 March 1863 gold was nearly five to one; [64] flour cost at least thirty dollars a barrel and in some places as much

[58] *Economist,* 21 Mar. 1863.

[59] *Index,* 26 Mar. 1863. The only government script at a premium, besides the Confederate, was the Portuguese, which was quoted at 2 to 3% premium. Russian scrip was quoted as par. For an analysis of the *Index* and its founder, Henry Hotze, see Charles P. Cullop, *Confederate Propaganda in Europe, 1861–1865* (Coral Gables, Fla.: University of Miami Press, 1969).

[60] *Index,* 26 Mar. 1863. See also J. K. Gilliat to George M. McCook, 1 Apr. 1863, Gilliat Papers.

[61] Edward Channing, *History of the United States* 6 vols. (New York: Macmillan, 1927–30), 6:361.

[62] J. K. Gilliat to F. L. Brauns & Co., Baltimore, 8 Apr. 1863, to A. H. Armistead, 24 Apr. 1863, Gilliat Papers.

[63] Erlanger Papers, book 3, 1863, p. 165. In March 1863 the bonds were selling at from 90% to 95% and then fell suddenly to 86% (J. C. Schwab, "The Confederate Foreign Loan: An Episode in the Financial History of the Civil War," *Yale Review* 1 (1892):175–86.

[64] I. R. Phillips to Persia, Frick & Ball, Baltimore, 11 Apr. 1863, Gilliat Papers.

as sixty or ninety dollars. Many items of common domestic usage and requirement were completely unobtainable.[65]

But the early jubilation was soon muted; in spite of their first success, the bonds began to sag slowly and by 3 April they were at 86% or 4% below par.[66] It was feared that confidence would soon fall completely, the bottom would drop out of the market, and perhaps bondholders would forfeit their 15% deposit already paid rather than meet the next installment, soon due. It was said that the bonds fell because of federal propaganda, but Erlanger's greediness was really at the root.[67] As Spence said, "This loan ought never to have been put before the public at 90%—a price which even well-established European Governments had been unable to sustain." [68]

Erlanger urged that Mason enter the market and buy the bonds to sustain the prices.[69] Erlanger claimed that he followed Slidell's advice in advising Mason to support the price of the Confederate loan in London.[70] J. C. Schwab has stated that the part which Erlanger and Company played in the attempt to manipulate the London market cannot be satisfactorily explained. He found it strange that the bankers who were directly, or indirectly through their clients, interested in sustaining the bonds should not have given facilities to unlucky bondholders to rid themselves on favorable terms of securities that were proving of doubtful value. Schwab has concluded that Erlangers were open to the grave suspicion of having been large holders of the bonds themselves and of having quietly unloaded them on the unsuspecting Confederate agents when

[65] *The Civil War Diary of General Josiah Gorgas*, ed. Frank E. Vandiver (University: University of Alabama Press, 1947), p. 27 (cited hereafter as *Gorgas Diary*). Butter cost $3 a pound, eggs $2 a dozen; a turkey cost $15; beef was $1.50 per pound (ibid.; *Times*, 10 Apr. 1863).

[66] Schwab, "Foreign Loan," pp. 181–82.

[67] J. K. Gilliat to D. Salomon, 10 Apr. 1863, Gilliat Papers. "The Federals are also believed to be trying for a loan here. It is thought that it will not go down, and if they are wise they will not attempt to offer it publicly, for a failure is worse than not attempting it at all" (Gilliat to James Thomas, Jr., Richmond, 28 Apr. 1863, ibid.).

[68] Mason, no. 32, p. 401; J. K. Gilliat to James Thomas, Jr., Richmond, 28 Apr. 1863, Gilliat Papers.

[69] Mr. Leban, of Tennessee, a member of the Confederate Congress, moved to approve Mason's removal from London because Russell would not acknowledge him as the representative of an independent power (*Richmond Dispatch*, 7 Apr. 1863; Richardson, 2:541–43).

[70] 3 Apr. 1863, Erlanger Papers; Schwab, "Foreign Loan," pp. 181–82; Erlanger to John Slidell, 9 Apr. 1863, Erlanger Papers.

the market showed signs of collapsing.[71] Such an explanation seems logical but is strictly within the realms of speculation. It is certain that on 7 April an agreement was signed between Mason and Erlanger by which Erlanger was authorized to buy on behalf of the Confederate government bonds to the value of £1 million or any smaller sum as might be deemed necessary to restore the value of the bonds.[72] Erlanger reserved the right to resell the bonds thus acquired at not less than 90%, with any profits going to the Confederate government. Slidell enthusiastically supported the agreement as being in the best interests of the government.[73]

So, from 8 April to the end of the month, the Confederate agents bulled the market, driving the bonds above par by the second day, but spending more than £1 million in doing so. On 20 April the *Times* reported that the loan was well maintained at 1% premium.[74] On the twenty-second J. K. Gilliat, the London merchant and banker, reported on the money situation to his American agent: "In our money market here there is some dullness and absence of speculation as the natural reaction from a speculative excitement and absorption of money in sundry foreign loans last month, the Confederate Cotton Loan of £3,000,000 among them. Money is easy at 2% and the bank rate for discount is expected to be lowered at the Bank Court tomorrow. Gold continues to pour into the bank—£107,000 came in yesterday."[75] Between 9 April and 24 April, £1,388,500 worth of bonds were bought in this way,[76] and Erlanger convinced Mason that a total of £1.5 million should be spent to strengthen the market.[77]

[71] Schwab, pp. 181–82.

[72] Articles of agreement between Mason and Erlanger, 7 Apr. 1863, Erlanger Papers. Witness to the signatures: J. H. Schroder of London.

[73] *O.R.N.*, ser. 2, 3:735–38, Articles of an engagement entered into 7 Apr. 1863 between Mason and Emile Erlanger & Company; John Slidell to Emile Erlanger & Co., 10 Apr. 1863, Erlanger Papers.

[74] On 11 April 1863 the Confederate loan did an enormous business and was steady from 1 to 1½ premium (*Times*, 11 Apr. 1863). In the face of the boom, Gorgas wrote, "It is undoubtedly the forerunner of recognition" (*Gorgas Diary*, pp. 31–32); *Times*, 20 Apr. 1863.

[75] J. K. Gilliat to Wilbur & Price, New York, 22 Apr. 1863; to B. D. Keesee, 23 Apr. 1863; to Watts Crane Co., New York, 24 Apr. 1863, Gilliat Papers.

[76] Mason, no. 34, 27 Apr. 1863; *Times*, 23 Apr. 1863; J. K. Gilliat to W. P. Arnold, Trenton, Ky., 23 Apr. 1863, Gilliat Papers.

[77] The *Richmond Sentinel* stated that Erlanger's profits amounted to $2.5 million. Schwab, "Foreign Loan," pp. 181–82.

This was not the only financial transaction in which Erlanger had an interest; he held a considerable amount of stock in the Cincinnati, New Orleans

This new plunge and the news from Charleston of the repulse of the federal attack allowed 1 May to pass with the bonds above par,[78] but despite constant purchases only ½% above premium.[79] Gilliat maintained that his company would not buy Confederate bonds because the cotton loan was at a premium and would probably not maintain that standing. He was confident that there would be plenty of opportunities to purchase bonds in the future, if it seemed desirable then.[80] It is true that all the Confederate bonds which came over from America late in April had a shadowy and speculative character in London; money could not be raised upon them in the ordinary way. Some went to contractors for supplies, since they could get nothing else from the agents at that time.[81]

However, the *Economist* encouraged the buying of Southern treasury notes in Great Britain,[82] because money was abundant at 2 to 2½%.[83] Erlanger wrote to Slidell that he had had a long conversation with a Mr. Holmes (the lawyer who secured the release of the *Alabama*), and on the basis of this talk he thought it wise to buy more bonds in the name of the government in order to prevent a panic. He sent Holmes to see Slidell in order to discuss the matter of further purchase.[84]

---

and Texas Pacific Railway Company. His holdings in America were vast. He was accustomed to American investment and had "the mind of the American financier" (Mathilde Slidell Erlanger to Erlanger, 18 Apr. 1863, Erlanger Papers).

[78] Gilliat wrote, "The Confederates are doing their own work alone, nobly and successfully and they have deserved and obtained the admiration and sympathy of the world" (J. K. Gilliat to William Barret, Richmond, 24 Apr. 1863; to R. D. Caldwell, Paris, Tenn., 29 Apr. 1863, Gilliat Papers). See also Mason, no. 35, 27 Apr. 1863.

[79] J. K. Gilliat to James Thomas, Jr., Richmond, 28 Apr. 1863, Gilliat Papers. The bank rate was reduced to 3% (Gilliat to W. H. Macfarland, 1 May, 1863, ibid.).

[80] J. K. Gilliat to J. P. Taylor, Richmond, 30 Apr. 1863, ibid.; Gilliat invested in Virginia state bonds (Gilliat to O., Richmond, 8 June 1863, ibid.). For Alabama state bonds and British investors, see Richardson, 2:498–505.

[81] Holders thought that matters would not improve overnight (J. K. Gilliat to I. R. Phillips, Liverpool, 2 May 1863; to John Smith & Co., Louisville, Ky.; to William Barret, Richmond, 4 May 1863, Gilliat Papers; *Bankers' Magazine*, 1863, p. 67).

[82] *Economist*, 2 May 1863. See also J. K. Gilliat to David Dunlop, Petersburg, Va., 6 May 1863, Gilliat Papers.

[83] J. K. Gilliat to A. J. Black, Augusta, Ga., 7 May 1863; to J. B. Daniel, Jr., president of the Richmond, Fredericksburg and Potomac Railway, 8 May 1863, Gilliat Papers.

[84] 9 May 1863, Erlanger Papers.

On 11 May the bonds closed at par,[85] perhaps as a result of the news that some federal ships had succeeded in running past Vicksburg.[86] On the twentieth the loan was at ½% below par;[87] and on the twenty-seventh the *Times* reported that the loan was dull the morning before at 2-to-1 discount, adding that rumors were circulating that France would mediate between the opposing American nations.[88] The *Index*, however, though pleading that Europe should exert its moral authority to make peace, was sure that the war would continue for an indefinite period.[89]

On 2 June the loan had slipped again, to as far as 2½ discount;[90] it rallied slightly during the month[91] and there was confidence in England that Vicksburg could not be taken by the Federals.[92] On the eighth Gilliat authorized J. P. Taylor of Richmond to purchase £5,000 worth of Confederate bonds, "drawing upon us in London for cost at current rates of exchange. We do this with very full confidence in both the stability and integrity of your new Government." These bonds were to be held by Taylor until Gilliat was able to have them safely transmitted.[93] Gilliat propounded that

[85] *O.R.N.*, ser. 2, 3:751–53. As a precaution Gilliat requested that insurance be provided on the cotton sent abroad. British consuls were used to help ship cotton out of the Confederate States (J. K. Gilliat to David B. Harris, 12 May 1863, Gilliat Papers.

[86] Mason, no. 36, 11 May 1863.

[87] J. K. Gilliat to K. F. Beaumont & Son, Clarksville, Tenn., 20 May 1863; to J. B. Daniel, Jr., 20 May 1863; to D. R. Burbank [Destination not given], 23 May 1863, Gilliat Papers.

[88] 27 May 1863. "From Federal sources in London there is as of yet, however, no symptom of an alteration in tone such as to encourage a hope of the probability of an early and reasonable effort for a Pacific adjustment" (ibid. See also J. K. Gilliat to J. P. Taylor, Richmond, 8 June 1863, Gilliat Papers).

[89] *Index*, 28 May 1863.

[90] *Times*, 2 June 1863. It was also reported that the Confederate commissioners were using their best efforts to open the way to peace, either by mediation or in any other way that would be consistent with the honor of the South.

[91] Ibid., 4 June 1863.

[92] J. K. Gilliat to S. T., New York, 12 June 1863, Gilliat Papers. By 8 June 1863 money was easy at 3½ to 4% (ibid., Gilliat to J. P. Taylor, Richmond, 8 June 1863). During this period Gilliat did a huge business in blockade-running, and profits were running high (Gilliat to William Gray, Richmond, 23 June 1863, ibid.).

[93] J. K. Gilliat to William Gray, 23 June 1863, ibid. Money was easy at 3½ to 4%. In London there were plenty of new schemes afloat to employ loose capital to support Confederate financial activity (Gilliat to E. J. Hudson, 23 June 1863, ibid.).

"the fate of Vicksburg depends upon the movements of Johnson." [94] Many bankers and merchants in London thought that the fall of Vicksburg and Port Hudson would be fatal to the Confederate cause. The status of Southern bonds depended on the outcome of the battle of Vicksburg.

By 9 July the loan was again at 1% discount,[95] and on the sixteenth it had risen to ½%, but by the twenty-third the market was concerned about rumors of the defeat of the Confederates at Vicksburg and the loan touched 5% discount.[96] By the end of July the rumors were confirmed: Vicksburg had fallen to the Federals, and on the thirteenth the stock fell as low as 20% discount.[97] Conflicting reports on the true fate of the Confederate armies held the price for a while, but on one occasion it dipped to 36% discount.[98] Luckily, once past the June payment bondholders were not likely to risk forfeiture, so the Confederate agents were not forced to go into the market again after the £1.5 million was spent.

In effect, the loan had failed. Over half the bonds had been bought back by the Confederate government by 14 May 1863, and very few were ever sold again.[99] This left $7.5 million purchased, but of this sum the Confederacy received only 77%, less 5% commission, less 1% to Erlanger for acting as collection agent, less 8% on deferred payments made before they were due. Added to this, one-twentieth of the bonds had to be redeemed each year, plus 8% interest. It is estimated that considerably less than $3 million

[94] J. K. Gilliat to William Pare, Baltimore 22 June 1863, ibid. It is surprising to learn just how well-informed London bankers and merchants were in regard to the military happenings in America.

[95] *Index*, 9 July 1863. The public were waiting for further news from America and, if favorable to the South, the *Index* felt there would be a considerable rise in the loan (ibid.).

[96] Ibid., 16 July 1863. On 18 July there had been a reaction of a ¼%, the last price being ¾ to ¼ discount (*Times*, 18 July 1863); *Index*, 23 July 1863.

[97] *A Cycle of Adams Letters, 1861–1865*, ed. Worthington C. Ford, 2 vols., (Boston: Houghton Mifflin, 1920), 1:65–66 (cited hereafter as *Adams Letters*); *Index*, 30 July 1863.

[98] *O.R.N.*, ser. 2, 3:875–81.

[99] Ernest A. Smith claims that the loan may be considered a success, in comparison with other financial affairs (pp. 107–10). See also note 121. For a comparison of the Erlanger Loan to Union issues in terms of relative purchasing power, see Paul Studenski and Herman E. Krooss, *Financial History of the United States: Fiscal, Monetary, Banking and Tariff, Including Financial Administration and State and Local Finance* (New York: McGraw-Hill, 1952), pp. 144–45, 153.

ever came into the hands of the Confederates as the result of Emile Erlanger's shrewd manipulation of John Slidell.[100]

In the South conditions were steadily worsening. Confederate notes were exchanged for gold at the rate of twelve or fifteen dollars to the dollar.[101] By August, flour was $40 a barrel, bacon $1.75 a pound, butter $3 a pound.[102] On 6 August 1863 Mason wrote of the failure of the loan, remarking that only the day before it had been as low as 30% discount and adding that it was obvious that the proceeds could not possibly cover the needs of the purchasing agents. By now Confederate reverses in the field were causing severe disquiet to some of the bondholders.[103] McRae was constrained to reply to inquiries and to make his statements public:

> On 1 March last the Government of the Confederate States had purchased about 320,000 bales of cotton. The purchasing was still going on, and it is fair to presume that by this time the quantity has been increased to at least 500,000 bales. This cotton is principally in the states of Georgia and Alabama, and some also in the Eastern part of Mississippi, North-Western Louisiana, and Texas, and is stored on the plantations of the planters from whom it was purchased, in the sheds or warehouses 300 feet from any other buildings, and in all cases the planters have agreed with the Government to take the same care of the cotton as if it still belonged to them, and deliver it to the order of the Government when wanted. The capture of our sea ports could not endanger the loss of a single pound of cotton, as there are no stocks of cotton at any of them, nor are there any considerable stocks of cotton at any one place in the interior, care having been taken by the Confederate, as well as the State Governments, that no cotton shall be stored at any point within five miles of a railroad station or navigable stream.

[100] The purchasing agents in England received the following amount of money from the Erlanger loan:

North	£30,000	2 Aug. 1863
Huse	£22,000	22 June 1863
Maury	£28,000	15 July 1863
Huse	£10,251	28 July 1863

Seventeen million francs were credited to the Confederate government on 1 October 1863 (Ledger Book, 1863, p. 134, Erlanger Papers).

[101] *New York Herald*, 1 July 1863; *Bankers' Magazine*, 1863, p. 394.

[102] John B. Jones, *A Rebel War Clerk's Diary*, 2 vols., ed. Howard Swiggert (New York: Old Hickory Bookshop, 1935), 2:5 (cited hereafter as Jones, *War Diary*). Jones wrote, "We are used to wounds and death; but can hardly bear starvation and nakedness." The value of the Jones diary is that it vividly presents the hopes and fears of the Confederate States, especially the city of Richmond, where he lived. A loaf of bread costing 5 cents at the beginning of the war cost $1 in April 1865 (*Confederate Veteran* 34, no. 4 (1926): 124.

[103] Mason, no. 43, pp. 444–45, ibid., pp. 412–14.

That portion of the crop of 1861 which have been brought to the various interior depots has long been taken back to the plantations by special order of the State Governments. The cotton will be delivered to any holder of the bonds on demand, as provided for in the fourth article of the contract. In the states of Alabama and Mississippi, where I have personal knowledge of the manner in which the business has been transacted, the cotton has been sampled, weighed, marked, and invoiced, and the agents of the bond holders can examine the samples at the offices of the chief agents of the loan in the different states and take their orders on the planters for the delivery of the cotton without trouble or expense. Cotton obtained under this loan will not be subject to tax or duty, except the export duty of one eighth of a cent per pound, existing at the date of the contract.[104]

On the following day the *Times* noted that "a very large and influential class of people who have made, are making, or hope to make fortunes out of the expenditure of war" were alarmed that the tide of victory seemed to have set so strongly in favor of federal arms,[105] and on 8 August the *Economist* roundly declared that the South's luck was over and it could now only expect the "natural consequences" of entering the war.[106]

Faced with these circumstances, the *Index* reported on 13 August that the loan stood at 26% discount.[107] Confederate agents in Europe used Erlanger bonds in their hands as collateral or even as a simple medium of exchange. With the failure of the loan, these bonds were no better than the ordinary cotton certificates.[108] Caleb Huse, for example, used repurchased Erlanger bonds to pay his debt to Isaac,

[104] *Index*, 6 Aug. 1863; *Manchester Guardian*, 7 Aug. 1863; *Bankers' Magazine*, 1863, p. 394.

[105] 7 Aug. 1863. The *Times* reported that "by the 1st July, 1864, the debt of the Federal Government would greatly exceed two thousand millions of dollars, or, at the ordinary rate of exchange, four hundred millions of pounds sterling. Great Britain owes £800,000,000 sterling." The Southern debt would have to be added to the Northern to arrive at the real money cost of the war. It is interesting to note that Americans in four years attained a state of indebtedness by their war that took England nearly 200 years to incur in battles by sea and land. See also the *Economist*, 8 Aug. 1863.

[106] *Economist*, 8 Aug. 1863. Memminger was now shipping gold out of the country ($20,000 by each steamer). This was probably with the aim of arresting the depreciation of Confederate currency. The standing of the loan may have made the use of gold essential to maintain a market for the bonds in London (Jones, *War Diary*, 2:11 [12 Aug. 1863], 2:18–19 [19 Aug.].

[107] *Index*, 13 Aug. 1863. This Confederate publication in England continually claimed that adverse influences were evidently at work to depress the price and that agents of the Northern government were at the bottom of these maneuvres.

[108] Company statements, 8, 10, 11 May 1863, Erlanger Papers.

Campbell and Company of London. On 25 May 1863 he owed them £515,000 on behalf of the Confederacy; half of this amount was paid off through Erlanger.[109] Fortunately for him—and unfortunately for Isaac, Campbell—Huse made his deal before the fall of Vicksburg; when the bottom dropped out of the market Isaac, Campbell could only sell at a great loss. This was indeed poetic justice, for the firm had systematically mulcted the Confederacy, keeping, as the agents soon discovered, a duplicate set of books to further their frauds.[110] With this news public among the agents, the company was left to enjoy its bonds; legal action was even discussed.[111]

The *Morning Post* of 18 August maintained that in the foreign market the Confederate loan was "not withstanding the more favourable news for the Confederate cause, quoted at 24 and 22 discount." It had heard that there were agents in London and Liverpool under directions to sell Confederate securities for Northern account at almost any sacrifice in order to damage Southern credit in England, but the *Post* was not certain whether this scheme would succeed.[112] By 20 August the loan stood at 30% discount;[113] on the twenty-fifth Erlanger wrote to Slidell that the loan was at 22% discount.[114] By the twenty-seventh it was at 23,[115] and in the autumn McRae was able to dispose of a further large number of bonds to pay for the debts of Huse and Bulloch and other purchasing agents.[116]

On 1 September, an installment of 15% on the dividend of the loan was paid, and on 1 October the last installment of 15% became due.[117] The fluctuations of the loan fully established that its fortunes varied with the fortunes of war, and Mason wrote to Benjamin that it would be "unwise to look at present to a future loan in Europe."[118]

109 Ledger Book, 1863, ibid.; see also *O.R.*, ser. 4, 2:845.

110 Jones, *War Diary* 2:11 (12 Aug. 1863); 2:42 (12 Sept. 1863).

111 *O.R.*, ser. 4, 2:1067–81.

112 There is some evidence in the Erlanger Papers to support the view that Slidell sold Confederate securities for Northern account; see Emile Erlanger to John Slidell, 4 Nov., 10 Nov. 1863.

113 *Index*, 20 Aug. 1863. See also *O.R.*, ser. 4, 2:735. Jones declared, "Our cause is dim in Europe" (*War Diary*, 2:20 [20 Aug. 1863]).

114 25 Aug. 1863, Erlanger Papers.

115 *Index*, 27 Aug. 1863.

116 Mason, p. 405. (See also Jones, *War Diary*, 2:42 [12 Sept. 1863]). *O.R.*, ser. 4, 2:979–83. But it was so difficult to provide the government steamers with cargoes of cotton that the *Cornubia* had to leave Wilmington empty (Eaton, p. 146; *O.R.*, ser. 4, 2:735).

117 *Index*, 3 Sept. 1863.

118 Richardson, 2:560–62; *Index*, 10 Sept. 1863.

The Confederate financial situation was now at a new low, one attributable to the great depreciation of the currency and to the lavish creation of paper money without taxation. Confederate currency depreciated more than 1,000% below gold and silver and 400% below suspended bank notes.[119] Financial troubles almost invariably beget spite, and about this time it was being said that Jefferson Davis and members of his cabinet had a large special fund in Europe, so that in the event the Confederacy lost the war their retirement would be provided for.[120]

In retrospect it is easy to see that the loan was useless as a financial measure, except insofar as it benefited the shipbuilders and bankers in Europe. Nevertheless, the fact that it was launched at all shows that it represented financial support of the Confederacy by the European commercial world. Although this support was of little practical value, especially to the purchasing agents, it must have given great satisfaction to the Richmond authorities, who were so signally unsuccessful in gaining substantial support from the established governments of Europe.

One of the principal reasons for the failure of the loan was its bad management. But under the most skilled management, it is doubtful that it could have done better, given the inherent weakness of the South. "Cotton is king," certainly, but as Professor Schwab has correctly indicated, the successful blockade of the coast by a Union navy restricted its export. Therefore, what the South supposed to be its greatest strength was also its greatest weakness. The concentration of all economic strength along such restricted lines reduced the possibility of Southern success in the Civil War to almost nothing, and final defeat became inevitable.[121]

In Great Britain some of the financial and commercial difficulties the Confederates faced were certainly of their own making. A major fault was their uncoordinated methods of securing supplies. At one time or another, a dozen or more purchasing agents might be active, sometimes even bidding one against another. When Spence had been appointed "financial agent," it was to be assumed

[119] *Times*, 10 Sept. 1863; 23 Jan. 1864; Jones, *War Diary*, 2:103 (23 Nov. 1863). On 17 Sept. the closing price of the loan was 25½ to 24½ (*Index*, 17 Sept. 1863). On 24 Sept. it was firmer at 31 discount (ibid., 24 Sept. 1863). For additional quotations, see App. II.

[120] Jones, *War Diary*, 2:67 (10 Oct. 1863), 2:83 (27 Oct. 1863).

[121] Schwab, "Foreign Loan," pp. 185–86. *Bankers' Magazine*, 1864, p. 935. In a well-researched and carefully documented article, Ms. Judith Gentry proposes that the Erlanger loan must be considered a successful Confederate effort in Europe ("A Confederate Success in Europe: The Erlanger Loan," *Journal of Southern History* 36, no. 2 [1970]: 157–188).

that he was to supervise and control all expenditure, but no sooner had he been appointed than Slidell broached the Erlanger loan. Yet McRae was given specific supervision of this loan, the negotiations for which effectively curtailed all other business for some months. In short, Spence was never given any real opportunity to exercise the overall authority that was so badly needed. Toward the end of 1863 he was advised that McRae would supplant him as general financial agent. No doubt McRae enjoyed greater confidence from the purchasing agents, which was important if he was to establish a central agency. But the main reason for Spence's dismissal was his attitude toward slavery. He would go about the country suggesting, or even offering, abolition in return for financial and commercial support for the Southern states, a proposal that was of course unacceptable to the Confederate government.[122]

McRae was an able man. From the time of his appointment until the end of the war, he worked steadily and effectively to perfect the purchasing system and to eliminate friction among agents.[123]

Bonds, certificates, loans—all had been tried.[124] Now, in the cold dawn of 1864, the Confederates had to resort to the systematic shipment of cotton to finance their foreign purchases.[125] As they had begun to realize in 1863, it was the only course left; all else had failed. Now was the time to act. Before the war a bale of cotton cost about £11; now the price was £40.[126] As early as December

[122] *O.R.N.*, ser. 2, 3:944–48; ibid., 3:948. However, it should be noted that Spence was a most active and effective propagandist for the Confederates in Great Britain (*Times*, 19 May 1862). Spence and his fellow British Confederates had launched a somewhat successful movement to create a situation that would demand continued English support for the Confederacy. See James Spence, *Southern Independence*, an address delivered at a public meeting in the City Hall, Glasgow, 16 Nov. 1863 (London: Richard Bentley, n.d.); and Spence, *The American Union and the Causes of the Disruption* (London: Richard Bentley, 1861).

[123] Richardson, 2:560–62; Mason, pp. 447–49. McRae was well versed in practically everything appertaining to the export of cotton (Richardson, ibid.; Jones, *War Diary*, 2:42 [12 Sept. 1863]). For an analysis of McRae's financial activities in Europe, see Charles S. Davis, *Colin J. McRae: Confederate Financial Agent* (Tuscaloosa: Ala., Confederate Publishing Co., 1961).

[124] The author has inspected a parcel of unissued cotton certificates (Schroder Papers, ref. no. 29, 1863). For mention of the Confederate loan, see Book of Issues, J. H. Schroder & Co., pp. 401, 680, 874, 1500, ibid.

[125] *Times*, 16 Jan. 1864.

[126] *Bankers' Magazine*, 1864, p. 393. The scarcity and high cost of cotton caused distress in Lancashire, where mills closed or put their men on short time. There were 42,973 people on short time; 33,725 people were out of work; 9,316 received relief from boards of guardians and district relief committees. At the height of the depression 114,600 operatives or their relatives were on re-

1863 Huse had purchased four English steamers for the official use of the government to ship in supplies and bring out cotton.[127] By autumn, these ships had run the blockade forty-four times without capture.[128] In September 1863 McRae recommended that the government should take blockade-running entirely into its own hands, and in October, in consultation with Slidell and other purchasing agents, he sent detailed recommendations to Memminger.[129]

They were acting not a moment too soon. The South was being steadily drained of what little gold it had left,[130] and as *Bankers' Magazine* pointed out at the turn of the year, the amount of cotton in store in the Confederate states represented £35 million value on the English market.[131] Tardily, almost too late, the South was now about to do what it should have done at the outset of the war. King Cotton was at last to be dethroned and made to work for his people. This was the plan of 1864.

Finally, on 6 February 1864 Congress passed a law prohibiting the shipment of cotton except under permit of the president and on the same day enacted a law forbidding the import of luxuries.[132] On this situation the *Times* commented, somewhat acidly: "The

---

lief. Lancashire started a public works program to aid the cotton workers, but this provided only a few with employment. However, not one person was known to have died by hunger in all Lancashire during the whole of the cotton famine (*Times*, 12 Oct. 1864). For the substantial profits made during the cotton famine, see W. O. Henderson, *The Lancashire Cotton Famine, 1861–1865* (Manchester: Manchester University Press, 1934), pp. 14–15. For rates of cotton before the war, see Minute Book of the American Chamber of Commerce, Liverpool, 27 Aug. 1861, p. 450.

127

Quarter ending	*Pounds of cotton exported per month*
30 Sept. 1861	24,312
31 Dec. 1861	664,716
31 Mar. 1862	351,586
30 June 1862	223,709
30 Sept. 1862	701,109
31 Dec. 1862	1,551,788
31 Mar. 1863	1,401,505
31 May 1863	2,197,716

For reference to the Huse steamers, see Richardson, 2:546–55.

128 *O.R.N.*, ser. 2, 3:882–89; Richardson, 2:546–55.

129 Richardson, 2:560–62. *O.R.*, ser. 2, 3:979–88.

130 *Times*, 1 Jan. 1864; *Gorgas Diary*, p. 61; *Bankers' Magazine*, 1864, pp. 934–35.

131 1864, pp. 934–35. For a comparative price list of the world cotton market, see Erlanger to Slidell, 22 Oct. 1863, Erlanger Papers.

132 *O.R.*, ser. 5, 3:79–82.

inevitable truths of finance are at length beginning to dawn upon the Southern mind. For three years past the acute and intelligent people of the States have been deluding themselves into a belief that by some fortunate privilege they could escape the operation of inexorable laws; that they could spend without paying and borrow without feeling the debt."[133] On 5 March 1864 regulations were issued providing that one-half the outbound cargo and one-half of the inbound should be on Confederate account at fixed rates; further, one-half of the private cargo exported from the Confederacy had to be invested in goods bought in the Confederacy.[134]

By spring 1864 the receipt of this news in London and the organizational efforts of McRae brought about a small but steady rise in prices of the Erlanger loan, a rise that continued all summer.[135] On 2 April the *Economist* reported that

> a joint-stock company (limited with a capital of £250,000) is now in formation in London, Liverpool and Paris—under the auspices of the Confederate States Government for blockade running on a large scale. It is proposed to purchase or build ten steamers specially for running the blockade. The shares in the company are to be allotted exclusively to holders of Confederate cotton bonds, the market price of which will, it is expected, be thus improved. Should the public respond to the company's appeal—the capital will be increased to £500,000 sterling. These steamers are to run from Bermuda, Nassau and Havana, to Mobile, Charleston and Wilmington. Their inward cargoes will be exclusively the property of the Confederate States Government, their outward cargoes cotton, for joint account of that Government and the shareholders. The promoters who had great experience in blockade running are sanguine of the scheme proving successful. We draw attention to this scheme—not because it is financially sound—but because it is politically curious.[136]

But, rather as the *Economist* anticipated, nothing came of this scheme. The only way the South could guard against continued depreciation of the currency was to frame a sound tax bill.

If the Confederacy was at least practicing a policy of partial financial realism, the new plan nevertheless brought many new problems. Cotton was plentiful in the South, but that which had been bought under the produce loans was mostly stored at plantations in the interior, often in inaccessible places, and the government was forced to purchase new supplies that were in the warehouse and could be shipped easily. To effect this, the government chose agents with

[133] 4 Mar. 1864. [134] *O.R.*, ser. 4, 2:187–89; see also *Times*, 1 July 1864.
[135] *Times*, 31 Mar. 1864. *Index*, 31 Mar., 19 May, 28 July 1864.
[136] 2 Apr. 1864. *Times*, 8 Apr. 1864.

the unhappy talent for creating chaos, a talent that seems to have been a feature of so many Southern financial negotiations. Each department began by purchasing its own cotton. By the summer of 1864 a score of agents were buying for shipment to Fraser, Trenholm and Company in Liverpool.[137] In the autumn this plan was abandoned, and all purchasing came under central authorities. The new realism of the South paid dividends. In July, McRae reported that he had been able to place large orders for essential supplies and for fourteen new steamers to run the blockade.[138]

A government report of 10 November 1864 gave some figures of the value of government cotton purchases.[139] The number of bales had by then reached 430,724 at a cost of $34,525,220. Of this amount 129,771 bales were lost by capture, burned by the Confederacy, or used for war purposes; 67,653 were held west of the Mississippi and subject to military uses; 6,961 were sold by the Treasury; and 19,683 were sent to England to pay the foreign debt, leaving a balance yet available of 191,041 bales.[140]

Three days earlier Jefferson Davis had made an interesting statement on finance to the Senate:[141]

> Your special attention is earnestly invited to the report of the Secretary of the Treasury, submitted in conformity with law. The facts therein disclosed are far from discouraging, and demonstrate that with judicious legislation we shall be enabled to meet all the exigencies of the war from our abundant resources and avoid at the same time such an accumulation of debt as would render at all doubtful our capacity to redeem it. The total receipts in the treasury for the two quarters ending on 30 September, 1864 were $415,191,550, which sum, added to the balance of $308,282,722 that remained in the Treasury on 1 April last, forms a total of $723,474,272. Of this total, not far from half—that is to say, $342,560,327 has been applied to the extinction of the public debt, while the total expenditures have been $272,378,505, leaving a balance in the Treasury on 1 October, 1864, of $108,535,440.
>
> The total amount of the public debt, as exhibited on the books of the Register of the Treasury on 1 October, 1864, was $1,147,970,208 of which $539,340,090 was funded debt bearing interest, $283,880,150 was Treasury notes of the new issue, and the remainder consisted of the former issue of Treasury notes, which will be converted into other forms of debt, and will cease to exist as currency on the 31st of next month.
>
> The report, however, explains that, in consequence of the absence of certain returns from distant officers, the true amount of the debt is

[137] *Times,* 19 Apr. 1864. See also Bulloch, 2:416. [138] *O.R.,* ser. 4, 3:525–30.
[139] *Times,* 1 July 1864. [140] Smith, pp. 193–94.
[141] For the president's message to the House of Representatives, see *Richardson,* 1:505–13.

less by about $21,500,000 than appeared in the books of the Register, and that the total public debt on the 1st of last month may be fairly considered to have been $1,126,381,095.

The increase of the public debt during the six months from 1 April to 1 October was $97,650,780, being rather more than $16,000,000 per month, and it will be apparent, on a perusal of the report, that this augmentation would have been avoided and a positive reduction of the amount would have been affected but for certain defects in the legislation on the subject of finances, which are pointed out in the report and which seem to admit of easy remedy.

In the statements just made the foreign debt is omitted. It consists only of the unpaid balance of the loan known as the cotton loan. This balance is but $2,200,000 and is adequately provided for by about 250,000 bales of cotton owned by the Government, even if the cotton be rated as worth but 6d per pound. . . .

The aggregate appropriations called for by the different departments of the Government, according to the estimates submitted with the reports, for the six months ending 30 June, 1865, amount to $438,102,679, while the Secretary estimates that there will remain unexpended out of former appropriations, on 1 January, 1865, a balance of $467,416,505. It would therefore seem that former estimates have been largely in excess of actual expenditures, and that no additional appropriations are required for meeting the needs of the public service up to 1 July of next year. Indeed if the estimates now presented should prove to be as much in excess of actual expenditures as has heretofore been the case, a considerable balance will still remain unexpended at the close of the first half of the ensuing year.

The chief difficulty to be appreciated in connection with our finances results from the depreciation of the Treasury notes, which seems justly to be attributed by the Secretary to two causes, redundancy in and want of confidence in ultimate redemption, for both of which remedies are suggested that will commend themselves to your consideration as being practical as well as efficient.

The main features of the plan presented are substantially these: First, that the faith of the Government be pledged that the notes shall ever remain exempt from taxation; second that no issue shall be made beyond that which is already authorised by law; third that a certain fixed portion of the annual receipts from taxation during the war shall be set apart, especially for the gradual extinction of the outstanding amount until it shall have been reduced to $150,000,000; and fourth, the pledge and appropriation of such proportion of the tax in kind and for such a number of years after the return of peace as shall be sufficient for a final redemption of the entire circulation.[142]

The *Times* said the report had the merit of frankness but gave its opinion that the depreciation of Confederate currency must be

[142] Ibid., 1:488–90.

arrested immediately "or the embarrassments of war will be insurmountable."[143] The *New York Shipping and Commercial List* acknowledged that Confederate currency had become scarcely worth the cost of printing it; that the attempt to fund it by compulsory process had proved a total failure; and that to meet financial obligations in England, Congress had adopted the expedient of fixing legal prices for the commodities it had to purchase.[144] English financial experts proclaimed that the only means of preserving paper notes from further depreciation was to issue no more. Currency depreciation of Confederate notes in England now meant that they were almost worthless to the purchasing agents. The *Times* claimed that never was a nation more sorely pressed for money and supplies than the Confederate States.[145]

However, the new financial policy aroused considerable confidence in other authoritative quarters. As early as June 1864 Memminger had been approached by the agent of a group of European bankers with a suggestion that they should establish a Confederate bank in Europe with a capital of £10 million. They were to establish branches in different cities in the South. Such a plan would facilitate bringing out new loans in Europe, and the bankers were prepared to give substantial backing for their scheme.[146] Negotiations proceeded with the utmost secrecy; in January 1865 a secret act went through Congress to issue a foreign loan not exceeding £15 million sterling. An agent was appointed to proceed to London and Paris to negotiate, but before these negotiations could be completed, the military disasters suffered by the Confederacy ended this enterprise.[147]

In February 1865 Mason wrote to Benjamin, "Not withstanding our late reverses, the Confederate loan maintains itself comparatively well."[148] In the same month, however, Erlanger was losing confidence. He thought that it would be best for the South to give up; yet he admitted that "nobody in Europe seems to have

143 29 Nov. 1864.

144 29 Oct. 1864. *Times*, 15 and 19 Feb., 29 Oct. 1864.

145 29 Nov. 1864. Richardson, 2:689–90; *Bankers' Magazine*, 1864, p. 941; Walker, p. 152.

146 Edward McPherson, *The Political History of the United States of American during the Great Rebellion* (Washington, D.C.: Phillip & Solomons, 1864), pp. 356–73. For the branch bank plan, see T. L. Bransford to G. A. Trenholm, 27 July 1864, Bransford Papers (MSS Section, Tennessee State Archives).

147 Charles W. Ramsdell, *Laws of the Last Confederate Congress* (Durham: N.C., Duke University Press, 1941), p. 15. McPherson, pp. 356–73; *Economist*, 10 Dec. 1864.

148 Richardson, 1:105.

a clear idea of events." With the approval of Slidell, Erlanger was prepared to sell all his Confederate holdings. "I will sell as soon as you approve of it." But his wife, Mathilde (Slidell's daughter), was against selling. "She feels it a national duty to hold on to our investment." The Erlanger holdings amounted to £12,000 of C.S.A. bonds[149] and also some federal bonds. Erlanger felt that the general attitude in Liverpool was one of continuing to help the South. "The Liverpool people do not yet seem to believe in peace."[150]

The cotton plan of 1864 was good but it had come too late, and in the face of Confederate reverses in the field early in 1865, it was powerless to save the Confederacy. By March of that year the Confederate government was paying a dollar in gold for sixty dollars of its own currency.[151] The Erlanger loan went into a new steady decline—its last.

On 23 April Slidell feared that his Confederate bonds would be confiscated, although he still believed that the federal government would take over the Confederate debt. Slidell considered turning his interests over to John C. William, an associate, rather than lose them to the government. Erlanger himself stood to lose by the defeat of the South, and Mathilde wrote to her husband, "Let us make up our minds to bear the storm bravely."[152]

By April the South was virtually defeated, the country in financial ruin and bankruptcy. *Bankers' Magazine* claimed that Confederate financial operations in England were now a rotten fabric of shoddy rearing.[153] When Richmond fell the government held less than $200,000 in specie, and the *New York Times* reported that the Confederate Congress, prior to its adjournment, empowered President Davis to seize specie deposited in banks.[154] It was the same all over the South; the agents in Europe were almost pen-

[149] Erlanger to Slidell, 2 Feb. 1865, Erlanger Papers. When it was suggested that Erlanger go to America to discuss financial matters, his business associates suggested that he need not go, for his "presence might possibly damage their interests and expose him to the risk of much personal annoyance" (L. G. Watson, New York, to Erlanger, 23 Mar. 1865, ibid.). For a list of major bond holders, see Appendix III.

[150] Some of the Liverpool cotton brokers believed that prices could be regulated and that juggling could save the Confederate currency as well as their own interests.

[151] 5 Mar. 1865, Erlanger Papers.

[152] Slidell to William, 23 Apr. 1865, Mathilde Erlanger to Erlanger, 28 Apr. 1865, ibid.

[153] 1865, p. 1178.

[154] *Times*, 20 May 1865; *New York Times*, 1 Apr. 1865.

niless.[155] In May, Erlanger feared that cotton would be destroyed and that not enough would be shipped abroad to meet bond payments.[156] The following month he sent a Mr. Hayne to America to salvage as much cotton as possible in order to pay Southern debts, but he was not hopeful of the outcome. He based his action on the rationale that none of the cotton in the South assigned as payment for the Confederate bonds in Europe would be safeguarded, but that all other cotton owned by neutrals could be shipped out. In the summer of 1865 immense quantities of cotton had been seized by the federal government but were lost to Erlanger and his financial associates. In fact, under a federal confiscation edict, Erlanger lost all legal rights to this cotton.[157]

The Confederate government still owed Fraser, Trenholm and Company a large amount of money. It was hoped that Confederate property in the hands of Bulloch would prove more than sufficient to pay that debt. It was agreed to divide what was left among all the government officers in Europe—civil, military, and diplomatic.[158]

The *Birkenhead and Cheshire Advertiser* declared that the suddenness of the Confederate collapse "has caught all and surprised all," and it predicted that many would lose money.[159] On 2 October 1865 Secretary of State William H. Seward informed the *Times* that there was no likelihood that any of the Confederate debts would be assumed or recognized by the United States government. In this Seward was correct, for the United States had always maintained that all Confederate debts contracted in Great Britain during the war were illegal, unconstitutional, and void. All British attempts to get the United States to assume these debts came to nothing.[160] In the same month the *Times* published a detailed

155 14 May 1865, Erlanger Papers; *Times*, 23 Dec. 1865.

156 May, 1865, Erlanger Papers.

157 *Index*, 8 June 1865; *Birkenhead and Cheshire Advertiser*, 10 June 1865.

158 Mason to Slidell, 4 June 1865, Erlanger Papers. See *United States* v. *Wagner*, the first important suit brought by the United States in England in connection with litigation resulting from the Civil War (Meade, p. 336). *United States* v. *McRae* (ibid., pp. 337–38). *Baltimore Sun*, 30 July 1872; *Liverpool Albion*, 15 Nov. 1866; *Times*, 1 Mar. 1867; *U.S. Congress, House Document* no. 304, 40th Congress, 2nd sess., 1868, p. 13, *Confederate Property in Europe*, letter from the secretary of the treasury, relative to certain efforts of that department for the recovery of Confederate property in Europe.

159 10 June 1865.

160 *Times*, 2, 11, 12 Oct. 1865. *New York Herald*, 4 Nov. 1865; *Schroder Papers*, p. 12; *Times*, 8 Feb. 1867. J. de Cordova of Clevedon, Somerset, called for a public meeting on 4 Feb. 1944 of British holders of bonds and claimants of monies invested abroad. The group he formed tried to collect from the United States on the Confederate loan. The meeting called for the establish-

analysis of Confederate debts and postulated a total of $3,450,766,000.[161]

So all ended in disaster. But what might have happened if the South, instead of proclaiming cotton king and placing on it an embargo in the vain hope of coercing Europe, had shipped every bale possible in 1861–62? It is not too much to say that the whole course of the war might have been different. By the time the Confederacy came to a realistic appreciation of the situation, even the right use of her greatest asset could not repair the ravages brought about by four years of ill-conceived and clumsily executed financial and procurement policies. It has often been said, and rightly so, that Confederate bureaucratic technique was largely

---

ment of a permanent debt protection and collecting authority (Schroder Papers, p. 3). Also, a committee was formed in or about the year 1918 to endeavor to obtain recognition of the Confederate bonds and some payment in respect thereof. The solicitors to the committee were Lindo & Co., 34, Coleman Street, London, E.C.2. (ibid., p. 22). After the war Confederate bonds had no market value except as collector's pieces (ibid., p. 29). See *Exchange Control Act*, 1947 (London: H. M. Stationery Office, 1947), part 3 (Securities), chapter 4, pp. 6–11.

[161] 13 Oct. 1865. Schwab's *Confederate States of America* gives a complete compilation of revenue and expenditure, but because he did not have access to the full range of primary sources, he was not able to deal with the problem of inflation of Confederate finance in the English money market. The *Times* figure for the Confederate debt is quite accurate and was arrived at as follows:

Funded debt	$ 297,871,000
Noninterest bearing notes	766,447,000
Interest bearing notes	102,000,000
Call certificates	89,000,000
Unpaid interest	181,000,000
Estimated expenses for 1864	1,427,448,000
Expenses until Lee's surrender in 1865	500,000,000
State debts	87,000,000
	$3,450,766,000

As a matter of interest, the conquest of the South was costly. It cost the North $3 billion, of which $350 million were spent by the Navy Department and $2.65 billion by the War Department (ibid., 11 Oct. 1865). When one adds the Federal war debt to the Confederate expenditure, the per capita cost becomes three times as great for the Southern people as for those of the North (James L. Sellers, "An Interpretation of Civil War Finance," *American Historical Review* 30, no 2 [1925]: 282–97; *New York Financial Chronicle*, 27 Apr. 1867; Frances Fessenden, *Life and Public Service of William Pitt Fessenden*, 2 vols. [Boston: Houghton Mifflin, 1907], 1:351–52). For Federal loan laws, see James P. Blaine, *Twenty Years of Congress: From Lincoln to Garfield*, 2 vols. (Norwich, Conn.: Henry Bill Publishing Co., 1886), 1:401. For Federal issue of paper money, see the *Annual Register for 1862* (London: Woodfal & Kinder, 1862), p. 228.

responsible for the difficulties experienced by the Confederate agents in Great Britain.[162] Mathilde Erlanger gave expression to the prayer on the lips of many Southerners when she wrote, toward the end of 1865, "May God in his mercy save us the trial we so much fear." [163]

[162] *Gorgas Diary*, pp. 165–66, 172–73. *American Heritage Reader* (New York: Dell 1956), p. 53. Robert Lowe, chancellor of the exchequer, informed Erlanger that Great Britain was determined not to submit to arbitration the question of indirect injuries and that Erlanger, although connected with the Confederacy by his financial dealings, would not be implicated in the proceedings (3 Mar. 1870, Erlanger Papers).

[163] Mathilde Erlanger to Erlanger, 5 May 1865, Erlanger Papers. In the final analysis, Schroder had no faith in Confederate finance (Schroder Papers, p. 10).

Part II

SPECIFIC ITEMS OF PURCHASE

CHAPTER III

THE CRUISERS

It would be difficult to adequately consider Confederate procurement of war material in Great Britain unless one understood its financial base of operation. For this reason chapters 1 and 2 dealt with Confederate fiscal policy, primarily in relation to Southern procurement interests in Great Britain. With this fiscal introduction, an account of the specific items that required such financing is easily understood.

The most dramatic, and perhaps most interesting, chapter in the history of Confederate procurement activities is that of the building of the cruisers. Although the American Civil War was fought mainly on land, the Confederacy, contrary to some opinion, had a navy that though inadequate by modern standards, played an important role by harrying the federal merchant marine. The Confederate Navy Department was never able to devise an efficient naval policy, and the Confederacy relied largely on privateers; nevertheless, the war at sea was significant and had far-reaching effects. Especially significant was the construction and procurement of war ships in Great Britain. The building and purchasing of these vessels were fraught with difficulties, and only a small number of British-built ships escaped the vigilance of Northern spies and British officials. But the few cruisers that finally got to sea practically destroyed the carrying trade of the North, and the resulting diplomatic and financial controversies continued for many years after the war.

In the early days of the war, the Confederate Congress recognized the need for commerce-destroyers, and a plan to provide a striking naval force became the chief objective of Southern naval activities, determining in large measure the policy of the Confederate government at home and in Great Britain.[1] In April 1861 Jeffer-

[1] In a strict modern sense, it can be argued that the Confederacy did not have a navy. It can also be said that the few cruisers it was possible to put afloat formed an irregular marine force that was too weak to act with any effective aggressive power and was therefore never collected for a united attack upon any given point. Further, the commanders of those few vessels

son Davis assured Congress that he was "fully alive" to the importance of a naval arm to the Confederate war machine.[2] Eventually a few cruisers were put afloat. While these were "too weak to act with any effective aggressive power . . . upon any given point," [3] the captains of these ships were able to inflict considerable damage on the merchant vessels of the North.

That as much as this was achieved was of considerable credit to the Confederacy, because as the nonindustrial part of the country the South was ill-adapted to the support of an adequate naval program.[4] Except for a few professional seamen, the Confederate government possessed almost no naval resources; its people were not given to seafaring pursuits.[5] At the outbreak of the war the South did not have one man-of-war, and there were few merchant vessels in its ports. In 1861 the Southern states did not own a single ship.[6] Their only shipyards were Norfolk and Pensacola.[7] They lacked skilled mechanics and possessed only three rolling mills, none of which was equipped for heavy work. There were hardly any machine shops, and except for an abundance of timber they possessed no raw materials for shipbuilding.[8] The navy yards of

---

were compelled to be content only with the injury they could inflict by the destruction of commercial ships. See James R. Soley, *The Navy in the Civil War: The Blockade and the Cruisers* (New York: Scribner's, 1883), p. 168; *Journal of the Confederate Congress*, 1:200; Thomas P. Abernathy, review of *The Confederate Privateers* by W. M. Robinson, Jr., *Mississippi Valley Historical Review* 15 (1929): 547–49. From 1865 to 1872 the question of the *Alabama* claims dominated Anglo-American relations. The United States suggested settlement by arbitration. The Treaty of Washington, which arranged for the settlement of the differences, led to the international tribunal at Geneva in 1872.

[2] *O.R.*, ser. 4, 1:256–58.

[3] Bulloch, 2:196; Winthrop L. Marvin, *The American Merchant Marine* (New York: Scribner's, 1919), p. 325. For a colorful analysis of the role played by the cruisers, see James P. Hill, *Sea Dogs of the Sixties* (Minneapolis: University of Minnesota Press, 1935).

[4] In 1860 over 92% of the total manufacturing output of the country (especially iron and steel) was located in the North (Ernest L. Bogart, *Economic History of the American People* [New York: Longmans, 1925], p. 485).

[5] *Confederate Veteran* 23, no. 2 (1915):76.

[6] J. Thomas Scharf, *History of the Confederate States Navy from Its Organization to the Surrender of Its Last Vessel* (New York: Rogers and Sherwood, 1887), p. 42.

[7] Norfolk was captured before the war was one-quarter over.

[8] Scharf, p. 42; Jefferson Davis, *The Rise and Fall of the Confederate Government*, 2 vols. (New York: D. Appleton, 1881), 1:314 (cited hereafter as Jefferson Davis).

the North had always built most of the vessels for the U.S. Navy,[9] and before the war only seven steam men-of-war had been built in the states forming the Confederacy. Of these, the engines of only two had been constructed in the South.[10]

The need for Confederate cruisers to operate on the high seas was noted again in May 1861 when Congress passed "an act recognising the existence of war between the United States and the Confederate States, and concerning letters of marque, prizes and prize goods."[11] In issuing such an act Congress authorized the engagement of all land and naval forces (i.e., cruisers) of the Confederate States and the use of private armed vessels by commissions or letters of mark for purposes of attack or defense in such manner as the president thought proper.[12] Although Jefferson Davis had a consistent naval policy in that he steadfastly pursued his desire for Confederate cruisers to be built or purchased in Great Britain, he placed too much reliance on the effectiveness of such cruisers. He had no practical insight and little judgment in naval matters.[13] With respect to Congress and the president, the *Times* observed that the conduct and language of Confederate legislative assemblies in the area of naval affairs lacked authority and went on to assert that Confederate naval authorities in the field wielded powers far beyond those given by the Constitution of the Confederate States.[14]

In May 1861 Congress took further action by passing an act "to purchase or to be constructed with the least possible delay in England (or France) one or two war steamers of the most modern and improved description." Two million dollars were appropriated for this purpose.[15] To encourage privateers Congress also passed an act which declared the government would pay to the captain of any armed vessel 20 percent of the value of each vessel sunk.[16] Ely Bruce of Kentucky submitted a resolution to the House of Representatives directing the attention of the Committee

[9] Scharf, p. 25. Lord John Russell maintained that by March 1862 the United States was ahead of Britain in ship construction (Russell to Palmerston, 31 Mar. 1862, Palmerston Papers [1784–1865] [in possession of the Mountbatten family, Broadlands].

[10] Scharf, p. 46. [11] *O.R.*, ser. 4, 1:281–85. [12] Ibid.

[13] *Atlantic Monthly*, Oct. 1865, p. 610; *United Service Magazine* (London), 1863, pt. 2, p. 426. See also Frank J. Merli, *Great Britain and the Confederate Navy* (Bloomington: Indiana University Press, 1971), p. 247.

[14] 31 Mar. 1865.

[15] *O.R.N.*, ser. 2, 2:66–67; *Journal of the Confederate Congress*, 1:208.

[16] *O.R.N.*, ser. 2, 2:63.

on Naval Affairs to the expediency of the privateering act. Bruce suggested that a duly commissioned officer should be allowed to enlist a crew anywhere and that the crew should be covered by his commission. He also proposed "to allow a privateer to destroy the enemy's property when it could not be brought into port and to receive payment therefor under suitable regulation. . . ."[17] The *Index* claimed that an increase in cruiser construction would aid the regular navy and that many such vessels would doubtless be able to run the blockade with cargoes. The main effect of the cruisers, continued the *Index*, would be the paralysis of Northern commerce, and this would "make the war felt by the cliques who were amassing riches on the ruin of their country, and the interests who were unsparing in their endeavours to prolong the contest."[18] Reaction in the North was rather different. The *Times* reported that the New York press had discussed the situation and felt assured that Britain would not support the Confederacy in cruiser construction and would regard Southern cruisers as potential belligerents.[19]

Meanwhile, on 13 April 1861 James D. Bulloch, a captain of the Merchant Marine, wrote a letter to J. P. Benjamin, attorney general of the Confederate States, requesting him to offer his services to the government.[20] In compliance with the request of Mallory, secretary of the navy, Bulloch called at the Navy Department on 9 May.[21] Before the meeting Bulloch believed that he would be called for service in relation to the Mississippi river defenses; he was rather taken aback by the secretary's laconic inquiry as to when he could start for Europe.[22] Mallory followed this by impressing upon Bulloch the urgent need for cruisers capable of raiding the sea-borne commerce of the North and possibly forcing the Federals to divert some war ships from the blockade of the South.[23] He warned Bulloch to be prudent and heedful not to

[17] McPherson, pp. 401–2; *Index*, 25 Sept. 1862; *Southampton Times*, 21 Nov. 1861.

[18] 25 Sept. 1861. [19] 3 Oct. 1861. [20] Bulloch, 1:33–34.

[21] Ibid., pp. 47–48. Stephen R. Mallory, of Florida, had, before the war, served as chairman of the Naval Affairs Committee in the U.S. Senate.

[22] Bulloch, 1:45.

[23] R. S. Henry, *The Story of the Confederacy* (New York: Home Library 1943), pp. 283–339; Alan Westcott, *American Sea Power since 1775* (Philadelphia: 1947), pp. 194–205; Joseph T. Durkin, *Stephen R. Mallory* (Chapel Hill: University of North Carolina Press, 1954), pp. 155–56. The chancellor of the exchequer anticipated that the Confederates would purchase more warships in Great Britain than in France because British yards were better prepared to meet Southern requirements (Gladstone Papers, box 29, 21 June 1861).

involve the diplomatic agents of the Confederate States in embarrassing complaints of alleged violation of neutral law and obligations, and he directed him to acquaint himself, as soon as possible after his arrival in England, with the nature and scope of the Foreign Enlistment Act, and the Queen's Proclamation of Neutrality.[24] Mallory closed the interview by once again speaking of the government's wish to get cruisers on the seas with the quickest possible dispatch.

Bulloch arrived at Liverpool on 3 June and lost no time in communicating with Fraser, Trenholm and Company, which furnished him with the address of the commissioners of the Confederate States in London.[25] Reporting to Mallory on 13 August, Bulloch complained that his movements were severely cramped because newspaper accounts had revealed exact details of his journey to England and precise information as to his mission.[26] As a result Bulloch could expect to be closely watched, since the U.S. consuls employed special detectives.[27]

Nevertheless, he set to work without delay, carefully examining the shipping lists. But close examination failed to reveal a single wooden steamer fit for his purposes, and he decided to make arrangements with a builder for the construction of two cruisers,[28] even though he was suffering from a shortage of funds the first weeks after his arrival. However, on 27 July a portion of the monies allotted in his orders came to Fraser, Trenholm and Company, and further sums followed the next week, amounting to a total of £131,000.[29] The sum was in the form of bills of exchange

[24] Bulloch, 1:47–48. The Proclamation of Neutrality (see App. IV) was not issued until 13 May, but on the ninth Mallory was certain it would be issued (Russell to Lyons, 21 June 1861, Gladstone Papers, box 72). "The question of belligerent rights [under British law] is one not of principle, but of fact; that the size and strength of the party contending against a Government, and not the goodness of their cause, entitle them to the character and treatment of belligerents" (*Times*, 15 May 1861; *Quarterly Review* 3 [1862]: 257, 259).

The Foreign Enlistment Act, dated 3 July 1819, was intended to prevent the enlisting or engagement of British subjects to serve in foreign service, and the fitting out or equipping, in British dominions, vessels for warlike purposes, without license.

[25] *O.R.N.*, ser. 2, 2:83–87. *Liverpool Mercury*, 9 Jan. 1901; *Liverpool Daily Post*, 8 Jan. 1901.

[26] *O.R.N.*, ser. 2, 2:90. *Belfast Telegraph*, 18 June 1954.

[27] *O.R.N.*, ser. 2, 2:90. Callahan, p. 99. The surveillance system of the United States consular agents was developed early in the war. Henry S. Sanford, in charge of federal espionage in Europe, was minister to Belgium and a close friend of Secretary Seward.

[28] Scharf, p. 41. [29] *O.R.N.*, ser. 2, 2:90.

on London and a letter of credit on the Bank of Liverpool.[30]

The *Florida,* the first of the Confederate cruisers built in England, was a wooden vessel. William C. Miller and Sons built the hull and supplied the masts, rigging, and boats and was responsible for the general outfitting. The senior partner of the firm had for many years served as a naval constructor in Her Majesty's dockyards and was prepared to build a vessel that could carry heavy weights on deck (i.e., guns) and berth large crews.[31] Miller and Sons was not an engineering firm, and Fawcett, Preston and Company of Liverpool was selected to design and construct the engines.[32] All the financial arrangements were also made through this company and the contract was signed by Bulloch as a private person, nothing being said about the ultimate destination of the ship.[33]

A scale drawing based on a British gunboat was prepared as a basis for the construction. The model was drawn out in the midships section, and the bottom was flattened to secure greater hold capacity. The increased length admitted finer entrance and clearance lines for greater speed. The rigging scale was also increased considerably so as to get a good spread of canvas.[34]

Oreto was chosen as the dockyard name of the ship. The workmen were told that she would probably be sent to a mercantile firm trading with Palermo; a local representative of the firm undertook the details of supervising and dispatching her. Meanwhile, federal officials were not inactive. Charles Francis Adams, the U.S. minister in England, learned from Thomas H. Dudley, the U.S. consul at Liverpool, that a screw gunboat called the *Oreto* (to be commissioned as the *Manassas*) had been fitted out with six months' provisions and was prepared to sail for Palermo.[35] Benjamin Moran, acting secretary of the U.S. legation in London informed Adams that his agents had been told the vessel was intended for the Italian government. Moran claimed that he had satisfactory evidence that the *Oreto* belonged to the Confederates and was designed as a privateer. He described the vessel as bark-rigged, having 2 funnels

[30] Ibid. Congress appropriated much larger sums for the navy, but Mallory wrote that Confederate exchange was quickly becoming exhausted (Capers, p. 182).

[31] Bulloch, 1:32–58. Horace White, *"Fossetts": A Record of Two Centuries of Engineering* (Bromborough, Cheshire: Fawcett, Preston, 1958), p. 47 (cited hereafter as White). *Index*, 27 Aug. 1863; *Ship Lovers' Digest, Sea Breezes,* n.s. 26, no. 153 (Sept. 1958): 180–213 (cited hereafter as *Sea Breezes*).

[32] *Sea Breezes*, n.s. 26, no. 153 (Sept. 1958): 180–213.

[33] White, p. 47; Bulloch, 1:32–58.

[34] Bulloch, 1:57–58. For a full description of the *Florida,* see App. V.

[35] Bulloch, 1:57–58; White, p. 47; *O.R.N.*, ser. 1, 1:364.

and 8 portholes on each side. He was also informed that she would be armed with 8 rifled cannons and 2 heavy swivel pivot guns to rake fore and aft.[36]

Following representations, the customs authorities closely inspected the ship. But although they found no armaments whatsoever and exacted an assurance on honor that no contraband of war would be placed in her, the American consul was loath to let the matter rest.[37] On 17 February 1862 Dudley reported to Adams that the *Oreto* was still at Liverpool and on that day she was making a trial trip up the Mersey. On that occasion she was described as a bark-rigged vessel having 2 funnels and 3 masts. No pains or expense had been spared in her construction, the report continued, and when armed she would be a formidable and dangerous craft.[38] William C. Miller, who built the hull, was questioned; he claimed to be employed by Fawcett, Preston and Company, which owned the vessel. But Dudley gathered information from a number of sources, and most of this information led him to believe that the *Oreto* was indeed intended as a Confederate privateer.[39] Dudley also reported to Adams that gun carriages had been taken on board. (This was false.) Primed with these reports, Adams wrote to Lord John Russell that he was convinced that the *Oreto* was destined for Confederate service.[40] As a result the Foreign Office directed the Treasury to effect immediate inquiries respecting the *Oreto* and "to take such steps as may be right and proper." [41] The treasury agent inspected the *Oreto,* which was lying in Toxteth Dock, and reported that she was a splendid steamer, suitable for a dispatch boat, pierced for guns but not carrying any, and without gun carriages. The builders were unaware that she was to be supplied with guns in England; her holds contained only coal and ballast.[42] The collector at Liverpool had every reason to believe that the vessel was intended for the Italian government, but the Foreign Office sent a telegram to Sir James Hudson, the British consul at Turin, to "ascertain whether a vessel called the *Oreto* was intended for the use of the Italian Government." [43] The reply from Turin was that Hudson had no knowledge of the ship but would cause further inquiry to be made.[44]

[36] *O.R.N.*, ser. 1, 1:364. [37] Ibid., p. 363.

[38] Great Britain, Foreign Office 5/1313, pp. 3–6, Public Record Office, London (hereafter cited as F.O. 5/1313); Great Britain, *Parliamentary Papers, Accounts and Papers,* 72 (1863):90; *O.R.N.*, ser. 1, 1:363.

[39] White, p. 47.

[40] F.O. 5/1313, pp. 7–8. Adams to Seward, 27 Feb. 1862, p. 39.

[41] F.O. 5/1313, p. 11. [42] Ibid., pp. 23–24; pp. 17–18. [43] Ibid., p. 25.

[44] Ibid., p. 28.

In the meantime Comdr. James H. North wrote to Mallory that the *Oreto* would leave Liverpool on 22 February. But the departure was delayed a month.[45] Although Mallory hoped that North would be her captain, he did not take command. He has often been criticized on this score, but he did not do so because the builders objected to an American captain for fear of seizure.[46] Dudley again reported that the *Oreto* was still in the river and that a flatboat had taken part of her armament to her. (This again was incorrect.) He also reported that Captain Bulloch would take command; that part of the crew of the steamer *Annie Childs*, which had brought cotton to Liverpool, would join him; and that the *Oreto* would make for Nassau.[47]

Adams was confirmed in his suspicions that the vessel was for the Confederacy and wrote to Lord Russell:

> It is with great reluctance that I am driven to the conviction that the representations made to your Lordship of the purposes and destination of that vessel were delusive, and that though at first it may have been intended for service in Sicily, yet that such an intention has long been abandoned in fact. . . . A very great proportion of the vessels which attempt to violate the blockade appear to be fitted out directly from Great Britain or some of her dependencies. . . . Disclaiming every wish to solicit more than my Government would in its turn be prepared under similar circumstances to concede and entertaining full confidence in the deposition of Her Majesty's Ministers on their part to act to the utmost of their ability in the same spirit.[48]

But when Adams wrote these words, the *Oreto*, temporarily called *Manassas* by the Confederates, had already sailed under the British flag with a British captain and crew. Three days after she left Liverpool Sir James Hudson reported to Lord Russell confirming his original dispatch that "the Italian Government knew nothing whatever of the vessel *Oreto*, said to be fitting out at Liverpool." [49] On 21 March 1862 Bulloch had reported to Mallory that the *Oreto* was ready for sea, with crew, provisions, and all boatswain's, carpenter's, and sailmaker's stores necessary for several months at sea. Bulloch declared that she would leave Liverpool on 23 March (she actually sailed on the twenty-second) for a West Indian port, whose name he would disclose in a subsequent letter. On the same day Bulloch notified John Low of the Confederate navy to take passage in the *Oreto*. Low was charged with the care of all Confederate property on board, and on arrival in the Bahamas he was instructed to communicate with Capt. J. N. Maffitt, Confederate navy. Bul-

[45] *O.R.N.*, ser. 2, 2:54–55.
[46] Owsley, *King Cotton Diplomacy*, p. 420.
[47] F.O. 5/1313, pp. 36–37.
[48] Ibid., pp. 30–33.
[49] Ibid., p. 38.

loch also asked Low to keep a careful memorandum of the ship's performance under steam and sail, noting her steering, stability, and all particulars of speed under different circumstances.[50] In a letter to Maffitt, Bulloch notified him that he would dispatch the *Oreto* for Nassau. He informed Maffitt that in all things except guns she was complete.[51]

Only by cautious management had this first cruiser escaped seizure or indefinite detention in a British port. Bulloch had not dared risk arming her before she left, but as the *Oreto* set forth from Liverpool, the *Bahama* left Hartlepool in Durham, loaded with cannon, rifles, shot, and shells—a cargo which would transform the peaceful *Oreto*, or *Manassas*, into the warlike *Florida*.[52] Her armament had been planned while she still lay in dock in England: one 7-inch rifled gun; one 68-pounder solid-shot gun on traversing carriages; four 42-cwt. 32-pounders as broadsides. The 7-inch gun was of Blakely pattern, complete with pivot belts and brass sweeps for the deck; 400 rounds of solid shot and 600 shells were loaded and fused in readiness. Low had with him a scale drawing marked to show precisely how the sweeps were to be laid down on the deck for the pivot guns.

The *Oreto* reached Nassau on 28 April 1862 after a voyage made chiefly under canvas, and on 1 May Low reported her safe arrival to Bulloch. He spoke of the ship most favorably, saying that under steam with smooth water she could do 10½ knots and under canvas alone, carrying the main topgallant studding sail, 13½. "As regards stability," he continued, "I do not think there is a stronger vessel afloat."[53] The *Oreto* was consigned to Adderley and Company, local correspondent of Fraser, Trenholm and Company, but on 21 May 1862 Captain Maffitt reported to G. W. Randolph, secretary of war, that he had taken command.[54] The British crew left the ship,[55] and Maffitt was faced with the formidable task of arming, victualing, and raising a crew for her.[56]

[50] *O.R.N.*, ser. 1, 1:756–57.

[51] Ibid., pp. 255–56. Nassau, Bahama Islands, is 4,500 miles via New York from Liverpool.

[52] George W. Dalzell, *The Flight from the Flag* (Chapel Hill: University of North Carolina Press, 1940), p. 96.

[53] *O.R.N.*, ser. 1, 1:756–57, 757–58; ibid., ser. 2, 2:29. *Liverpool Journal of Commerce*, 27 Feb. 1863.

[54] *O.R.N.*, ser. 1, 1:758.

[55] Ibid.; Dalzell, p. 96. For the enlistment of British subjects in the Confederate armed forces, see *Annual Register for 1864*, p. 131.

[56] *O.R.N.*, ser. 2, 2:204–5; True Copy victualing bill, F.O. 5/1313, p. 56; *Oreto* Bonded Stores no. 662, Bill of Entry Office Custom House (Geneva Arbitration) 23 Oct. 1871, F.O. 5/1390.

Although the *Bahama* had arrived safely, Maffitt was hampered by the constant surveillance of the British. Strict injunctions had been sent to Nassau following the continued protests of Adams. On 30 April, only two days after her arrival, Comdr. H. F. McKillop of H.M.S. *Bulldog* informed his commander-in-chief, Vice Adm. Sir Alex Milne, that he had no doubt at all that the *Oreto* was destined for Confederate service.[57] On 9 May C. R. Nesbitt, the colonial secretary at Nassau, warned the shipping agents that if any attempt was made to arm the *Oreto* she would be seized immediately.[58] On 10 May Adderley and Company denied that it had any intention of arming "the British steamer" *Oreto*. But on 6 June, after further representations from Samuel Whiting, the U.S. consul at Nassau, the commander of H.M.S. *Bulldog* visited the *Oreto* and advised the governor that she was in every way fitted as a man-of-war and not as a merchant vessel. Captain Maffitt did not deny the allegation. Two days later the commander of H.M.S. *Bulldog* wrote even more strongly to the colonial secretary, saying that should the *Oreto* take on guns or ammunition he would consider it his duty to seize her.[59] She was arrested by Commander H. D. Hickley, the senior naval officer at Nassau, who placed British naval officers and men on board. But although Commander Hickley was himself convinced that the *Oreto* was a Confederate privateer, on 16 June he reported to C. J. Bayley, governor of the Bahamas, that he could not further detain her in view of the legal opinion which had been obtained, and he withdrew his prize crew.[60]

The British government however, was more anxious than ever to preserve its neutrality in the face of the continued protests from the U.S. consul, and on 21 June the governor reported that the Queen's advocate had received instructions to prosecute the *Oreto* in the Colonial Court of the Vice Admiralty.[61] The *Oreto* was once more placed in the hands of a prize crew from H.M.S. *Greyhound*,[62] and the case was heard before John Campbell Lees, a judge of the Vice Admiralty Court of the Bahamas. It was alleged that the *Oreto* had violated the Foreign Enlistment Act, but on 2 August Judge Lees, after a careful summary of the evidence on both sides, ordered that the *Oreto* should be released, adding, however, that he thought Commander Hickley had prima facie grounds for

[57] F.O. 5/1313, pp. 70–71.

[58] Ibid., pp. 91–92; see Whiting to Bayley, ibid., pp. 83–85.

[59] Ibid., 10 May 1862, pp. 93–94. Ibid., 4 June 1862, p. 107. Ibid., 6 June 1862, p. 114. Ibid., 8 June 1862, p. 117.

[60] Ibid., pp. 146–49. [61] Ibid., pp. 74–82.

[62] Gorsevoort to Welles, 4 Aug. 1862, *O.R.N.*, ser. 1, 1:769–70.

the seizure; he thus ordered each party to pay their costs.[63] The next day the *Oreto* was released and sailed to Green Bay, sixty miles distant. There she met a schooner from Nassau with her armament and was regularly commissioned a man-of-war, officially named the *Florida*, and so began a period of distinguished service in the Confederate navy.[64] She had escaped Nassau by concealing her Confederate ownership; shortly afterwards she had occasion to do so again. Yellow fever broke out on board, and in five days the working force was reduced to one fireman and four deck hands.[65] The ship was run into Cardenas, Cuba, but because of the stringency of the Spanish quarantine regulations, Maffitt determined to make a Confederate port where he could have the sick attended to and generally outfit his ship.[66] On 4 September 1862 he approached Mobile and, hoisting the British colors, stood toward the federal blockading ships.[67] Captain Preble, of the *Oneida*, thought the *Florida* was a British ship examining the blockade and fired a warning shot across her bow, whereupon she hauled down her flag and with superior speed ran through the federal ships into Mobile.[68] On 15 January 1863 the *Florida*, fully fitted out and manned, made her escape to sea and captured or sank thirty-six enemy ships before she herself was taken as a prize in October 1864.[69]

To return to England and the summer of 1861. Soon after Bulloch had arranged for the building of the *Florida* he visited Birkenhead Ironworks and was introduced to the Laird brothers. After an examination of their extensive yards, Bulloch led the conversation to the subject of wooden dispatch vessels and described with some care the type of vessel which would best meet the need of the Confederacy. A few days later he called again and further discussed the possibility of building a screw dispatch vessel. On this occasion Bulloch invited Lairds to prepare the necessary calculations, draw

[63] Decree of His Honour John Campbell Lees, 2 Aug. 1862, F.O. 5/1313, pp. 219–34. On 31 October the *Manchester Guardian* declared "that all United States ships bound from Liverpool to any of the Northern ports, undergo, before leaving the Mersey, a system of piercing, in order that they may be able to carry guns."

[64] Scharf, p. 790; *O.R.N.*, ser. 1, 1:760. [65] *O.R.N.*, ser. 1, 1:760.

[66] Dalzell, p. 99; Alabama *Claims: the Case of the United States* (Washington, D.C.: Government Printing Office, 1871), p. 350 (cited hereafter as Alabama *Claims*). *O.R.N.*, ser. 1, 1:421–22.

[67] *O.R.N.*, ser. 1, 1:460–68; D. G. Farragut to Gideon Wells, 8 Sept. 1862, ibid., 1:431; extract from the *National Republican*, 22 Sept. 1862, F.O. 5/1313, p. 241.

[68] *O.R.N.*, ser. 1, 1:436–40, 433–34.

[69] Scharf, p. 793; *Times*, 7, 23, 28 Nov.; 28 Dec. 1864; *Annual Register for 1864*, p. 281; Channing, 6:508–9.

up specifications, and make a working model. He also satisfied Lairds as to his financial status, and the details of the second of the Confederate cruisers, eventually to be called the *Alabama*, were settled to their common satisfaction.[70] On 13 August 1861 Bulloch reported to Mallory that the details of a second gun vessel, to measure 210 feet, had been arranged, but that Lairds could not deliver until some time in the spring of 1862.[71] The *Alabama* was to be the 290th vessel built at Lairds; in accordance with custom, she was assigned the dockyard number of 290.[72]

By 14 March 1862 Bulloch was able to report to his associate, James H. North, that he had carefully inspected the ship and was delighted with her.[73] A few days later he wrote to Maffitt, the future captain of the *Florida*, that he hoped the 290 would be ready for sea in about two months. Bulloch had originally hoped to command the *Florida*, but when she sailed he was in America; he now remarked to Maffitt that he hoped to be given the captaincy of the 290.[74] As the 290 took shape in the Lairds yard, federal spy activity became feverish. On 28 March 1862 a detective had reported that no one could or would tell him for whom the vessel was intended.[75] Both Bulloch and Lairds were acting with caution and prudence. On 11 April Bulloch reported to Mallory that Lairds had advised him to leave out the bolts for the broadside guns, to avoid arousing suspicions still further, and a week later he was able to report that the 290 "now lies in the graving dock, with all her engines and boilers and the topmasts on end." [76] During the time Bulloch had been in America, the building of 290 had fallen somewhat in arrears. Lairds were meticulous in their standard of craftsmanship, and wood as a material for shipbuilding had gone almost entirely out of use. Thus there was some difficulty in obtaining the quantities and qualities required.[77] The *Alabama* was 220 feet in length; 32 feet in breadth, with a loaded draft of 15 feet and a ton-

[70] Bulloch, 1:58–59. The working model of the *Alabama* is in the possession of Mrs. Helen Roosevelt Robinson, Mohawk, N.Y. *Liverpool Mercury*, 9 Jan. 1901; *Liverpool Daily Post*, 8 Jan. 1901; Channing, 6:49, 358–60; Benson J. Lossing, *The Civil War in America* (Hartford: T. Belknap, 1868), 2:568.

[71] *O.R.N.*, ser. 2, 2:83–87.

[72] Account Records, p. 57, Laird Papers, Cammell, Laird & Co., Ltd., Berkenhead, Eng., *O.R.N.*, ser. 1, 1:777–78.

[73] *O.R.N.*, ser. 2, 2:165–66. [74] Ibid., 1:755–56.

[75] An unsigned report written by a detective employed by persons unknown to spy on the activities of Lairds (in the possession of Mrs. Helen Roosevelt Robinson). See also F.O. 5/1318, pp. 11–12; *Liverpool Mail*, 5 Dec. 1874.

[76] *O.R.N.*, ser. 2, 2:183–85, 185–86. [77] Bulloch, 1:60–62.

nage of 1,040. She was bark-rigged with two horizontal engines of 300 horsepower.[78]

On 15 May the ship was launched.[79] Since it was necessary to provide a name that would not reveal her purpose, she was christened *Enrica*, which she bore until she ceased to be a British merchantman.[80] On the following day a spy reported that the gunboat at Lairds was a sister ship to the *Oreto* but "far superior," and he went on to state that she was built of the best timber available and was comparable in every way with a ship turned out by Her Majesty's dockyards.[81]

The *Enrica* was now nearing completion, and on 15 June she was taken for a trial run that proved satisfactory. The spies reported that a number of American gentlemen were seen on board. Meanwhile, Bulloch appointed a British captain, Mathew J. Butcher, to take the vessel out.[82] Since he knew it would be impossible to arm the *Enrica* in England, he had already decided that she should make a rendezvous with a vessel carrying her armament off the island of Terceira in the Azores.[83] Although intelligence reports continued to pour in, they were mostly compounded of rumors, and it was not until nearly eleven months after the order for the *Enrica* had been placed that Adams had any worthwhile evidence to submit to the Foreign Office.[84] On 21 June 1862 Dudley, the U.S. consul at Liverpool, reported that "the evidence I have is entirely conclusive to my mind," and he added that the foreman at Lairds had admitted that the *Enrica* was a sister ship to the *Oreto*, the armament of the *Enrica* would consist of 11 guns, and she would be completed in nine or ten days. In Dudley's opinion, she would be a most formidable and dangerous craft, and if she were not prevented from going to sea would be a menace to federal shipping.[85] Early in July he

[78] Ibid. For a full description of the *Alabama*, see App. VI; *Alabama*, Specification of a Screw Steam Vessel and her Machinery, 1 Aug. 1861, p. 7, Laird Papers (Birkenhead); Specifications of a Pair of Marine Steam Engines with Screw Propeller of 300 H.P., p. 16, ibid.; List of Iron and Wood Vessels and Engines, built at the Birkenhead Iron Works, p. 13, ibid.

[79] Dalzell, p. 130.

[80] Bulloch, 1:229; Dalzell, p. 130.

[81] Reports in the possession of Mrs. Helen Roosevelt Robinson; Account Records, Hull Woodwork, p. 57, Laird Papers, (Birkenhead).

[82] Bulloch, 1:230–32.

[83] *O.R.N.*, ser. 1, 1, Letter of Instruction drawn up by Bulloch in regard to a meeting at Terceira and transfer of cargo to the steamer *Enrica* (afterwards the C.S.S. *Alabama*), London, 28 July 1862.

[84] Dalzell, p. 130.

[85] F.O. 5/1318, pp. 11–12.

reiterated his views to the collector of customs at Liverpool, stating that "everything about the vessel shows her to be a war vessel—she has well constructed magazines—she has a number of canisters of a peculiar and expensive construction for containing powder—she has platforms already screwed to her decks for the reception of swivel guns."[86] Apparently Lairds had not denied that she was a war vessel but had said she was intended for the Spanish government. On 21 July Dudley made a formal deposition accusing the *Enrica* of being intended as a privateer and stating that Bulloch would sail in her.[87] (But this was not to be; Bulloch was ordered to remain in England and was advised that Captain Semmes would take eventual command.)[88] On 23 June Adams had already lodged a complaint with Lord John Russell, the foreign secretary, but on the advice of a customs solicitor the foreign secretary assured the federal minister that no offense had been committed since the *Enrica* carried no guns or gun carriages.[89] However, the Foreign Office had no alternative but to take notice of Dudley's deposition, and further affidavits together with urgent requests for the seizure were filed on 23, 24, 25 and 26 July.[90] The depositions included one from Henry Wilding, U.S. vice-consul at Liverpool, who made a codeposition with Matthew Maguire, a secret agent who had been specially detailed to watch Bulloch's movements.[91] Another was filed by William Passmore, a sailor who had signed for service on the *Enrica*, who swore that Captain Butcher had told him that the vessel was to fight for the government of the Confederate States of America.[92] On the twenty-second these and other depositions were

[86] Ibid., pp. 114–18; *Alabama*, Constructional Profile, Plan of Lower Deck, Laird Papers (Birkenhead); Dudley to Adams, 8 July 1862, Gladstone Papers, box 72; see also Adams to Russell, 11 July 1862, ibid.

[87] Deposition of Dudley, Gladstone Papers, 21 July 1862, pp. 34–35; see also Edwards to Treasury, 21 July 1862, ibid., p. 51; Deposition of William Passmore, 21 July 1862, ibid., pp. 44, 47; Adams to Russell, 22 July 1862, ibid., p. 32; Deposition of ship's carpenter, 22 July 1862, ibid., p. 73.

[88] Bulloch, 1:235, 242. Raphael Semmes, *Memoirs of Secret Service Afloat* (Baltimore: Kelly Piet & Co., 1869), p. 369.

[89] Rupert C. Jarvis, *The* Alabama *and the Law*, (London: Confederate Research Club of Great Britain, 1959), pp. 4–5; F.O. 5/1318, p. 114.

[90] Jarvis, p. 5; Gardner (Treasury) to F. Peck, 23 July 1862, F.O. 5/1318, p. 77; Affidavit of Henry Redden, 24 July 1862, ibid., p. 93; Deposition of Mr. Maguire, 25 July 1862, ibid., p. 36; Affidavit of M. Squarey, 26 July 1862, ibid., p. 15.

[91] Deposition of Henry Wilding, 21 July 1862, F.O. 5/1318, p. 42; Bulloch, 1:226–27.

[92] Deposition of William Passmore, 21 July 1862, F.O. 5/1318, pp. 44–47; Bulloch, 1:230–32; *Army and Navy Register*, June 1882, p. 177.

transmitted by Adams to Lord Russell; a further affidavit was taken on the twenty-fourth. None of these, however, proved that the *Enrica* had taken on arms or enlisted men in the service of the Confederate navy.[93] Nevertheless, Bulloch had reason to fear detention. On the twenty-sixth he received information that it would not be safe to leave the ship in Liverpool another forty-eight hours, and he made immediate preparation for her departure.[94] On the twenty-eighth he ordered Captain McQueen of the brig *Agrippina* to proceed to the Bay of Praya in the island of Terceira, there to meet the *Enrica* and place her armament on board. As his representative on board the *Enrica,* Bulloch apointed C. R. Younge acting assistant paymaster, instructing him to check all invoices and store rooms. He also instructed Captain Butcher to join the *Agrippina* in the Azores and particularly instructed him regarding the proper placing of the armament and its care until Captain Semmes could relieve Butcher of his command.[95]

On 28 July, a Monday morning, the *Enrica* came out of dock, ostensibly for another trial run, attended by the tug *Hercules.* She was decked in flags and had a party on board. After luncheon Bulloch told his guests that he had decided to keep the ship out all night and returned them in the tug, while the *Enrica* proceeded down the Anglesey shore to Point Lynas. Bulloch returned with his guests to collect a crew, which was being hastily recruited by the shipping master.[96] About four in the afternoon on the following day, the tug came alongside the *Enrica,* and after a delay caused by the crew's women, who had come aboard the tug and now demanded their men's pay in advance, the seamen's articles were signed and the *Enrica* weighed anchor. Bulloch was anxious for her to be away with all speed, for he had been advised that the federal ship *Tuscarora* was searching for *Enrica.*[97] On 30 July, E. Morgan, a surveyor, inspected the *Hercules* and reported that there was nothing suspicious on board.[98] Bulloch had acted none too soon, because on the thirty-first the law officers of the Crown gave au-

[93] Adams to Russell, 22 July 1862, F.O. 5/1318, p. 32; Deposition of Henry Redden, 24 July 1862, ibid., p. 93; Jarvis, p. 6.

[94] *Liverpool Mercury,* 7 July 1865; Bulloch, 1:235–42.

[95] *O.R.N.,* ser. 1, 1:771–72, 773, 773–74; Bulloch, 1:235–42.

[96] *O.R.N.,* ser. 1, 1:775; Gardner to Peel, 29 July 1862, F.O. 5/1318, p. 102; the report of E. Morgan, the customs surveyor, stated that the *Enrica* had neither "guns" nor "carriages" on board (Liverpool, 28 July 1862, ibid.); see also *Cammell Laird Magazine* 1, no. 4 (April 1958): 13; John W. Foster, *A Century of American Diplomacy* (New York: Houghton Mifflin, 1901), p. 386.

[97] Bulloch, 1:235–42; *Times,* 4 Aug. 1862; *Liverpool Albion,* 4 Aug. 1862.

[98] F.O. 5/1318, pp. 136–37, 134–35; Bulloch, 1:257–62.

thority for the seizure of the *Enrica.*[99] On the same day a telegram was sent from the secretary of customs, London, to the collector of customs, Liverpool, for her detention "if she return or can be met with." Meanwhile, the *Enrica* laid a course round the north of Ireland and Bulloch and the pilot were set down. On 3 August Bulloch was back in Liverpool, reporting to Mallory the safe departure of *Enrica* and expressing his sorrow at not being permitted to command her—a ship, he added, to which he had given so much care.[100] A few days later he reported to Mallory on the armament of the future *Alabama:* "When finally armed the *A*[*labama*] will have a battery consisting of a 7-inch 100-pounder rifled gun, Blakely pattern, 84 cwt.; one 8-inch solid shot 68-pounder, smooth bore, 108 cwt., and six 6-inch 32-pounder guns, 55 cwts. each." Bulloch went on to say that he had provided the guns with adequate supplies of ammunition.[101] Meanwhile the commander of the *Tuscarora* was forced to report to Gideon Welles, secretary of the U.S. Navy, that the *Enrica* had escaped from Liverpool. He regretted his inability to give chase across the Atlantic, as had been suggested by Adams, because of the limited coal capacity of the *Tuscarora.*[102]

The *Enrica* arrived at Praya to find the *Agrippina* already awaiting her, with guns, ammunition, and coal. On 20 August the *Bahama* arrived, bringing both Bulloch and Semmes.[103] Semmes lost no time in taking on his arms and making sure that all was shipshape. On the twenty-third they finished coaling and the following day sailed some four or five miles out from Angra, fired the starboard bow gun, hauled down the English flag and hoisted the Confederate colors, which they saluted by playing "Dixie." Then Semmes addressed the crew, inviting them to sign up for the cruise. In all he got eighty men, but only by paying them much higher than usual terms, so that seamen received £4.10.0., petty officers £5 or £6, and firemen £7 a month.[104]

99 F.O. 5/1318, p. 108. 100 *O.R.N.*, ser. 1, 1:775.

101 Ibid., ser. 2, 2:235–39; Bulloch, 1:235, 242. See William Dayton, Jr., to William Dayton, 22 June 1864, Dayton Papers (MSS division, Princeton University Library). The vessel was named after the state. Most of the cotton sent to England to pay for the cruiser came from Alabama. See Selected Letters, Secretary of War, W.R. 46–399, Relating to Josiah Gorgas, 1861–65, Rebel Archives, Ordnance Dept., Library of Congress (cited hereafter as W.R.).

102 Bulloch, 1:414–19; ibid., p. 415.

103 British Vice Consul, Terceira, to Foreign Office, 25 Aug. 1862, F.O. 5/1318, pp. 138–41; *O.R.N.*, ser. 1, 1:776–77; *Liverpool Albion*, 12 Oct. 1869.

104 *O.R.N.*, ser. 1, 1:785; Deposition of Henry Redden, 3 Sept. 1862, F.O. 5/1318, p. 146. *Belfast Telegraph*, 18 June 1954.

So on 24 August 1862 the *Enrica* became the C.S.S. *Alabama*. Her life was no more than twenty-two months, for she was sunk off Cherbourg on 19 June 1864, but during the interval she herself sank or took as prizes no less than sixty-six ships.[105]

On 1 September 1862 Bulloch was back in England and able to report: "The *Alabama* is safely at sea, fully equipped under our own national flag, and with a crew of 82 able seamen, besides a staff of 27 officers. . . . On Sunday night, before last, at midnight, I bade Captain Semmes farewell. . . ." [106]

The third of the Confederate cruisers, the *Georgia*, was purchased for the Confederate navy by Capt. M. F. Maury in March 1863.[107] Unlike the *Florida* and the *Alabama*, she was not expressly commissioned by the Confederates but was originally designed for commercial service and had been named the *Japan*. Maury, who had been sent to England with "authority to buy and despatch a vessel to cruise against the Commerce of the U.S. whenever he thought the attempt practicable," [108] found the *Japan* in dock at Dumbarton, Scotland.[109] He made the purchase through Thomas Bold of Fraser, Trenholm and Company, paying by means of Confederate cotton certificates.[110] Launched on 10 January 1863, the *Japan* was originally named the *Virginia* by the Confederates, but when she was put into official commission she was rechristened the *Georgia*.[111] She is described as being an "iron screw steamer of 600 tons burden and 200 horse power." [112]

In spite of her commercial design federal agents quickly suspected

[105] Scharf, p. 815. For accounts of some sinkings and captures, see F.O. 5/1318, p. 278; ibid., pp. 275–76; *New York Times*, 22 Oct. 1862, p. 91; Minutes of the New York Chamber of Commerce, 31 Oct. 1862, p. 220; *New York Herald*, 7 Nov. 1862, James Dischitt, underwriter at Lloyds, to his relative, James Stransfeld, 20 Nov. 1862, F.O. 5/1318, p. 343; Mr. Lawless to Russell, 26 Nov. 1862, ibid., pp. 361–73; Draft to Brown Shipley & Son, Rathbone & Co., Liverpool, 29 Nov. 1862, ibid., pp. 332–333; Office of Committee of Privy Council for Trade to the Under Secretary Foreign Affairs, 21 Oct. 1862, ibid., p. 349; Russell to Lyons, 26 Dec. 1862, ibid., pp. 419–20; *New York Times*, 7 Mar. 1862; *Times*, 31 July 1863; *Index*, 30 July 1863; *Porcupine*, 31 Oct. 1868; Minute Book of the American Chamber of Commerce, Liverpool, 27 Nov. 1862, p. 465; Palmerston Papers, 25 Jan. 1864; *Liverpool Courier*, 13 June 1865; *Birkenhead Tomahawk*, 15 July 1865.

[106] *O.R.N.*, ser. 1, 1:775–76.

[107] Scharf, p. 803; Alabama *Claims*, p. 503; Soley, p. 214; Bulloch, 2:261.

[108] *O.R.N.*, ser. 2, 2:325. [109] Scharf, p. 803.

[110] Maury to Fraser Trenholm & Co., 23 Oct. 1863; Maury to J. H. Schroder & Co., 10 July 1863; Maury to C. J. McRae, 23 Oct. 1863, Schroder Papers.

[111] Alabama *Claims*, pp. 256–57; Soley, p. 214; Bulloch, 2:261.

[112] Scharf, p. 803.

her true purpose, and it was deemed wise that she should sail as soon as possible. She thus left Greenock on 1 April 1863, her crew having signed articles for a voyage to Singapore and intermediate ports. The departure was timely, for a detention order reached Greenock the day after she had passed down the Clyde,[113] even though she was registered in Bold's name as a British vessel. (Those who were parties to this subterfuge and recruited the crew in the knowledge that she was destined for Confederate service were subsequently proceeded against under the Foreign Enlistment Act and were fined £50 each.)[114]

Prior to her sailing, the *Japan*, as she was still called at that time, was described by the American consul at Glasgow as a "screw-steamer—about 500 tons register, built by Denny Brothers, Dumbarton—clipper-built—figurehead, fiddle bow—short thick funnel—got a number of apartments forward on both sides and from eight to ten feet square and stronger than a jail—strong doors to them with hinges about three inches thick and brass padlock accordingly—a strong magazine forward in the bow." The consul was under the mistaken impression that the *Georgia* was intended to act as a tender for the *Alabama*.[115]

The *Georgia* sailed with a skeleton crew from Greenock to Liverpool, where the full complement of men was taken on board.[116] Thence she sailed to the French coast, where she met the steamer *Alar*, which had been charted by another employee of Fraser, Trenholm and which was freighted with guns, ammunition, and stores.[117] William S. Maury, a cousin of Capt. M. F. Maury, took charge of the ship, the Confederate flag was hoisted, and she was formally put into commission as the C.S.S. *Georgia*, a man-of-war with a battery consisting of five Whitworth guns: two 100-pounders, two 24-pounders, and one 32-pounder.[118] The new captain announced that the ship was not bound for Singapore but that she was going to sail under the Confederate flag "to sink, burn and destroy vessels belonging to the U.S." Those seamen who refused to sail under the Confederate flag were returned to England, and the *Georgia* set forth on her cruise.[119]

But Great Britain had not heard the last of the *Georgia*. As a privateer she had only a short career—until May 1864—but during

[113] Ibid. [114] Soley, pp. 214–15.

[115] General Correspondence: Geneva Arbitration, July to Nov. 1871, F.O. 5/1390, p. 4. For a full description of the *Georgia*, see App. VII.

[116] Ibid. [117] Ibid. Scharf, p. 803; Bulloch, 2:262.

[118] Alabama *Claims*, pp. 671–72; Scharf, p. 803. [119] *Index*, 20 May 1863.

that time she made prizes to the value of $406,000.[120] Then, in spring 1864 the Confederates decided that because her inadequate sail power necessitated frequent coaling, her continuance as a cruiser was not worthwhile, and she was taken to Liverpool, where she arrived on 2 May 1864.[121] On the same day Morgan, the surveyor at Liverpool, reported to the customs collector:

> I have the honour to report the arrival at 4 A.M. today of the steamer *Georgia*, which vessel now lies at Anchor abreast of the entrance to Birkenhead Docks with the pendant and flag flying of the Confederate Navy. On my visiting the vessel I found her fully equipped for warlike purposes and in reply to my enquiry as to the object of his visit to this port, her Commander, Captain Evans, informed me the intention was to dismantle and lay her up in the great float at Birkenhead. I am of opinion that his statement is to be relied upon: I will not fail, however, to watch the movements on board and report any occurrence worthy of notice.[122]

On the same day the arrival of the *Georgia* was reported to the Treasury, the customs stating that she carried a crew of sixty men and five guns.[123] The day following the Foreign Office suggested that the Board of Customs should be instructed to apply strictly to the *Georgia* the regulations of 31 January 1862 and "to take every precaution to prevent any collision within any British waters" between the *Georgia* and the U.S.S. *Kearsarge,* which had arrived in the Dover Roads.[124] Four days later the captain of H.M.S. *Majestic* reported that the *Georgia* had moved into the Great Float at Birkenhead, having discharged her ammunition, and that the crew were about to be paid off.[125] Adams was not slow to lodge a complaint with Lord Russell. He questioned the right of the *Georgia* to remain at Liverpool "in virtue of her former character," casting doubts on the seriousness of the Confederate intentions to lay her up.[126] Accordingly, on 16 May the Foreign Office communicated to the Treasury Lord Russell's opinion that the *Georgia* should either be sold or ordered out of Liverpool.[127]

Fletcher, Hull and Stone, of Liverpool, now advised the customs

[120] Alabama *Claims,* pp. 671–72. [121] Ibid.

[122] Morgan to Edwards, 2 May 1864, F.O. 5/1317.

[123] Gardner to Hamilton, 2 May 1864, ibid., p. 289.

[124] F.O., to Treasury, 3 May 1864, ibid.

[125] Paynter to Cmr. Controller General of the Coast Guard, 7 May 1864, ibid.

[126] Adams to Russell, 9 May 1864, ibid.

[127] F.O., to Treasury, 16 May 1864, ibid.

that the *Georgia* was in fact to be sold and that on their advice the captain had removed all munitions of war, discharged her crew, and landed and warehoused her stores.[128] Advertisements appeared in the Liverpool papers, offering the *Georgia,* a "splendid screw steamer . . . about 750 tons." [129] Meanwhile, her stores were put up for sale by Curry, Kellock and Company, shipbrokers.[130]

The Federals suspected, however, that all this was merely a Confederate stratagem, and the Foreign Office urged the Treasury to do all in their power to ensure that the sale was a bona-fide one.[131] On 4 June the Customs House put in a report that the vessel had been sold to Edward Bates, "one of the largest and wealthiest ship owners of Liverpool," and that in the opinion of the collector the sale was genuine.[132] Adams, however, was far from satisfied and wrote to Lord Russell that the U.S. government declined to recognize the validity of the sale and claimed the right of seizing the ship "whenever it may be found on the high seas." [133] The British government would not agree to take any further action,[134] but a month later the Federals felt no less unhappy about the situation, and on 26 July the vice-consul at Liverpool feared that "the recorded sale of this vessel is all a sham and that there is no intention of converting her into a merchant vessel." He asserted that nothing had been done to alter the character of the *Georgia* beyond unshipping her guns and that these were in warehouse in Birkenhead and easily obtainable. He also suspected that Bates, who had paid £15,000 for the *Georgia,* was sympathetic to the Confederate cause.[135] On 8 August Russell advised Adams that he had no grounds for believing that the *Georgia* would again be used as a man-of-war, but he gave an understanding that for the future "no ship of war of either belligerent should be allowed to be dismantled or sold in a British port." [136]

On 11 August 1864 the *Georgia* left port for Lisbon, where Bates intended to charter her to the Portuguese government. The surveyor at Liverpool stated that she had been searched shortly before sailing, and nothing suspicious had been found on board. He was convinced that she was now a genuine merchantman.[137] Adams, however, fearing that the British government would not detain the *Georgia,* had already instructed Commander Craven, the captain of

[128] Fletcher Hall & Stone to Edwards, 19 May 1864, ibid. [129] Ibid.
[130] Edwards to Cmmrs. of H.M. Customs, 20 May 1864, ibid.
[131] 25 May 1864, ibid. [132] Dickins to Hamilton, 4 June 1864, ibid.
[133] 7 June 1864, ibid. [134] F.O. to Treasury, 9 June 1864, ibid.
[135] U.S. Consul, Liverpool, to Adams, 26 July 1864, ibid. [136] Ibid.
[137] Morgan (Statement for the Record), 12 Aug. 1864, ibid.

the U.S. frigate *Niagara,* to sail from Antwerp and to intercept and capture the converted Confederate cruiser, in spite of the fact that she was now on the British register and flew the British flag. Off the mouth of the Tagus river the *Georgia* was seized by the *Niagara.*[138] On 25 August the *Times* reported that the *Niagara* was back in Dover Roads and with the captain and crew of the *Georgia,* captured "under the British flag" on Monday 15 August about twenty miles off Lisbon.[139] Bates made a protest to the government but was told that the case of the *Georgia* must go before a prize court in the United States and that he must prepare a defense there. The *Georgia* was sent to Boston, where she was condemned by a prize court, though eventually the owner received £6,000 insurance money from the British courts.[140]

The history of the fourth cruiser purchased in England, the *Rappahannock,* is comparatively brief. Unlike the *Florida, Alabama,* and *Georgia,* she was of small service to the Confederate cause. Originally H.M.S. Victor, the *Rappahannock* had been a screw gunboat in the service of the British navy. She was reputed to be a handsome vessel of some 500 tons, but in 1861 the Admiralty had removed her from service on the grounds that she was defective and worn out, beyond economic repair.[141] In 1862 she was examined by Capt. Sherard Osborne, acting for the Chinese government, but he declined to purchase her on the grounds that she was rotten. In July 1863, however, Gordon Coleman and Company, acting on behalf of Maury, applied to be allowed to purchase her. The dock yard officers recommended the Admiralty's acceptance of the offer and reported her value as £9,375 with fixtures. On 9 October 1863 the *Victor* was docked for inspection and Coleman offered to buy the mast yards and sails.[142] This request was referred to Lord Russell, who said, "There can be no objection to the sale of the rotten hull of the *Victor,*" but asked that the masts and sails should be reserved "at present." On 10 December the *Victor* was given over to her purchasers and it was observed that the name *Scylla* had been painted on her stern. It was given out that she would be engaged in the China trade.[143]

[138] *Times,* 25 Aug., 12 Sept., 28 Jan. 1864. [139] Ibid., 25 Aug. 1864.

[140] Ibid., 12 Sept. 1864; Scharf, p. 803; Soley, pp. 214–15.

[141] *The Navy List Corrected to the 20 December, 1855* (London: John Murray, 1856), p. 174; M. Bernard, *Neutrality of Great Britain* (London: Longmans Green, Reader & Dyer, 1870), p. 357; Bulloch, 2:262. For a description of the *Rappahannock,* see App. VIII.

[142] F.O. 5/1052, pp. 74–79; see also ibid., pp. 4–5; Memo by Russell, ibid., p. 3.

[143] Memo by Russell, ibid., p. 3; ibid., pp. 74–99.

Meanwhile, Adams had been informed that the fitting out of the ship indicated that she might be intended for the Confederates. But though the British government was now more concerned to preserve strict neutrality, he hesitated to make a complaint because he lacked definite evidence.[144] In October the Admiralty itself had considered whether the *Victor* could be destined for Confederate service. The customs inspections, however, failed to engender any suspicions, although Russell's refusal to sell the masts and sails was an indication of growing caution on the part of the British government.[145]

The Confederates, aware of the more stringent attitude of the government and sensitive to the rumors of forthcoming inquiries, resolved to have the *Scylla,* as she was now called, at sea at the earliest possible moment. On 19 November she was masted by H.M.S. *Cumberland*—an action for which the captain of the *Cumberland* was later reprimanded, for he acted without the sanction of higher authority.[146] As the days went by the Confederates became increasingly certain that the *Scylla* would be detained. On the evening before her departure a customs officer found her only partially rigged, "her spars and ropes lying about the deck," and with no captain or regular crew on board,[147] but she did in fact sail from Sheerness on 24 November,[148] in great haste, without water tanks or proper coaling. Since she had not received a bill of clearance, it was thought she had merely gone on a run to try out her engines. In her sailed some of the riggers, their work still uncompleted, and a number of dockyard workers, against some of whom disciplinary action was taken later.[149] In the light of previous experience, the Confederates had of course decided that the *Scylla* must sail unarmed and as a merchantman, her armaments to be taken on at an appointed rendezvous, as the other cruisers had done in the past.

Captain Campbell, C.S.N., was designated to command the *Rappahannock,* but in passing down the Thames her brasses blew out and she drifted across the Channel.[150] In mid-Channel she was formally commissioned as a Confederate man-of-war and christened the *Rappahannock.*[151] It was decided she must put into Calais, where she arrived on 26 November.[152] On the same day the British consul at

144 Alabama *Claims,* p. 726. 145 F.O. 5/1052, p. 15; ibid., p. 68.

146 Ibid., p. 96; Detective officer's special report, metropolitan police office, Scotland Yard, ibid., p. 97.

147 Ibid., p. 22. 148 Scharf, p. 802. 149 F.O. 5/1052, pp. 22, 99.

150 Scharf, p. 802. 151 Soley, pp. 213–14.

152 *London Daily News* 28 Nov. 1863; *O.R.N.*, ser. 2, 3:969; Alabama *Claims,* p. 583; F.O. 5/1052, pp. 6–7. John Bigelow, *Retrospections of an Active Life,* 5 vols. (New York: Baber and Taylor Co., 1909), 2:350.

Christopher G. Memminger, first Confederate secretary of the treasury, 1861–64. (*O.R.N.*, ser. 2, 3:373)

James M. Mason, Confederate commissioner to England. (*O.R.N.*, ser. 2, 3:110)

Colin J. McRae, special Confederate financial agent for the Erlanger loan. (Courtesy of Charles S. Davis, president, Winthrop College, Rock Hill, S.C.)

Baron Frederick Emile von Erlanger. (Courtesy of D. S. Ramsay, Hill Samuel and Co., Ltd., London)

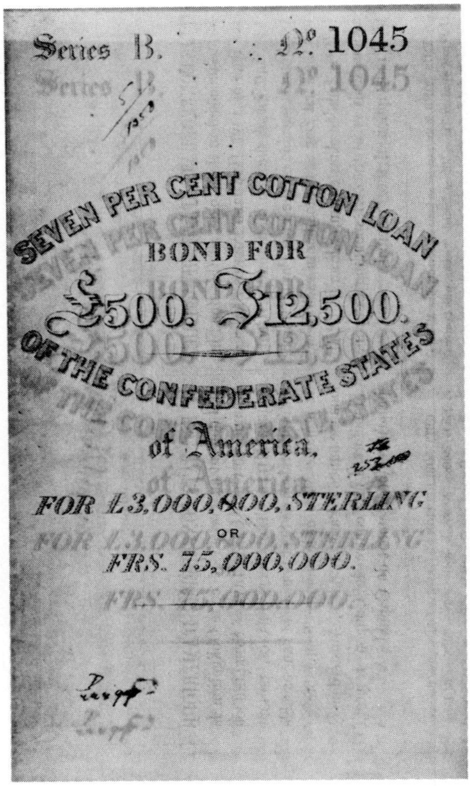

Series B. Nº 1045

SEVEN PER CENT COTTON LOAN
BOND FOR
£500. F12,500.
OF THE CONFEDERATE STATES
of America.

FOR £3,000,000, STERLING
OR
FRS. 75,000,000.

Cover of a 7-percent Erlanger contracted cotton loan bond, stamped London 4–8–63.

John Laird, English shipbuilder. (Courtesy of Elsam, Mann and Cooper, Ltd., Liverpool)

Model of the C.S.S. *Alabama* constructed by Bassett-Louke, Ltd., Northampton, England, from original specifications. (Courtesy of The Smithsonian Institution)

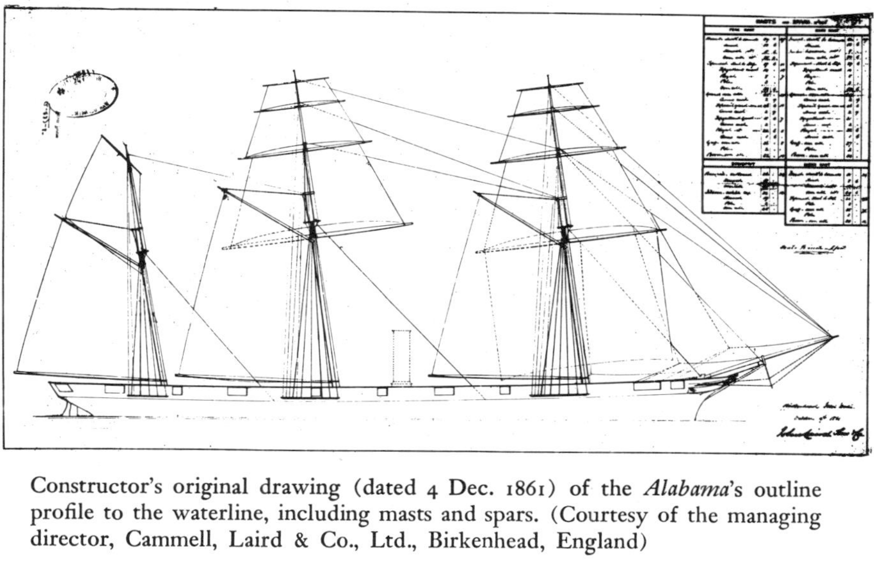

Constructor's original drawing (dated 4 Dec. 1861) of the *Alabama*'s outline profile to the waterline, including masts and spars. (Courtesy of the managing director, Cammell, Laird & Co., Ltd., Birkenhead, England)

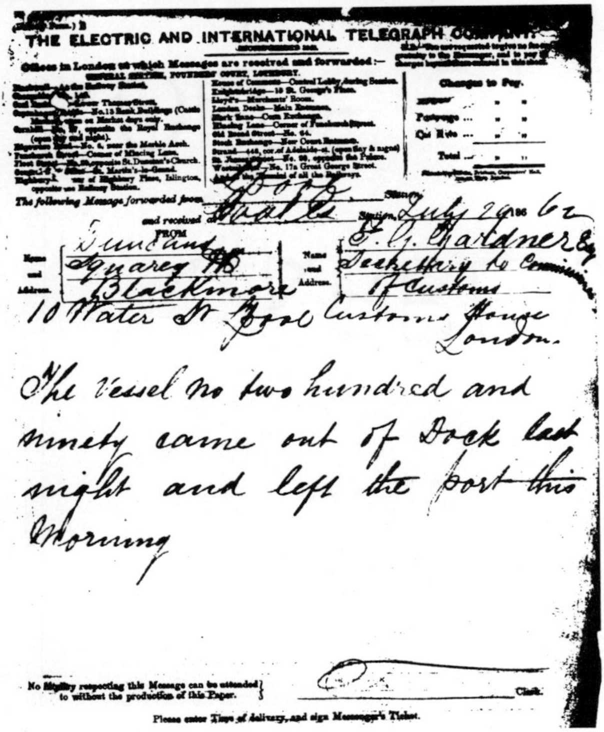
THE ELECTRIC AND INTERNATIONAL TELEGRAPH COMPANY.

The following Message forwarded from L'pool Station July 29 1862

and received at Station

FROM Duncan Squarey & Blackmore 10 Water St L'pool

TO F. G. Gardner Esq Secretary to Commissioners of Customs Customs House London.

The vessel no two hundred and ninety came out of Dock last night and left the port this Morning

No inquiry respecting this Message can be attended to without the production of this Paper. Clerk.

Please enter Time of delivery, and sign Messenger's Ticket.

Telegram from Liverpool Customs to London Customs, 29 July 1862, concerning the C.S.S. *Alabama* ("290"). (Courtesy of the Library, H.M. Customs and Excise, London)

Telegram from secretary of customs, London, to collector of customs, Liverpool, 31 July 1862. (Courtesy of the Library, H.M. Customs and Excise, London)

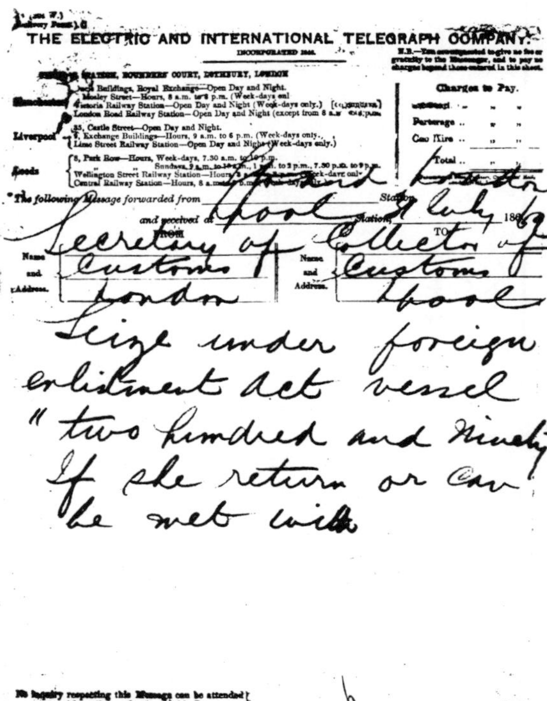
THE ELECTRIC AND INTERNATIONAL TELEGRAPH COMPANY.

INCORPORATED 1846.

The following Message forwarded from London Station

and received at L'pool Station 31 July 1862

FROM Secretary of Customs London

TO Collector of Customs L'pool

Seize under foreign enlistment act vessel "two hundred and Ninety" If she return or can be met with

No inquiry respecting this Message can be attended to without the production of this Paper. Clerk.

Please enter Time of delivery, and sign Messenger's Ticket.

Stephen R. Mallory, Confederate secretary of the navy, 1861–65. (Courtesy the Library of Congress)

James D. Bulloch, chief agent of the Confederate States Navy in Great Britain. (Courtesy of Putnam's)

Model of the blockade-runner *Fergus*, built in Scotland by Alexander Stephen and Son. (Courtesy of The Smithsonian Institution)

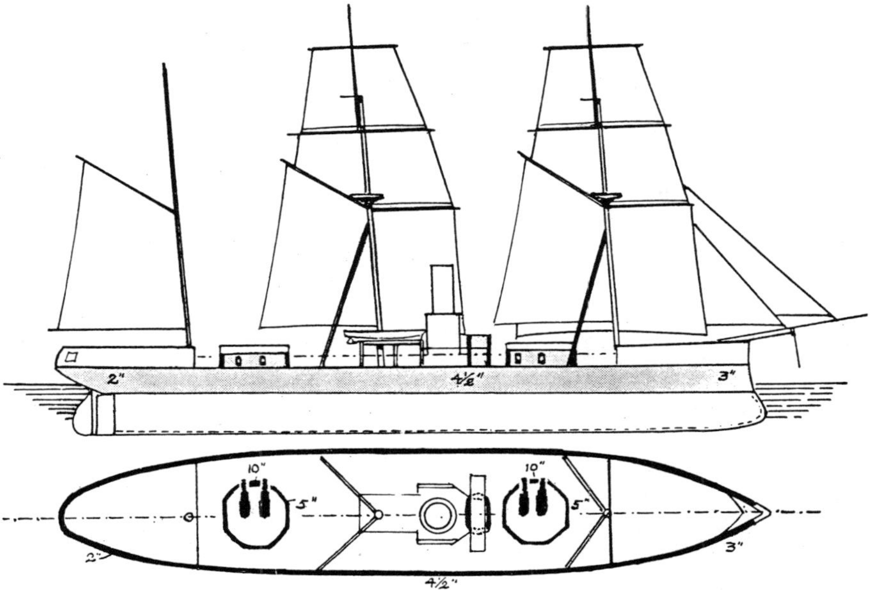

General diagram of the *Scorpion* and *Wivern.* (Imperial War Museum, London)

The *Wivern* at anchor, 1865. (Imperial War Museum, London)

Caleb Huse, purchasing agent for the Confederate War Department. (Courtesy of T. R. Marvin & Son)

Great Seal of the Confederacy, made by Joseph S. Wyon, chief engraver of Her Majesty's seals. (Courtesy of The Museum of the Confederacy)

Calais reported her arrival to Russell, stating she had hoisted the Confederate colors. He reported her rigging and spars as incomplete and her crew as small and of "shipwright class" rather than sailors.[153] The next day the consul reported that the French customs authorities had given the *Rappahannock* permission to leave whenever she wished, presumably on the grounds that she was a bona-fide ship of war in distress and needing repairs. At that time she was in no condition to take advantage of this freedom.[154]

Following the escape of the *Rappahannock*, investigations were begun by the British government. Statements were taken from a number of men who had sailed in her from Sheerness. One of them, Richard Spendiff, deposed that when they reached Calais he and the rest of the crew were invited by Captain Campbell to enter the Confederate service and were offered a bounty of £10 besides £8 per month if they would sign articles for twelve months. Captain Campbell told them that the *Rappahannock* would carry eight guns but that when fitted out she would have to run through the American cruisers, of which three had already gathered outside the harbor.[155]

The repair and servicing of the *Rappahannock* did not prove to be an easy task. The diplomatic controversy she aroused was a source of considerable embarrassment to the French authorities, who had to reconsider their decision that the *Rappahannock* was free to sail whenever she chose. Nor did a dispute with a French merchant ship, the *Nil*, regarding berthing, endear the *Rappahannock* to them.[156] There was also some dispute among the Confederates as to whether she would ever be a serviceable craft. A board of survey finally found her entirely unsuited as a cruiser, as she was slow under steam or sail and could carry only eleven days' coal and six weeks' provisions.[157] By permission of the French government, the *Rappahannock* thus remained in Calais until March 1865 when Bulloch decided to sell her because of the low ebb of Confederate finances. The ship was turned over to a broker who took her to England; ultimately she fell into the possession of the U.S. government.[158]

The *Rappahannock* appropriately was called the Confederate white elephant by her officers. Her only service to the Confederate cause lay in the fact that the Federals were forced to deplay cruisers

[153] F.O. 5/1052, pp. 5–7, 22–25. A shipwright is a skilled workman engaged on the building of the hull of a vessel of any kind.

[154] F.O. 5/1052, pp. 26–27, 120; F.O. to Home Office, 29 Nov. 1863, ibid.; Report of F. Williamson, detective, metropolitan police officer, Scotland Yard, 10 Dec. 1863, ibid.

[155] Ibid., pp. 150–54. [156] Ibid. [157] Scharf, p. 802.

[158] *O.R.N.*, ser. 2, 1:364; Bulloch, 2:367–69.

to blockade Calais harbor to forestall any attempt to run out of port.

In autumn of 1863 Bulloch, on a visit to the Clyde, "caught sight of a fine, composite, full-rigged ship, with something more than auxiliary steam-power, and all the necessary arrangements for disconnecting and lifting her screw."[159] He was charmed with her but at the time could only make a hasty and imperfect inspection since she was in all the bustle of loading for her first foreign voyage. Some ten months later a broker reported to him that the vessel was back from Bombay and had just been discharged. Bulloch telegraphed the broker to buy without delay.[160] So came into being the *Shenandoah*, the last of the Confederate cruisers.

Originally constructed by Alexander Stephen and Sons, the vessel that Bulloch had so much admired was the *Sea King*. Her transformation from an innocent tea clipper to a crack war vessel, the terror of the Yankee whalers, was one of the triumphs of the Confederate navy. The *Sea King* was launched on 17 August 1963 from the shipyard of Alexander Stephen and Sons, at Kelvenhaugh. She was described then as a fine screw steamer of about 1,200 tons, specially constructed for the China trade. She was fitted with simple compound steam engines and rigged as a full three-masted sailing ship, beautifully finished.[161] Bulloch felt that her fitness for conversion into a cruiser would be as evident to the spies of the U. S. consul as it was to him, and, the purchase made, he lost no time in preparing for her departure.[162] Her purchase was officially made by Richard Wright of Liverpool, whose son-in-law was a partner of Fraser, Trenholm and Company, on 20 September 1864. Wright hastened to ballast her with coal and arranged her clearance for Bombay. Captain Corbett, the British master, was given a power of attorney to sell her any time after leaving London,[163] and the Confederates arranged that Lt. James Iredell Waddell should command *Sea King* when she was commissioned as *Shenandoah*.[164]

Everything was accomplished so speedily that the Federals hardly

[159] Dalzell, p. 178. [160] Bulloch, 2:125–26; *O.R.N.*, ser. 2, 1:264.

[161] *North British Daily Mail*, 18 Aug. 1863. The *Sea King* was the first screw steamship in the world built on the principle of iron frames and wooden planking, and also the first steamship that had been specially constructed for the China trade, having been built with the view of competing with the fastest ships in the trade from China to London for bringing home the first teas of the season. For a description of the *Shenandoah*, see App. IX.

[162] Bulloch, 2:127. [163] F.O. 5/1384, pp. 35–38, ibid. p. 21.

[164] For an interesting analysis of Waddell and the exploits of the *Shenandoah*, see *C.S.S. Shenandoah: The Memoirs of Lieutenant Commander James I. Waddell*, ed. James D. Horan (New York: Crown Publishers, 1960).

had time to formulate their suspicions. On 8 October 1864 the *Sea King* cleared London, well ballasted with coal and provisions but without armament except for two 12-pounders that had been on board when she was purchased.[165] On the same day the steamer *Laurel* left Liverpool, being cleared for Nassau. On board were Waddell and several other Confederate officers and a cargo of cases marked "machinery," but which in reality contained the guns and armament for the future *Shenandoah*.[166] The true purpose of the voyage was well concealed. The *Laurel* habitually carried passengers as well as cargo, and the sailing of the ship was advertised in the usual way. All her "passengers" held tickets. Her captain, Ramsey, held a master mariner's certificate issued by the Board of Trade, but he was also an officer in the Confederate navy. In accordance with his usual practice, Bulloch had placed a single Confederate officer aboard the *Sea King* to watch over his interests. This time he was Lieutenant William C. Whittle, who traveled under the name Brown and was charged with the checking and supervision of the stores.[167]

The *Laurel* dropped anchor in Funchal Bay, Madeira on 16 October; at midnight on the eighteenth the *Sea King* arrived and, having made herself known to the *Laurel*, steamed off toward the north. Next day both vessels dropped anchor off Las Desertas. *Sea King* was formally handed over to the Confederates and christened the *Shenandoah*. The *Laurel* was lashed alongside, and the armament and stores safely transferred. Then Captain Waddell tried to recruit members of the British crew, which had brought out the *Sea King*, but only a small proportion volunteered, and Waddell wrote to Bulloch, despairing of ever reducing the chaos on the ship to order and of doing all that was expected of him.[168] Nevertheless, within a few days the *Shenandoah* was ready to embark on a most creditable career in the service of the Confederacy. She was specifically commissioned to attack and destroy the whaling ships of the North. All together she captured more than forty ships with cargoes of sperm oil, pork, beef, tea, molasses, rope, flour, tobacco, railroad iron, soap, and beer. After the war had ended, even as late as 28 June 1865, the *Shenandoah* captured eight ships in the Bering Straits; it was not until 2 August that Waddell learned from a British ship that the Confederate cause had been lost. On receiving the news Waddell proceeded to Liverpool, where the last of the Confederate flags was furled on 6 November 1865. After a visit from a British naval officer,

[165] F.O. 5/1384, pp. 23–26.
[166] Ibid.; Bulloch, 2:129.
[167] F.O. 5/1384, pp. 4–7.
[168] Ibid.; Bulloch, 2:116–18.

Captain Waddell formally surrendered the *Shenandoah* to the British government on behalf of the United States. Her officers and crew were released, but the *Shenandoah* became the property of the U.S. government. Later she was acquired by the Sultan of Zanzibar who used her for cruising and trading purposes for fourteen years until this once proud ship foundered on a coral reef and was allowed to crumble away.[169]

Meanwhile, the news of the transformation of the *Sea King* into the *Shenandoah* did not take long to reach England. On 18 November 1864 Adams asserted to Russell that there had been a breach of the Foreign Enlistment Act, stating that the "owner," Richard Wright, was a British subject, as were her officers and crew, and that indeed everything on board was British—"an English transaction from beginning to end." [170] On 29 October Corbett, who took the *Sea King* out, made a statement to the British consul at Teneriffe, stating he was not aware that by transacting the sale as instructed he had in any way breached the Foreign Enlistment Act. Forty-two of the crew of *Sea King*, who did not wish to serve in her as a Confederate cruiser, were landed at Teneriffe and made depositions. This, in the opinion of the consul, was sufficient to substantiate a charge against Corbett. The consul thus sent him forward to England in custody.[171] One of the seamen, John Wilson, made a detailed statement of the events that led to the commissioning of the *Shenandoah*. When the *Laurel* came aside, he said, the crew of *Sea King* were ordered to get ready to lift guns.

> The cases weighed three tons and a half and contained 68 and 32 pounders, with a quantity of shot and shell; and there were a number of barrels, 60 or more, containing powder . . . while transshipping the guns one of the cases caught the rail and caused the seam to open, so that I could put my hand in which I did and felt the gun. . . . We were then called aft and as we went an iron safe was hoisted from the *Laurel* and I and a number of others were ordered to carry it aft into the cabin which we did. It was as much as four of us could manage and by the rattling sound we judged it contained money.

Wilson contended that it was Captain Corbett who appealed for volunteers and offered them bounty money.[172]

Meanwhile, in England inquiries were pursued regarding the purchasing of the vessel, and Captain Corbett instructed solicitors

[169] Eaton, p. 188; Soley, pp. 218–20; Bulloch, 2:146–48; Hill, p. 250.
[170] F.O. 5/1384, pp. 35–38. [171] Ibid., p. 21; pp. 4–7.
[172] Ibid., pp. 47–55, 79–81.

in his defense. However, at his trial the evidence of the seamen varied considerably, and after long deliberations the jury acquitted him and he was discharged.[173]

And so ended all Southern efforts to construct or procure Confederate cruisers in Great Britain. Given the Confederacy's extremely limited resource—and the legal and technical difficulties involved—in terms of cost-benefit ratio, the Anglo-Confederate cruiser venture must be termed a success.

[173] Ibid., p. 75.

CHAPTER IV

OTHER SHIPS

In addition to the procurement of cruisers intended to harry and destroy federal commerce on the high seas, the Confederates had a clear need for other ships, notably blockade-runners and other vessels to export cotton to England and to carry, by return passage, urgently needed war supplies.

On 19 April 1861, a week after the firing on Fort Sumter, President Lincoln proclaimed a blockade of Southern ports.[1] News of the blockade reached England on 4 May 1861,[2] and on the fifteenth the *Times* reported that "the blockade is to be enforced immediately" and that fifty vessels with steam transports and 20,000 men were ready to support the blockade.[3]

[1] William N. Still, Jr., *Confederate Shipbuilding* (Athens: University of Georgia Press, 1969), pp. 7, 8, 9. Thomas A. Bailey, *A Diplomatic History of the American People* (New York: Appleton-Century-Crofts, 1955), p. 347.

[2] "The following is President Lincoln's proclamation of the blockade of the Southern ports: 'An insurrection against the Government of the United States has broken out in the States of South Carolina, Georgia, Alabama, Florida, Mississippi, Louisiana, and Texas, and the laws of the United States cannot be executed effectually therein conformably to that provision of the Constitution which requires duties to be uniform throughout the United States, and further a combination of persons engaged in such insurrection have threatened people. The President calls out a naval force to blockade Southern ports and vessels attempting to enter or leave a blockaded port will be captured and sent to the nearest convenient port for such proceedings against her and her cargo as may be deemed advisable'" (*Times*, 4 May 1861).

Nearly everyone in America, including the highest naval authorities, thought that the blockade could not be rigorously enforced and that it would result in a paper blockade (Francis Bradlee, *Blockade-Running during the Civil War* [Salem, Mass.: Essex Institute, 1925], pp. 9–10; Mary E. Massey, *Ersatz in the Confederacy* [Columbia: University of South Carolina Press, 1952], p. 11). The great powers, however, did recognize the blockade as binding (*Annual Register for 1863*, p. 314). Blockade was a belligerent right (Channing, 6:345; Theodore A. Dodge, *A Bird's-Eye View of Our Civil War* [Boston: James R. Osgood, 1884], p. 33; *Times*, 24 Feb. 1862).

[3] *Times*, 15 May 1861; Memorandum relative to the Blockade, Gladstone Papers, box 6, 5 Mar. 1862. It is now a well-settled principle of international jurisprudence that a lawful maritime blockade of a port requires the actual presence of the blockading force. Blockades are effective when maintained by sufficient force to shut the access of the enemy's ships and other vessels

In a short time the effect of the Northern blockade was felt by the South, but the control of thirty-five hundred miles of coastline was never completely effective.[4] Within seven days of the announcement of the blockade, the Confederate secretary of the navy reported that he proposed to adopt a class of vessels "hitherto unknown to naval service"—vessels built exclusively for speed, at a low cost, and with a battery of only one or two guns.[5] The primary purpose of this fleet was to *evade*, not engage, the enemy. On 9 May 1861 Mallory had ordered Bulloch to proceed to England for the purchasing of "six steam propellers," [6] and on the same date he asked the chairman of the Committee of Naval Affairs to recommend an appropriation of £1,000,000.[7] On 25 July Mallory urged upon Bulloch the urgent need for small, strong, light-draft gunboats, saying that the U.S. Navy was already building many of these with the object of attacking privateers carrying cargoes for Confederate ports.[8]

On May Day 1861 Commodore Josiah Tattnall of the Confederate

(*International Law, Lectures Delivered at the Naval War College* [Washington, D.C.: Government Printing Office, 1895], p. 151; U.S., Department of State, *Papers Relating to Foreign Affairs* [Washington, D.C.: Government Printing Office, 1863], pp. 36, 42, 59 [hereafter cited as *Papers Relating to Foreign Affairs*]).

The blockade of Southern ports was an outstanding example of the proper use of sea power under the principles of economy of force and objective. Though lamentably unprepared for war in 1861, the federal navy by 1864 had become formidable:

U.S. Official Naval Report before the War		
Year	*No. vessels*	*Tonnage*
1858	33	12,684
1859	49	21,308
1860	41	13,683
3 yrs.	123	47,675

U.S. Official Naval Report during the War		
Year	*No. vessels*	*Tonnage*
1861	126	71,673
1862	135	64,578
1863	348	252,379
1864	106	92,052
4 yrs.	715	480,682

In 1864 the Royal Navy possessed 608 vessels with a tonnage of 454,525 tons (F.O. 5/1384, pp. 104–12, 120).

4 Herbert J. Fielder, *Life and Times of Joseph E. Brown* (Springfield, Mass.:, Press of Springfield Printing Co., 1883), p. 237. The naval blockade was a strategic weapon (Walter Millis, *Arms and Men* [London: Lowe & Brydone, 1958], p. 126). The blockade was the controlling condition of Union success. Cut off from the outside world and all exterior sources of supply, reduced to a state of collapse, the Confederacy died a slow and painful death (*Papers Relating to Foreign Affairs*, pp. 225, 234; *Times*, 27 Jan. 1862).

5 *O.R.N.*, ser. 2, 2:61. See also Still, p. 5.

6 Ibid., pp. 64–65; Bulloch, 1:376–79.

7 *O.R.N.*, ser. 2, 2:66.

8 Ibid., p. 82.

navy was reported to have remarked, "I have no fleet. Long before the Southern Confederacy has a fleet that can cope with the Stars and Stripes my bones will be white in the grave." [9] But though the Confederates were woefully unprepared and ill-equipped at the beginning of the war, they pursued their plans for a navy with energy and determination, and in this they were aided by the uncertain neutrality of the great powers. The Confederates had but little choice. At the outbreak of war, the Confederate States had, for all practical purposes, no navy at all. Only 10 ships, some of them very small, and 15 light naval guns were seized by the Southern states when they seceded. In comparison, at the beginning of the war the United States had navy yards, of which they lost only two (Norfolk and Pensacola) to the Confederates.

The shipbuilding ports of Great Britain furnished the largest proportion of the blockade-runners that kept the South supplied for four years.[10] For example, one yard on the Mersey launched 5 blockade-runners in a single day; Lairds built 7 or 8 such vessels.[11] However, these activities were not allowed to go forward without active protest on the part of the federal government, and Confederate agents were often greatly hampered in their plans. Nevertheless, it has been estimated that by their efforts over 1,200 vessels owned by, or carrying supplies for, the Confederates came into or left Liverpool during 1861.[12] In 1862 it was reported that insurance was being effected daily on ships and cargoes about to run the blockade of Sourthern ports.

In some quarters the Confederate government was criticized for not placing adequate funds at the disposal of its agents. It has been claimed that if it had adopted a bolder policy, the blockade might have been broken completely. The government's critics were of the

[9] Russell, *Diary*, 1:227; *O.R.N.*, ser. 2, 2:99–105.

[10] Great Britain had undertaken to be neutral between the belligerents. But neutrality is always easier to promise than to practice. It was difficult for Great Britain to be impartial (F. W. Seward, *Seward at Washington, as Senator and Secretary of State* [New York: Derby & Miller, 1891], p. 627; Arthur C. Wardle, "Address Given before the Members of the Liverpool Nautical Society on 7 November 1942," *Mariner's Mirror*, 1942, pp. 179–88). Every government has the right to determine the standard of its own neutrality, subject only to the requirements of international law, as noted in App. IV. Great Britain laid down at a very early date the rules of neutrality by which it would be guided.

[11] Company report, Laird Papers (Birkenhead), p. 7. Extensive enlistments for the Confederate naval service were also made in British Ports (*Times*, 14 Jan. 1864).

[12] *London Post*, 7 Nov. 1863; *New York Herald*, 20 Nov. 1863.

opinion that an appropriation of 10 million raised on bonds invested in cotton could have been the means of acquiring such a fleet, and it has been said that the East India Company offered to sell to the Confederater "a fleet of ten swift and stout steamers, built for armament and capable of long voyages." [13] Thus the critics maintained that for $ten million covered by bonds for 40 bales of cotton, these ships could have been manned, armed, and placed in American waters within six months of the outbreak of the war.[14] The cotton crop of 1860 was good, and many planters wished to cooperate with just such a project, but the feasibility of this plan can be vigorously questioned. It is not clear, says Schwab, where the government could have found these ships to carry the cotton to Europe before the federal fleet closed the Southern ports, nor is it likely that the Treasury Department could have obtained at such short notice the means with which to buy the cotton from the planters. Schwab rightly concludes that such a scheme was far too ambitious for the Confederate government to have undertaken.[15]

Whichever of these conflicting views is accepted, there is no doubt that Bulloch and the other Confederate agents in England did succeed in securing a large number of vessels for Confederate service—exactly how many it is impossible to estimate.[16] Some of these ships had been private yachts; some were engaged in trade between British ports or between England and France. Others had been built for the China trade, and some were built specially for the Confederates.[17]

As the war proceeded, more and more emphasis was placed on ships that could be armed and used for blockade-running. In the

[13] Gladstone Papers, box 62, 1 May 1861.

[14] Joseph T. Durkin, *Stephen R. Mallory* (Chapel Hill: University of North Carolina Press, 1954), p. 151–52.

[15] Schwab, *Confederate States of America*, pp. 233–34. See also C. G. Memminger's very complete description of the impracticality of the plan, in Capers, pp. 348–57.

[16] For a list and description of British blockade-runners purchased, constructed, or chartered in part or in whole for use in support of Confederate activities, see App. X.

Bulloch was the most effective naval procurement agent. Other Confederate agents accomplished comparatively little for the Navy Department. Other than Bulloch, these purchasing officers had little technical knowledge of details such as cost, structure, or the time necessary to construct a vessel. In the main, they did not understand British maritime law, especially the influence of the Foreign Enlistment Act and other obstacles to be overcome in getting ships out of Great Britain. Bulloch was effective because he had a firm grasp of these essential elements.

[17] Huse, p. 25.

summer of 1864 Mallory instructed Bulloch that each vesssel should have the following qualities:

1. The first and greatest requisite is speed at sea.
2. Draft of water should not exceed, deep loaded, ten feet.
3. Strength to stand heavy sea and weather. She will be used to carry heavy weights.
4. Carrying capacity of 200 to 250 tons, or as much as may be found consistent with speed, strength and power.
5. Deck frames forward, aft, and amidships extra strong and three guns, say 30-pounder Whitworth's.
6. Power to be applied to one screw, if speed can be had, if not, then to two; and if they can be so arranged as to be readily disconnected when under sail it would be advisable.
7. Every necessary arrangement should be made to prevent the display of smoke.
8. Coal bunkers, if practicable, should protect the boilers.
9. Boilers should be so constructed as to be readily kept clear of scale.
10. A berth deck and a room suitable for magazine should be fitted up. If this might beget suspicion, the space for it might be decided upon, and the partitions for it prepared and put on board to be fitted subsequently.
11. The decks, rooms, quarters, etc. prepared for a crew of 100 all told, but every appearance of a man-of-war avoided.
12. A clear sweep for the forward and after pivot gun to be secured.
13. Three fore-to-aft sails, with flying topsails, to be arranged for; and the lower masts, topmasts, yard, etc. to be arranged in general harmony with the speed of the vessel.[18]

Blockade-runners were swift, the swiftest craft of their day. They were low-built ships, equipped with raked masts, sails, and steam-driven propellers that could navigate easily in shallow water. Painted grey and burning anthracite coal, usually cardiff coal, which was relatively smokeless, they would sail into Southern ports on moonless nights or during stormy weather.

Appendix 10 lists 104 vessels other than the cruisers used in Confederate service; the following are selected as representative of the varying types of ships purchased or commissioned and the difficulties with which the Confederate agents had to contend.

Not long after the diplomatic furor over the sailing of the *Florida* had died down, there was another uproar, this time over the *Alexandra*, which had been built at Liverpool by Miller and Sons for Fawcett, Preston and Company, which put in the engines. She was launched on 7 March 1863 and towed into Toxteth Dock for fitting

[18] *O.R.N.*, ser. 2, 2:707.

out. There she was immediately a center of interest to federal spies.[19] On 11 March 1863 Dudley, the U.S. consul at Liverpool, discouraged by his experiences with the *Florida* and the *Alabama*, wrote that while he would do all possible to stop the vessel from sailing, his task was made difficult by what he felt to be the uncooperative attitude of the British government.[20]

Nevertheless, various depositions were taken. For example, on 28 March Neil Black, a ship's carpenter of Liverpool, made a formal statement to the effect that in his opinion the *Alexandra* was intended as a gunboat. He described her as being very strongly built of thick teakwood, with beams of about 13 inches. Her bulwarks, he said, were very strong and low and her upper deck was of pitch pine. Henry Hotze, the opinion-molding Southern propagandist, reported in the London-based *Index* that the ship had iron beams of double angle iron and was more than a foot lower than would be found on vessels for the merchant service; it is interesting to note that pitch pine decks were never seen in Great Britain during this period, except in ships of war.[21] O. R. Mumford, a Yankee merchant captain, made a similar deposition and swore that the *Alexandra* was fitted out as a gunboat.[22] Other depositions were taken, and on the same day Morgan, the customs surveyor at Liverpool, reported that the *Alexandra* was well adapted to be a small gunboat; he gave her length as 125 feet, her breadth as 22 feet, her draft 9 feet, and her tonnage as between 200 to 300 tons. This report caused a special watch to be placed over the vessel, and orders were given that she be detained until further instructions were given. The only opinion which was formed in these ex parte affidavits was that the *Alexandra* was intended for other than mercantile purposes. However, no law of the period could prevent a British shipowner from building a steamer of any strength he pleased.[23]

Meanwhile, two days earlier the U.S. minister, Adams, who was incensed at the possibility of the escape of another Confederate war-

[19] F.O., 5/1318, pp. 162–63; *Index*, 25 June 1863. The *Alexandra* was intended as a gift to the Confederate government from Fraser, Trenholm & Co. (*O.R.N.*, ser. 2, 2:125–26, 141–45, 147).

[20] C. C. Beaman, *The National and Private "Alabama Claims"* (Washington, D.C.: W. H. Moore, 1871), p. 150.

[21] Alexandra Black's deposition, 28 March, 1863, F.O. 5/1048; *Index*, 25 June 1863.

[22] Mumford's deposition, 28 Mar. 1863, F.O., 5/1048. The *Alexandra* was unsuitable for the merchant service. Her hatchways were too small, and she was fitted with 3 pumps of a description used only in warships (Deposition of John De Costa, 28 Mar. 1863, F.O. 5/1048).

[23] Ibid., F.O. 5/1048.

ship, if only a comparatively small one, had told Lord Russell, "England is at war with the United States, while the United States is not at war with England." [24] On 28 March, when the depositions were taken, Dudley formally applied to the collector of customs at Liverpool to seize and detain the *Alexandra.*[25] On the same day the collector reported his own impression that the vessel was indeed intended for Confederate service,[26] and on 30 March Adams denounced the *Alexandra* to Lord Russell. On 1 April Adams claimed that the same individuals who were concerned in the outfit of the *Alabama* were now directing the outfit of the *Alexandra.* (This of course was not true.) In any case Sir George Grey, the British home secretary, requested that immediate inquiries be made in order to ascertain whether the ship was being equipped for Confederate service.[27]

Grey placed the evidence Adams had collected before the law officers of the Crown; [28] however, the final decision of seizure rested with the foreign secretary. On 4 April the law officers recommended that the *Alexandra* should be seized immediately under the Foreign Enlistment Act.[29] Next day Russell was able to report to Adams that orders had been sent to Liverpool for the seizure of the *Alexandra* and asked that the United States prepare its evidence so that proceedings might be started.[30] The law officers of the Crown regarded the *Alexandra* case as raising an important question as to the true construction of the Foreign Enlistment Act.

Morgan, the surveyor, duly reported his seizure of the *Alexandra.*[31] The *Times* reported that at about noon Morgan had gone aboard, marked a broad arrow on one of the masts, and remained on board, keeping the vessel under surveillance. The *Times* described the *Alexandra* as a fine tidy-looking craft, "nicely coppered and copper fastened," and presenting an appearance of speed, but with no gun ports, or shell room. Nor had the engines been fitted at this

[24] Brooks Adams, "The Seizure of the Laird Rams, "*Proceedings of the Massachusetts Historical Society*, 45 (1912):276–88.

[25] Dudley to Price Edwards, 28 Mar. 1863, F.O. 5/1048.

[26] S. Price Edwards to Honourable Commissioners, 28 Mar. 1863, ibid.

[27] Adams to Russell, 20 Mar. 1863, ibid.

[28] Brooks Adams, pp. 276–88; F.O. 5/1048, Gardner to G. A. Hamilton, 2 Apr. 1863.

[29] Great Britain, Treasury Board Papers, Public Record Office, London. T 1/6445 and A/16196, 4 Apr. 1863.

[30] Russell to Adams, 5 Apr. 1863, F.O. 5/1048.

[31] Morgan to Price Edwards, 5 Apr. 1863, ibid.; *Index,* 25 June 1863; *Times,* 7, 10 Apr. 1863.

stage. In short, this account concluded, "she presents the appearance of a fast schooner-rigged steam yacht." [32]

On 6 April Adams expressed to Russell his "lively satisfaction" at the decision to detain the vessel,[33] and on the eleventh he wrote suggesting that action be taken under the seventh and eighth sections of the enlistment act.[34]

Fawcett, Preston quickly lodged a protest against the seizure of the *Alexandra.* The company claimed to have built her as a speculative venture. She was described as a three-masted schooner of under 300 tons with engines upon the screw principle of 60 horsepower, calculated to drive her at a speed of 9 to 10 knots and designed to be fitted out either as a passenger boat, mailboat, or yacht.[35]

But despite Fawcett, Preston's expressions of outraged virtue and angry protests in the House of Commons, the British government pressed the case, and it was brought to trial on 22 June 1863.[36] Sir William Atherton, the attorney general, Sir Roundell Palmer, the solicitor general, and Sir Robert Phillimore, Queen's advocate, appeared for the Crown; Sir Hugh Cairns led the defense. The Crown sought two major convictions under the Foreign Enlistment Act: first, an indictment of the vessel itself with a view to its condemnation: second, a verdict against the persons implicated in the fitting out of the vessel.[37] The substance for these charges was contained in ninety-eight counts, but the basis of all of them was that "the defendants did on 5 April, equip the said vessel to employ her in the service of the Confederate States of America with intent to cruise and commit hostilities against the Republic of the United States of America." [38]

After a three-day trial the defendants were acquitted, the judge, Sir Frederick Pollock, advising the jury that "if you think the

[32] 7 Apr. 1863; *Illustrated London News,* 9 May 1863. An arrow is a mark distinguishing British Government Stores.

[33] Adams to Russell, 6 Apr. 1863, F.O. 5/1048; *Papers Relating to Foreign Affairs,* p. 196.

[34] F.O. 5/1048, ibid.; *Times,* 29 Apr. 1863.

[35] *Index,* 25 June 1863; *Times,* 7 Apr. 1863.

[36] *Times,* 23 June 1863.

[37] Duncan Squarry & Blackmore to H. Wilding, 27 Apr. 1863, F.O. 5/1048; F.O. Draft to Home Office, 3 June 1863, ibid. The attorney general is the legal officer empowered to act in all cases in which the state is a party. The solicitor general, Crown law officer, ranks below the attorney general and, like him, is appointed by the government, advising and representing it in legal matters. The Queen's advocate is a professional pleader in the court of justice. (In English law this should not be confused with the lord advocate, who is the principal law officer of the Crown in Scotland.)

[38] *Index,* 25 June 1863.

object was to build a ship in obedience to an order, and in compliance with a contract, leaving it to those who bought it to make what use they thought fit of it, then it appears to be that the Foreign Enlistment Act has not been in any degree broken." The verdict was one that met with the approval of public opinion. Adams, of course, claimed that the verdict was a scandal.[39]

A few days afterwards Fawcett, Preston made application for the restoration of the *Alexandra*,[40] but this was refused pending the lodging of an appeal to the House of Lords.[41] Fawcett, Preston was seriously concerned by the deterioration of the vessel in dry dock and proposed that she should be bought by the British navy, but this request was also refused after considerable deliberations, although in some quarters the solution was favored for political reasons, and a decision to purchase would certainly have met with the approbation of the U.S. government. It was also considered, at one point, whether the government of Venezuela could properly purchase this vessel as a means of overcoming the somewhat embarrassing impasse, but Lord Russell finally decided against this because Venezuela was itself at war.[42]

The appeal to the House of Lords failed, but it was not until April 1864, a year after her seizure, that the *Alexandra* was released. Fawcett, Preston claimed £6,370 compensation for her detention but finally settled for a payment of £3,700.[43] The legal battles over, the *Alexandra* was sold and rechristened *Mary*.[44] On 10 September 1864 the U.S. consul at Halifax, Nova Scotia, reported her arrival in

[39] White, pp. 49–50; *Index*, 25 June 1863; Birkenhead *Guardian*, 7 Nov. 1874; *Times*, 2 Nov. 1863. Confederate agents, elated by their legal success, now undertook to obtain recognition from Parliament (ibid., 17 Nov. 1866).

[40] Fletcher & Hull to Price Edwards, 29 June 1863, F.O. 5/1048. They were anxious for immediate possession as the ship was suffering damage each day during the warm weather (Fletcher & Hull to the Commissioners of H.M. Customs, 4 July 1863, ibid).

[41] Report of the Solicitor of Customs, 3 July 1863; ibid.; *Adams Letters*, 2:100.

[42] Pro-secretary to the under secretary of state, 20 July 1863; Romaine to the under secretary of state, 3 Aug. 1863; F. J. Hamel, on Fletcher & Hull's recommendation, proposed that the *Alexandra* be purchased by H.M. government, 13 July 1863; Fletcher & Hull to the commissioners of H.M. Customs, 13 July 1863; draft to Admiralty, 23 July 1863; draft to Treasury, 24 July 1863; Memo signed "R" (Russell), 23 Oct. 1863, F.O. 5/1048.

[43] White, pp. 49–50; Detailed statement of the damages sustained by Preston, Fawcett & Co., by reason of the seizure, n.d., F.O. 5/1049; with respect to repairs while in port, see E. Morgan to the collector of customs, 25 Feb. 1864, F.O. 5/1048.

[44] White, pp. 49–50.

that port and stated that he believed she intended to take on arms, but no action was taken against her on that occasion.[45] In December 1864, however, she was detained while loading at Nassau. Revenue officers found a 12-pounder rifled gun and cases of shells in her afterhold. The gun was stamped "Fawcett Preston & Co. 1862" and had been shipped in the steamer *Powerful* to Bermuda, where it had been transferred to the *Mary*. Another court hearing followed, but she was again freed—this time too late to be of service to the Confederates, for by now the war was over.[46]

In autumn 1862 Lt. George T. Sinclair made arrangements with J. and G. Thomson and Company, of Glasgow, for the building of a new cruiser, which was eventually to be named the *Pampero*.[47] She was to be built on lines similar to the *Alabama*, but larger and of greater horsepower.[48] Her ultimate true ownership was disguised by the use of several intermediaries, and the initial contract was signed by the Thomsons and Edward Pembroke, a London shipping broker, who agreed to pay £46,000 in five equal installments. Pembroke then contracted to sell her to Sinclair for £51,250, payable in the form of 246 cotton certificates, each valued at £208.6.8d.[49]

The *Pampero* did not long escape the notice of federal spies, although it was not until March 1863 that there were any official interchanges on the subject. On 21 March Lord Russell wrote to Adams that they had two steamers in the Thomson yard under surveillance, but that neither vessel could possibly sail for some months. This uninvited report by Russell was an indication of the steadily growing vigilance of the British authorities, but no further action was taken that summer. On 9 October, however, Warner Lewis Underwood, the American consul in Glasgow, reported that "there is nearly ready to be launched a finely rigged clipper screw sail steamer . . . being bent according to universal report for the Confederate Government." [50] Meanwhile, Sinclair was hoping to get the *Pampero* to sea early in November, following the now well-estab-

[45] Jackson to Tupper, 10 Sept. 1864; George Hamilton to commissioners of customs, 14 Sept. 1863; case of the *Alexandra*, Oct. to Nov. 1865 F.O. 5/1049; H. Hemming to W. G. Romaine, 13 Oct. 1863 ibid. 5/1048; O. L. Bekeley and W. R. Grey to the lords commissioners of Her Majesty's Treasury, 26 Nov. 1864 ibid. 5/1049.

[46] White, pp. 49–50; Soley, p. 213.

[47] E. D. Adams, *Great Britain and the American Civil War* (New York: Longmans Green, 1925), 2:156–57.

[48] *O.R.N.*, ser. 2, 2:518, 295–96.

[49] Thomson to Bemrose, 10 Oct. 1862, Pembroke to Thomson, 17 Oct. 1962, F.O. 5/1051.

[50] Beaman, p. 158.

lished procedure of arranging for her guns and powder to be shipped separately to a prearranged rendezvous.[51]

A few days later Adams received further details concerning the *Pampero*. She was described as being 280 to 300 feet long with a beam of 36 feet, a frame of iron boarded up with teakwood about 5-inches thick, and 8 large and 8 small portholes (the large ones suitable for the use of pivot guns).[52] On 17 October Adams called for an investigation by the British government,[53] and on the nineteenth Russell replied that inquiries would be made promptly. The senior naval officer on the Clyde, the Treasury, and the Home Office were all ordered to cooperate, and the sheriff of Lanarkshire was ordered to prevent any breach of the Foreign Enlistment Act.

The customs surveyor reported peculiarities in the bulkhead of the topgallant forecastle, which was hinged so that it could be folded up and either secured to the underside of the forecastle deck or removed; [54] he stated that her cabin accommodation was also unusual for a merchant vessel. But he refused to commit himself further because of her unfinished state. The collector interviewed the shipbuilders, who stated that the *Pampero* would be launched very soon and then taken to Finnieston Quay to receive her engines. Thomson stated that she was being built for Patrick Henderson and Company of Glasgow, acting as the agent of a London firm. The collector informed Thomson that the *Pampero* must not sail until directions were received from the government, and he further informed the customs commissioners she could be converted into an armed vessel very easily.[55] Meanwhile the Home Office had launched its own inquiry. A Crown agent questioned George Thomson, who continued to assert that he had no knowledge of the *Pampero's* warlike purpose. At the same time Captain Farquhar, of the gunboat *Hogue*, inspected the *Pampero*, and although he was also rebuffed by the builders, he reported that "she is evidently built for aggressive purposes and from her fine lines will probably have great speed." [56]

It was evident that the launching of the *Pampero* would be accomplished any day, and the Federals consulted legal experts as to what steps could be taken to prevent her from sailing. Apart from

[51] *O.R.N.*, ser. 2, 2:108–9. [52] Ibid.

[53] Adams to Russell, 17 Oct. 1863, F.O. 5/1051.

[54] F.O. to Admiralty, 19 Oct. 1863; F.O. to Treasury, 19 Oct. 1863; F.O. to Home Office, 19 Oct. 1863, ibid. The topgallant forecastle was probably hinged so as to provide greater access to the windlass.

[55] Costello to Treasury, 20 Oct. 1863, ibid.

[56] Hart to Alison, 23 Oct. 1863, Farquhar to Admiralty, 22 Oct. 1863, ibid.

the collection of evidence by deposition, it was suggested that by Scottish law witnesses could be examined under oath at a hearing preliminary to any formal court proceedings that might follow. This suggestion was passed to the Foreign Office, which accordingly called on Sir George Grey, the home secretary, to institute a full investigation under the Scottish provision.[57]

The *Pampero* was launched on 29 October. Investigations were intensified, both by the British government and by federal agents, but the days slipped by without conclusive action. Federal sympathizers in Scotland were now growing alarmed lest the *Pampero* get away as the *Alabama* had escaped the previous year. On 4 November the Glasgow Emancipation Society sent an urgent memorial to Lord Russell, warning him that preparations were in hand for the vessel's early departure. On 7 November Lord Russell acknowledged the memorial but stated that investigations had not been completed.[58] The following day however, he asked the Home Office for an immediate report on the vessel and for the facilities offered by Scottish law for her detention.[59]

The lord advocate and the solicitor general for Scotland duly submitted their report, but it did not warrant Lord Russell taking immediate and clear-cut action, for it was much concerned with the intricacies of Scottish law. The report suggested that further evidence was still required. The Admiralty's report did not aid matters, for it stated that investigators were unable to discover any positive evidence of warlike purposes in the specifications of the *Pampero*, although they felt there were some grounds for suspicion.[60]

As October gave way to November, Sinclair was jubilant that preparations for the *Pampero*'s sailing grew daily more complete, although the news that the case of the *Alexandra* was to go to the Court of Appeal must have come as a disappointment to him. Russell still did not believe there was sufficient evidence to proceed against the *Pampero*, but on 13 November the Home Office asked the lord advocate if an interdict could be justified.[61]

Captain Farquhar had never relaxed his guard of the *Pampero* and on 14 November reported that she was being rapidly equipped

[57] Underwood to Adams, 24 Oct. 1863, ibid., F.O. to Home Office, 27 Oct. 1863, ibid.

[58] *Times*, 12 Nov. 1863.

[59] F.O. to Home Office, 6 Nov. 1863, F.O. 5/1051.

[60] Admiralty to F.O., 11 Nov. 1863, ibid.

[61] Home Office to F.O., 13 Nov. 1863, ibid. The lord advocate was also requested to attempt to discover whether Captain Maffitt of the Confederate navy was actually in Glasgow.

for sea and within several days was to be taken down river to a point unspecified, where her fittings could be completed.[62] On the same day Adams sent to Russell a number of depositions which he, Adams, considered conclusive that the *Pampero* was intended as a Confederate ship. In the days ensuing further depositions were collected. One Robert Mitchell deposed that the *Pampero* was pierced for eighteen guns but that the portholes had been temporarily covered up. He also declared that she had a telescopic funnel.[63]

It was now obvious that if the *Pampero* was to be detained at all, decisive and swift action was necessary. She had her boilers and all machinery on board, and the collector estimated she could sail within forty-eight hours. Trevor, the lord advocate immediately instructed that the *Pampero* should be detained if she attempted to set sail. Impatient of further delays, the U.S. government made formal application for the seizure of the *Pampero* under the seventh section of the Foreign Enlistment Act, but still the lord advocate would not recommend such a step until he had more conclusive evidence in his hands. The Federals made great efforts to supply evidence that Captain Maffitt of the *Florida* was in Glasgow and would sail as captain of the *Pampero*, but nothing came of this.[64]

The *Pampero* had not applied for a certificate of registry or a declaration of nationality. During this interim period between suspicion and proof, the British government depended on the 19th and 102nd clauses of the Merchant Shipping Act to detain her, should she attempt to set sail. Two gunboats were stationed nearby and kept at the ready to enforce the act.[65]

The collection of evidence continued steadily. By 24 November the lord advocate was more optimistic about the prospects of indicting the *Pampero*,[66] and the agitations of federal sympathizers on the Clyde grew daily more vehement, the *Caledonian Mercury* being instrumental in whipping up popular feeling against the Confederates.[67] As the *North British Daily Mail* commented, the investi-

[62] Farquhar to Admiralty, 14 Nov. 1863, ibid.

[63] Adams to Russell, 14 Nov. 1863, Deposition of Robert Mitchell, 16 Nov. 1863, ibid.

[64] Trevor to Customs House, 16 Nov. 1863, Underwood to Trevor, 17 Nov. 1863, Moncrieff to Waddington, 16 Nov. 1863, Underwood to Seward, 8 Jan. 1864, ibid. It appears that Maffitt and Seward of the *Florida* crew were waiting in Glasgow for the purpose of serving on the *Pampero*.

[65] Murray to Moncrief, 18 Nov. 1864, ibid. This act of 1854 provided that a new vessel is required to have a certificate of registry and a declaration of nationality before sailing.

[66] Trevor to Grey, 24 Nov. 1864, ibid.

[67] *Caledonian Mercury*, 19, 23, 25 Nov. 1864.

gations "still drag their slow length along,"[68] but at last the lord advocate was satisfied that he had sufficient evidence to bring the case to trial. On 9 December 1863 the Glasgow customs collector was instructed to seize her, and the seizure was effected the following day.[69]

For greater security the collector prepared to move the *Pampero* to Bowling Bay, and Russell meanwhile advised the Treasury and the Home Office that the seizure would be maintained until the case was brought to court; on this occasion no overtures for the purchase of the vessel would be considered. Patrick Henderson and Company lost no time in registering a protest against the seizure and threatened to sue for "the heaviest damages."[70] At this stage the Confederates considered it possible, in the light of previous experience, that the *Pampero* would eventually be returned to them.[71]

Russell's instructions that the purchase of the *Pampero* could not be entertained were no doubt issued to safeguard against her once more falling into Confederate hands, but early in 1864 it was suggested that the Admiralty should consider her purchase for the British navy. The Admiralty surveyors duly made their inspection but did not recommend purchase.[72]

Although the *Pampero* was to all intents and purposes safely in British hands, the Federals feared a Confederate plot to seize her, and on 28 December 1863 Adams had sent an urgent message to Russell urging greater security measures. As a result Captain Farquhar was alerted.[73] Inquiries by the customs officials failed to unearth any plot such as the one suspected by Adams, but as the New Year dawned the Confederates were still hopeful that the *Pampero* would be cleared of any violation of the Foreign Enlistment Act.[74]

The legal proceedings against the *Pampero* began formally on 16 January 1864 when the Crown laid an appraisement of seizure before the Court of Session.[75] Alarmed by the determination of the British government, the owners placed compromise suggestions before the lord advocate, undertaking to guarantee that if the *Pampero* was released, she would not pass into the service of the Confederate States.[76] While this suggestion was under consideration, 5 May 1864 was appointed as the opening date for the trial. After consulting with Russell, the lord advocate replied that he could not accept the owners' proposition but instead submitted a counterproposal:

[68] 28 Nov. 1863. [69] Moncrieff to Grey, 1 Dec. 1863, F.O. 5/1051.
[70] Farquhar to Admiralty, 11 Dec. 1863, ibid. [71] *O.R.N.*, ser. 2, 2:567.
[72] F.O. to Admiralty, 6 Jan. 1864, F.O. 5/1051.
[73] Adams to Russell, 28 Dec. 1863, ibid.
[74] *O.R.N.*, ser. 2, 2:574–75. [75] *Morning Star*, 23 Mar. 1864.
[76] Galbraith to Bouverie, 17 Mar. 1864, F.O. 5/1051.

The Crown to take a verdict on one of the counts in the information. The defendants may select the Court in which the verdict is to proceed, and state, if they think fit, the circumstances under which they violated the statute. No further proceeding to take place on the part of the Crown, with a view to the appreciation of the verdict, provided the rest of the arrangement is duly carried out. The owners therefore to execute on the vessel such alterations as the Crown may require to make her in all respects a merchant ship. These alterations being completed, the Crown to permit the owners to trade with the vessel for their own behoof, they giving bond for the due employment of the vessel under such penalties as may be fixed. The amount to be arranged before this arrangement is completed. The registry of the vessel to be so effected as to prevent the owners from transferring her without the consent of the Crown. . . . Lastly, after such interval as may seem reasonable and provided the above stipulations have in the meantime been faithfully carried out, the Crown to release the vessel as far as the title acquired by the judgement is concerned, the bond still subsisting should the Crown so require.[77]

The owners agreed to this proposal, and on 5 April stated to the Court of Session that "although they adhered to their statement that all the counts were unfounded in fact, they had ascertained that George T. Sinclair had attempted to furnish the vessel with the intent mentioned in the 37th count (which charged that the defendants did attempt and endeavour to furnish the *Pampero* for belligerent purposes) and being advised that the vessel might be liable to seizure, although the owners had not themselves infringed the statute, they had agreed with the pursuer for a settlement of the case." Both the Crown and the defendants agreed that a verdict should be taken on the thirty-seventh count without a jury trial and that no liability or expenses would be imposed upon either party.[78]

On 5 May 1864 the Crown formally announced its verdict in accordance with this agreement and the case of the *Pampero* was at an end.[79] The Confederates had not made a deposit on the building of the *Pampero,* but on the basis of fragmentary references to her in the records of the Confederate navy, it is possible that the owners continued to intrigue with Southern agents.[80] If this is so, the Federals had no inkling of the situation, for there is no further mention of the *Pampero* in their dispatches. But it is curious that the agreement between the lord advocate and the defendants was never put into effect; the *Pampero* remained in the hands of the customs officials until after the end of the war—apparently without the knowl-

[77] Moncrieff to Bouverie, 24 Mar. 1864, ibid. [78] *O.R.N.*, ser. 2, 3:1088.
[79] Beaman, p. 161. [80] *O.R.N.*, ser. 2, 2:652–53, 772, 789.

edge of Russell, the Foreign Office, or the Treasury. So it was not until October 1865 that the *Pampero* was finally returned to her owners.[81]

The *Tallahassee*, cruiser and blockade-runner, was of greater service to the Confederate cause. Originally named the *Atalanta*, she was built at Cubitt Town on the Thames by J. and W. Dudgeon, ostensibly for the use of the London, Chatham and Dover railway; and, as number 48722, was registered in the Port of London on 30 March 1864, owner, George Sutherland of Woodford, Essex.[82]

Having made her trials in March, she was transferred on 12 April to Jefferson Wallace, a merchant living in Bermuda, who was given authority to dispose of her at will for not less than £20,000.[83] While the *Atalanta* was building, she does not appear to have aroused the suspicions of either federal agents or customs officials and was allowed to sail unmolested. In Confederate naval records the *Tallahassee* is described as "a small English built propeller, square stern, no bowsprit, schooner-rigged, small masts, bottom painted red, hull and smoke stacks painted white. Burns hard coal and is not fast." [84] She was also described at being 230 feet long, with a 20-foot beam, fore-to-aft schooner rig, 3 guns (2 pivot and 1 light gun on the forecastle), carrying a crew of about 120 and able to steam 14 knots.[85]

As the *Atalanta*, the ship twice ran the blockade into Wilmington, North Carolina, but in late summer of 1864 she was commissioned as the C.S.S. *Tallahassee* under the command of Comdr. J. T. Wood,[86] and on 18 August 1864 the lieutenant governor of Halifax reported her arrival in Nova Scotia. Her commander told the governor that the *Tallahassee* was an iron vessel of about 300 tons, manned by 125 men, with double screw, very fast, and carrying 3 guns, namely, a 100- 30- and 12-pounder, respectively.[87] On 23 August the governor wrote of the swiftness with which the *Tallahassee* had established her reputation—"reported to have captured or destroyed between thirty and forty vessels in about twelve days and

[81] F.O. to Treasury, 6 Oct. 1865, F.O. 5/1051.

[82] *Sea Breezes*, n.s. 19, no. 110 (1955): 128–130. See *Illustrated London News*, 29 Nov. 1862.

[83] Horace Greeley, *The American Conflict*, 2 vols. (Hartford, Conn.: O. D. Case, 1867), 2:645. Bermuda during the Civil War was full of blockade-runners; Wallace and Sutherland were probably Southern sympathizers.

[84] *O.R.N.*, ser. 1, 2:138. The *Tallahassee* could not be considered a slow vessel (ibid., p. 145).

[85] Ibid., pp. 137–38, 148–49.

[86] Scharf, pp. 806–7; *O.R.N.*, ser. 2, 2:707.

[87] *O.R.N.*, ser. 1, 2:137.

said to have a speed exceeding by five knots that of the *Alabama*." Under these circumstances, it was resolved to carry out strictly the provisions of Her Majesty's government, and compel the commander of the *Tallahassee* to discharge every pound of coal he had put on board in excess of the quantity that would suffice to take her to the nearest Confederate port.[88]

In her short career she had already burned sixteen vessels, scuttled ten, bonded five, and released two.[89] The *Tallahassee* has been called the "ship of seven names"; by October she had become the *Olustee*. In Wilmington her battery was taken out and she was renamed the *Chameleon*, and under the command of Capt. John Wilkinson, C.S.N., she sailed for Bermuda to provide a cargo of provisions for General Lee's army.[90]

On 20 January 1865 the lieutenant-governor of Bermuda reported that "a merchant steamer" *Chameleon* had come into Saint George's harbor and that she was formerly the *Tallahassee*, formerly the *Atalanta*. The governor ended his dispatch rather pathetically: "It seems most desirable from the practice of the Confederate States to change the character of their vessels from merchantmen to men-of-war and from their having in this instance returned the ship to her original mercantile calling, which reversion they may at any time repeat—that the Law Officers of the Crown should give an opinion on such cases to guide officers administering Colonial Governments." [91]

In February of 1865 Mallory instructed Maffitt, "Sell the *Tallahassee* if you can do so," adding that the original cost of the vessel in England was about £17,000 and that the Confederates paid £25,000 for her. If the vessel could not be sold, Maffitt was ordered to exchange *Tallahassee* for a fast steamer drawing under six feet of water when fully laden.[92] The reason for the projected sale of a ship with a proud if brief career was the fast-diminishing resources of the Confederacy. But the war was drawing to its close, and Wilkinson, hearing of the evacuation of Charleston, resolved to take the ship to England, where he arrived on 9 April.[93] She was seized by the British government and was about to enter the merchant service under the name *Amelia* when the United States entered suit

[88] Ibid., pp. 145–49; *Times*, 9 Sept. 1864.

[89] Scharf, pp. 806–7, *Times*, 9 Sept. 1864.

[90] Scharf, pp. 806–7. [91] F.O. 5/1094, pp. 177–79, 171–72.

[92] *O.R.N.*, ser. 2, 2:804–6.

[93] Scharf, pp. 806–7; The *Tallahassee* was reported to be docked at Liverpool (*Manchester Courier*, 11 Apr. 1865).

for possession. The court awarded the vessel and she was handed to federal officials on 23 April 1866.[94]

During her short period of active service, the *Tallahassee* had captured twenty-nine U.S. vessels,[95] but even now her adventures were not quite at an end. In 1867 yards were crossed upon her masts and the brig *Haya Maro* entered the registry. For two years she traded with Japan; on 17 June 1869 she struck a rock while on passage from Yokohama to Hiogo and sank. Her Captain and twenty-one of her crew lost their lives.

As already indicated, the blockade-runners either purchased or constructed in Great Britain, or chartered in part or in whole from British owners are numerous. The following have been selected as representative of the varying types of vessels used and their varying fortunes.[96]

The *Robert E. Lee* was one of the most famous of all blockade-runners. She was originally the *Giraffe*, an iron paddle steamer of 600 tons burden and 290 horsepower, once engaged on the Glasgow-Belfast run. She was a fast ship, making about 13½ knots.[97] The *Robert E. Lee* was purchased by the Confederates for £32,000. Scharf describes her as a very long and narrow side-wheel steamer, of light draft, very strongly built, with 2 short masts on which fore and aft sails could be set and which were only serviceable to keep her steady in a sea abeam.[98] Under the command of Capt. John Wilkinson, she ran the blockade twenty-one times in ten months and carried out thousands of bales of cotton.[99] She was finally captured in 1863 while flying the Confederate flag.[100]

Several blockade-runners were specially built on the Clyde. The initiative came from Bulloch, who found great difficulty in obtaining vessels which combined strength with speed in the required degree. One of the first of these was the *Hawk*, of 900 to 1000 tons register,

[94] *Sea Breezes*, n.s. 19, no. 110 (Feb. 1955): 134, 135. There is no record of her actually sailing from Liverpool under the name *Amelia*. In May, Dudley called upon C. W. Kelloch & Co. to evaluate the vessel and was given a figure of between £4,000 to £4,500. The *Tallahassee* was placed in their hands for sale at public auction (ibid.).

[95] Scharf, pp. 806–7. [96] *Sea Breezes*, n.s. 19, no. 110 (Feb. 1955): 135.

[97] Scharf, p. 468; *O.R.*, ser. 4, 2:601–2.

[98] P. 468. Her beautiful saloon and cabins were dismantled, and bulkheads constructed to separate the quarters for officers and men from the space used for storage of her cargo (ibid.).

[99] Owsley, *King Cotton Diplomacy* p. 268.

[100] *O.R.N.*, ser. 1, 9:287–88. No Confederate papers were found on board (ibid.).

150 horsepower (nominal), 254 feet long, 14 feet draft, iron plates ¼-inch thick, screw-propelled, and with 1 funnel.[101] Ostensibly owned by a London merchant, Thomas Begbie, she was made a test case by Adams, who strenuously tried to detain her.[102] However, while under investigation, she escaped from the Clyde to London and thence to Bermuda. There she was closely watched by U.S. warships, and after lying idle for six months she returned to London. On 14 January 1865 Adams again asked for seizure, but after further investigation Russell refused to take any action, and she was never seized or captured.[103]

The *Georgiana* was a blockade-runner built by Lairds in 1862–63. She is described by Scharf as a "fast and powerful steamer." [104] She escaped from British jurisdiction under the pretense of being destined for the China service and left Liverpool for Nassau on 22 January 1863, the intention being to run the blockade into Charleston, where the ship was to be armed and fitted out as a cruiser. After being detained some time at Nassau, she started for Charleston but was surprised off the port by U.S. ships. Her captain ran her ashore on Long Island beach to avoid capture. The U.S. ships made strenuous efforts to get at her cargo, which was partly of military stores, but the Confederates kept their landing parties at bay by bringing field batteries to bear on them, although in the process they destroyed the *Georgiana*, a serious loss to the Confederacy since she would have made a fast and strong vessel.[105]

The exigencies of war, bearing upon an inadequate and hard-pressed navy, often forced Confederate ships to change their character. As a further example the *Chickamauga* may be instanced. Originally the *Edith*, she was built on the Clyde, purchased by the Confederate government, and for a time operated as a blockade-runner.[106] Then, in autumn 1864, she was renamed the *Chickamauga*, placed under the command of Captain Wilkinson (previously of the *Robert E. Lee*) and sent out as a commerce-destroyer or cruiser. It was also thought that she could be used to cause the withdrawal of a fleet of fast federal steamers from the blockading force of Wilmington, N.C.[107] She is described as having a double screw propeller, 2 smokestacks, and of being very fast (once she was chased five

[101] Grey to Baring, 19 Jan. 1865, F.O. 5/1050; *O.R.N.*, ser. 2, 2:671. The vessel was built in December 1863.

[102] *O.R.N.*, ser. 2, 2:671. [103] F.O., 5/1050, p. 146.

[104] A list of vessels built for the year 1862–63, Laird Papers (Hereford); Scharf, p. 803.

[105] *Times*, 25 Feb. 1864. [106] See Greeley, 2:645.

[107] Scharf, p. 808. *O.R.N.*, ser. 1, 10:802–3.

times on one trip). She was armed "the same as the *Tallahassee*," with 5 guns: one 84-pounder, two 24-pounders and two 32-pounders.[108]

On her first cruise she destroyed several ships before running the blockade back into Wilmington. Wilkinson said she was more sturdily constructed than most of the blockade-runners, and very speedy, but altogether unfit as a cruiser since she could only keep at sea while her coal supply lasted, her masts being very short and only really serviceable to steady her in a rough sea.[109] Wilkinson believed that she may have done more harm than good to the Confederate cause by attracting the Federals' attention to Wilmington and possibly precipitating the attack that resulted in the capture, in January 1865, of Fort Fisher, which controlled the port of Wilmington.[110] The *Chickamauga* was eventually destroyed by fire, early in 1865. Among the notable U.S. ships she sank were *Albion Lincoln*, the *Emma L. Hall*, and *Shooting Star*.[111]

The *Fingal* was yet another Confederate ship that changed her character as the war proceeded. In autumn 1861 Bulloch was seeking a ship strong and swift enough to take out a large shipment of arms to the Confederate forces in Virginia; he discovered the *Fingal* at Greenock.[112] She was a new ship, having made only one or two trips to the north of Scotland, and was in good condition, with a speed of 13 knots in good steaming weather.[113] The *Fingal* attracted Federal attention while she was loading, and on 7 October 1861 Benjamin Moran, the first secretary of the U.S. embassy, noted that she was "taking on a heavy cargo of contraband." [114] A spy drew a sketch of her that was sent to the Union to be copied for circulation among the blockading ships.[115] Until her departure she was, of course, kept under the British flag, and a British master was engaged.[116]

She got safely away at eight in the morning on 10 October 1861. She was "very deep laden" and drew ten feet of water forward and

[108] *O.R.N.*, ser. 1, 10:44–55, 60; 508–10, 793–94. [109] Bradlee, pp. 82–83.

[110] *O.R.N.*, ser. 2, 1:725–733–74; D. D. Porter, *Naval History of the Civil War* (New York: Sherman Publishing Co., 1886), p. 820.

[111] *O.R.N.*, ser. 1, 12:57; Scharf, p. 818. For a photograph of the *Chickamauga* see *O.R.N.*, ser. 2, 2:251.

[112] Bullock was so instructed by the Richmond authorities. The *Fingal*'s cost was £17,500. After the purchase the balance of the department in England was £10,207.2.9 (*O.R.N.*, ser. 2, 2:114–16).

[113] Bulloch, 1:110. See *Adams Letters*, 1:60–61.

[114] Benjamin Moran, *The Journal of . . .*, ed. Sara Wallace and Frances E. Gillespie, 2 vols. (Chicago: University of Chicago Press, 1949), 2:88. See *O.R.N.*, ser. 1, 12:330.

[115] *O.R.N.*, ser. 1, 6:368; Bradlee, p. 52. [116] Bulloch, 1:113.

eleven feet aft, her gunwales being not more than nine feet or so above the waterline. A sketch of her, made as she left port, shows that she had a long black hull with gilding on the stern and 2 masts painted very bright. She had a single long black smokestack and was rigged with a long boom for a spanker. Her bridge was white.[117]

So laden, she ran into a fierce gale that continued for two or three days. Then came the intelligence that she had collided with the brig, or bark, *Siccardi*, variously reported to be Austrian or Sardinian.[118] The *Siccardi* sank immediately, but the *Fingal* being iron, was hardly damaged and was able to resume her voyage.[119] After a stormy passage (Bulloch had now joined the ship), the *Fingal* arrived at Bermuda on 2 November 1861.[120] At that time she was described in Confederate records as an iron screw steamer, schooner rigged, with 2 masts, the bust of a man for a head. She had a deck and a poop and was 186 feet long and 25 feet wide, of 500 tons.[121]

After repairs the *Fingal* set sail again and ran through the blockading fleet into Savannah harbor, anchoring there on 12 November 1861.[122] On 25 November Bulloch reported to Mallory that her cargo had been discharged and she was ready to receive freight. On 30 November Bulloch was instructed to take her back to Great Britain with a cargo of cotton and resin, where he was to hand over command to Lt. G. T. Sinclair. On the same date Bulloch was given authority to arm her, should he judge it expedient.[123] Since federal ships were massed in considerable force outside the harbor, it proved impossible for the *Fingal* to run the blockade.[124] Bulloch was subsequently instructed to return to England without her, and thus handed command to Sinclair on 19 January 1862.[125]

The Confederates realized that Savannah was now sealed by the enemy, and the Navy Department took the *Fingal* into service, converting her into an armor-clad and rechristening her *Atlanta*.[126] To effect this conversion, she was cut down to her deck and widened, armor plated, and provided with a beak, or ram, at the bow, and a pole and a lever that could fire a percussion torpedo. She was armed

[117] *O.R.N.*, ser. 1, 6:370; 12:226–27; 368; sketch, p. 369.

[118] Bulloch, 1:113–14, 115; *O.R.N.*, ser. 1, 6:406.

[119] Bulloch, 1:115–16.

[120] Ibid., p. 117.

[121] *O.R.N.*, ser. 1, 6:355–56.

[122] Bulloch, 1:127.

[123] *O.R.N.*, ser. 2, 2:132, 113–14, 112.

[124] Bulloch, 1:340–50.

[125] *O.R.N.*, ser. 2, 2:127–28, 129, 130, 132, 142–43.

[126] Bulloch, 1:144; *O.R.N.*, ser. 1, 15:708. There were five ships of war at the entrance of Romerly Marsh. The *Fingal*, with speed of only 9½ or 10 knots, could scarcely keep away from the enemy's paddle wheel cruisers (ibid., ser. 2, 2:120–21).

with two 7-inch rifled guns on bow and stern pivots and two 6-inch rifled guns in broadside.[127]

Comdr. William A. Webb was put in command of the new warship. On 17 June 1863 he sailed but went aground just outside the harbor and was pounded by the U.S. ship *Weehawken,* which hit the *Atlanta* four times. After a sorry engagement of fifteen minutes, the *Atlanta* had no option but to haul down her flag and surrender.[128]

The annals of the American Civil War are full of passing references to numerous other blockade-runners and ships, but often their individual histories are lost. Some blockade-runners were purchased outright by the Confederates, a few were built specially, others were owned in part by the Confederates, and still others were leased to them for varying periods. The record is also complicated by the fact that a change of name frequently accompanied a transfer of ownership. To take only one example, the Bristol ship *Alfred* was employed as a blockade-runner under the name *Old Dominion* and was later reregistered as the *Sheffield.*[129]

While the blockade-runners were drawn from ports all over Great Britain, the majority came from the Clyde. In the *Times* reports such as this one are not uncommon:

> The favourite and crack steamer *Iona* was withdrawn from her station between Glasgow and Ardishaig on Monday last, the beautiful saloon steamer *Fairy* taking her place. We are told that this withdrawal is caused by the *Iona* having been sold to the Confederates in America. It is also rumoured that the fine Belfast paddle steamer *Giraffe* and the West Highland steamer *Clydesdale* have also been disposed of to the same parties. If this be true, then the very flower of our Clyde passenger steamers will have been withdrawn, to make room, it is hoped, for others equal at least, if not superior to those we shall have lost.[140]

John Brown and Company, the famous Clydebank shipbuilders, quote an unnamed authority as stating that 111 ships were taken over by the Confederate naval forces, having a total of over 60,000 gross tons and costing £1.7 million.[131] These vessels were taken from

[127] *O.R.N.*, ser. 2, 120–21.

[128] *Index,* 9 July 1863; Clarence E. Macartney, *Mr. Lincoln's Admirals* (New York: Funk and Wagnalls, 1956), p. 304.

[129] A. S. E. Browning, curator of technology, Glasgow Museums and Art Galleries, to Richard Lester, 2 Dec. 1958.

[130] 18 Sept. 1862.

[131] H. D. Brown, John Brown & Co. (Clydebank) Ltd., Clydebank Engineering and Shipbuilding Works, to Richard Lester, 23 Sept. 1958.

river services on the Clyde, the northwest highland routes and the cross-channel services. They varied from fast river paddle steamers to coastal vessels and deep-sea cross-channel ships.[132] In a letter to Commander G. Gansevoort, U.S.N., Gideon Welles mentions that "among the vessels that have been reported as having arms, munitions of war, etc., and as having sailed from Europe with the intention of violating the blockade or throwing their cargoes into the Southern States by transshipments, are the steamers, *Julia*, *Usher*, *Bahama*, *Melita*, *Sylph*, *Stanley*, *Leopard*, *Columbia*, *Merrimac*, *Memphis*, *Anglia*, *Scotia*, *Herald*, *Sophia*, *Phoebe Ann*, *Tubal Cain*, *Southwick*, *Economist*, *Minho*, *Londona*, and *Adela*." [133]

Many of these ships emanated from the Clyde. Browns built at least five vessels for blockade-running: the *Lilian*, *Little Hattie*, *Wild Rover*, *Emma Henry*, and *Corcovado*, although the last was built too late to see active service.[134]

Many of the most successful of these runners were engined by Fawcett, Preston, famous then as now for their marine engines. One ship, the *Phantom*, was reported to have a remarkable turn of speed of not less than 17 knots.[135] Blockade-running, which sometimes realized a 700 percent profit,[136] was naturally a hazardous occupation and losses were heavy, but one blockade-runner, the *Chicora*, was in existence as recently as 1938. Originally named the *Let Me B*, she was a 740-ton iron paddle ship launched in 1864. The following year she was the last blockade-runner to get out of Charleston. Later she was transferred to Canadian registry and converted into a passenger vessel for service on Lake Superior. Later still she went into service on the Niagara river, and in 1901 carried the Duke and Duchess of Cornwall, later King George V and Queen Mary, on their visit to the falls. In 1919 she sank, was raised again and became a coal barge on Lake Ontario, and was finally broken up in 1938.[137]

Two ships that were built on the Clyde for the Confederates were the *Ajax* and the *Hercules*. These were intended as gunboats for the defense of Wilmington, rather than as blockade-runners. Bulloch was charged with their building, and they were to have an exceptionally light draft of 7 feet 6 inches, each to be armed with one 9-inch pivot gun. Mallory was confident that they would escape interference from the British authorities, since the vessels were

[132] *Times*, 25 Nov. 1863. [133] *O.R.N.*, ser. 1, 1:399–400.

[134] H. D. Brown to Richard Lester, 7 May 1958. [135] White, p. 50.

[136] George McHenry, *Approaching Cotton Crises* (Richmond: Otley & Co., 1863), p. 31; Callahan, p. 106.

[137] White, p. 51.

planned to resemble commercial ships, except that they would have reinforced decks.[138] Bulloch contracted for the building at the Denny shipyard in Dumbarton and towards the end of the year was able to report their favorable progress.[139] On 16 December Mallory announced that they were to be renamed *Olustre* and *Vicksburg*.[140] Early in January the *Ajax* was completed and Bulloch made arrangements for sending her to Nassau. Denny was registered as the owner and the vessel was put under the command of a Captain Adams. However, Lt. John Low, C.S.N., was ordered aboard to take command when the *Ajax* reached Nassau and then to attempt to run her into Wilmington.[141] The American consul, unaware of her belligerent character, described her as "a small double screw, reported to be built for a tug boat, 340 tons gross, 202 tons Customs House register, with a crew of twenty seven men." [142]

The *Ajax* sailed without interference. One of the sailors, John Melley, was suspicious, and when they arrived at Kingstown, Ireland, he confided his suspicions to the crew, fifteen of whom refused to do duty. They were prosecuted, and although their spokesman, one Robert Browne, was sentenced to a month in prison, the majority refused to return to the ship. Two others were then sentenced to six weeks' imprisonment. At the trial the defendants testified that the *Ajax* had 3 decks, berths before the funnel, and engines and boilers with 2 safety valves under the water line. She was inspected by the Dublin customs surveyor, who declared she would need alterations before she could be used as a gunboat. In this contention he was supported by the collector. Upon receiving these reports, the Irish law officers asserted that there were no grounds for action against the *Ajax*, and she sailed from Kingstown on 25 January 1865.[143]

By now, however, the U.S. authorities were thoroughly aroused, and the quest for statements and depositions followed the familiar pattern. On 7 February Adams protested hotly to Russell. Adams's sheaf of depositions included one from an employee of Denny's, who stated that the *Ajax* and *Hercules* were the strongest ships for their size he had ever seen; that they had portholes for guns; that their decks were strong enough to take the recoil of heavy artillery; that their sides were very thick and strong, being composed of lay-

[138] *O.R.N.*, ser. 2, 2:695. [139] Ibid., pp. 767–69. [140] Ibid., p. 779.

[141] Ibid., pp. 787–88. [142] Ibid.

[143] Report of Armstrong, Dublin police officer, 18 Jan. 1865, Report of Dublin customs surveyor, 19 Jan. 1865, Gardner to Larcom, 19 Jan. 1865, Dublin Castle to Home Office, 19 Jan. 1865, Baring to Hammond, 25 Jan. 1865, West to Cannellan, 21 Jan. 1865, F.O. 5/1050.

ers of iron, wood, and cement; and that the vessels were referred to as gunboats in the yard. As a result of these protestations, two customs officials were placed on board the *Ajax* when she arrived at Nassau on 11 March, but nothing suspicious was discovered and she was allowed to sail for Bermuda, although a request was sent forward to the acting governor of the colony to watch her. As soon as the *Ajax* arrived in Bermuda, she made application to ship guns, but this was refused and the local privy council upheld the prohibition.[144]

Meanwhile, the *Hercules* was receiving attention. Dudley, the U.S. consul at Liverpool, reported to Adams that he believed the *Hercules* was intended as a Confederate warship. He described her as a double screw boat of 220 tons registered and 500 tons burden, with 2 engines combining 150 horsepower nominal. The hull, he said, was 170 feet long with a beam of 25 feet, 11½ feet of hold and drawing about 8 feet of water. She had a funnel, 2 masts, the foremast rigged, the aft schooner rigged, and the decks flush fore and aft. The timbers, he asserted, were of angle iron, heavy and very close to give great strength, plated over with iron, the hull 6-inches thick beside the iron plate, and with deck beams strong enough to hold guns of any size. The bulwarks were so low that guns could be fired over them, and there were watertight compartments in the hull.[145]

On 7 February 1865 Adams submitted his report to Russell, who promised an investigation, remonstrating, however, that Adams had given him very little time since the *Hercules* was reported due to sail in a few days. On the eleventh the treasury solicitor reported that although the *Hercules* was clearly a warship, there was no evidence that she was intended for the Confederates so that he had no grounds for detaining her under the Foreign Enlistment Act. The Glasgow customs collector went further, declaring that the *Hercules* was a tug and had no warlike characteristics whatsoever.[146] As the legal wrangles continued, the Confederacy collapsed and the war ended before either the *Ajax* or the *Hercules* could be brought into action.[147]

144 Seward to Cardwell, 11 Feb. 1865, Smith's deposition, 7 Feb. 1865, Rawson to Cardwell, 1 Apr. 1865, Rawson to acting governor of Bermuda, 29 Mar. 1865, Hamley to Cardwell, 5 May 1865, ibid.

145 Dudley to Adams, 2 Feb. 1865, ibid.

146 Adams to Russell, 7 Feb. 1865, Russell to Adams, 8 Feb. 1865, Greenwood to Hamilton, 11 Feb. 1865, Waddington to Hammond, 18 June 1865; Mulvaney to Williamson, 13 June 1865; Russell to Adams, 28 June 1865, ibid.

147 *O.R.N.*, ser. 2, 2:805–6, 808; *Case of the Ajax*, F.O. 5/1050.

Two of the blockade-runners built on the Clyde are of particular interest, not on account of their records, but because their plans still exist. The *Fergus* and the *Dare* were both built by Alexander Stephen and Sons "in record time." Both ships were 210 feet long, with a beam of 23 feet and a draft of 9 feet 6 inches. Both were of 552 tons.[148] The *Dare* was launched on 11 September 1863 and was a two-funneled, two-masted paddle steamer. Her funnels were hinged and she was fired by two dome-topped vertical high-pressure boilers, which could be stoked fore or aft, or from both sides. Her poop deck was 36 feet 6 inches long.[149] She had wood deckings fore and aft with iron deck beams and stringers.[150]

The *Fergus*, launched 1 August 1863, was similar in appearance. Both ships were strongly constructed with ample cargo space. The crew's quarters were well forward; the galley was behind the forward boiler room and there was a saloon and accommodation for first-class passengers behind the deckhouse.[151]

Finally, mention should be made of the torpedo boats. In July 1864 Mallory wrote to Bulloch that under certain conditions torpedo boats could operate effectively against the blockading ships, and Bulloch was instructed to have six built as soon as possible.[152] These ships were intended to be small swift steamers with explosives attached to long spars on the bows. They would ram Union ships, explode the "torpedo," and then retreat.[153] Mallory advised Bulloch that these vessels would select their own time for operating in a smooth sea, and that as they must operate at night it was important that they be low in the water.[154] They were expected to

148 The secretary of Alexander Stephen & Sons Ltd., shipbuilders and engineers, Glasgow, to Richard Lester, 10 Oct. 1958.

149 *The Dare,* Outline of external profile. Plan in the possession of Alexander Stephen & Sons, Glasgow. She also possessed an elliptic counter, emergency steering gear, gaff mainsail, gaff head, feathering paddle floats, funnel guts, alleyway to fore and aft on each side of the engine room, paddle blade 8′10″ by 2′5″.

150 *Fergus* and *The Dare,* Detailed construction of section; paddle wheel arrangement, Alexander Stephen & Sons, Company records.

151 *Fergus:* Half section of longitudinal construction; outline construction plan, Alexander Stephen & Sons. Owing to their shallow draft and length, with a beam ratio to length of 9 to 13, their safety factor for deep-water ocean voyages was limited. Both vessels were fitted with turtle decks forward for safety purposes.

152 *O.R.N.*, ser. 2, 2:688–89.

153 Milton F. Perry, curator of the museum, Harry S. Truman Library, Independence, Mo., to Richard Lester, 9 Sept. 1958. Torpedo boats were the grandfathers of modern destroyers.

154 *O.R.N.*, ser. 2, 2:688–89.

carry from five to seven men, coal for twenty-four hours, and 4 torpedoes. Mallory stated that the torpedo was to be made of copper or iron boiler plate, containing forty to one hundred pounds of powder prepared with three sensitive tubes which exploded the powder on impact below the waterline. He hoped that the boats might be completed without interference from the British authorities or federal spies but if this proved impossible suggested they should be built in sections and sent to the Confederate States part by part, although he hoped such a course of action would not be necessary since "we are so destitute of mechanics." [155]

In September 1864 Bulloch was able to report that the torpedo boats were under construction, but discussions followed as to their best design.[156] The last winter of the war came and passed, and the Confederacy fell before the torpedo boats could be delivered.[157]

[155] Ibid. [156] Ibid., pp. 724–25, 769–71.

[157] Milton F. Perry to Richard Lester, 9 Sept. 1958.

CHAPTER V

THE IRONCLADS

At the beginning of the American Civil War, the fighting power of the world's navies was still largely vested in wooden ships.[1] These were two- or three-decked line-of-battle vessels of anything up to 130 guns and were powered by steam and sail. They were usually armed with the traditional iron or bronze 68- or 32-pounder smoothbore guns and cannonade. But the Crimean War had demonstrated the vulnerability of wooden bulwarks to the increasing power of shellfire.[2] Experimentation during the war indicated that vessels clothed in rolled iron of 4½-inch thickness were, to all practical purposes, invulnerable against any projectile. Immediately after the war, however, developments in the rifling of cannon led to a further increase in the range and destructive power of artillery both on land and at sea, and the naval powers of the world became aware—in some cases reluctantly—that armored ships were necessary to withstand rifled ordnance.[3]

The French saw ironclads, or rams, as a possible means of avenging the defeat of Trafalgar and in 1858 ordered four such vessels to be built. French shipbuilders proposed fast ironclad frigates of 20 to 34 guns, with displacements ranging from 1,800 to 4,000 tons. An agent of John Laird, the famous English shipbuilder from Birkenhead (near Liverpool), declared that one early French ironclad, *La Gloire*, looked "hogged," her plates appearing as though every slam were loose.[4] Nevertheless, French ironclad construction spurred the

[1] Oscar Parkes, *British Battleships* (London: Seeley Service & Co., 1956), p. 2.

[2] Millis, p. 113; *Times*, 15 Mar. 1861; *Morning Star* (London) 2 Apr. 1862; *Edinburgh Review* 118 (1863): 192, 169; W. H. Russell, *The Capture of Kinburn* (London: Routledge, 1856), pp. 287, 291.

[3] Parkes, p. 2. During the Crimean War, both on shipboard and in the batteries at Sebastopol, the Royal Navy had tried a rifled gun, the invention of a Mr. Lancaster, which had an oval bore. This was a truly excellent weapon, perhaps the best of its weight in the world (W. E. M. Reilly, *Siege of Sebastopol: An Account of the Artillery Operations* [London: George Eyre and William Spottiswoode, 1859], p. 205; W. H. Russell, *The British Expedition to the Crimea* [London: Routledge, 1858], p. 563).

[4] *Times*, 15 Mar. 1861; *O.R.N.*, ser. 2, 2:67, 69; (name illegible) to John Laird, 13 Dec. 1861, Laird Papers (Hereford).

British Government to action, and in 1859 the first British ironclads, *Warrior* and *Black Prince*, were ordered. The rationale was that if England could produce iron-cased vessels attaining anything like the speed of ordinary men-of-war, and as seaworthy, other vessels would have not the slightest chance against them. The first British ironclads were armored with 4½-inch rolled iron plate backed by 18 inches of teak; the bow and stern of each vessel were unarmored, but the ships were designed so that they could float and fight with both extremities blown away.[5]

In the United States experiments in the construction of armorclad vessels had been carried out in desultory fashion. Actually, the resistance of iron plates cast over any unyielding surface to the direct action of heavy ordnance had been tested first by Robert L. Stevens of New York in 1845. At the outbreak of the Civil War, the Union quickly laid plans to build up an ironclad fleet that could operate in shallow waters. Secretary of the Navy Gideon Welles had earlier urged that Congress launch a program of ironclad construction to provide ships to prevent Confederate ironclads from disrupting the blockade of Southern ports and to attack blockade-runners.[6] Meanwhile, the Confederates were no less aware of their need for ironclads to carry forward the war at sea, and indeed there is considerable evidence in the Laird papers that long before the outbreak of hostilities in 1861, Southern businessmen had been interested in the development of armored vessels.[7]

In 1861 Stephen R. Mallory, Confederate secretary of the navy,

[5] (Name illegible) to John Laird, 25 Oct. 1863, Laird Papers (Hereford); Robert S. McCordoch, *The Yankee Cheese Box* (Philadelphia: Dorrance, 1938), p. 254; *United Service Magazine*, pt. 1 (1863): 435, 129, 275. The seaworthiness and the stability of iron ships were not known (ibid., pt. 2[1861]: 412; *Army & Navy Gazette*, 23 Feb. 1861).

[6] *Times*, 24 Dec. 1861; *O.R.N.*, ser. 2, 2:67, 69; R. S. West, Jr., *Gideon Welles* (New York: Bobbs-Merrill, 1943), p. 185; James F. Rhodes, *History of the United States*, 8 vols. (New York: Harper & Macmillan, 1919), 4:614; *Quarterly Review* 3 (1862): 347; William N. Still, Jr., *Iron Afloat* (Nashville, Tenn.: Vanderbilt University Press, 1971), p. 5 (cited hereafter as Still, *Iron*).

[7] Wm. Scarborough to Wm. Laird & Son, Sundry letters as to John Randolph and Iron Vessels for America, 1834–37; G. B. Larmar to Wm. Laird & Son, 9 July 1835; C. MacIver to Wm. Laird & Son, Erskine Hagard to Wm. Laird & Son, E. T. Miller to Wm. Laird & Son, and Charles C. Mills to Wm. Laird & Son, Sundry letters as to Iron Ships for America, 1837–1841; Isaac Gage to John Laird, 6 Feb. 1839; F. B. Ogden to John Laird, Sundry letters as to Iron Vessels for America, 1839–1840, Laird Papers, (Hereford). See also list of iron and wood vessels and engines built at the Birkenhead iron works, ibid. *New York Herald*, 30 Oct. 1868; *Annual Register for 1862*, p. 221.

noted that "rifled cannon may destroy wooden ships at 5,000 yards, but such guns are harmless against ironclads [5.1 to 2.5 inches in thickness] at a greater distance than 400 yards." [8] On the same date he reported that an agent of the Confederate Navy Department was leaving for England "in a day or two," charged with the duty of purchasing ironclad vessels. This agent was Lt. (later Comdr.) James North, C.S.N.,[9] who was ordered a few days later to proceed to London to purchase ironclads of *La Gloire* class.[10] For the Confederates, procurement abroad was the only viable option for securing ironclads of high quality. Because proprietors of Southern ironworks found it impossible to undertake the rolling of iron plates, the Confederates were incapable of building ships of this type in their own shipyards. North had no immediate success in England, and in June 1861 Mallory sent him an urgent message in code instructing him to purchase an ironclad warship "upon any terms." Mallory staked the success of the Confederate navy on two projects: the construction of commerce-destroyers, such as the *Alabama,* and the construction of ironclads that would break through the blockade and carry the war to the enemy.[11]

In July, North still being silent, Mallory sent terse instructions that he should be informed as to North's progress.[12] But on 16 August North replied that, money shortage apart, he could not purchase any ironclad ready for sea because England and France were indulging in an arms race for this latest instrument of warfare. In September he reported that if money were available, he could arrange for the building of ironclads. (But this came to nothing.) And in March the Confederate Navy Department, perhaps wearied by North's procrastination (though he was certainly hampered by a serious lack of funds), ordered James D. Bulloch to supplement North's mission.[13] Although the Confederate Congress had appropriated $2 million for the purchase or construction of warships, North and Bulloch's subsequent work in Great Britain was continually held up for lack of ready funds.[14]

In January 1862 Mallory instructed North to continue his efforts

[8] *O.R.N.*, ser. 2, 2:68. For Mallory's policy toward ironclads, see Still, *Iron,* pp. 16, 17.

[9] *O.R.N.*, ser. 2, 2:69, 72, 73, 74, 75–79, 191, 204–5. [10] Ibid., pp. 70–72.

[11] Ibid., p. 107; Foster, p. 387; James P. Baxter, *The Introduction of Ironclad Warships* (Cambridge: Harvard University Press, 1933), p. 237.

[12] *O.R.N.*, ser. 2, 2:81–82.

[13] Ibid., pp. 87–88; *Manchester Examiner and Times,* 25 Mar. 1862.

[14] *O.R.N.*, ser. 2, 2:95, 96. Mallory suggested the aid of John Fraser & Co. (ibid., 97–98, 98–99, 106; Bulloch, 1:79–88).

to secure an ironclad builder.[15] A few days later wrote to Bulloch that he required an armored steam sloop of about 2,000 tons that could carry 8 or 10 heavy guns. Mallory believed the completion of *La Gloire*, the *Warrior*, and the *Prince* would furnish extensive information and many useful hints for the construction of such a vessel. He went on to suggest to North that the vessel might be contracted for in the name of a Brazilian, Sardinian, or Spanish house and delivered to a neutral port, where her armament could be placed on board.[16]

In March 1862 North, once again urging upon Mallory the need for funds to be available in England, reported that he had a bid for the construction of gunboats cased with armor plates from stem to stern and for iron-screw corvettes of between 1,800 and 2,000 tons. North stated that these vessels would have 4½-inch plates and 9-inch teak amidships, tapering off to 6 inches of teak and 3½-inch plates at each end, the armor extending from stern to stem.[17] On 6 April North further reported that he had found two gunboats of about 500 tons each, armor-plated with 2¼- to 2½-inch iron, that were due for completion in a short while.[18] But nothing seems to have come of this suggestion. A few days later, however, North was in communication with George Thomson of J. and G. Thomson, the Glasgow shipbuilders, asking the firm to prepare a model, plans, and specifications for an armor-clad steamship.[19]

Meanwhile, Bulloch himself was finding that there were considerable obstacles in the way of obtaining ironclads. The principal difficulty was the time required for construction, which he estimated at a minimum of twelve months. Other impediments were the high cost and the fact that it was impossible to conceal the true character of an ironclad. The engagement between the *Merrimack* and the *Monitor* had decisively changed the plan of iron shipbuilding for the British navy. Several of the largest screw liners had already been selected for cutting down and conversion to ironclad vessels, and four entirely new ones were to be built.[20]

On 14 April North again sought funds, reporting to Mallory that he had arranged for the building and equipping of an armored vessel of 3,000 tons that would cost £200,000.[21] Coincidentally, the

[15] *O.R.N.*, ser. 2, 2:128–29. [16] Ibid., p. 131.

[17] Ibid., pp. 166–68. The *Manchester Guardian* claimed that although the Confederates were seeking ironclads, the war would be settled by armies (26 Mar., 1 Apr. 1862).

[18] *O.R.N.*, ser. 2, 2:181. [19] Ibid., p. 183. [20] Ibid., pp. 183–85, 186–87.

[21] Ibid., p. 185; *Annual Register for the Year 1864*, pp. 123, 134; Estimate of an additional appropriation required for the service of the government from 1 Apr. to 30 Nov. 1862, dated 25 Mar. 1862, (ibid., p. 173).

Confederate Congress two days later passed an act authorizing the purchase of a maximum of 6 iron-plated vessels of war.[22] The building of these ships was to be financed by a private citizen of the Confederacy (the name of the citizen was not given), and the Confederate States were to pay for them in cotton on delivery.[23]

Early in May J. and G. Thomson reported to North that their engineers had prepared the plans and made a model of his ironclad, but that after weights and displacements had been calculated, they had found it necessary, for stability, to increase the beam to 50 feet to obtain the draft required.[24] On 20 May the specifications of North's ironclad were set down. She was to be 270 feet long, with a beam of 50 feet and a draft of 30 feet. Her displacement was to be 3,200 tons.[25] Her keel was to be of hammered scrap iron, 14 inches deep and 4 inches thick, and she was to have a ram projecting from her bow. She was to be completely armored, both internally and externally, and the builders proposed that her forepeak should be specially strengthened. It was planned that she should be bark-rigged, and her engines were to be of a nominal 500 horsepower. She was to have tubular boilers, and her coal bunkers were to have a capacity of 1,000 tons. With these specifications, the ship would be the largest of her kind in the world.[26]

The next day Thomsons and North entered into an agreement for her construction. The cost was to be £182,000, payable in eight installments over a twelve-month period. Early in June North sent to Mallory a further urgent request for funds. Thomsons had pledged delivery by 1 June 1863; the first deposit was paid, and the work began.[27]

In June 1862, however, Bulloch received orders from the Confederate Navy Department to give North command of a ship, and he instructed North to join him in Liverpool. Bulloch was not enthusiastic about taking over North's project, which he felt to be too large and costly, and Thomsons did not look with favor on the proposed transfer of the contract, pointing out that the agreement was based on personal confidence in North. Nevertheless, the contract was transferred to Bulloch.[28]

A few days later the command of the *Alabama*, which North had hoped for, was given to Commander Semmes.[29] Much to his chagrin, North, who throughout this period was continually seeking the

22 *O.R.N.*, ser. 2, 2:182–83. 23 Ibid., pp. 181–82. 24 Ibid., pp. 191–93.

25 Specification of hull, masts, spars, rigging, outfit, engines, boilers, etc., of an armored iron Steamship, ibid., pp. 192, 198; *Times*, 22 May 1862.

26 *O.R.N.*, ser. 2, 2:192, 198. 27 Ibid. pp. 199–204, 206.

28 Ibid., pp. 207–8, 212–13. 29 Ibid., pp. 213, 214.

command of a high-seas Confederate vessel, was forced to turn his thoughts back to the ram.[30] So the building went on, although Bulloch continued to maintain that the ship was too large, expensive, and deep-drafted for the Confederate service.[31]

In late July the problems of financing North's ironclad ram became increasingly severe. The first two installments had been paid,[32] but Confederate currency was depreciating rapidly.[33] Early in August, North advised Mallory that the ram would cost between $2 million and $2.5 million, and that only a quarter of that sum was available.[34] He went on to suggest that the Confederates issue bonds based on cotton, which he believed he could successfully dispose of in Britain. On 6 August he again urged on Mallory the need for funds, stating that a third installment on his ram was almost due.[35]

Further difficulties now beset North. In September the ram came to the attention of Prettyman, the American consul in Glasgow. Prettyman warned Seward, the U.S. secretary of state, that the ship would be "a formidable vessel, equal in her protection against shot to anything yet afloat." He added that it was rumored among her workers that she was intended for the Confederacy and was referred to as the *Merrimack.* The consul promised to watch her closely. Meanwhile, the money for the next installment having been found from Bulloch's funds, work went on, and at the end of September North reported to Mallory that he hoped the ram would be completed by May 1863. In November Thomsons asked for the next installment, announcing that the plating of the forebody had begun and predicting that if the weather remained good, the ship would be half-plated in the New Year.[36]

By late November North was sufficiently encouraged to begin negotiations for acquiring arms and other equipment for the ram. He made inquiries with the Whitworth Ordnance and Rifle Company of Manchester, a firm that was pioneering in the manufacture of rifled artillery and experimenting with steel shot and shell.[37] But, reporting to Bulloch on these negotiations, North went on to say that the cost of such artillery frightened him: "£700. for each gun and £5. for each flat-head shell almost takes away one's breath." [38] Nevertheless, North proceeded to negotiate with Whitworth for four 70-pounders, together with ammunition, carriages, and other equipment, to be delivered in the spring of 1863. When spring came North was again having difficulties meeting his obliga-

30 North was always seeking to command a high seas vessel.

31 *O.R.N.*, ser. 2, 2:228. 32 Ibid., p. 223. 33 E. D. Adams, 2:156–57.

34 *O.R.N.*, ser. 2, 2:234. 35 Ibid.; ibid., p. 269. 36 *Ibid.*, p. 301.

37 *Ibid.*, p. 300. 38 *Ibid.*, p. 301.

tions for the ram, but Capt. Matthew F. Maury, who was also in England, managed to send him an unspecified sum on 1 February 1863.[39]

During the early part of 1863, however, Charles F. Adams was exerting pressure on Lord Russell to prevent the sailing of Confederate ships then under construction in British ports. As a result, it was proposed to Bulloch that the ram should be transferred to France for completion. Since France at this time had resolved to maintain a strict neutrality in the American Civil War, this suggestion was not feasible.[40]

No solution was possible for North, who was harassed by shortage of money. James Mason and John Slidell, the Confederate commissioners, advised him to sell his ship. However, on 27 June 1863 North received orders to proceed with construction.[41]

Although the Glasgow ironclad was ignored in Adams's dispatches, it came to the attention of abolition and other pro-Union groups who were pressing the British government on the subject of Confederate warships. The London Emancipation Society, in a memorial addressed to the British government, called for the arrest of Confederate ships.[42] A similar memorial was sent by the Glasgow Emancipation Society on 8 September 1863.[43] Even newspapers that had previously tended to be pro-Confederate were critical of the building of Confederate ironclads in Britain, and the public was made to feel that if the ships were allowed to escape, Britain might find herself at war with the United States.[44]

North, after weary months of doubt and indecision, was once more ordered to sell his ship. Now named the *Pampero*, the ironclad had been seized as being in violation of British neutrality laws, and the Confederates were seriously worried.[45] On 18 February 1864 North reported to Mallory from Paris, where he had fled in consequence of increasing federal espionage in Glasgow, that the seized ship had been sold by her builders to the Danish government for the sum of £240,000.[46] This action, a noted Southern historian claims, was evidence that the British government's seizures of Confederate ships were based on policy, not on law.[47]

So ended a venture that had been fraught with difficulties and

[39] *Ibid.*, pp. 301, 342, 348.
[40] Ibid., pp. 413, 414, 415–16, 421–22. *O.R.N.*, ser. 2, 2:439–40.
[41] *O.R.N.*, sec. 2, 2:443. [42] *Glasgow Herald*, 27 Aug. 1863.
[43] Glasgow Emancipation Society Minute Book, 8 Sept. 1863.
[44] *Glasgow Herald*, 1 Sept. 1863; *Times*, 7 Sept. 1863.
[45] *O.R.N.*, ser. 2, 2:566, 567, 574–75, 581–83.
[46] Ibid., pp. 587–88. [47] Owsley, *King Cotton Diplomacy*, p. 443.

frustrations from the beginning. North wrote to Mallory, "It has been a sad, sad disappointment to me after so many months of labour to find it was necessary to part with so noble a ship when I felt confident she would have done us most valuable service."

Meanwhile, in the summer of 1862, Bulloch, receiving instructions to proceed with the buildings of ironclads, had made contact with Lairds, who had built the *Alabama*.[48] A contract was soon formulated providing for the construction of two ironclads, one to be delivered in March 1863 and the other in May 1863.[49] Before closing the contract both Bulloch and Lairds sought legal advice to determine whether "armor-plating a ship would be violating British neutrality." They were advised that there was nothing illegal in the transaction.[50]

The Birkenhead, or Laird, rams, as they came to be called, were about half the size of North's vessel. They were to be heavily armored and also equipped at the bows with a piercer, or ram, of considerable strength.[51]

While under construction these ships were known as the 294 and 295, and in the Laird records are shown to have been sister ships, identical in nearly every detail. They were both screw vessels, 220 feet long, 42 feet wide, and 18 feet 3 inches deep in the hold. Their displacement builder's measurement was 1,827 tons. The engines were also made at Lairds, and each vessel had a nominal 400 horsepower (developing 1,450) with a projected top speed of 14 knots.[52] The 294 was launched on 4 July 1863, the 295 on 29 August.[53]

These vessels were to cost £93,750 each, exclusive of arms and ammunition.[54] The contract provided for the sterns to be forged solid of the best hammered scrap iron and formed as projecting beaks below the waterline; they were designed to inflict blows when the vessel was used as a ram. The stern frame was formed with a

[48] *O.R.N.*, ser. 2, 2:587.

[49] Ibid., p. 226; Owsley, *King Cotton Diplomacy*, p. 42; E. D. Adams, 2:122; *Birkenhead Guardian*, 3 June 1865; Company report, p. 11, Laird Papers (Birkenhead); *London Daily Mail*, 3 June 1865.

[50] Bulloch, 1:387–88; *Index*, 10 Sept. 1863; *Times*, *Economist*, 12 Sept. 1863; *Times*, 17 Oct. 1863; *The Later Correspondence of Lord John Russell, 1840–78*, ed. G. P. Gooch, 2 vols. (New York: Longmans Green, 1925), 2:334–35.

[51] *Times*, 20 Sept. 1862; ibid, 28 Aug. 1863; Owsley, *King Cotton Diplomacy*, p. 42; E. D. Adams, 2:122; Lower deck, iron cased cupola screw steam rams, contract for general outfit, midship section, Laird Papers (Birkenhead).

[52] Iron and wood vessels and engines built at the Birkenhead Iron Works, 1829–69, Laird Papers (Hereford), Laird Diary, p. 31; *Illustrated Times*, 21 Nov. 1863.

[53] Laird Diary, ibid.

[54] Account records, pp. 70, 71, Laird Papers (Birkenhead).

suitable aperture for the screw propeller.[55] The floorings throughout were to be of plate iron, ½-inch thick and 2 feet 3 inches deep at the vertical keel plate, tapering off toward the longitudinal frame. Near the beak of the stern the plates were to be increased to a thickness of one inch to withstand the shock of collision. The deck beams were to be of bulb iron, ½-inch thick, strengthened with bars of angle iron and were to be properly secured to the longitudinal bulkheads or side framing of the ships. The contract also provided for 12 watertight bulkheads extending to the upper deck and 5 extending to the lower. Three of these bulkheads, located amidships, were to be of plates 7⁄16-inch thick up to the lower deck and ⅜-inch thick from the lower deck to the upper. Great attention was paid to these bulkheads to insure that they were watertight. The Laird records indicate that the longitudinal watertight bulkhead was to extend for a length of about 95 feet on each side of the ship. Half bulkheads were to extend from this longitudinal bulkhead. The bulkheads were to be carefully fitted throughout and so riveted that they could be caulked watertight. The coal bunkers were designed to hold about three hundred tons of coal, giving the ships a cruising radius of approximately 1,210 miles at 10 knots. These coal bunkers were to be built of iron plates 3⁄16- or ⅛-inch thick. The backing of both vessels was to be of East India teak, over which the armor plating was to be laid. This plating was to be 3 inches thick at the bows, 4½ inches amidships, and 2 inches astern. The teak was to be between 6 and 9 inches thick. The armor plates were to be secured outside the teak by bolts passing through the teak and the side plating. The plates were to be fitted edge to edge.[56]

The engines were to be driven by four tubular boilers designed to work independently and capable of carrying steam pressure of 20 pounds per square inch. These were contained in specification of a pair of marine steam engines (horizontal direct-acting) with a 3-bladed screw 14 feet in diameter, pitch 20 degrees, of 350 horsepower nominal by English Admiralty rule. The pistons were to be fitted with metallic packing and the piston-rod glands were to be

[55] General outfit and stern, ibid.; see E. C. Rollason, *Metallurgy for Engineers* (London: Edward Arnold, 1940), pp. 118, 120.

[56] Floorings, deck beams (they were properly secured to the longitudinal bulkheads or side framing of the ships), pp. 4, 5, watertight bulkheads, coal bunkers, p. 7, system of armour plating, the backing, p. 12, account records, Laird Papers (Birkenhead); Great Britain, *Patent Office Papers* (H. M. Stationery Office, Love and Malcomson, 1855–65), fastening for armour plates, 17 Feb. 1864, no. 411, p. 1; ibid., ships of war, 6 Aug. 1864, no. 1961, p. 1 (cited hereafter as *Patent Office Papers*).

double.[57] The vessels were to carry 3 masts, each about 60 feet high.

At the time of construction, it was proposed to fit the topsails on the plan generally known as double topsail yards, but with the upper sail to reef on the Cunningham patent.[58] The lower rigging was to be of steel wire-rope, the running gear of hemp or manilla. The steps and handrails up the struts were designed so as not to obstruct the firing arcs.[59]

As cruising ships, the rams were heavily rigged for their size but with different types of masting. The Laird papers indicate that both ships were dressed as barks, with lower masts and topmasts in one piece. However, while 294 carried double topsails, 295 was given struts to her foremasts and mainmasts instead of shrouds and hoisted single topsails, topgallants, and royals. Thus 295 was the first ship in the world to carry tripod masts. This arrangement was an expedient to prevent the masking of gunfire by standing rigging. Aloft was another unique feature. The topgallant masts were fidded on the after side of the topmast crosstrees and the topgallants were struck abaft, thus allowing them to be sent down without lowering the topsails. On balance, these vessels were unique. They were the first turret ships in the world with both a forecastle and a poop and thus could fight in high seas, unlike ships of the low-freeboard monitor type, which could not fight their guns in a seaway. They were also the first ironclads in the world with movable bulwarks that could be lowered to expose the turret guns; the hammocks were stowed around the turret crowns to form rifle pits.[60]

The development of rifled shot and of armor plate presented serious problems to designers during this innovative period of naval construction. The heavy guns required large crews, and a shot striking among the guns would result in mass execution; the force of the recoil was another potential danger. On completion both Laird rams carried four 9-inch M.L.R., the heaviest weapon in the Royal Navy.[61] With these difficulties in mind the brilliant Cowper Phipps Coles, captain, R.N., had designed a turret, revolving and heavily armored, which was both shotproof and easy to maneuver.

[57] *Patent Office Papers*, specifications of a pair of marine steam engines, ibid., p. 17; *Index*, 3 Sept. 1863.

[58] Company report, p. 15 Laird Papers.

[59] *O.R.N.*, ser. 2, 2:222, 226; *Edinburgh Review* 116 (1862):219.

[60] This was distinct from the low-freeboard monitor type vessels (Parkes, p. 78). For a rather detailed table of specifications of load draft of water from top of keel, displacement, tonnage, center of effort of sail and other vital statistics, see Book of Elements for 294 and 295, Laird Papers (Birkenhead).

[61] Parkes, p. 79.

Such turrets were constructed on a framework of plate and angle iron so arranged that, above deck, the teak backing and armor plates could be fitted and, below deck, the necessary fittings and turning gear for training the guns could be accommodated. Each turret tower was adapted for two guns.[62] In 1859 Coles applied for and received letters patent for the invention under the title "An Apparatus for Defending Guns and Gunners in Ships of War, Gun Boats, and Land Batteries." [63] Coles is one of the forgotten men of history. Without doubt, he was one of the great maritime engineers of the nineteenth century. Bulloch was enthusiastic about the Coles principle and decided that each of his rams should have fixed turrets, made of 5½-inch iron backed with 12-inch teak. The floors of these turrets were to be made of iron to bear the guns.[64] Lairds applied for and received licenses for the use of the Coles turret on payment of £209.17.0. for each vessel.[65]

In the summer of 1862, all details settled, work began on the two rams. As armored vessels, however, they soon attracted the notice of federal agents,[66] and as early as September 1862 the *Times* reported that "a large iron-plated ram is now being constructed on the Mersey without much attempt at concealment." [67] By January 1863 Lord Russell, beset by protests from Adams, had indicated fairly clearly to Bulloch that although the *Alabama* had escaped, the two rams would not.[68] Bulloch then arranged for a French banking firm, M. Bravay and Company, to purchase the ships, ostensibly on behalf of the Egyptian government. His object was to secure their free sailing from the Mersey; the ships would be transferred at sea to Confederate agents. To further this plan of a "sale" to the Egyptian government, 294 and 295 were named *El Tousson* and *El Mounasser*. In the contract with Bravay, Lairds stipulated a price of £55,000, one-fourth to be paid on the launching of the first ship, one-fourth on its completion, and further quarter payments on the

[62] *Times*, 14 May 1862, 27 Oct. 1864; *Manchester Guardian*, 22 Apr. 1862; Company report, p. 12 Laird Papers (Birkenhead), *Patent Office Papers*, Working and Loading Ordnance, 14 Dec. 1864, No. 3103, pp. 1, 8; ibid., Protecting Ships' Bottom, 21 May 1864, No. 1285, pp. 1, 3; ibid., Protecting Ships' Bottom and Sides, 22 Nov., No. 3000, pp. 1, 5.

[63] *Patent Office Papers*, Apparatus for Defending Guns, etc., 30 Mar. 1859, No. 798, p. 1; *Edinburgh Review* 118 (1864):166.

[64] *Patent Office Papers*, ibid., p. 2; *O.R.N.*, sec. 2, 2:222–26. See *Times*, 10 Apr. 1862; *Liverpool Post*, 11 Apr. 1862.

[65] License to use Captain Cowper Phipps Coles's shield and patent apparatus, 5 Dec. 1862, pp. 1–11, Laird Papers (Birkenhead).

[66] *O.R.N.*, ser. 2, 2:345.

[67] *Times*, 20 Sept. 1862.

[68] *O.R.N.*, ser. 2, 2:345.

launching and completion of the second ship. The vessels were to be insured by Lairds. In a letter dated 16 June 1863, the firm promised to deliver the first ship in three months and the second in five "unless prevented by unforeseen circumstances." [69]

The transfer did nothing to satisfy Adams, who considered the construction of the vessels a direct violation of British neutrality. Under the circumstances, the familiar process of collecting depositions and reports from federal spies continued unabated. In April 1863 Clarence Randolph Yonge, former paymaster on the *Alabama*, deposed that he had seen the plans, drawings, and specifications for the rams in June 1862, while they were in Bulloch's possession, and that the plans had been approved by the Confederate government. A deposition by a W. H. Russell (master mariner) and a Joseph Ellis (master shipwright) stated that they were present 4 July 1863 when an ironclad steam vessel was launched by Lairds. Russell and Ellis described the ship as a vessel of war in all respects—"an ironclad ram of the most formidable description." [70] These and other depositions Adams forwarded to Lord Russell.

On 11 July Adams wrote to Russell, "All the appliances of British skill to the arts of destruction appear to have been resorted to for the purpose of doing injury to the people of the United States." Russell submitted the depositions to the law officers of the crown, but on 24 July was advised that "there was no evidence capable of being presented to a Court of Justice that the ships were intended for the Confederates." [71] The law officers added that, in their opinion, the government ought not to detain the vessels or interfere with them in any way.[72]

Russell nevertheless pursued further inquiries, and Adams sent more affidavits and requests for seizure—on 16 July, 14 August, and 3 September. On 25 July Adams wrote to Russell that the report that the vessels were being built for the French had been denied by the French consul. However, on 1 September Russell responded

[69] Bulloch, 1:405–7; Parkes, p. 77; Rhodes, 2:378; Company report, p. 11, Laird Papers (Birkenhead); Great Britain, Admiralty Papers, Report of Survey no. 17165, and Controller of the Navy, D.C. 3467, folio 7, National Maritime Museum, Greenwich (cited hereafter as Admiralty Papers [Greenwich]); extract from correspondence with Bravay (6 rue de Londres, Paris) forming contract for completing two iron screw steamers (No. 294–295), Contract Book C, p. 240, Laird Papers (Hereford).

[70] Deposition of Clarence Randolph Yonge, 6 Apr. 1863, Deposition of W. H. Russell and Joseph Ellis, 7 July 1863, F.O. 5/1000.

[71] Dudley to Edwards, 7 July 1863, Dudley to Adams, 8 July 1863, Adams to Russell, ibid.; *Parliamentary Papers*, 62:145–148.

[72] Brooks Adams, pp. 243, 244, 333. *Parliamentary Papers*, 62:147.

that the evidence submitted failed to show any infringement of British neutrality and that he thus could take no action. Russell assured Adams that a careful watch would continue to be maintained and that if any action contrary to the statutes of neutrality was observed, the foreign secretary would apply to the Treasury to prevent the ships' departure.

Russell's letter reached Adams on 4 September; meanwhile, the work on the first ram, *El Tousson,* proceeded apace.[73] Her engines had been fitted by Fawcett, Preston and Company and she was taking on coal. Adams was enraged. The next day he wrote to Russell: "I trust I need not express how profound is my regret at the conclusion to which Her Majesty's Government have arrived. I can regard it in no other wise than as practically opening to the insurgents full liberty in the Kingdom. It would be superfluous in me to point out to your Lordship that this is war." [74]

"This is war." Perhaps Russell had an inkling that Adams was not to be balked this time, for on 3 September, unknown to Adams, he had already given instructions that the rams were to be stopped should they attempt to put to sea. Further orders were given on the fifth,[75] and on the eighth Adams was advised, somewhat tardily, of the action of the British government. On replying to Adams, Russell declared, "It has been the aim of the Government of Great Britain to maintain a strict neutrality between the parties who for two years have carried on a civil war of unusual extent and loss of life." [76] Finally, Lairds was notified that the ships must not be allowed to sail or to make a trial run without permission.

On 14 September a report was sent to the solicitor of the Treasury that one of the rams was completed and ready for sea, except for the turrets on deck, which were not armor-plated. Completion, the report added, was being pressed with all possible speed, and the

[73] Russell to Adams, 1 Sept. 1863; see also additional deposition, Dudley to Edwards, 1 Sept. 1863; Joseph Ellis to Customs House; Thomas Sweeney, 2 Sept. 1863; Adams to Russell, 3 Sept. 1863; Dudley to Edwards, F.O. 5/1000. It was thought that some of the *Florida*'s crew would be used to man the rams (Maffitt to Bulloch, 3 Sept. 1863, ibid.). Again Adams issued a solemn protest (Adams to Russell, 4 Sept. 1863, ibid.). On the same day Russell assured Adams that the matter was under the serious and anxious consideration of Her Majesty's Government (ibid). *Times,* 4 Sept. 1863.

[74] Adams to Russell, 5 Sept. 1863, F.O. 5/1000; *Liverpool Daily Post,* 13 June 1865; *Birkenhead and Cheshire Advertiser,* 24 June 1865; *Tomahawk Review,* 1 July 1865.

[75] Layard to Stuart, 5 Sept. 1863, F.O. 5/1000; Seward was confidentially informed (ibid.). *Liverpool Mercury,* 12 July 1865.

[76] Russell to Adams, 8 Sept. 1863, Russell to Adams, 11 Sept. 1863; Adams to Russell, 16 Sept. 1863, F.O. 5/1000.

carpenters were working overtime. (Lairds employed 256 carpenters; average pay was 37 shillings a week, with 2 shillings for overtime.) Bulloch, it seemed, was still hoping the rams would be allowed to sail.[77]

A month of correspondence followed, during which Adams and Russell exchanged long and sometimes heated letters. Lairds was invited to furnish proof that the vessels were not intended for the Confederacy but failed to do so. An offer by the British government to purchase the vessels for resale was refused.[78] The firm was granted permission for a trial trip for *El Tousson;* the permission was withdrawn, then extended again if Lairds would accept a contingent of Royal Navy sailors and marines on board. The firm declined.

On 9 October both vessels were seized by the Royal Navy, and armed guards were placed on board.[79] Work on the ships virtually ceased. Captain Inglefield of H.M.S. *Majestic*, who was put in charge of the two rams, received from Lairds a stream of protests for unauthorized occupancy and requests that he leave.[80]

On 31 October the London *Evening Standard* supported the Laird contention that the seizure was being enforced in an unsympathetic

[77] "Townsend and Jackson," 30 Hamilton Square, Birkenhead, 14 Sept. 1863, to the Solicitor of the Treasury, Whitehall; the memorial of the committee of the Union and Emancipation Society of Hull to Russell, 18 Sept. 1863, F.O. 5/1001. Company report, p. 13, Laird Papers (Birkenhead); *Laird Diary*, p. 50, ibid. (Hereford); *Cheshire Observer*, 10 June 1865; *Times*, 14 and 16 Sept. 1863; *Liverpool Daily Post*, 3 July 1865.

[78] Admiralty to E. J. Reed, 20 Sept. 1863, Admiralty to the Turkish Embassy, Adams to Russell, 24 Sept. 1863, Russell to Adams, 25 Sept. 1863, E. J. Reed to the secretary of the Admiralty, 28 Sept. 1863, Adams to Russell, 29 Sept. 1863, F.O. 5/1001. When the Admiralty failed to purchase the rams afterward to be transferred to the Turkish government, the F.O. suggested in October that the Turkish chargé d'affaires apply directly to the builders (F.O. to Sir Henry Bulwer, 1 Oct. 1863, F.O. to Mr. Grey, F.O. to Lord Napier, W. G. Romaine to Hammond, 2 Oct. 1863, printed memorandum of the Duke of Argyll, sent to cabinet members, 3 Oct. 1863, Russell to Adams, 5 Oct. 1863, ibid.).

[79] Company report, p. 15, Laird Papers (Birkenhead). See also *Liverpool Albion*, 5 June 1863; *Liverpool Courier*, 7 June 1865; *Liverpool Advertiser*, 10 June 1865; *Birkenhead and Cheshire Advertiser, Times*, 27 and 28 Oct. 1863; *Annual Register for 1864*, p. 125.

[80] Great Britain, Admiralty Papers 1/5828, Laird Bros. to Captain Inglefield, 29 Oct. 1863; separate letter, same date; ibid., 31 Oct. 1863; Laird Bros. to Inglefield, 14 Oct. 1863, Public Record Office, London (cited hereafter as Admiralty Papers 1/5828). Inglefield forwarded the Laird correspondence to the secretary of the admiralty (23 Oct. 1863; Laird to Inglefield, 31 Oct. 1863, ibid.). *Times*, 2 Nov. 1863.

manner that might harm the vessels, and they suggested the rams were not for the Confederates at all.[81] The following day Captain Inglefield reported to the secretary of the Admiralty that he had moved *El Tousson* out of dock into the Mersey immediately above his ship *Majestic* and added that he could now assure the Admiralty that *El Tousson* was "secure against all ordinary accident or the possibility of any illegal interference," two officers, twelve marines, and twenty bluejackets having been placed on board to insure that she not escape.[82]

During the last months of 1863 and January of 1864, Lairds energetically pressed the government for some solution of the deadlock, but Russell, having acted, remained adamant, and the rams were kept under close surveillance. The British government devoted the early part of 1864 to a diligent search for evidence against the rams, even sending a commission to Egypt to question the viceroy and his grand vizier as to their business relations with Bravay.[83] In January a report of Mallory's fell into the hands of Adams, who lost no time in forwarding it to Russell. His letter stated: "I am directed to convey the opinion of my Government that the proof thus furnished is sufficient to remove all doubt that may yet be lingering over the objects, character, and designs of the builders of the steam-rams now under detention in the ports of this Kingdom." [84]

Finally, the date of the trial run was fixed for 27 May 1864. By that time, however, negotiations had been concluded for the purchase of the vessels by the British government.[85] In reaching the decision to sell them, the Confederates were influenced by their desperate shortage of money and the fear of months of expensive and tedious litigation.

So ended all Confederate hopes of obtaining ironclads from Great Britain. "This is war," Adams had written to Russell. In spite of all his efforts, Adams had seen the *Alabama* sail away; apart from his understandable chagrin, he may have feared that if North and Bulloch's rams had been allowed to sail, the Confederate navy could have altered the whole course of the war—a view shared by some

[81] 31 Oct. 1863; 31 Oct. 1863, Admiralty Papers 1/5828. For Britain's rationale in seizing the rams, see Wilbur D. Jones, *The Confederate Rams at Birkenhead* (Tuscaloosa, Ala.: Confederate Publishing Co., 1961).

[82] Captain Inglefield to secretary of the admiralty, 1 Nov. 1863; Inglefield to Clarence Paget, 1 Nov. 1863, Admiralty Papers 1/5828.

[83] Bulloch, 1:434–39, 440–42; *Times*, 23 Oct. 1863.

[84] Adams to Russell, 19 Jan. 1864, F.O. 5/1000.

[85] Bulloch, 1:440–42, 2:96–100, 1:434–39; *Birkenhead Guardian*, 3 June 1865; Brooks Adams, p. 325.

historians.[86] According to one able student of American diplomacy, "If the rams had put to sea the South would probably have won its independence, and the North would almost certainly have declared war on Britain." [87] There can be no doubt that the rams were designed to smash the blockade, and if they had gone free they could have inflicted considerable damage on the wooden federal ships. But on the showing of Bulloch's rams as ships of the Royal Navy, the conclusion that they could have changed the course of the war seems altogether too dramatic. In the smooth waters around the blockaded ports the rams might have wrought havoc among the Union ships and possibly laid some cities under contribution, but it is reasonable to doubt whether these ships could have even made the Atlantic crossing safely without the refitting and improvements later carried out by the Royal Navy. Adams was of course in no position to assess these possibilities in 1863, but in 1867 he attended the great naval review at Portsmouth, where one of the two Laird rams, already obsolete, was pointed out to him. He afterward wrote, "As I looked on the little mean thing I could not help a doubt whether she was really worthy of all the anxiety she had cost us." [88] If the historian's verdict that the South would have won the war if the rams had escaped is an exaggeration, perhaps Adam's remark is an understatement, and the truth lies between the two.

One question remains: what did Adams really mean when he made his famous statement "This is war"? He must have known full well that the Northern leadership would not rashly commit the United States to go to war with Great Britain. Despite the opinions of some historians, it is surely reasonable to assume that Adams, in writing to Russell, was exerting the utmost diplomatic pressure to prevent the sailing of the rams, but it is doubtful that his statement implied any threat of an American declaration of war. It seems almost certain that he intended to convey simply that in failing to detain the rams, Great Britain was responsible for a hostile act against the United States that, in Adam's opinion, amounted to war.

Financially, the sale of the rams was satisfactory to the Confederates. The Admiralty valued them with scrupulous regard for their intrinsic worth and paid about £30,000 in excess of the original contract price. The Confederates received a portion of this "profit," determined by the amount they had already paid on ac-

[86] Baxter, p. 237.

[87] T. A. Bailey, *A Diplomatic History of the American People* (New York: Appleton-Century-Crofts, 1955), p. 373.

[88] *Adams Letters,* 1:316.

count. The funds were most welcome.[89] Indeed, if the funds had not been received at that particular time, other contracts would have had to be canceled; in September 1863 Bulloch had reported that the financial needs of the Navy Department were £705,300 in excess of their visible assets.[90]

As ships of the Royal Navy, the rams became H.M.S. *Scorpion* and H.M.S. *Wivern.* They were finally completed in October 1865, *Scorpion* costing a total of £111,614 and *Wivern* £118,769.[91] (E. J. Reed gives these figures as £112,587 and £119,672, respectively.) They were equipped with four 9-inch guns, and each carried a complement of 153 men. During trials, *Scorpion* attained a speed of 10½ knots, *Wivern* about 10 knots.[92]

The ships were not popular in the Royal Navy, and the Admiralty's experiences are cause for speculation as to how well they would have served the Confederates. To test their behavior in a seaway, the vessels were taken into the Portland Race during a gale of force 10 to 11. (A whole gale is wind force 10 on the Beaufort scale. Average wind velocity in nautical miles per hour is 52.) *Scorpion* was laid broadside on with the sea on her quarter and proved buoyant and steady, but her captain thought that her constantly wet decks and the resulting discomfort to the crew materially affected her efficiency as a cruiser.[93] *Wivern*, tested with weights instead of guns in her turrets, proved to be by far the inferior vessel, although this was thought to be due to her tripod masts.[94] However, later reports show that both ships were heavy rollers. *Scorpion* once registered a list of over 30 degrees in the Dover Straits; how much more could not be ascertained because the pendulum on board did not register over that figure. (*Rolling angle* is any degree between 0 and 45 each way according to the size of waves and type of vessel.)[95] It was also found that the pilothouse forward of the funnel was useless because the view was obstructed by the stanchions and ladders of the light bridge erected atop it, although this condition was greatly improved after a refit in 1867.[96]

Against the wooden vessels of the Federals, *Scorpion* and *Wivern* could admittedly have caused some damage, but in the Royal Navy they were thought of as "the weakest of our armour-clads," [97] and

[89] Bulloch, 1:442–43. [90] Ibid. [91] Parkes, p. 78.

[92] E. J. Reed, *Our Iron-Clad Ships* (London: John Murray, 1869), pp. 219, 96.

[93] Parkes, p. 80. See also *Times*, 20 Jan. 1863.

[94] Parkes, p. 80. See Patent Office specification in *Patent Office Papers*, Improvements in masts for ships, 10 Apr. 1862, No. 1027, pp. 1, 4.

[95] Parkes, p. 8. [96] Ibid. [97] Reed, p. 32.

it was decided that they should be employed in local defense duties abroad.[98]

Wivern served in the channel during 1865 and 1866 and was paid off in reserve at Devonport in August 1868 for a refit. During 1870 she served as a coastguard ship at Hull and then was again placed on the reserve list. Later in the same year she was sent to Hong Kong as a harbor defense vessel and once more put on the reserve, eventually becoming a distilling ship; she was sold in June 1922.[99]

Scorpion also served in the Channel during 1865 and 1866, and again, after a refit, in 1868 and 1869. In '69 she was fitted for service in Bermuda; arriving there in November, she was paid off the following month. She remained in Bermuda as a harbor ship, being fitted with searchlights and quick-firing guns in 1880. At the beginning of the century she was used as a target ship and was sunk in 1901. Raised the following year, she was sold for £736 in February 1903 but foundered on her way to Boston.[100]

[98] Parkes, pp. 78–79. [99] Ibid. [100] Ibid.

CHAPTER VI

ORDNANCE

THE OUTBREAK of the Civil War found the Confederate States as deficient in ordnance as they were in nearly every other sinew of war.[1] There was not a single privately owned arms factory within their borders. And, being almost wholly without industrial resources, the South was soon engaged in a desperate scramble for arms.[2] Some ordnance was seized when the Confederate States seceded; some was imported before the blockade became effective; some was smuggled in from the North or gathered on the battle field. In the opinion of one writer, no government department deserved greater credit than the Ordnance Bureau in Richmond, under General Josiah Gorgas.[3] "Although economical of ammunition yet we never lost any action for lack of it." [4]

The American Civil War saw the first general use of rifled weapons and the appearance of breech-loading and magazine arms.[5] The first rifled field pieces of the nineteenth century were the British Lancaster guns used in the Crimean War. They were cast iron and oval bored and were used in the siege of Sebastopol as an experiment. On the whole they were a failure, because, in most cases, the straight-sided projectile then used jammed on the spiral bore and upturned the case.[6] But even after the successful introduc-

[1] E. P. Alexander, *Military Memoirs of a Confederate* (New York: Scribner's, 1907), p. 54. An illustration of the scarcity of material is the fact that Arkansas found it necessary in 1862 to use public documents of the State Library for cartridge paper.

[2] *O.R.*, ser. 4, 1:292–94.

[3] At an early date Gorgas insisted upon the use of cotton and tobacco to procure military supplies. The Bureau of Foreign Supplies was formed as a result of his suggestion (J. Gorgas, "The Confederate Soldier in the Civil War: A Paper on Confederate Ordnance," [Louisville, Ky.: Job Printing Co., 1895]). In 1877 Gorgas became president of the University of Alabama. See W. H. Albaugh III and E. N. Simmons, *Confederate Arms* (Harrisburg, Pa.: Stackpole Co., 1957), p. 139.

[4] Alexander, p. 54.

[5] Gordon B. Turner, *A History of Military Affairs in Western Society Since the Eighteenth Century* (New York: Harcourt, Brace, 1953), p. 145.

[6] F. S. Storey and C. Jones, *A Text Book of the Construction and Manufacture of the Rifled Ordnance in the British Service* (London: George E.

tion of rifled artillery, smoothbores were retained, not only because of the difficulty of replacing them, but because their shotgun discharge of grape at close quarters was remarkably effective.[7] Thus many of the cannon used in the American Civil War were virtually models made of the materials and in the style which had been known for three hundred years. Until the introduction of the rifled gun, little progress had been made in artillery since the sixteenth century.[8]

In 1861 the Confederates were short not only of small arms but of all types of artillery.[9] What cannon they had were mainly smoothbore 6- and 12-pounders.[10] Immediate steps were taken to manufacture rifled guns, but throughout the war the South lacked copper and brass and the mechanical skill necessary to turn out first-class weapons and ammunition. As time went by, purchases from abroad and the capture of federal guns did something to remedy the deficiency, but the South was always handicapped by the poor quality of its ammunition.[11] Early Confederate guns were likely to burst because of poor manufacture. The charge often went

---

Eyre and William Spottiswoode, 1872), p. 3. The British used breech-loaders in the Crimea and in the Opium War with China. In the American Civil War, breech-loading guns were in action in 1862 at Seven Pines and during the siege of Vicksburg.

[7] Millis, p. 128.

[8] The general adoption of rifled small arms necessitated the introduction of rifled ordnance in order that artillery might still retain its superiority over infantry and remain as before the principal arm in the field. Long-range rifled small arms could put a battery out of action before its short-ranged smoothbore guns could be brought into action against the advancing columns. The introduction of rifled ordnance brought about a revolution in the whole conception of artillery, the science of which had been almost static since the time of the Tudors. Cast steel was used in the manufacture of rifled ordnance for the first time during the Civil War. The invention of the steam hammer also enabled, for the first time, very large guns to be cast. Rifling machines were also greatly improved and were able to work to tolerances of 1000th of an inch. Whitworth's micrometer was also of great assistance in the manufacture of more accurate guns. For Whitworth's contributions to machine-tool equipment, see C. Singer et al., *History of Technology* (Oxford: Clarendon Press, 1958), pp. 637–38.

[9] There were no batteries of serviceable field artillery at any of the Southern arsenals (C. Fuller and R. Steuart, *Fire Arms of the Confederacy* [Huntington, W.Va.: Standard Publications, 1944], p. 113). For actual figures, see Russell, 1:307–8. See also Warren Ripley, *Artillery and Ammunition of the Civil War* (New York: Van Nostrand 1970), p. 137.

[10] "Lecture on the Moncrieff System of Working Artillery as applied to Coasts Defence," *Proceedings of the Royal Artillery Institution*, 4 (London, 1869).

[11] Ibid.

off at the breech end, thus causing a swift rise in temperature and the consequent explosion of the gun.[12] All through the war, the Southern workman's lack of technical skill reduced the effectiveness of the Southern army in the field. Although the Confederates learned swiftly how to mass artillery to the best effect (as Napoleon did), their artillery was, by and large, insufficiently developed to face the might of the federal army.[13]

Throughout the war, Tredegar Iron Works was the principal source of supply of Confederate arms. Situated just outside Richmond, it made the city's defense imperative and was an important factor in determining the choice of Richmond as the permanent capital of the Confederacy.[14] In 1861 Tredegar was the only foundry in the South capable of casting heavy guns. Here the plates for Confederate-built ironclads were rolled, heavy ordnance for the forts and shells and shot manufactured. Tredegar also made torpedoes. As the war went on, the Tredegar works expanded to include rolling mills, machine shops, forges, coal mines, and sawmills; it even possessed its own blockade-runner. It employed some 2,500 men and produced some 1,000 cannon for the Confederacy. If technical skill and materials were often lacking, enthusiasm was not, and Tredegar was a pillar of the Confederate cause. Indeed, the Tredegar works so greatly aided the Confederacy that the length of the war may be, in large measure, attributed to its efforts.[15]

But the best Tredegar could do was not enough. Arms had to be imported, and in spite of the difficulties, some of the biggest cannon of the war came from England, as did railway artillery,[16] incendiary bombs, and machine guns.[17] The Confederates were hungry for the weapons of war, and they turned avid eyes upon the technical skills and materials available in Great Britain. The Royal

[12] Commager, 2:1067. [13] Millis, pp. 128–29.

[14] T. C. De Leon, *Four Years in Rebel Capitals* (Mobile, Ala.: Gossip Printing Co., 1890), pp. 91–92.

[15] De Leon, pp. 91–92. This firm is also believed to have made machinery for the manufacture of arms. At the close of the war, the firm was in better condition as a production unit than at the beginning of the war.

[16] The earliest railway artillery of which there appears to be any record was employed in the Confederate army under Maj. Gen. J. Bankhead Magruder, on 29 and 30 June 1862, at Savage Station, on the Richmond and York River Railway, about ten miles east of Richmond. For characteristics of Railway artillery in the Civil War, see U.S. Ordnance Dept., document no. 2034, *Railway Artillery* (Washington, D.C.: Government Printing Office, 1921), 1:9–13, 15.

[17] Milton F. Perry to Richard Lester, 9 Sept. 1958. Perry, a Civil War expert, was formerly curator of the Military Museum, United States Military Academy, West Point, New York.

Arsenal at Woolwich was probably the largest, best equipped, and most efficiently organized establishment of its kind in the world.[18] General Gorgas was so sure of the urgent need for arms from abroad that he organized his own blockade-runners for the Ordnance Bureau.[19]

A detailed consideration of the principal kinds of weapons purchased will clarify the problems the Confederates faced in their arms transactions in Great Britain.

One of the most important weapons was the Armstrong gun, which was invented by a Tyneside civil engineer in December 1854.[20] William Armstrong's gun was built on an entirely new principle. Instead of cast iron, he used thin, wrought-iron coils or layers shrunk onto an inner tube, to give increased strength to the bore.[21] In 1859 two variants on the original gun, the 12-pounder for field artillery and the 9-pounder for horse artillery, were accepted for issue to the British army.[22] In 1858 John Anderson, inspector of

[18] Interview between Brigadier O. F. Y. Hogg, C.B.E., F.S.A., and Richard Lester, 28 Oct. 1958. Brigadier Hogg, a well-known authority on English ordnance, is the official historian of the Royal Arsenal at Woolwich and was secretary of the Ordnance Select Committee.

[19] Fuller and Steuart, p. 120.

[20] Lt. W. Wilson, R.A., *The Story of the Gun* (Woolwich: Royal Artillery Institution, 1944), pp. 46–47. In 1854 a few Armstrong guns were ordered for trial; the first of these, a 3-pounder, was delivered in July 1855 and was reported on favorably by the Ordnance Select Committee, who expressed the desire to make further experiments (*Report of the Select Committee on Ordnance Expenditure,* in Storey and Jones, p. 4). The gun was subsequently rebored to a 5-pounder, and in Dec. 1856 was tried near Newcastle. Col. E. Wilmot, R.A., reported that "at 1,500 yards and at 2,000 yards the gun had made remarkably good practice." A second gun, an 18-pounder of the same weight as the experimental gun, showed great strength, precision, and range (ibid.; see also *Edinburgh Review* 119 [1864]: 514). Armstrong guns were thought best for naval work (*United Service Magazine,* 1863, p. 377); Lord Brassey, K.C.B., *Naval Annual,* 1886 (Portsmouth: J. Griffin & Co., 1886), p. 364.

[21] Armstrong used the polygroove system for his rifling, which consists of a number of shallow grooves in the bore of the gun. The elongated projectile was coated with lead and made slightly larger than the bore so that the whole of the shell acted as a driving band. The bore at the breech end was made slightly larger to enable the shell to be loaded into the chamber. The breech was closed by means of a ventpiece that dropped into place from above and was pressed against the chamber by a breech screw (Great Britain, War Office Reports 33/6, pp. 811–23, Public Record Office, London (cited hereafter as W.O. 33/6); *Manchester Guardian,* 26 Oct. 1861; *O.R.,* ser. 4, 1:343–46).

[22] Wilson, pp. 46–47. Armstrong had his guns manufactured at the Royal Arsenal, Woolwich; his first government contract was gained in Jan. 1859. England hoped that this gun would give it supremacy over other countries in the field of ordnance. In Feb. 1859 he was appointed Engineer of Rifled Ordnance (Storey and Jones, p. 4).

machinery at the Royal Arsenal, reported most favorably on this weapon, describing it as "a mechanical structure involving great care in its manufacture" and displaying "extreme accuracy." His report concluded with the significant remark that if the Armstrong were required in large numbers, it would cost considerably less than the traditional form of cast-iron or brass cannon.[23] In November 1858, a Committee on Rifled Cannon reported on Armstrong's gun. The committee mentioned that the shrapnel shell used had a "very great" power and commented with favor on the percussion arrangement, which insured that the shell would explode immediately if it passed through the slightest obstacle.[24] Penetration was found to be excellent, and the range of a 32-pounder Armstrong set a record of 9,175 yards.[25] With the 18-pounder, also under test, 100 rounds were fired in two hours and twelve minutes.

In June 1861 the *Manchester Guardian* commented on the astonishing effectiveness of the Armstrong, which was indeed the beginning of a revolution in artillery equipment after the three-centuries-old cast-iron or bronze smoothbore, muzzle-loading ordnance that discharged round shot or shell.[26] The *Guardian* described an experiment in which Armstrongs were tested against a screen of eight- and ten-inch bars backed by eight feet of masonry and brickwork. Leveled against this fortification were a 100-pounder and a 120-pounder Armstrong, which speedily broke the bars, cracking the masonry and forcing the whole structure backwards.[27]

However, no invention is without its detractors. In November 1861 Armstrong, by then Sir William Armstrong, was called upon to defend his gun, and in so doing stated his contract prices.

[23] *Report of the Committee on Rifled Cannon upon Guns Adapted for Field Service—Armstrong's Breech-loading and Rifled Cannon* London: War Office, 16 Nov. 1858). An extensive series of experiments was conducted throughout which the gun exhibited most extraordinary powers of range, combined with an equally extraordinary precision of fire (ibid.).

The Armstrong field guns were always most effective where a long-range or great precision was required. They could be loaded and fired very quickly with time and concussion fuses. Armstrongs were used with excellent results in China in 1861 and in New Zealand 1861–64 (Storey and Jones, p. 6); WO/3316, pp. 811–23).

[24] Armstrong submitted for use with his shrapnel shell a percussion arrangement, a percussion nozzle, and a time fuse. The object of the arrangement was to explode the shell upon its striking the ground, or an object; the percussion nozzle was so arranged so as to explode immediately, thus giving great power to the shell (*Committee Report*).

[25] Finally, the committee remarked upon the great mechanical ability and completeness which were exhibited in all the details of Armstrong's gun and projectile (ibid.); see also *Manchester Guardian*, 19 June 1861.

[26] 19 June 1861; Wilson, p. 46. [27] 19 June 1861.

The 100-pounder cost £650; the 40-pounder, £285; the 25-pounder, £195; and the 6-pounder, £120. By 1861, 1,622 Armstrongs had been proved, and of these not one had burst.[28] Armstrong described his gun as being of "unprecedented strength" and considered it a matter of congratulation that his invention had been perfected without "loss of either life or limb, or even injury to a single individual." He also stressed that his gun represented a new system of artillery, with new projectiles, fuses, and accessories. Huse reported that he held in his possession detailed drawings of the Armstrong gun, which he would forward to the Confederate authorities.[29]

Nevertheless, although short of guns, according to a *Times* correspondent, the Confederates were far from sharing the inventor's enthusiasm. This writer said that British artillery was often criticized by both North and South and that there was a dislike of the "rapid twist of the rifling in the rifled ordnance of England." Another report, in the *Manchester Guardian,* indicated that the Americans might not be satisfied with the Armstrong because there were instances where the muzzles as well as ventpieces had been blown away; and indicated that the Armstrong gun was alarmingly liable to fracture.[30] The Brooke and Parrott guns (both American) were felt by many to be durable and powerful.[31] American criticism was not so much of the Armstrong in particular, but of rifled cannon in general, and it is likely that many of the objections to rifled ordnance voiced in North and South came about as a result of poor ordnance and unsuitable ammunition. One disadvantage of the rifled cannon, from the Confederate point of view, was the greater accuracy necessary in the manufacture of the shells.[32]

[28] *Times,* 28 Nov. 1861. Half of these had been issued for use and half retained in store.

[29] Ibid.; *O.R.*, ser. 4, 1:343–46.

[30] *Times,* 17 Dec. 1863, *Manchester Guardian,* 26 Oct. 1861.

[31] The rifling of the Brooke gun was very gradual, consisting of one complete turn in 40 feet, or one-fourth of a turn in each gun of 10 feet. The initial velocity of British ordnance was very low and the grooves wore rapidly. For the relative magnitude and powering of British and American artillery, see *Times,* 22 Dec. 1863.

[32] Ibid., 17 Dec. 1863. The first Brooke cannon was built at Tredegar Iron Works, Richmond, in Nov. 1862 and was a 7-inch rifled gun carrying a 160-pound bolt. It was a Brooke rifle that punctured the turret of the U.S.S. *Weehawken* in Apr. 1863 (Albaugh and Simmons, p. 205). There can be no question that so far as heavy rifled ordnance are concerned, the two great successes of the Civil War were the Brooke and Parrot guns. How far these guns outshone the Armstrong and Whitworth, their rifled competitors in Europe, it is difficult to say, without additional research. However, the superiority of rifled ordnance over smoothbores had been entirely established.

How much store the manufacturers themselves placed on the correct use of the correct ammunition is shown in a letter from Bulloch to Mallory, which enclosed a letter from Armstrong and Company [33] regarding the fuses furnished for some 150-pounder guns shipped by that firm. It appears that the company did not consider the fuses suitable. Bulloch replied that as the guns had been shipped, an exchange could not be effected. He continued, "Unwilling, however, that their guns should be used with any but the most perfect fuses they . . . stated they had packed 200 to replace those erroneously sent." [34] In correspondence Armstrong and Company made a point of asking that Bulloch should request the "officer in charge of the guns to see that the fuses first delivered are put out of the way until they can be returned to us for alteration." The company enclosed directions to be observed in the use of its guns and drew special attention to the importance of cartridges being made "as near as possible to the length specified." [35]

Another important British gun in the Civil War was the Whitworth. This gun was also breech-loading and rifled, but somewhat different in construction from the Armstrong, the breech being closed by a screw that had to be removed when loading the gun.[36] The bore was hexagonal in section and the projectile so shaped that it fitted the bore mechanically. Invented by Joseph Whitworth (later Sir Joseph Whitworth) almost simultaneously with the Armstrong, it was never as satisfactory; there was a tendency, never overcome, for the shell or projectile to jam in the bore. Principally for this reason the Whitworth was never adopted by the British Army.[37] Whitworth submitted his gun to the Ordnance Committee in 1857, and the Committee on Rifled Cannon reported on it in 1858.[38] The committee felt that the Whitworth lacked accuracy, had a tendency to jam, and was generally inferior to the Armstrong.[39]

[33] *O.R.N.*, ser. 2, 2:781–82.

[34] Ibid. Armstrongs sent from England were covered with a composition of white lead and tallow and were packed in wooden cases (Huse to Gorgas, 23 Jan. 1863, W. R. 46–399).

[35] *O.R.N.*, ser. 2, 2:781–82.

[36] Wilson, p. 48. Later this was to some extent corrected.

[37] Wilson, p. 48. The records of the Ordnance Select Committee up to 1855 suggest that experiments had been made with rifled guns and projectiles for half a century in England, without satisfactory results. The projectiles tried were very numerous, and most of them were intended to be fired from smoothbore pieces, the necessary rotation being obtained either by the action of gas in the gun or the action of the air on the peculiar shape of the shot.

[38] W.O. 33/6, pp. 811–23; see also p. 813.

[39] Ibid. Whitworth succeeded in obtaining a certain degree of accuracy with his hexagonally bored 9-pounder, weighing 13¾ cwts. But the committee main-

However, rifled guns were new; as already noted, the Armstrong had been the subject of considerable criticism from certain quarters, and a similar controversy arose about the Whitworth. The inventor defended his gun with vigor.[40]

During the first year of the war, before the blockade became stringent, four Whitworth guns were purchased by the Confederates.[41] Two of these were sent to the Army of Northern Virginia and enjoyed a great reputation for range and accuracy of fire; they were used for the shelling of distant columns and trains. Otherwise, they were something of a disappointment. They were large and heavy to handle, and their clumsiness in loading reduced their efficiency in battle.[42] In action in the Civil War, the Whitworth usually fired a solid metal bolt that made a strange whirring sound as it flew through the air. Although judged unsatisfactory by British army standards, on the whole the Whitworth acquitted itself well in the Civil War, comparing favorably in power with the medley of Napoleon and other bronze smoothbore cannon. The Whitworths used in northern Virginia had a bore of 2.75 inches with an overall length of 104 inches. Each weighed 1,092 pounds and was capable of firing 12-pound projectiles.[43]

Bulloch showed an early interest in the Whitworth, and in November 1862 wrote to North that he had obtained estimates from Whitworth covering a wide variety of ordnance, "from the smallest field piece up to the 70-pounder naval gun." [44] A few days later he sent North details of a 32-pounder Whitworth, showing the length

---

tained that guns rifled upon Whitworth's principle presented some serious objections. First, the results of practice showed that Whitworth's projectiles had a large and rapidly increasing deflection to the right. Second, the shot and shell appeared to give different results of accuracy, the accuracy of the shot being considerably greater than that of the shell. Last, very careful washing and drying were found to be necessary after each round in order to enable the shot to go home without jamming. However, the later use of wads composed of beeswax and tallow appeared to overcome this difficulty.

[40] See *Manchester Guardian*, 1 Nov. 1861.

[41] David Gregg McIntosh, "The Confederate Artillery: Its Organisation and Development," *Photographic History of the Civil War* 10 vols. (New York: Review of Reviews Co., 1911), 5:63.

[42] McIntosh, p. 63.

[43] J. W. Mallet and O. E. Hunt, "The Ordnance of the Confederacy," *Photographic History of the Civil War*, 5:163. These cannon took a hexagonal bolt which at first were imported from England with the cannon, but in May 1863, the Confederates began to make Whitworth shot and shell at Richmond and their efforts were successful (Albaugh and Simmons, p. 274). See also Fuller and Steuart, p. 228.

[44] *O.R.N.*, ser. 2, 2:288.

of bore as 87 inches, the diameter as 4.14 inches, and the pitch of the rifling as 75. The gun was to weigh 32 hundredweight and at 100 elevation had a maximum range of 4,800 yards. It was to cost £400. Solid projectiles were offered at £30 per 100, hollow over at £35 per 100, and "flat fronted for penetrating armor, £4 each." [45] In the same letter Bulloch gave details of a 70-pounder naval gun, weighing 75 hundredweight, with a bore-length of 114 inches and a diameter of 5.5 inches. The rifling was pitched at 100; at 10° it had a maximum range of 5,000 yards. Its cost was £700; solid projectiles were £60 per 100, hollow, £65 per 100; armor piercing cost £5 each.[46]

In his letter, Bulloch reported that, in his opinion, Whitworth "is a very clever mechanic and seems to be pushing hard to supersede Sir W. Armstrong in the snug berth he has thus far held against all competitors in England." [47] In 1863 a *New York Tribune* report appearing in the *Times* claimed that half the battery that had laid Charleston in ruins was of British manufacture and included Whitworth artillery. This assertion led a correspondent to ask how it was that Whitworths could be exported from a British port when there was such an outcry about the rams.[48] The answer, of course, was that even the largest gun could be discreetly stowed in the hold of a ship, whereas the building of the rams (and other ships) could not be so easily concealed.

The Blakely was another notable British cannon that figured in the Civil War. It had been invented by Capt. A. T. Blakely of the Royal Artillery [49] who, in 1855, patented his method of manufacturing the barrel of a gun by using an internal tube with cast-iron

[45] Ibid., p. 290. The prices were:

	£	s	d
1 150-pounder gun	1,140	0	0
75 segment shells	121	17	6
75 common shells	97	10	0
100 fuses @ 2/9d	13	15	0
100 fuses @ 1/10d	4	11	8
	£1,377	14	2

The Whitworth 32-pounder required a charge of powder of 5¼ lbs. and obtained average ranges of 90 yards at 1° and 2,800 yards at 5° (ibid).

[46] Ibid. Particulars of the Whitworth gun show that it was a 70-pounder for naval use, with a charge of 12 pounds. At 1° it had a range of 1,000 yards; at 5° 2,900 yards and at 10° 5,000 yards.

[47] Ibid., p. 289. [48] *Times*, 23 Sept. 1863.

[49] See *List of Officers of the Royal Regiment of Artillery, 1716–1899* (London: William Clowes and Sons), p. 56.

or steel rings heated and shrunk over it.[50] The object of this device was to secure a better protection against the stresses and strains of the powder explosion. The Blakely gun had a rifled barrel and was muzzle-loading.[51] The Blakely Ordnance Company was founded, and made many guns, during the period of the Civil War. It also supplied some of the biggest guns seen in action during the conflict. Two in particular became famous. They were giants, 12¾-inch muzzle loaders, 16 feet 2 inches long and weighing 27 American tons each. Their steel carriages weighed 730 pounds apiece. They cost a total of £22,763—"a fearful cost," wrote General Gorgas.[52] They were cast for Captain Blakely at the Vauxhall Foundry, Liverpool, by George Forrester and Company and were purchased by Huse through Fraser, Trenholm and Company.[53] The Liverpool customs bill of entry shows the guns as weighing 22 (English) tons each, with bores of 13½ inches. The carriages are entered as weighing 38 tons each. They were purchased by Huse at £5,000 each, which included 50 rounds of 700-pound shells.[54]

On 3 July 1863 the *Gibraltar*, once the *Sumter*, sailed from Liverpool with the giant Blakelys.[55] They were landed at Wilmington in August and became a center of great interest and speculation. Rumor said they had a range of seven miles.[56] They reached Charleston in time to go into action. Soon the story was spread about that one of them had burst, but this was later denied, and it was said that it was a Richmond-made gun that had failed.[57] But

[50] General Lefroy, *Hand-book for Field Service, 1866* (London: H.M. Stationery Office, 1866), p. 329; O.R., ser. 4, 1:343–46.

[51] See exhibits in the hall of the Model Room, Royal Artillery Institute Library, Woolwich Arsenal, Woolwich. The shot was designed by Captain Blakely and made by the Blakely Ordnance Company about 1861 or 1862. The gun was a 120-pounder, diameter 7 inches, weight of shot 128.9 pounds. Blakely supplied shot to the Admiralty as well.

[52] Josiah A. Gorgas, "Notes on the Ordnance Department of the Confederate Government," *Southern Historical Society Papers* 12 (1884): 94. These giant weapons, and the sheer enormity of their size and weight, are still impressive.

[53] Milton F. Perry to Richard Lester, 9 Sept. 1958.

[54] Liverpool Customs Bill of Entry, bill A. no. 13749, Customs and Excises Papers, The Library, Customs and Excise, King's Beam House, Mark Lane, London; *O.R.N.*, ser. 1, 9:127–29. For Caleb Huse, see Samuel E. Morison and Henry S. Commager, *The Growth of the American Republic*, 2 vols. (New York: Oxford University Press, 1962), 1:650.

[55] *O.R.N.*, ser. 1, 9:127–29. Welles thought these guns were intended to work in the turret of the ironclads (ibid.).

[56] Jones, *War Diary*, 2:21.

[57] *Times*, 17 Oct. 1863. It was also thought that the piece could have been the Prince Alfred gun, manufactured by the Mersey Steel Co., which was at this time the property of Captain Blakely (ibid.).

it was one of the Blakelys that had exploded; its remains can be seen today at West Point. The Blakely was an interesting gun; some of its principles are embodied in present-day artillery. Its main innovation was the application of "initial tension"—intentional strain in the metal of the gun, scientifically placed so as to counteract the strain set up by the powder discharge.[58]

To turn to small arms, at the beginning of the war the old smoothbore musket, .69 caliber, made up the bulk of Confederate armament, and even as late as the end of 1862 some of the guns were old flintlocks. Every effort was made to replace these muskets with rifled weapons captured in battle, brought through the blockade from England, or manufactured in the South.[59] By 1863 the small arms of the South were extremely mixed: smoothbore muskets were still in evidence; other soldiers had .54 rifles;[60] .58 Springfield muskets, captured from the North, were also quite common.[61] There was also a sprinkling of Belgian rifles, caliber .70, and various British arms. Lewis R. Berkeley, in his *Small Arms and Ammunition in the United States Service*, says that so many foreign arms were used that anything approaching a comprehensive list is impossible to compile.[62] He goes on to evaluate some of the early weapons. The British model 1836 percussion musket, last of the smoothbores, was "little better than the old flintlock Brown Bess" and had an effective range of only 125 to 150 yards.[63]

Many of the first Southern weapons were obtained by the act of secession. Alabama seceded on 11 January 1861 and took pos-

[58] "The Defenses of Charleston," *Photographic History of the Civil War*, 5:109–22. The Blakely was among the earliest fieldpieces to be successful with this principle of "initial tension," which was a fundamental element in the scientific design of the best modern built-up guns of the day (James A. Longridge, *Construction of Artillery* [London: William Clowes, 1859–60], 19:16, 24.

[59] Berkeley R. Lewis, *Small Arms and Ammunition in the United States Service* (Washington, D.C.: Smithsonian Institution, 1956), p. 67. The Confederate States obtained French arms as well (particularly revolvers). For a drawing of the Le Mat revolver, see *The American Rifleman* 108, no. 11 (1960):35. For its successful use, see *Richmond Daily Examiner*, 28 June 1861. These pistols were delivered and inspected in London. Two hundred had been delivered and paid for by 30 July 1862 (*O.R.N.*, ser. 2, 2:230).

[60] The U.S. rifled musket model 1861, caliber .58, percussion 40-inch barrel, 40-inch stock, total length 58.5 inches, was the principal infantry weapon of the Civil War (Chapel, p. 289).

[61] Alexander, pp. 53–54. There is reason to believe that had Union infantry been armed from the first with even the breech-loaders available in 1861, the war would have been terminated within a year.

[62] For a list of foreign-made arms used by Confederate forces, see *O.R.*, ser. 1, 47:180.

[63] Lewis, p. 103.

session of Fort Morgan, thus acquiring 5,000 rounds of shot and shell; at the Mount Vernon arsenal the Confederates took 20,000 arms, 1,500 barrels of powder, and some cannon.[64] When Florida seceded a day earlier, the South gained 500,000 rounds of musket cartridges, 300,000 rifle cartridges, and 50,000 pounds of gunpowder. Arkansas provided the arsenal at Little Rock, 9,000 small arms, 40 cannon, and some ammunition.[65] Texas brought 35,000 small arms, 26 pieces of mounted artillery (44 dismounted), and ammunition. Louisiana contributed 50,000 small arms, 4 howitzers, 20 heavy cannons, 2 batteries, and 300 barrels of powder.[66] Georgia gave two 12-pounder cannons, 22,000 muskets and rifles, and large stores of gunpowder, balls, and grape.[67]

These figures show that the South had a small nucleus of arms at the outbreak of the war,[68] even if they were not always of the most modern design. It had been federal policy to store all rifles and muskets in Northern arsenals. But with growing unrest in the South, the government decided in 1860 to transfer the Southern quota of arms from Northern arsenals. Under the Constitution, the South had a right to such arms and the transfer was, of course, made before there was any thought of secession or war. In this way, the South gained 114,868 muskets and rifles.[69] However, lacking the means of manufacturing accurate modern rifles in quantity, the South was soon forced to purchase from Europe.[70]

The Enfield rifle was one of the most popular small arms—whether purchased, captured, or in some cases copied by Southern factories.[71] It had a caliber of .577, with a barrel-length of 39 inches, or, with bayonet fixed, 73 inches. It weighed 9.19 pounds complete

[64] *O.R.*, ser. 4, 1:292, 120–22.

[65] Scharf, p. 21. In the literature on the Civil War, information concerning ammunition supply is almost entirely lacking.

[66] Ibid. [67] *O.R.*, ser. 4, 1:168–70.

[68] Ibid., pp. 113–14; see also ibid., pp. 118–19. For the distribution of arms at the various Southern forts, see ibid., pp. 277–78.

[69] Scharf, pp. 16–17. The attack of John Brown upon Virginia and the numerous efforts of Northern emissaries to incite slaves to insurrection suggested the importance of distributing their quota of arms among the Southern states. Accordingly, orders were issued in 1860, by Secretary Floyd, to transfer the Southern quota of arms from the Northern arsenals. The order was made on 30 May 1860 (ibid.). See also the Constitution of the United States, Amendment II.

[70] For domestic manufacture see *O.R.*, ser. 4, 1:107–8; 127–31. The South looked primarily to the North for arms (ibid., pp. 210, 212–13, 216, 217). For purchases in Havana see ibid., p. 272. For purchases in British provinces, see ibid., p. 275.

[71] *O.R.N.*, ser. 2, 2:80–81.

with bayonet, was rifled and very accurate.[72] It had been officially adopted by the British Army in 1853 and was used in the Crimea.[73] The Enfield rifle was so called because the first experiments, ordered by Lord Hardinge, master general of the ordnance, were carried out at the Royal Small Arms Factory at Enfield, Middlesex. In its original form the Enfield had an overall length of 4 feet 7 inches, a net weight (without bayonet) of 8¾ pounds, and was sighted up to 900 yards. The original barrel was 39 inches in length.[74] The Enfields fired the Pritchard bullet with a perfectly smooth exterior.[75]

The Confederates made considerable use of the Enfield. For example, on November 1861 the U.S. consul in London reported to Capt. J. B. Marchand, commander of the U.S.S. *James Adger*, that the *Gladiator*, a Confederate steamer, "has on board 20,240 guns and Enfield rifles." The consul also maintained that Confederate arms were under the protection of the "English flag and English papers." [76] In the same month, a Confederate agent in Havana reported that he had in store 1,800 Enfield rifles awaiting shipment on payment of the freight costs.[77]

The Whitworth rifle was also used. In 1858 Joseph Whitworth had proposed a rifle with a .450 bore,[78] and the Enfield and Whitworth Committee, convened by the secretary of state for war, were favorable to the idea, although it was untried.[79] The bore on the Whitworth rifle was hexagonal, so that the bullet emerged with an increasing twist.[80] A special hard-alloy bullet, with its sides molded in the same shape as the interior of the bore, was used.[81] The results

[72] Ibid. The charge was 2½ grains (Army Book no. 127, p. 118, Hogg Papers, in possession of Brigadier O. F. G. Hogg, C.B.E., F.S.A., RA., London); Report of the Enfield and Whitworth Committee called for by the secretary of state for war, 5 Nov. 1858, W.O. 33/7.

[73] Army Book no. 127, p. 118, Hogg Papers.

[74] J. N. George, *English Guns and Rifles* (Plantersville, N.C.: Small Arms Technical Publishing Co., 1947). The official records indicate that a considerable number of Enfields were purchased by both the federal and Confederate governments during the war.

[75] Colonel J. Gorgas, *Ordnance Manual for the Use of Officers of the Confederate States Army* (Richmond: West and Johnston, 1863), cited hereafter as *Ordnance Manual.*

[76] *O.R.N.*, ser. 1, 1:227. [77] Richardson, 2:114–15.

[78] The key to Whitworth's success, in an engineering sense, was a reduction of bore from .577 inch to .450 inch, with the use of a longer bullet that would expand into a barrel (Army Book no. 127, p. 119, Hogg Papers).

[79] W.O. 33/7, pp. 59–79.

[80] Army Book no. 127, p. 119, Hogg Papers. The rifling had a pitch of 20 inches in order to give the bullet the necessary velocity of rotation.

[81] George, pp. 308–10. It was claimed that system was also adaptable to an ordinary cylindrical expanding bullet (ibid.).

of the first practical tests were excellent, but in spite of its great accuracy, it never became the official arm of the British services, although it was issued to the Rifle Brigade for a time.[82] The Whitworth was used by the Confederates for long-range sharpshooting and was quite capable of striking a target with force at 2,000 yards. In penetration and range, it was the superior of the Enfield.

Less well known, the Brunswick rifle was also used by the Confederates. This British rifle had two grooves that diminished in depth to a certain distance in the barrel, where they were eased off smooth with the bore.[83] The Brunswick had a .0704 caliber and used spherical belted bullets to fit the special rifling.[84] At short range it was moderately effective, but at 500 yards or more it was wild.[85] Loading was so difficult that a man's hand became too unsteady for accurate shooting.[86] The rifle was also heavy, weighing over 11¼ pounds. The Royal Manufactory as Enfield condemned it in 1852 as being "very much inferior to every arm hitherto noticed." [87]

Another gun supplied to the Confederates from England was the Vandenburg Volley Gun—a crude predecessor of the modern machine gun. This was invested by Origen Vandenburg, a North American.[88] The gun was a cluster of rifled barrels in a brass jacket, with as many as 169 barrels to some guns.[89] On 13 April 1860 "Origen Vandenburg of the City of Syracuse and State of New York, temporarily residing in London" applied to the British Patent Office for Letters Patent for his invention of "Improvements in Projectiles and Appliances of Projection, Imparting great Precision and great Range of Flight to Projectiles forced through the Air by Gunpowder or other Explosive Compound with Facility for Rapid Discharge, and for Discharging many Projectiles simultaneously by

[82] Army Book no. 127, p. 119, Hogg Papers; George, pp. 308–10.

[83] *Ordnance Manual.* Caliber about .70 (ibid.).

[84] Army Book no. 127, p. 117, Hogg Papers. The ammunition consisted to 2½ grains of powder enclosed in a paper cartridge, weight 557 grams, diameter .696 inches (ibid.).

[85] Lt. Col. A. Gordon to Sir C. E. Trevelyan, K.C.B., *Remarks on National Defence Volunteers, and Rifles, with a Report on Experiments with Small Arms, Carried on at the Royal Manufactory at Enfield in 1852* (London: Military Library, Whitehall, 1853).

[86] Ibid. [87] Lewis, p. 104; Gordon to Trevelyan, "Remarks."

[88] *Patent Office Papers,* Improvements in the Breech-Pieces of Breech-Loading Cannon, p. 1, 13 Dec, 1860, no. 3065.

[89] Gen. O. Vandenburg, "A New System of Artillery," *Journal of the Royal United Services Institution* 6:377–90. Vandenburg also tried to increase the weight of the breech-piece in proportion to the weight of the projectile so that the inertia of the breech-piece would be considerably greater than that of the shot (*Patent Office Papers,* no. 3065, p. 1).

One Projecting Appliance with the same Advantage, giving increased Area to the Space covered by the Destructive Projectile Matter, and Light Weight and Small Space to the Appliance for Projection."[90] These volley guns were made for Vandenburg by Robinson and Cottum of London; one still exists at West Point and shows fine workmanship.[91] Vandenburg first tried to sell his guns to the U.S. Ordnance Department but was turned down. Soon afterwards they appeared in Confederate hands, and while no proof exists that Vandenburg actually made the sale, it seems likely that he did so: he grew extremely bitter at the refusal of the Federals to take him seriously, even when he offered to supply them with the guns at cost.[92]

Some Carbines—weapons of intermediate weight and length, between the rifle and the pistol—were also supplied to the Confederates from Great Britain. Most notable was the Terry Carbine, with a .566 or .568 caliber, firing a bullet of 530 grams.[93]

Very little information exists about gunpowder shipped to the Confederates, but rather considerable quantities must have been sold from Britain.[94] In March 1862 Bulloch, writing to Mallory, notes that "the order for 100 tons of cannon powder" will be filled as soon as possible, and that powder "will be shipped in lots as opportunity can be found."[95] As the *Economist* noted, lead and gunpowder were pressing needs of the South throughout the war.[96] The Confederates did not solve the problem of producing powder in quantity until the end of the war was upon them.[97] Nor was the quality of home-produced powder as good as the British product.[98] A permanent blockade-runner, the *Anne Child,* otherwise the *Julia Usher,* frequently ran powder consigned by Fraser, Trenholm and Company.[99]

[90] *Patent Office Papers,* 13 Apr. 1860, no. 921, Vandenburg's specifications. In the barrels there were a number of ignition passages, which converged on the ignition chamber (ibid., 19 Nov. 1860, no. 2837, p. 1).

[91] Milton F. Perry to Richard Lester, 9 Sept. 1958. [92] Ibid., 5 Mar. 1959.

[93] *Ordnance Manual.* In the Terry carbine the cartridge had a thick felt wad at the base that was pushed forward by the bullet of the next cartridge after firing (Army Book no. 127, p. 117 Hogg Papers).

[94] *O.R.*, ser. 4, 1:496–98; *O.R.N.*, ser. 2, 2:82. It seems that powder was shipped in lots of 200 tons (ibid., 2:82–83).

[95] *O.R.N.*, ser. 1, 1:753. [96] 12 Sept. 1863.

[97] Channing, 6:617. Early in the war L. P. Walker, secretary of war, saw the need for the establishment of powder mills (*O.R.*, ser. 4, 1:250).

[98] Although the Southern army lacked much in the way of powder manufacturing equipment, the gunpowder in their cartridges was better than that used by the Federals.

[99] Great Britain, *Hansard's Parliamentary Debates* (Commons), 3d ser., 72 (1863):639.

Of all the Confederate agents in England, Caleb Huse was particularly concerned with the purchase of arms and munitions.[100] His immediate orders, on landing, were to purchase 12,000 rifles and battery of field artillery and to procure one or two guns of larger caliber as models. He contacted the London Armoury Company,[101] and after some negotiations he was able to secure all their output under contract, an arrangement which, Huse said, lasted until the end of the war.[102] From the official records, however, it seems likely that he was less successful at the time than he says. There is much evidence that to obtain the arms required, the Confederate agents had to make the rounds of the many small-arms factories in the country; the Confederates were in competition with both federal agents and the British army.[103]

Years afterwards Huse stated that the purchase of supplies was reasonably simple.[104] But his dispatches for the years 1861 and 1862 do not give this impression. The shipping of supplies was more difficult, for he was shadowed and harried by detectives, as were Bulloch and the other Confederate agents. Most consignments got through, but the Federals scored one success with the capture of the *Stephen Hart*, a schooner of American origin purchased by an English firm and put under the British flag for Confederate use.[105] The proof that she was loaded with army supplies was so complete that there was no defense, and after this episode all army supplies were carried by steamer, either to a Confederate port direct or to Nassau or Bermuda.[106] There was little difficulty in shipping to the British West Indies. Since ship and cargo generally belonged to British subjects and the voyage was from one British port to another, everything appeared lawful. From the West Indies, supplies were taken to Confederate ports by speedy steamers of light draught, such as the *Merrimac*.[107] Sometimes shipments were sent to Mexico, where a friendly government allowed their reexportation.[108]

In after years Huse was inclined to make light of the difficulties he had experienced throughout the war in obtaining supplies at fair prices. But there is no doubt that the supply of acceptable arms was seldom equal to the demand, for the revolution in the manufacture

[100] Richardson, 2:19, 42; *O.R.*, ser. 4, 1:211, 333.

[101] *O.R.*, sec. 4, 1:220, 343–46. [102] Huse, pp. 19–20.

[103] *O.R.*, ser. 4, 1:565–67, 538–42; *O.R.N.*, ser. 2, 2:83–87.

[104] Huse, pp. 24–25. [105] *O.R.*, ser. 4, 1:565–67, 493–94.

[106] *O.R.N.*, ser. 2, 2:81–82. [107] Huse, p. 25.

[108] *O.R.*, ser. 4, 1, W. F. Robertson to L. P. Walker, 21 May, 1861. A Confederate agent would purchase articles and consign them to a similar agent in Matamoros, where they were sent across the Rio Grande into Texas and then distributed to any part of the Confederate states (ibid., 1861 pp. 486–87).

of armament—the replacement of the old smoothbore cannon by rifled artillery[109] and of the musket by the rifle—had only just preceded the beginning of the Civil War, and the great powers of Europe were themselves short of new weapons. For this reason the South was never able to overcome completely the endless variety of weapons and calibers its soldiers were forced to use. However, after the battle of Gettysburg, the whole Army of Northern Virginia was equipped with the rifled musket,[110] and General Gorgas estimated that by 1863 the Confederates had 300,000 infantry, "pretty well armed." General Gorgas estimated that 185,000 rifles and muskets had been imported from 1 January 1862 until 1 January 1863. These included 70,980 long Enfield rifles, 9,715 short Enfields, 354 Carbine Enfields, 20 small-bore Enfields, 21,040 miscellaneous British muskets, and 2,020 Brunswick rifles.[111] In addition, in the year ending 30 September 1863, the Ordance Bureau's own fleet of 4 blockade-runners brought in 113,504 arms.[112]

Huse was also responsible, up to February 1863, for shipping 139 pieces of heavy ordnance that played a large and important part in the coastal defense of the Confederacy.[113] Among these cannon were fifty-four 6-pounder smoothbore bronze guns; 18 howitzer smoothbore bronze guns; 2 howitzer rifled iron guns with carriages; 6 rifled Blakely cannons with carriages, 18,000 shells and 2,000 fuses; three 8-inch rifled Blakely cannon with 680 shells; twelve 12-pounder rifled steel guns with shot and shell; 2 rifled bronze guns with 200 shells and fuses, 756 rounds of shrapnel shells and 9,280 wooden fuses; and four 9-pounder rifled steel cannon with 1,008 shells and fuses.[114]

Huse also concerned himself with all necessary adjuncts of the arms he shipped. By 3 February 1863 he had sent 484,500 pounds of powder to the South, 89,900 friction tubes, 4,137,000 cartridges for small arms, and 10,100,000 percussion caps. By the summer of 1863 he had sent a further 2,012,000 cartridges and 3,000,000 percussion caps.[115] By early 1863 it must have seemed that the efforts of Huse

[109] Ibid., pp. 538–42. [110] Alexander, pp. 53–54.

[111] Gorgas, "Notes on the Ordnance Department of the Confederate Government," pp. 67–94.

[112] *O.R.*, ser. 4, 2:956.

[113] Ibid., p. 382. There is no record of how many of these guns actually reached the Confederate armies and how many were lost on route. But the chances are that only a relatively small portion were captured on their way through the blockade, for it has been estimated that the ratio of successful blockade-running, even in 1863, was approximately four to one (Owsley, *King Cotton Diplomacy* p. 285).

[114] *O.R.*, ser. 4, 3:930. [115] Ibid., 2:383, 889.

and his fellow agents would succeed and the arms famine would be beaten. But just then the beginnings of the financial collapse of the Confederacy threatened their credit, never very stable, and delayed supplies.[116] The figures on arms shipped for the last year of the war are less easily ascertained, but by the time of the collapse, it seems likely that the Confederates had received between 500,000 and 600,000 arms from foreign sources, of which a substantial portion came from Great Britain.[117] Many of these weapons were Enfields, Whitworths, Brunswicks, or Terrys. In addition the Confederates made use of the .75 Tower musket, the .577 rifled Musketoon, the .45 Sharpshooter rifle, and the .44 Kerr rifle.[118]

By the end of the war, Huse had left Confederate debts of $500,000. His original commission was limited to £10,000, and although this limit was soon waived and he was given powers to purchase at his discretion,[119] there were continual worries over remittances.

Judah Benjamin was one of the most determined opponents of the policy "Cotton is King." Early in 1861 he was strongly in favor of shipping 100,000 bales of cotton and using it for the immediate purchase of at least 150,000 stand of small arms, guns, and munitions in corresponding amounts.[120] But the rest of the government disagreed, and by the time Huse was appointed and had reached Europe, valuable time had been lost.

Shortly after Huse's appointment, Maj. Edward C. Anderson was sent after him to supplement and, if necessary, direct his work. Huse, however, proved more forceful and enterprising than his superior, and on 22 July 1861 both agents were authorized to purchase as they thought fit and at their discretion.[121]

From time to time Bulloch was also instructed to purchase arms,

[116] With purchases cut down by financial embarrassment and lack of confidence in the chances of the Confederacy for success, records of Confederate imports of arms became vague to the point of inconsistency. From 1 Nov. 1863 to 8 Dec. of the following year, 3,146 cases of rifles and carbines, a total of approximately 69,000 stand of arms, were imported by the Confederate government through Wilmington and Charleston, the most important points of entry (ibid., 3:930).

[117] This estimate is based on the available records. It is probable, however, that those for 1864 are incomplete. See Great Britain, *Parliamentary Papers* (*Accounts and Papers*, vol. 58, 1864), "Munitions of War: An account of the Guns and other Munitions of War shipped from the port of Liverpool to America during the years 1861 and 1862, showing the quantity, description, value and port of destination," p. 555.

[118] Lewis, pp. 67–68.

[119] *O.R.*, ser. 4, 1:343–46, 493–94.

[120] Meade, pp. 165–67; *O.R.*, ser. 4, 1:623, 633–34.

[121] *O.R.*, ser. 4, 1:443–44.

mainly on behalf of the navy.[122] For example, on 23 July 1861 Mallory advised both Bulloch and North to purchase "10,000 good Enfield rifles, or rifled muskets with bayonets." [123] In the same letter Mallory also mentioned that rifled cannon were no longer so urgently required since "we can make them," but small arms remained an urgent need. Another continuing requirement was powder.[124] On 25 July 1861 Mallory wrote to Bulloch to send "200 or 500 tons of powder." [125] This need continued throughout the war, for the Confederacy lacked many essential materials, such as saltpeter.

A more detailed consideration of some of the negotiations outlined on preceding pages is worthwhile. Anderson and Huse began to see the first real fruits of their labors in the late summer and early autumn of 1861. When they first arrived, the Federals, who had sent their agents more expeditiously, were in control of the market. This was not so unfortunate as it first appeared to be. Some of these Northern agents had been unselective in their purchase and, in their eagerness, had bought up old, worn-out muskets which Anderson and Huse described as "the merest rubbish in the world, very far inferior to the old George Law muskets, and will surely prove more dangerous to those who may venture to use them than the troops against whom they are pointed." As a general rule, it can be said that having looked carefully over all the arms within their reach, Confederate agents abstained from the purchase of worn-out muskets. The Confederates were more selective than the Federal agents. This was largely true because federal procurement agents were eager to buy all and any arms in order to prevent them from falling into Southern hands.[126] At that time, August 1861, Confederate agents' purchases had been confined to the Enfield rifle, and the first of their contracts were on the point of delivery. Both Anderson and Huse were assured that these weapons would give confidence to any soldiers in whose hands they were placed.[127] A few days later Anderson reported that their money was almost exhausted, although the governor of Georgia had sent $100,000 and asked for a further prompt supply so that they could establish the success they were beginning to gain over the Northern agents.[128] On 17 August Leroy P. Walker, the secretary of war, was able to

[122] *O.R.N.*, ser. 2, 2:83–87. [123] Ibid., pp. 80–81.

[124] *O.R.*, ser. 4, 1, Walker to the president, 24 July, 1861.

[125] *O.R.N.*, ser. 2, 2:82. [126] *O.R.*, ser. 4, 1:538–42. [127] Ibid.

[128] Ibid. Anderson deemed it his duty to mention the fact of having been requested to purchase arms for the state of Georgia, and in consenting to do so he felt that he should have the same sanction of the War Department, because he was not a state, but rather a Confederate, agent (ibid.).

advise Huse and Anderson that a remittance of nearly $250,000 was being sent. He instructed them to invest this sum in the purchase of arms with all possible speed. At this point it was hoped that the procurement agents in the arms business would no longer confine their efforts to Great Britain alone, which up to this point was the principal source of supply. It was hoped that in the interest of casting a wider net, agents such as Huse and Anderson would visit other countries in order to procure arms. Although other countries were visited, Great Britain continued to be the primary source of procurement of arms for the remainder of the war. The money helped, but Huse, writing a few weeks earlier to Gorgas, summed up his early difficulties with some terseness. He was embarrassed by the shortage of money, and his efforts suffered from intense competition with Northern agents, who had large means at their disposal.[129] Soon afterwards Bulloch made the same point to Mallory[130] but in the same letter mentioned that Anderson and Huse hoped to have a large supply of arms ready in about five weeks and that they were planning to unite their remaining funds to buy a ship to carry the ordnance to the Confederates.[131] Bulloch also wrote of his searches for suitable guns for the ships he was building and mentioned that he had selected the Blakely and had also contracted for 1,200 Bashley Britten shells. In addition, he mentioned that he could not obtain navy-service rifles ready made but that he had been successful in purchasing ammunition with 1 million military caps. Three days later North wrote to Mallory of financial pressure which prevented him from sending rifled cannon. In spite of the agents' efforts to do all possible in the face of a grave shortage of funds, on 20 August Walker sent Huse and Anderson an exhortation to do more, saying that thousands of "brave volunteers" had been refused service for want of arms.[132] At the end of August Henry Hotze was sent to supplement the work of the agents already in Europe; Hotze also received a solemn exhortation from Walker, this time, however, backed with some real promise of substantial finance on the way. The record indicates that requisitions amounting in all to $907,055.50 had been drawn and transmitted for procurement purposes through Samuel Smith, of New Orleans, and John Fraser

[129] Ibid., pp. 564–65, 566–67.

[130] *O.R.N.*, ser. 2, 2:83–87. Bulloch declared: "I soon learned that no contracts or purchases could be made without cash actually in hand. . . . I could therefore only examine arms and visit dockyards and great gun factories . . . arranging for contracts as soon as the means of payment should arrive" (ibid.).

[131] Ibid. Bulloch was in charge of this project. Ibid. pp. 87–88.

[132] *O.R.*, ser. 4, 1:577–78.

and Company, Charleston. Walker informed Hotze of the importance of this mission: "We could bring into the field and maintain there with ease 500,000 men with arms and munitions sufficiently abundant." The Secretary concluded, "May God speed you and crown you with success, thus assuring victory to our standard and independence of our people." [133]

In September Mallory wrote to Bulloch of the Confederate army's urgent need for powder, and further remittances were made to cover naval ordnance and supplies.[134] In every letter the agents heard the *cri-de-coeur* of a nation starved for arms. The plea "Send us more, more!" was always in their ears. But by then supplies *were* beginning to arrive. In October 1861, for example, the *New York Tribune* announced the cargo of the *Bermuda*, which ran the blockade into Charleston: 18 large rifled guns, 2 Whitworth 124-pounders, 7,500 Enfield rifles, and 18,000 Belgian rifles with fixed ammunition.[135]

In December, the Queen's Proclamation on the Export of Arms was issued and it was prohibited to export "or carry coastwise" arms, ammunition, gunpowder, military and naval stores on penalty of forfeit. Immediately after this proclamation was issued, orders to arms manufacturers dropped, and a period of uncertainty set in that did nothing to help the Confederate cause.[136] However, the Proclamation was never rigorously enforced.[137] It was really intended as a notification of possible powers to be taken should England find herself at war with some foreign nation.[138]

The arms were distributed as fast as they flowed in. In March 1862 Benjamin reported to President Davis that in spite of all the efforts of the agents and of all the Confederate factories [139] could manufacture, there was never more than 1,000 to 2,000 small arms in reserve.[140] The agents continued to labor without respite. The capture of the *Stephen Hart* was a blow. But in March Huse was able to report to Gorgas that the *Southwick* was outward bound with 5,000 rifles, 1,500 cavalry sabres, 1,500 cavalry belts, 10,000

[133] Ibid., pp. 596–97.

[134] *O.R.N.*, ser. 2, 2:95–96. These remittances amounted to $100,000.

[135] 14 Oct. 1861. For the *Bermuda*, see O.R., ser. 4, 1:623, 633–34.

[136] This was of short duration (*O.R.*, ser. 4, 1:806–7, 818–19.

[137] The *New York Herald*, angered over British arms being sent into the Confederacy, declared: "England in her jealousy of the American Republic desires to see it split into powerless fragments. Between Vermont and Minnesota we could pour 150,000 troops into Canada in a week, and overrun the Province in three weeks more."

[138] *Times*, 7 Dec. 1861; *O.R.N.*, ser. 1, 1:168–69.

[139] For such efforts see *O.R.*, ser. 4, 2:863–65.

[140] Ibid., 1:971–72.

friction tubes, and 500 barrels of gunpowder. Consignments of this size were frequent, but Huse mentioned in his report that he was narrowly watched wherever he went and that the utmost discretion was always essential.[141] He also asked for more funds, mentioning that in view of the recent reverses in the field, Confederate credit stood extremely low. It was at this time that he was negotiating his contract with the London Armoury Company, designed to gain control of their whole output for three years.[142] Their rifles were to cost £3 each, and the company asked for a deposit of £15,000 against forfeit by the Confederate government.[143]

On 1 April 1862 Huse was able to report a further shipment leaving London with about 10,000 rifles, 2,000 barrels of powder, and considerable miscellaneous purchases,[144] but in the same letter he spoke of severe money shortage that prevented him from entering into new contracts.[145] On 11 April Bulloch reported the impending shipment of 1,000 barrels of gunpowder and of navy revolvers. On 19 April he reported a further consignment for the Navy Department of 2,000 barrels of powder and 380 revolvers with cartridges, caps, and spare parts.[146] Shipments continued steadily although, as will have been noted, the individual consignments were small when compared with the number of men which the Confederates could put into the field.

Another difficulty was the long lapse of time between shipment from England and actual delivery in the Confederate States. Losses, although small, are mentioned from time to time in the official dispatches. For example, on 12 July 1862 Mallory acknowledged the safe arrival of 862 barrels of powder from Bulloch, but mentioned

[141] Ibid., pp. 1003–5.

[142] With this plan projected, Gorgas notified Benjamin that the Ordnance Department would require at least $700,000 to carry on until 1 April (Gorgas to Benjamin, 18 and 25 Mar. 1862, W.R. 46–399). In the opinion of C. F. Adams, the Confederates wasted "floods" of money in their "voluminous intrigues" (*Adams Letters*, 2:259).

[143] *O.R.*, ser. 4, 1:1003–5.

[144] *O.R.N.*, ser. 2, 2:177–80.

[145] Ibid., pp. 177–80. The situation was made more difficult because in many instances bonds were useless since creditors refused to receive them at par, alleging with truth that their contracts were based upon payment in currency (Memminger to Seddon, 7 Apr. 1862, W.R. 46–399).

[146] *O.R.N.*, ser. 2, 2:185. On the same date Gorgas notified Memminger that it was difficult to persuade anyone to take more than half of a contract in bonds. Also heavy contractors generally objected to the large bonds for the reason that they could frequently use the small ones in payment of debts and the purchase of material, where otherwise they would have to sell the large ones at a discount to buy the cast (Gorgas to Memminger, 11 Apr. 1862, W.R. 46–399). *O.R.N.*, ser. 2, 2:185–86.

the loss of 400 barrels in the *Cecile* between Charleston and Nassau.[147] On the same date Mallory asked Bulloch for at least two coil-made smoothbore guns of the Armstrong pattern, for navy use,[148] and on 27 October he acknowledged the arrival of two 7-inch rifled guns with projectiles.[149] On 11 November 1862 the *Manchester Guardian* reported the stoppage of a vessel laden with powder for the South, following protests from the Federals at the impunity with which the British government allowed privateers to be loaded at British ports.[150] To a large extent, these charges appeared to be correct; on the other hand, the Federals themselves shipped large quantities of ordnance from England without undue interference.

By November 1862 the shortage of iron in the Confederacy was grave, and cannon from Europe were greatly in demand.[151] In December a Southern writer noted that Huse had, to date, purchased 157,000 stand of arms, "besides many cannon, much ammunition, quartermaster's stores etc.," and that he was reputed to have obtained $6 million of credit.[152]

During 1861–62 Huse had proved himself to be an able and resourceful purchasing officer, battling immense difficulties. His methods of obtaining credit might be deemed reckless by conservative financiers, but the plight of the South demanded desperate measures. Without a doubt Huse was a key man in the Confederate military campaigns, and without him the South would have been beaten to her knees much sooner. However, not all successful men are wise ones, and during 1862 Huse had been the object of vague accusations of treachery and a fair amount of malicious gossip.[153] These allegations were renewed in 1863 by B. F. Ficklin, who accused Huse of robbing the Confederate government and asked that the secretary of war bring charges. The secretary asked for specific de-

147 *O.R.N.*, ser. 2, 2:215–17.

148 Ibid. With working drawings and descriptions for making them. Some breech-loading guns shipped to the Confederacy had been tried in battle and condemned, because the escape of gas soon rendered them unfit for service.

149 Ibid., p. 284.

150 For munitions shipped into Charleston, see G. V. Fox to D. G. Farragut, 9 Sept. 1862, in R. M. Thompson and R. Wainwright, *Confidential Correspondence of Gustavus V. Fox* (New York: De Vinne Press, 1918, 1919), p. 317.

151 Gorgas to Seddon, 26 Nov. 1862, W.R. 46–399. In the Confederacy armament construction was at a standstill. Gorgas recommended that the government seize one half of the stock of iron at the furnaces, paying for it at $125 per ton (ibid.).

152 Jones, *War Diary*, 1:210.

153 See, for instance, *O.R.N.*, ser. 2, 2:204–5.

tails, but Ficklin replied that as he was not an officer of the Confederacy, he could not properly bring such charges against Huse. Gorgas rushed to Huse's defense and stated that he was satisfied that the charges were misrepresentations. To some degree, the charges may have been aroused by jealousy of the courageous and independent way in which Gorgas himself administered the Ordnance Bureau. So the matter rested for the time being. Huse certainly had enough difficulties without having to contend with malice: his credit was at its limit and he was harried on all sides.[154]

In February a statement of supplies purchased and shipped by Huse was published. Details of the ordnance have been given earlier, but the total value of his purchases, including miscellaneous supplies, freight, and insurance, amounted to £249,853.1.0d. In addition the statement showed that besides miscellaneous supplies, 23,000 rifles, 2,012,000 cartridges and 3 million percussion caps were in London awaiting consignment; 30,000 rifles were in Vienna. For these a total of £117,750 was to be expended. Total indebtedness was £1,186,472.19.3d, of which Fraser, Trenholm and Company had received £613,589, leaving a total deficiency of £572,883.[155]

In the Spring of 1863 the charges against Huse became more specific. In April North had reported that Isaac, Campbell and Company had offered to split with him a commission of five percent on business transactions for the Confederate government, which he declined.[156] In May Major Ferguson, Confederate quartermaster in London, stated that Huse admitted to him that he had received a commission on certain purchases made through Isaac, Campbell and Company, but that some of this money had been used to pay his traveling expenses, and the balance, amounting to £1,000, he intended to use to purchase a military library for the Ordnance Department. Ferguson replied that, in his opinion, the commission should have been deducted from the face of the invoices in the shape of a discount and that the purchase of the library should be postponed until Confederate debts were paid and the army shod and clad. Ferguson went on to charge Huse with buying supplies at extortionate rates.[157]

[154] Fickling to Seddon, 3 Jan., 10 Jan., 13 Jan., and Huse to Seddon, 23 Jan. 1863, *W.R.* 46–399.

[155] *O.R.*, ser. 4, 2:382–84. [156] Ibid., p. 558.

[157] Ibid., pp. 556–57. A few evenings after this (16 May 1863), there was a general meeting of all the government agents, including Spence and Prioleau, Captains Maury, Bulloch, and North of the navy, Major Huse, and Major Ferguson. It was determined to withdraw all securities from the market and wait the result of the Erlanger proposition.

Nothing immediate came of this, although at this time none of the agents were on the friendliest of terms. Their credit was nearly exhausted, and all financial operations had been suspended pending the negotiation of the Erlanger loan. Long and unprofitable squabbles about the amount of authority enjoyed by Huse followed.[158]

As a consequence of the shortage of money, the supply of arms dropped off. On 24 May Gorgas wrote to Huse of the urgent need of arms for Texas, offering cotton in payment.[159] The general's faith in Huse remained unshaken, and on 22 May 1863 he wrote in his defense to James A. Seddon, secretary of war, that as an officer of fifteen years' service, Huse knew that the taking of commission on purchases would result in his dismissal from the service with disgrace, yet it was alleged he made such a statement to an unfriendly brother officer.[160] He also defended Huse's purchases at high prices. These were necessitated, he argued, by the circumstances prevailing and were authorized by the general character of his instructions.[161] But the attacks against Huse continued, exacerbated by the general shortage of funds and the fact that each agent's responsibilities were not precisely defined. In June Huse wrote to Gorgas that he would not commit himself to new contracts until funds were forthcoming.[162] The supply of ordnance to the Confederacy was slowing, and the organization so painstakingly brought into being in the years 1861–62 was crumbling. All through the summer of 1863 the agents

[158] Ibid., pp. 535–47, 555–56, 628.

[159] Memminger suggested that treasury bonds be turned over to Seddon for sale abroad and that the money realized from the bonds should be placed in Huse's account (Memminger to Seddon, 11 May 1863), W.R. 46–399). *O.R.*, ser. 4, 2:567–68.

[160] *O.R.*, ser. 4, 2:564.

[161] Ibid. Gorgas maintained that if Huse had applied for instructions as to whether he should procure supplies at high prices, authority would have been given him "without a moment's hesitation. Purchases made at those rates have saved my department and that of the Quartermaster-General millions of dollars if compared with the charges made by Confederate houses." At his own request Huse was directed to confine his purchases to the Ordnance and Medical Departments.

[162] Ibid., pp. 645–47. Huse refused to furnish other agents with funds. He claimed that "the whole question of finance for the War Department on this side of the water is full of difficulties." McRae, the agent of the Treasury Department for the Erlanger loan, had manifested every desire to cooperate with Huse and iron out these financial "difficulties." Later Huse requested McRae to audit the account of Isaac, Campbell and Company. Being relieved of this debt, Confederate agents could then purchase once again in the open market (ibid., p. 644). Memorandum of proposition for settlement of the debt due by the government of the Confederate States of America to Isaac, Campbell and Co., London, 18 July 1863, ibid., p. 647).

were necessarily more concerned to meet the pressure of their creditors than to secure further supplies.[163] A few shipments were still made, however. For instance, on 3 July 1863 the *Gibraltar* sailed from Liverpool for Nassau with cannon and ammunition valued at £22,763, but supplies were only a trickle compared with those of 1862.[164] All this came at the worst possible time for the Confederacy: on 4 July Vicksburg surrendered and 170 cannon and 60,000 muskets were lost—mostly supplies from Europe.[165]

On 24 July, however, Huse was able to report to Gorgas that he hoped to dispatch the supplies for Texas at "an early day" but asked that supplies of cotton, 3,000 bales, should be dispatched in payment.[166] The next day, Gorgas wrote to Seddon of the urgent need for £100,000 in Europe for the credit of Huse.[167]

In August news of Huse's alleged dealings became public knowledge in the Confederacy. Capt. W. G. Crenshaw, an agent in London, and apparently an implacable enemy of Huse, was now the chief accuser. Huse was alleged to have contracted for 50,000 muskets at four dollars above the current price.[168] Again, nothing seems to have come of this accusation.

By autumn 1863 the position of the agents had somewhat eased. Some of the proceeds of the Erlanger loan and of the cotton certificates were available, and cotton and tobacco were at last being shipped.[169] Supplies began to flow again, but the demands of the hard-pressed Confederate army were growing. Knoxville had been evacuated. Losses of arms to the North were severe. At Fort Sumter the guns were using 1,000 rounds a day—25 tons of ammunition—and then, as has been mentioned, one of the great Blakelys exploded.[170] Powder was again in short supply; at Bermuda, in September, there were only 1,000 pounds in reserve.[171] At this time came news of the capture of the schooner *Caroline Goodyear*, laden with arms.[172]

[163] See, for instance, ibid., pp. 586, 626, 627.

[164] See Ships Manifest (The Library, Customs and Excise, Mark Lane, London). Contrary to the records, Jones recorded in his diary that Gorgas was in daily receipt of immense amounts of ordnance stores from Europe (Jones, *War Diary*, 1:377).

[165] Eaton, p. 206.

[166] *O.R.*, ser. 4, 2:670. Huse believed, and correctly so, that it would strengthen his hand very much to have an amount of cotton on the way to England at the same time that supplies were on the way from England.

[167] Gorgas to Seddon, 25 July 1863, W.R. 46–399. [168] Jones, 2:14–15.

[169] Ibid., p. 18. [170] *Gorgas Diary*, pp. 60, 61–62.

[171] Vandiver, *Confederate Blockade-Running*, pp. 46–47.

[172] Richardson, 2:567–69.

Early in 1864 desultory slanders against Huse's character continued. A few months before, McRae, the agent for the Erlanger loan, defended him, as did his chief, Gorgas. Now Erlanger himself sprang to his aid. Slidell also wrote most favorably on his behalf.[173]

The Erlanger loan may have temporarily assuaged the direct needs of the agents, but on 14 April 1864 Huse's debts were stated to be £129,593.12.4d. (Gorgas was always trying to get more money for Huse.)[174] Nevertheless, in May General Gorgas was able to say that the immediate and most pressing need for supplies was, for the moment, overcome.[175] But the odds were too great against the Confederates. A shipment of 5,000 arms safely received after months of planning and organization was a matter for jubilation. Yet by September 1864 it was estimated that the North, working through thirty-eight armories, could produce just that number of arms in a single day.[176]

In October Gorgas's review of the situation was not optimistic. During the year only some 30,000 small arms had been imported.[177] It had been hoped that Southern armories would contribute between 50,000 and 60,000, but they manufactured only 20,000. Some 45,000 weapons had been captured during the year, but against this figure had to be set a loss of 30,000.[178] Gorgas reported that about 20,000 arms were in transit from Europe and 50,000 had been ordered. He estimated that a further minimum of 50,000 would be necessary for the coming year. The major difficulties in the production of powder had been overcome, except for some shortages of saltpeter and sulphur. Niter had to be largely imported.[179] The situation in relation to artillery was relatively good, but cavalry arms were in very short supply.[180] At the end of the year Gorgas stated the final figures of importations received: 39,798 rifles, 1,716 pistols and 4,740 carbines. He also remarked that the shortage of funds had greatly limited supplies. He estimated that there might be a further 10,000 to 12,000 arms in the West Indies awaiting shipment.[181]

[173] *O.R.*, ser. 4, 3:158, 958.

[174] The whole amount advanced to Huse and others for account of the War Department out of the Erlanger loan was £544,976 (ibid., p. 240). Ibid., 3:302; Gorgas to Seddon, 5 Oct. 1864, and Seddon to McRae, 8 Oct. 1864. W.R. 46–399.

[175] Jones, *War Diary* 2:197. [176] *O.R.*, ser. 4, 3:676.

[177] Ibid., pp. 733–34; Gorgas to Seddon, 23 Dec. 1863, W.R. 46–399.

[178] *O.R.*, ser. 4, 3:733–34. [179] Ibid.

[180] However, from deficiency in the supply of copper, the manufacture of bronze fieldpieces was suspended and an iron gun tightly banded was substituted for the 12-pounder Napoleon, which gave entire satisfaction (ibid.).

[181] Ibid., pp. 986–88.

As the year waned so did the accusations against Huse, and the affair ended in mystery. It appears that no formal charges were ever brought against him, and nothing was ever proved. Thus the truth must be a matter for speculation. Perhaps indiscretion and enthusiasm rather than dishonesty were the faults of this clever, hardworking officer who did so much to further the cause of his government.

At the end of 1864 the war, for the armies in the field, had still a few months to run, but for the agents in Europe, it was virtually at an end. As the Confederates lost battle after battle, their credit slipped even further, chaos ensued, and the agents could only cease operations, wind up their affairs as best they could, and depart, leaving their debts behind them.

CHAPTER VII

MISCELLANEOUS PURCHASES

PREVIOUS CHAPTERS HAVE noted the paucity of Confederate industrial resources and have described how weaknesses in this respect necessitated the importation of a large part of Confederate naval and ordnance requirements, from Great Britain. Confederate manufacturing capacity was no less deficient in nearly every other commodity required, both for waging the war and for sustaining the people. Importation of shoes, machinery, all types of tools, paper, buttons, and saddles—to name only a few urgent requirements—was needed to sustain the Confederacy, and if some of these needs were not as obvious as guns and cruisers, they were no less essential.

To cite one example of the Confederate plight: before treasury notes could be printed on a large scale, it was necessary to smuggle through the blockade the paper, the presses, all the equipment for a large lithography establishment, and the craftsmen required for the printing. The craftsmen were drawn from the famous London printing firm of S. Straker and Sons and were offered $20 a week in gold, with a liberal rate of piecework pay. Each man also received between £40 and £60 for the expenses of his journey.[1]

Most of the printing of Confederate paper money was carried on in Charleston, South Carolina. Evans and Coggswell printed notes of small denominations, $1 and $2 bills, as well as the thousands of cotton bonds the Confederacy issued; Keatings and Ball printed the large-denomination notes, $100 and $500, while the printing works of Colonel Blanton Duncan printed $5, $10, and $20.[2]

Some seventy-five craftsmen were employed by these establishments, and it is significant that nearly all were Englishmen, as were the designers. The paper too was manufactured in England and was stamped at the mill with the mark of the Confederacy, a small palmetto encircled by the motto Treasury Department, C.S.A.[3]

Major Evans, of Evans and Coggswell, made most of the arrangements described above; Maj. Benjamin F. Ficklin was sent to Eng-

[1] "Memoirs of a C.S.A. Treasury Note Lithographer," *New York Sun*, 13 Dec. 1896. The article refers to "*Charles* Straker & Sons" (my emphasis), but this is incorrect.

[2] Ibid. [3] Ibid.

land to employ engravers, lithographers, and printers, and he too was commissioned to purchase steel dies, presses, lithographic stones, inks, paper, and so on—a comprehensive list clearly showing the Confederacy's lack of the materials required to carry on the business of government.[4]

Even Confederate stamps were printed in England. When the British paddle steamer *Bermuda* was taken by the Federal warship *Mercedita* near the coral island of Abaco in the Bahamas, watchers on the shore saw two boxes tossed into the sea from the *Bermuda*.[5] These boxes contained postage stamps and were a part of a consignment of twenty-six cases of some five million stamps printed for the Confederate States by Thomas De la Rue and Company in London.[6]

Major Ficklin had been instructed to buy these stamps. He reached an agreement with the De la Rue Company to print a five-cent blue stamp bearing the head of Jefferson Davis and a one-cent red with the head of John C. Calhoun. Also on board the *Bermuda* were a number of Scottish lithographic artists recruited by Major Ficklin.[7] Although the first shipment of De la Rue stamps came to a sorry end (those not thrown overboard were pulped by the Federals), something like seventeen million were shipped through the blockade, as well as considerable quantities of printing presses, printing plates, ink, and paper.[8]

Later some of the De la Rue stamps were printed in the Confederacy, but the company retained the original engravings, and only electroplates of those engravings were supplied to the Confederate government. The original die of the five-cent stamp is still in the possession of the firm, but that of the one-cent is lost. (This stamp, incidentally, was never issued.) [9]

[4] For Major Ficklin's activities, see August Dietz, *The Postal Service of the Confederate States of America* (Richmond: Dietz Printing Co., 1929), p. 164. See also Private Day Book A, 30 Nov. 1857 to 30 June 1864, p. 108, De La Rue Papers (De La Rue & Co., London).

[5] "The Lost Shipment", *De La Rue Journal*, no. 13 (July 1951). This article incorrectly gives the date of the seizure as 1861, but it was in fact 1862.

[6] Ibid. In 1851 Thomas De La Rue introduced surface-printed stamps by the letterpress method, using a rectangle of metal upon which the design was raised in relief *Stars and Stripes*, 28 Apr. 1960). For the major firms that did business with the Confederacy, see App. XI.

[7] *De La Rue Journal*, no. 13 (July 1951). The work was put in hand at once, the engraving of the founder being carried out by Joubert de la Ferte.

[8] The presence of the De La Rue stamps sealed her fate, for it was impossible to pretend her destination could have been anywhere but a Confederate port.

[9] There was some forgery of Confederate stamps. The work was done in Birmingham, England. The design might be considered an improvement on the

The De la Rue day book shows that the original printing of the five million five-cent postage stamps cost £372.9.2, including a perforating machine and case. Between January and the end of March 1862, the Confederacy spent £3,359,12.4 with De la Rue.[10]

The shortage of materials and labor just in the sphere of printing is an indication of the immense Confederate deficiencies in general manufacturing. The lading bills of ships leaving English ports and bound, however circuitously, for the Confederacy show cargoes of almost every kind of goods. There was, in fact, no commodity (except cotton) that the Confederacy did not have to seek abroad.[11]

Two or three examples may serve to illustrate this fact. In June 1863 the *Gibraltar* was loading in Liverpool, bound for Nassau. Her cargo manifest is typical of such shipments. It included mapping paper, pigs of lead, steel, shovels, axes, pickaxes, screws, wire, chains, iron beams, wheels and hubs, basins, rails, axles, cranes, planks, as well as guns and fittings. Other typical shipments included shoes, haberdashery, hardware, millboard, books, turnip seed, wool, and umbrellas.[12]

Also extant is an order from Fraser, Trenholm and Company of 28 July 1863 for heavy engineering equipment. It included high-pressure horizontal engines, Cornish boilers, donkey pumps, an iron tank, iron girders, milling machines, presses, bullet-compressing machines, machines for making lead rods, machinery for manufacturing bayonets, lathes, boring machines, and many other items—ten foolscap pages in all.[13] All this machinery was manufactured by Greenwood and Batley, of Leeds.

As with naval and ordnance supplies, the whole structure of general purchasing had to be created from nothing at the outbreak of war, and initial proposals and schemes for shipments were quite uncoordinated. One of the earliest proposals on record came from Andrew Low and Company, merchants of Savannah, who wrote to the secretary of war, L. P. Walker, in April 1861 offering to send a

---

original, and it can be identified by the absence of the dots after C.S.A. (interviews between Richard Lester and G. L. Newman, archivist of the Thomas De La Rue Company, the Dufferin Works, Bunhill Row, London, 20 Aug. 1958).

[10] De La Rue Papers, Day Book, p. 108.

[11] These lading bills are in the Library, Customs and Excise, King's Bream House, Mark Lane, London.

[12] Copy Manifest of the cargo shipped via the S. S. *Gibraltar* for Nassau, 1 July 1863, ibid.

[13] Order from Fraser, Trenholm & Co. to Greenwood Batley, Albion Works, Leeds (copy supplied by managing director of Greenwood Batley to Richard Lester, 4 Feb. 1959).

ship through the blockade laden with beef, pork, and fish, provided that the secretary would fill her with cotton and guarantee the owners of the ship against losses by seizure. The papers for these provisions were to be made out in Low's name as a British subject.[14] Such were the haphazard beginnings of the blockade-runners. In June 1861 the *Manchester Guardian* reported that there were more American ships in the Clyde than ever before, all presumably awaiting suitable cargoes.[15] In the same month, Lord Russell claimed that the government was desirous of observing the strictest neutrality in the contest.[16]

While Anderson and Huse were primarily concerned with the purchase of ordnance, they also had to be responsible for purchasing general supplies, and on 11 August 1861 they reported to Walker that they had forwarded leather in large quantities for harness, as well as buckles, thread, awls, knives, and samples of saddles and knapsacks. At this stage British contractors were prepared to furnish any quantity of equipment and essentials required.[17] Bulloch assumed primary responsibility for naval requirements, and during 1861 shipped quantities of clothing for seamen and marines. But he was sensitive to the problems involved. On 13 August 1861 Bulloch wrote: "The Queen's Neutrality Proclamation is more than embarrassing. It is almost an exclusive barrier against shipments to the South." In the same month some leading Confederate merchants realized that the blockade could only be raised by Great Britain or France and that unless this was done, shipping war materials to Southern parts would become increasingly difficult.[18]

Previous chapters have already noted that supplies sent by the purchasing agents seldom equaled the demand; this was also true of miscellaneous requirements. In October 1861 Abraham C. Myers, the acting quartermaster general, wrote to Benjamin, acting secretary of war, that increased supplies from Europe were essential. Myers was much harassed by the offers of war profiteers, who played on the urgency of his needs to send shipments at exorbitant prices. He reported to Benjamin that between the beginning of

[14] *O.R.*, ser. 4, 1:237.

[15] 18 June 1861. It was anticipated at the outset of hostilities that British shipping would benefit to a very great extent from the withdrawal of American vessels from the general carrying trade. In the early part of the war these anticipations were not realized (ibid.).

[16] *Hansard's Parliamentary Debates*, 3d ser., vol. 163 (Commons), 3 June 1861.

[17] *O.R.*, ser. 4, 1:538–42.

[18] *O.R.N.*, ser. 2, 2:83–87; *O.R.*, ser. 4, 1:562–64.

September and 10 October 1861, the price of materials for clothing had advanced 100 percent.[19]

The early policy of the Confederate government in relying on the privateer was disastrous, because the importer who successfully ran the blockade could practically name his own prices.[20] The realization of this fact led the government to place more and more power in the hands of the purchasing agents in Europe, allowing them to buy goods direct from the factories and then make their own arrangements for shipping; but these arrangements were never entirely effective for goods that were not top priority.

The blockade was not nearly so effective as the Federals wished. In a letter to his son dated 25 October 1861, Charles F. Adams mentioned that the *Alliance*, *Goudar*, *Thomas Watson*, *Bermuda*, *Fingal*, and *Amelia* had all gotten successfully through the Northern blockade with quantities of clothing "and military equipment of every description." He added that federal ships did nothing but catch fishing schooners. Adams believed that successful blockade-running provided the South with the material for carrying on the war indefinitely and gave to all Europe the idea of an ineffective blockade —"the most dangerous thing of all to our ultimate success." [21]

In the early months of the war, Confederate agents in Nassau appear to have purchased without regard to price. On 2 December 1861 G. B. Lamar, a merchant of Savannah, reported to Benjamin that he could offer goods for sale on board the *Cheshire* at Nassau.[22] He asked, "Will you buy them, and at what advance on the cost in England?" But he then went on to criticize other Confederate commissaries who, he alleged, were buying coffee at $1 to $1.20 per pound when it could be purchased at 30 to 40 cents. An anonymous endorsement to the letter denies this allegation and states that the maximum ever paid by the agents was 40 cents.[23]

The wide variety of the Confederacy's needs is further illustrated by a study of the goods on board the *Cheshire*, which included 721 bags of coffee, 4,000 sacks of salt, 500 boxes of coke terre plates, 500 boxes of charcoal tin plates, 38 casks of pickles, 75 crates of earthenware, 2 cases of cotton twist, 5 bales of twine, 60 bales and 2 packages of blankets, 1 case of pins and needles, 1 package of drugs and

[19] *O.R.*, ser. 4, 1:688. Myers suggested that bills be drawn in the Confederate States payable to the orders of Mason in London, or Slidell in Paris, who might then pay the drafts of the agents (ibid.).

[20] Ibid. [21] *Adams Letters*, 1:60–61.

[22] For Lamar's other activities, see *Atlanta Century*, 3 Feb. 1861.

[23] *O.R.*, ser. 4, 1:770–71. He was offered some at 80 cents (ibid.).

cotton lint, 1 bale of buntings, 1 bale of counterpanes, 1 case of boots, and 12 boxes of block tin.[24]

A good example of the sort of arrangement the Confederate government entered into with private individuals during the first year of the war is the agreement reached between Benjamin and an O. Chauvin, who was staying at the Pulaski Hotel, Savannah. This agreement provided that Chauvin should introduce into "some port of the Confederate States" an agreed list of articles that would be purchased as reasonably as possible and that he was to receive their cost plus 50 percent profit, plus freight, packing, and loading costs. Freight costs were to be allowed at twice the normal rate for neutral vessels. Payment, in cotton, was to be made on delivery,[25] but the Confederate government assumed no responsibility in the event of nondelivery, and Chauvin also had to export his cotton at his own expense and risk. The government also stipulated that a purchasing officer in Europe should examine the goods before shipment. The agreement called for 1,000 tons of saltpeter; 500 tons of cannon powder; 100 tons of rifle or musket powder; 50,000 rifles or rifled muskets, with bayonets; 5,000 carbines; 5,000 revolving pistols for the cavalry; 10,000 sabers for the cavalry, with belts; 5,000 sabers for artillerists, with belts; 100 tons of bar steel, assorted sizes from 1-inch square upwards, chiefly small sizes; 500 gross of files, assorted sizes, for armorers and finishing purposes; 2,000 gross assorted screws, from 1¼ inches up to 2½ inches, 200 carboys of nitric acid; 500 carboys of sulphuric acid; and 100,000 pounds of leather suitable for harnesses and bridles.[26]

At the end of 1861 the value of exports from Great Britain to the South since the beginning of the war in April was estimated at £240,160, while the Federals, with their superior resources and powers of organization—and no blockade—had been able to obtain supplies to the value of £8,405,862.[27] The articles exported to the South included agricultural implements, soda alkali, miscellaneous clothing, bags, beer and ale, bleaching materials, books, bread and biscuits, bricks, brushes and brooms, cabinet and upholstery wares, tallow candles, coals, copper, cordage, cables, a wide variety of cotton manufactures, drugs and chemical preparations, earthenware

[24] Ibid. For other cargoes see ibid., pp. 800–802, 816–17. Goods were shipped at the rate of £8 per ton with 5% primage, to be paid in cash on the sailing of the vessel from England (ibid., pp. 817–18).

[25] At current market prices. He was at liberty to export cotton on his own account and risk (ibid., pp. 817–18).

[26] Ibid., p. 820.

[27] Great Britain, Customs Papers 8/94, Public Record Office, London.

and porcelain pottery, glass, glass windows and bottles, glue, hardware and cutlery, iron in various forms (cast and uncast), leather, linen manufactures, mathematical instruments, mats and matting, naphtha oil, printers' and dyers' colors and materials, pickles and sauces, printing types and materials, saddlery and harness, salt, seeds, silk manufactures, soap, paper, stones and slates, sugar, tiles, tin, toys, turpentine and woollen manufacturers—not to mention, of course, primary military supplies.[28]

As mentioned previously, the war gave merchants and blockade-runners the opportunity to make quick, if hazardous, profits.[29] They were aided by the lack of official Confederate organization. Throughout the greater part of the war Confederate policy was simple in relation to shipments from Europe: it consisted only in specifying that vessels running the blockade were to carry, first, arms and ammunition; second, clothes; and third, drugs and chemicals in short supply. Any goods not purchased by the Confederate government were auctioned to private dealers.[30] Internally, Confederate policy was much the same for controlling its own manufacture: the only direct controls imposed were, first, on the manufacture of arms and munitions under the Ordnance Bureau; and second, on a more diverse group of goods which included clothing, blankets, tents, shoes, wagons, saddles, and harness, which came under the Quartermaster's Bureau.[31] The unsystematic purchasing methods of the Confederates, especially in the first year of the war, arose in part from the realization of their desperate need for almost every type of commodity, and the president himself said, "Let supplies be had by purchase, or borrowing, or other possible mode." [32]

The wild, and sometimes extravagant, Confederate purchases of the first twelve months brought prosperity to many British firms and helped to offset the depression caused by the shortage of cotton. For example, the district of Northampton, then as now, was famed for its association with the boot and shoe trade and secured many

[28] Ibid. In the field of Confederate history, little attention has been given to the actual materials imported and to their quantity. Although some good work has been recently done in this area, the definitive study is yet to be written.

[29] John Lewis Peyton, *The American Crisis; or, Pages from the Notebook of a State Agent during the Civil War* (London: Saunders Otley, 1867), pp. 1, 20.

[30] Ina Van Noppen, *The South* (Princeton: Van Nostrand, 1958), p. 308.

[31] C. W. Ramsdell, "The Control of Manufacturing by the Confederate Government," *Mississippi Valley Historical Review* 8 (1921):231–49.

[32] J. F. C. Fuller, *Grant and Lee* (Indianapolis: Indiana University Press, 1957), p. 124.

contracts from the Confederacy.[33] In particular, the firm of Isaac, Campbell owned a large factory on the Mounts, Northampton, and appeared to have contracted for the supply of boots on a large scale.[34] In 1862 the *Northampton Mercury* reported that the town was enjoying "a great amount of prosperity as there was a very large demand for shoes for both armies." [35]

Prosperity for makers of guns and ammunition and for shipbuilders was to be expected, but other manufacturers, such as those making buttons, also benefited. Buttons played an important part in the Civil War. At the beginning of the war there was not a single button factory in the South, and nearly all supplies came from England.[36] J. R. Grant and Son [37] and Firmen and Sons of Birmingham are two firms still in existence which sold buttons to the Confederates; [38] Smith and Wright sold insignia.[39]

Confederate purchases in Great Britain during the nine months of the war were less than 3 percent of the total purchases of the Federals. The Federal blockade and lack of organization were certainly contributory causes of the Confederate failure to export more, but shortage of funds was probably the most important factor. Two agents, writing to Toombs in August 1861, summed up this aspect of the situation:

> The Commission has felt almost daily the want of contingent funds, and even of authority to employ and send dispatches by special paid agents.
>
> It has no authoritative information of affairs in the Confederate States since your dispatch No. 6, and all our sources of information are the

[33] Information on any aspect of the history of the boot and shoe industry is difficult to obtain, but it is fairly certain that several firms in the borough were interested in securing orders from the C.S.A.

[34] Howard Halliday, chief librarian, County Borough of Northampton, Central Public Library, Abington Street, Northampton, to Richard Lester, 4 Oct. 1958. The fortunes of this firm waned with the fortunes of the Confederacy, and the firm went out of existence sometime during the late sixties (*Northampton Mercury*, 12 June 1869). There are no local business records available for this period, and what information there is can be gleaned only from scattered references in the local press.

[35] 15 Nov. 1862.

[36] *Stars and Stripes*, 30 Sept. 1959.

[37] W. E. Sanders, J. R. Grant and Son, to Richard Lester, 20 Nov. 1958.

[38] W. Allcock, director, Firmen & Sons, Birmingham, to Richard Lester, 8 Nov. 1958. Firmen & Sons also sold badges, ornaments, and metal smallwares to the Confederacy.

[39] Harold Wright, director, Smith & Wright, Briarley Street, Birmingham, to Richard Lester, 3 Sept. 1958.

New York and Baltimore papers. The diplomatic representatives of the United States, we have every reason to believe, have a large contingent fund, which is freely used in obtaining information of the movements of every agent or friend of the Confederate States; and this, in addition to their being representatives of a recognised government, with high salaries and distinguished positions, places the agents of the Confederate States here at a great disadvantage.[40]

As 1862 began the Confederates gave some consideration to proposals for the better organization of their blockade-running,[41] and on 2 January R. Salas of Charleston proposed the following to Benjamin:

It being every day more and more apparent that the existing war between the Confederate States and the United States will be one of long continuance, during which our Government will necessarily require from abroad a large amount of clothing (chiefly woollens, military accouterments, arms, ammunition, etc., especially lead, gunpowder, and the ingredients for making it), I would most respectfully propose to the consideration of your Department the following suggestions. . . . Until recently numerous vessels on private account were employed in running the blockade from our principal ports, but now very few can be induced to run the risk in consequence of the number which have been recently taken by the enemy. What I propose is that the Government should undertake to do what individaul enterprise will certainly hereafter be unwilling to do. I would propose to have, in charge of proper agents, three or four depots nearby in the West Indies constantly supplied from Europe with such articles as may be needed for the prosecution of the war.[42]

By nearly every ship which reached Confederate or West Indian ports or which docked in Great Britain, messages were carried from or to the purchasing agents. These agents were always open to the pressures of the situation. Thus on 1 January 1862 an agent was able to report that the cargo of the *Justitia*, consisting of medicines, blankets, boots, shoes, and clothing to the value of £93,000, had all been warehoused in Nassau;[43] a few days later Mallory, writing to Bulloch, increased an order for 50 tons of powder to 100 tons, de-

[40] Richardson, 2:53–54.

[41] For statistics on blockade-running, see James T. Adams, *Dictionary of American History* (New York: Scribner's, 1951), p. 201.

[42] *O.R.*, ser. 4, 1:829–30. The little harbor of Mosquito on the Florida Coast also offered a chance of sucess (ibid., pp. 828–29).

[43] Vandiver, *Confederate Blockade-Running*, p. 34.

scribing it as "a most pressing necessity," and hoping for 100 tons of saltpeter as well.[44]

With the general rise in prices in the Confederacy and the growing shortage of all kinds of manufactured goods, increasing pressure was brought upon Benjamin to organize and systematize Confederate purchasing and shipping. In the middle of January D. T. Bisbie of Richmond wrote to Benjamin:

One of the objects of the interview requested was to lay before you that plan for an organised system and effort for obtaining supplies by importation. These supplies are those needed by Government: by merchants of general merchandise, the want of which is manifested by double and treble and in some cases quadruple and quintuple prices; by railroads, for want of which every road in Southern Confederacy is crippled, and by the arts and manufactures which are perhaps more imperiously demanded than any other. Many new manufacturing establishments, otherwise ready to go into operation, are kept back for want of one or two indispensable articles, and many old establishments will soon be compelled to suspend without them. One article is named which ordinarily costs two cents per pound, and now brings one dollar; and a list of 500 articles can be shown which are selling from ten to forty fold advance on former cost. Probably each 1,000 dollars worth of these key articles would make at least 50,000 dollars worth of Southern manufactures immediately available to the pressing wants of the people. It would seem, then, that any plan which would ensure these much needed importations would be of the greatest public and private benefit. The Government can of course get its own immediate wants filled, but not so the others without other combinations. The Government cannot of course be indifferent to the condition of the manufactures from which it draws many of its own supplies, nor that of the railroads upon which it is dependent not only for supplies but for strategic combinations. I submit, too, whether the Government could not, through the suggested combination, get its own importations more surely, promptly, and cheaply than through any other method. The combination here is simply that the Government combined for a part of its own supplies with the importers of merchandise, manufactures, and the railway companies, making their orders from the English combination named below. It will be seen that the organisation is designed to cover large operations. The profit on the wants of a single interest would not be sufficient to induce it, while the aggregate profits of the whole would. The European combination is simply an association of European capital and enterprise for the purpose of sending goods to the Confederate States during the war. Without such a combination I am certain that no such exportations will be made to any extent. Trade is nowhere so perfectly systematized—I may say channelized—as in England, where

[44] *O.R.N.*, ser. 2, 2:129.

the base of expected operations will be located. It is governed by rules which have almost the force of legal enactments. One of these rules is to make no ventures outside the scope of legitimate traffic, and it is considered destructive to commercial character to do so. Firms, then, as business operations, will not send goods to this country in any quantities, and only when stimulated by extraordinary profits. In proof of this I may cite the fact that the extremely high prices that have ruled since last spring have not induced these exports, notwithstanding the great efforts made by myself and others to start them. Why? First the rules of trade above named, the great risk if a firm owned the entire cargo, and the publicity given by any attempt for a small combination; the want of knowledge as to what was wanted here and the prices they would command; and finally, because they were not sufficiently interested to insugurate and perfect a system that would include the elements of secrecy, security, and knowledge of what was wanted and the prices they would command. Again, they wanted reliable information of the risks of capture, of the ports on this side, of pilotage, etc., which even the few disposed to venture could not get except in rare cases. A combination of interests here could supply these all-important desiderati upon which the European combination will be built up, which will ensure exportations to this country. For while, for the reasons above named, the merchants—as business operations—will not make large ventures, they as a mass are friendly to the South, are looking eagerly to the future 600,000,000 dollars of annual reciprocal trade between Europe and the Confederate States, and are exceedingly desirous of placing themselves favourably with our people, and will each contribute to an export fund, the inducement being the placing of the proof of friendly interest so important to their future trade, while properly conducted there is not only a moral certainty of no loss but of large profit. The plan is for, say, 100 firms to contribute an average of £2,000 each, or in all 1,000,000 dollars, placing the whole matter under the control of a single manager. This is for the purpose of securing the necessary elements of secrecy. Then to get up other similar organisations, say to the number of five, making a total capital of 5,000,000 dollars. Then for the five managers to contribute equally to the cargoes; thus if their average cost was 250,000 dollars each man's venture would be distributed in twenty bottoms, which brings in the element of mutual insurance. Under a proper system there would be a virtual certainty that three-fourths of four-fifths would get in safely, as can be proved by the operations of Fraser & Company and others. At an average profit of only 100% (many articles paying from 500 to 1,000%) but one half would have to go in to save loss. If two-thirds, three-fourths, or four-fifths, there would be respective profits of 1,750,000 dollars, 2,500,000 dollars and 3,000,000 dollars on each 5,000,000 dollars exported, with a still larger profit on the return cargoes at far less risk. While, therefore, there would be an almost absolute certainty of no loss there would be a moral assurance of a large profit. Here, then, are combined all the inducements that can be supposed to influence English merchants, the placing with our people, so anxiously desired, the proof of a disposition to aid us, so important to their future standing, combined with perfect safety against loss and the moral certainty of profit. I am certain this European combination can be made. It would, of course, have to be properly managed, and would require active, intelligent, and persevering in its organisation, as do most important enterprises. So certain am I of success that I am ready to give it my personal attention on terms that will involve neither risk nor expense of any moment to the Government. The plan of shipments might be in part the one I had the honor of submitting to you from Nassau, or other plans, one of which I propose shall be made to no human being on this side of the Atlantic except yourself, and to no others on the other side except the managers of the European combination. I forgot to mention that the European combination would expect the privilege of taking return cargoes of cotton, naval stores, etc., and the remission from Government duties during the war. I would state that this communication is in part made at the instance of distinguished merchants and railroad officials, for which reason I respectfully request a reply at your early convenience.[45]

However, this plan and others like it came to nothing.[46] By the beginning of 1862 more money had become a pressing necessity for all the Confederate officers in Europe. Semmes in C.S.S. *Sumter*, lying of Gibraltar, reported on 24 January 1862: "I am now lying perfectly idle, waiting for funds. I cannot strike the first stroke towards repairing my ship until I am in funds; and, even if my ship were in a condition to go to sea, I have not even the wherewithal to coal her!"[47] Semmes received his supplies three weeks later;[48] but in March Benjamin himself was forced to write to Isaac, Campbell and Company, explaining delays in sending remittances. This letter makes it plain that in spite of appeals Benjamin had no intention of persuading the government to organize its own blockade-running.[49]

A few days later Benjamin wrote to Huse of the need for medical supplies to the extent of £20,000, but went on, "I again repeat, send

[45] *O.R.*, ser. 4, 1:843–45. [46] Ibid., pp. 882–83.

[47] *O.R.N.*, ser. 2, 2:136–37. His crew was also in need of clothing (ibid., pp. 140–41, 145–46; Richardson, 2:166).

[48] *O.R.N.*, ser. 2, 2:143–46.

[49] *O.R.*, ser. 4, 1:1007–8. The amount was $1,261,600. Benjamin concluded that Confederate demands for supplies from England would continue to be large.

us small arms and powder or saltpeter, to neglect of everything else, if necessary."[50] On 1 April 1862 Huse was able to report the consignment of 5,900 knapsacks and boards, 5,690 sets of accounterments, 1,840 gun slings, 992 saber belts, 4,500 yards of light blue cloth, 1,850 sabres, 5,700 rifles, 300 pairs of shoes, and 16 sets of saddlery.[51]

During the early part of 1862 concern was expressed in both Houses of Parliament that most of the blockade-running was being carried out by British vessels and that such voyages might be deemed an infringement of declared neutrality.[52] Replying to these allegations, the solicitor general made it clear that the Foreign Enlistment Act was irrelevant so far as these shipments were concerned, but he went on to state that while the British government could not interfere with British vessels carrying supplies for the Confederates, it would not interfere if these vessels were seized by the Federals.[53] A few days earlier it had been stated in the House of Lords that some 600 to 700 ships had already broken the blockade,[54] and many British officers and seamen were growing rich on the fruits of their enterprise. The *Times* of 23 April 1862 reported that the captain of a blockade-runner received £1,000 in gold for the voyage, his chief officer £250, the second and third officers £150 each, the chief engineer £500, the pilot £750, and each ordinary seaman £50.[55] George W. Randolph replaced Benjamin as secretary of war early in 1862, and from time to time requests were submitted to him, as they had been to Benjamin, to organize government blockade-runners. Larkin Smith, assistant quartermaster general, wrote on 31 July 1862:

[50] Ibid., p. 1018. The surgeon general was also in need of drugs. At this time there was so much difficulty in sending bills abroad that the secretary of the treasury was shipping cotton in lieu of remittances.

[51] *O.R.N.*, ser. 2, 2:177–80.

[52] *Hansard's Parliamentary Debates* (Commons), 3d ser., vol. 165 (1862), 20 Feb. 1862. It was also mentioned that although the attention of the government had been called to the fact that vessels were loading in English ports with munitions of war for the Southern states, no steps had been taken to prevent them accomplishing their voyages.

[53] Ibid. The *Richmond Enquirer* (13 Oct. 1862) claimed that British policy was to let the war continue long enough to destroy the strength of both South and North.

[54] *Hansard's Parliamentary Debates* (Lords), 10 Feb. 1862. The Earl of Malmesbury claimed that his source of information was Mason (ibid., 10 Mar., 22 Apr, 1862).

[55] 23 Apr. 1862.

To obtain a full supply of clothing for the army is becoming more embarrassing and difficult as the raw material is diminishing and the machinery employed in its manufacture becomes worn out. Every exertion has been made to render all the resources of the country available; but if, in the matter of clothing and shoes, there were ample supplies of raw material the capacity to manufacture them is wanting, thereby rendering it certain that a reliance upon our own sources of supply will be in vain. The prices of all goods are enormous, those from abroad bringing readily in open market 300 or 400% on their cost in Europe. In view of these facts, I respectfully recommend as the only effective mode of relief from these difficulties and embarrassments that an officer be dispatched to Europe to purchase cloth, shoes, blankets, and other indispensable articles of issue to the troops. The Government would save largely by purchasing abroad, even if one of every three cargoes were lost. To depend on private enterprise to import these goods is to trust a very unreliable source of supply and to pay enormous profits to the importers. Major Ferguson of this department, who has been employed in providing materials for the clothing department at Richmond, is fully competent to purchase goods abroad, as, in addition to his knowledge of quality and prices, he has the mercantile ability and integrity to disburse advantageously the large sums which would be intrusted to such agents as may be sent to Europe. The necessity of almost immediate arrangements of these supplies leads me to ask for your early consideration on this subject.[56]

No action on the part of the secretary was forthcoming, however, although the *Manchester Guardian* stated that British government officials at Liverpool had received instructions to prevent "as far as possible" the shipment of any warlike stores, intended for the Confederates, at that port.[57]

Ready money continued to be in short supply for the purchasing agents, and they would have fared very badly indeed if firms like Isaac, Campbell and Co. had not been prepared to accommodate them—even if at considerable profit to the firms themselves. Although there were profits to be made, there were also some risks. Federal waships heavily armed were dispatched from Fort Monroe and other points to cruise and search for blockade-runners.[58] In No-

[56] *O.R.*, ser. 4, 2:30–31.

[57] 13 Nov. 1862. The progress of the war in America was an increasing stimulant to the munitions trade with the Confederates. Within two months no fewer than eight vessels, laden to their fullest capacity with military stores, left Queensland to run the blockade (ibid., 14 June 1862; *O.R.*, ser. 4, 2:8–9; 18–20).

[58] *O.R.*, ser. 4, 2:56–58; *Times*, 3 Sept. 1862; *Richmond Dispatch*, 29 Sept. 1862.

vember 1862 Benjamin W. Hart wrote to the secretary of war, mentioning the capture of a vessel with clothing and equipment for 100,000 men but stating that Isaac, Campbell were prepared to replace this equipment within three months.[59] Hart continued:

My friends have taken into consideration the difficulty experienced by the Confederate Government in placing funds in Europe in the present state of affairs, and propose to execute the order on terms of payment which they judge will be acceptable to your Department and greatly facilitate your Government and promote its success in the struggle in which it is engaged. The order in question will occasion the outlay of a large amount of ready money, and Messrs. S. Isaac, Campbell & Co., having up to this time advanced to the Government about $400,000 sterling, that active means are so far diminished as to require that some portion of the payment will be made in cash or sterling bills of exchange.

Following my instructions, I beg leave at the same time to bring to your attention the state of the account between Messrs. S. Isaac, Campbell & Co. and the Government for equipments and other war material already furnished. They have been given to understand the Government has matured plans for the issue of certificates for certain specified quantities of cotton, which are to be made applicable to the liquidation of debts contracted abroad for war materials and for future purchases. The details of the measure are unknown to us, but assume they are such as will be entirely acceptable, and accept them in advance of the information which you will greatly oblige by forwarding with your reply in duplicate by first steamer leaving for this port.

At the end of 1862 Gorgas reported to Seddon, now secretary of war, on the activities of Huse, one of the most active of the purchasing agents. In addition to the arms, which were his main concern, Gorgas stated that Huse had bought "large quantities" of infantry equipments, harness, swords, saltpeter, and lead. He had also been responsible for the purchase and shipment of clothing, blankets, cloth, and shoes for the Quartermaster's Department.[60] This report contained a statement of Huse's liabilities, which amounted to £444,850, and an appeal from Gorgas for their liquidation. To pay for these purchases, funds had been sent to Huse from time to time by the Treasury Department on requisitions from the War Department.[61]

Mentioning that a large proportion of Huse's purchases had fallen into enemy hands, Gorgas appealed to the navy for a service of light-

[59] *O.R.*, ser. 5, 2:190–91. Captured vessels were immediately reported to the Northern press (F.O. 5/1318, p. 243; *Times*, 29 Nov. 1862).

[60] *O.R.*, ser. 4, 2, Gorgas to Seddon, 5 December, 1862. [61] Ibid.

draft steamers that could ply between Bermuda and Confederate ports and bring in supplies landed there from England.[62] The increasing vigilance of federal ships was leading the Confederates to prefer Bermuda to the original choice of Nassau for the unloading of cargoes en route for the Confederacy. The following letter is quoted at length because it gives a vivid picture of Confederate shipping problems in the West Indies at the end of 1862. Writing to Randolph, L. Heylinger, the agent in Nassau, said:

My last dispatch was under date of the 12th ultimo by the *Kate*, since which the steamers *Herald* (now *Antonica*) and *Leopard* have arrived from Charleston. I have shipped by the *Antonica* the following remnants ex *Melita:* 5 cases of knapsacks, 3 cases of boots, 3 cases of percussion-caps, 1 case of saddlery, 2 cases of cavalry saddlery, 1 case of friction-tubes, 2 cases of bayonet scabbards, 5 bales of army cloth, 2 bales army cloth.

Also to Dr. Chisolm, Medical Department, South Carolina and Georgia, 6 cases and 3 barrels medicines. By the *Leopard*, to leave in three days, I should clear up the odds and ends of the *Melita's* cargo, besides 50 cases Enfield rifles, some medicines for Dr. Chisolm, and about 2 tons of steel to Captain Childs. Both the *Antonica* and *Leopard* carry a large quantity of iron plates, a considerable shipment of woollens, all the blankets and shoes that could be got together, and a variety of other useful stuff on private account.

Mr. S. G. Porter, Government agent, arrived here on the *Herald*, bound to Bermuda, but was detained for some time by sickness. The communication between here and Bermuda being so sparse, Mr. Porter concluded to charter a schooner, and would have left ere this but for a violent storm that has prevailed for some days past. I expect he will get off by the day after tomorrow. Mr. Porter has fully explained to me the important nature of the business confided to him, but I am apprehensive he may be partially thwarted by the paucity of suitable steamers to transship Government property from Bermuda to the Confederacy. As far as I can learn, all the suitable steamers from England are bound to this place, the owners deeming it the best policy to load at Nassau. It is very certain they have taken a strong objection to Bermuda. Mr. George Wigg, formerly of New Orleans, and a very intimate personal friend, expects several steamers here, but is unwilling to divert them to Bermuda unless at a difference of freight, which I consider to be admissible. Still, he is anxious to further the interests of Government and will give us the preference of room over all other parties. If Mr. Porter should be blocked in his operations at Bermuda I have counseled him to send a cargo here, which I could dispatch in a very brief period.

Captain Malcolm, the naval commander at this station, assured me the

[62] Ibid.

day before yesterday that the Federal cruisers have received express instructions from their Navy Department not to molest neutral vessels bound from a neutral to a neutral port, even if laden with munitions of war, unless the course of the vessel should justify a reasonable suspicion that she intended to violate the blockade. To use his own language, she would be in the legal prosecution of her voyage, and her seizure under such circumstances would be decidedly illegal. This source of apprehension removed, it might perhaps be good policy to divert some of the accumulation of stuff at Bermuda to this place, so as to get it into the Confederacy at the earliest moment. The steamer *Antonica,* one of George Wigg's vessels, left England on the 3rd ultimo for Saint Thomas, and instructions have been sent to her to proceed to Havana, where she will take a pilot and run the blockade at Mobile. She is a clear eleven-and-a-half knot boat and has a very valuable cargo, consisting in part of 22,000 pairs of shoes, 30 tons of gunpowder, blankets, etc. The steamers *Pearl* and *Eagle* (paddle), sixteen to eighteen miles an hour certain, are expected here every moment. The *Thistle* (a fast screw) will be due in eight days. Then there is a new screw, under a builder's guaranty of £5,000 to run fourteen miles an hour, carrying 700 tons of cargo, which will be out on the 20th proximo. All these are George Wigg's vessels, so that you will perceive the facilities offered for the transshipment of cargo. In addition to these, there are no less than six steamers to make their appearance within the next sixty days. Before that time no less than 100,000 pairs of shoes and a vast quantity of blankets will reach this place, irrespective of some private ventures which will increase the amount.[63]

During the latter part of 1862 the uncoordinated methods of purchasing and shipping came in for some general criticism in the South.[64] Various schemes were mooted with a view to organizing the blockade-running, but without result.[65] Yet it must be admitted that the medley of officers, agents, business firms, and private individuals seeking to issue orders, supervise finance, and purchase supplies provided a vast quantity of materials for relatively little money.[66] Confederate importations, when compared with those of the Federals, were indeed tiny, but it is surprising, not how little, but how much got into the Confederate States, considering the shortage of money, the blockade, and the lack of organization at the executive level.

[63] Ibid., 2:233–34. [64] See Jones, *War Diary,* 1:223–34.

[65] *Times* (15 Dec. 1862) claimed, "The whole war has been a war of blockade." It believed that intervention was the only hope the South had of neutralizing the blockade.

[66] The judgment of this writer is that if there had not been so much jealousy among the agents, even more could have been accomplished.

In November 1862 the *Charleston Mercury* strongly repudiated allegations that the wrong goods were being imported and that Confederate cotton was falling into the hands of the United States. The paper stated that John Fraser and Company, of Charleston, had shipped about seven-eighths of the cotton that had been dispatched from the ports of the Confederacy and that "not one pound of cotton shipped by that house had gone to the United States, either by sale or capture." The *Mercury* also affirmed that ordnance was always given priority on ships out of Europe and that lighter goods were only packed in the ships to complete the cargoes. The landing bills of such ships were handed to government agents at the Confederate port of entry. The agents took whatever they wanted, fixing the prices themselves, the remainder of the cargoes being sold by auction. The newspaper instanced the *Minlo*, which had just run the blockade into Charleston. She carried 7,340 rifles, 21,000 swords, 87 cases of ammunition, and 80 cases of caps—as much heavy freight "as she could safely take." In addition, she carried salt, shoes, and miscellaneous goods. The *Mercury* concluded: "If the Confederate States had twenty mercantile houses with the enterprise and patriotic liberality of John Fraser & Co., we would not want for arms and ordnance, our army would not now be in rags, and our people would not want many of the comforts of life. If other Southern cities had done as much for the purposes of war as Charleston, the South would be in a much better condition.[67]

A previous chapter has detailed how active the agent Caleb Huse was in sending ordnance to the Confederate States. He was no less active in attempting to supply the multifarious needs of an agricultural nation at war. Indeed, he was probably the most successful and versatile Confederate agent in Europe. During the first two years of the war, apart from ordnance he shipped to the Confederacy the following: 1,226 cavalry equipments, 16,178 cavalry sabers, 5,392 saber belts and knots, 1,386 surcingles and pads, 34,731 sets of accouterments, 10,000 pouch pins, 40,240 gun slings, 34,655 knapsacks, 4,000 canteen straps, 81,406 bayonet scabbards, 650 sets of sergeants' accouterments, 3,336 pieces of serge for cartridge bags, and 2,000 completed bags.[68] He also bought large quantities of

[67] 7 Nov. 1862.

[68] *O.R.*, ser. 4, 2:382–84. The agents purchased swords, and in the thirteen months ending 8 Dec. 1864, 134 cases of them actually reached the Confederacy (ibid., 3:930). There were no major sword factories in the South before the war, and swords were mainly imported from Europe and Northern manufacturers. Some naval cutlasses were made in the South (*Confederate Veteran* 34, no. 1 (1926):12–13.

powder and the materials from which it could be made. It has been estimated that at the start of the war, there was hardly enough powder in the Confederacy for a month of action. The Ordnance Bureau was almost completely dependent on foreign supplies, since the caves of Tennessee, Alabama, Georgia, and Arkansas could not produce nearly enough niter.[69] In the first twenty months of the war, Huse shipped 1,024 hundredweight of saltpeter and 2,800 pounds of potassium chlorate.[70] Lead was also an essential raw material, and by February 1863 Huse had exported 1,013 hundredweight and 10,000 pounds of copper.[71] In addition, this indefatigable officer was responsible for many miscellaneous items such as machinery, screws, castings, grate bars, bearers, boilers, steam chests, picks, wire, files, vices, bellows, anvils, axes, spades, rasps, horseshoes, and horseshoe nails, swords, puncheons, bridles, twine, belting, and hose.[72]

But in spite of all Huse could do, the Confederacy's demands must have seemed to him well-nigh insatiable. For example, it was always a struggle to keep up with the South's lead requirements. Until the summer of 1862 supplies more or less equaled the demand, but heavy fighting subsequently strained resources to the utmost. By March 1863 the position was so serious that the superintendent

[69] According to the report of the Niter and Mining Bureau, the importation of niter until the end of 1862 exceeded the home production (O.R., ser. 4, 2:222). Even the requirements of the commissary general gave way before the orders for niter (ibid., p. 877). The director of the Confederate powder works estimated that 2,700,000 pounds of niter were received from Europe and sent to the Confederate powder factories at Augusta, Ga. (George W. Rains, *History of the Confederate Powder Works* [Newburgh, N.Y.: Newburgh Daily News Prints, 1882], p. 7).

[70] William Diamond, "Imports of the Confederate Government from Europe and Mexico," *Journal of Southern History* 6 (1940):480–81. Unfortunately, the records are deficient. All that can be said with any degree of certainty is that imports remained one of the chief sources of the Confederacy's supply of saltpeter (*O.R.*, ser. 2, 3:733). From 1 Nov. 1863 to 8 Dec. 1864, the astonishing total of 1,933,000 pounds safety arrived in the ports of Wilmington and Charleston (ibid., p. 930).

[71] Lead, like saltpeter, was one of the essential war materials urgently needed, and the Confederate States were forced to depend to a great extent on foreign supplies. In the summer of 1862 the superintendent of the Niter and Mining Bureau reported that all deficiencies in lead had been met by importations (*O.R.*, ser. 4, 2:30). From 1 Jan. 1863 to 1 Jan. 1864, the Niter and Mining Bureau imported and received 1,909,800 pounds of the metal. This was 39.8% of the total supply of the Confederacy. It is difficult to estimate how much of this amount actually came from England. Gorgas considered it a very precious metal indeed (ibid., p. 733).

[72] Diamond, pp. 480–81.

of Confederate ordnance laboratories, John W. Mallet, wrote to Gorgas that supplies of small-arms ammunition were almost exhausted. As a possible remedy, Mallet suggested that all blockade-runners should carry a certain proportion of lead in each cargo. Mallet added that at that particular period of the war, lead was as vital as niter. The situation was not helped by the fact that the captains of blockade-runners tended to throw cargoes of lead overboard if chased, so as to lighten their loads.[73]

Another serious shortage at this time—and indeed for the greater part of the war—was shoes. Many Confederate soldiers were forced to go barefoot, even in winter.[74] Often they were compelled to try to protect their feet from sharp stones by tying cloth round them. In all, the Confederates imported 550,000 pairs of boots and shoes from Europe, but supply never equaled the demand.[75]

Mines are a commonplace of modern warfare, but it is not generally known that the Confederate States of America was the first government to use them in a practicable form.[76] Matthew F. Maury was sent to England in June 1862 with the express purpose of experimenting with underwater explosives. As a result of his experiments, he shipped mine components, such as electrical cable and magnetos, to the South.[77] On 12 December 1862 the U.S. ironclad *Cairo* was sunk by a Confederate mine; on 13 July 1863 the *De Kalb* suffered a similar fate.[78] Records are incomplete, but it seems likely

[73] Mallet suggested that blockade-runners be required to bring some fixed amount of lead as part cargo at a set price. He said, "The question of lead supply is nearly if not altogether as vital as that of nitre" (*O.R.*, ser. 4, 2:31).

[74] It should be noted, however, that some troops were accustomed to going barefoot in summer, and they would at times remove their heavy army shoes in order to walk more comfortably.

[75] This figure could go as high as three-quarters of a million pairs of footwear (*O.R.*, ser. 4, 3:930).

[76] However, as early as 1810, Robert Fulton had experienced with torpedoes (Taylor Peck, *Round-Shot to Rockets: A History of the Washington Navy Yard and United States Naval Gun Factory* [Annapolis: United States Naval Institute, 1949], p. 35; A. J. Hanna, *Flight into Oblivion* [Richmond: Johnson Publishing Co., 1938], p. 243).

[77] Captain Maury invented an electric mine in the summer of 1861 but could not obtain insulated wire for its production (Theodore Roscoe and Fred Freeman, *Picture History of the United States Navy* [New York: Scribner's, 1956], p. 658). For an interesting analysis of Confederate infernal machines and other unusual Confederate devices, see Milton F. Perry, *Infernal Machines: The Story of Confederate Submarine and Mine Warfare* (Baton Rouge: Louisiana State University Press, 1965).

[78] Isaac N. Brown, "Confederate Torpedoes in the Yazoo," *Battles and Leaders of the Civil War*, 4 vols. (New York: T. Yoseloff, 1956), III:580. For photograph of the *De Kalb*, see 1:340. Both vessels were sunk in the Yazoo River in the Delta region of Blackbelt, Mississippi.

that the materials for these primitive mines emanated from England.[79] They were sometimes made from a five-gallon glass demijohn filled with black powder and set off on contact by an artillery friction tube.[80] Others were made from beer barrels fixed with conical heads and coated inside and out with resin dissolved in coal tar, or from cast iron, copper, or tin.[81]

At the beginning of 1863, shipments on route to Confederate ports were passing through Nassau and Bermuda at a steady rate. On 10 January 1863 the agent in Nassau was able to report that most of the government supplies had been cleared, with the exception of some field artillery, 230 boxes and packages of steel, 200 boxes of fixed ammunition, and a quantity of lead. The *Antonica* was about to sail from England with a cargo of army stores, woollens, medicines, iron plates, and so on, and the *Douglas*, *Thistle*, *Nicolai I*, *Dairo* and *Calypse* were soon to arrive. The *Flora*, *Ruby*, *Ingle*, *Pearl*, and two unnamed ships were expected shortly. The *Calypso* included in her cargo 148 cases of sorely needed shoes for the army. But costs were always rising and blockade-runners were now demanding £60 per ton for freight, whether or not the cargo arrived safely.[82]

Early in 1863 the agents already in England were joined by Capt. J. M. Robinson, who was sent by Seddon to buy supplies for the Engineer's Bureau and the railway companies in the Confederacy.[83] To carry these supplies, the Confederate government was at last actively interesting itself in the purchase of blockade-runners. On 30 March W. G. Crenshaw reported to Seddon on the building of four iron steamers and the impending purchase of another three, ready to put to sea. The emphasis he placed on speed makes it clear

[79] Applying Electricity for Discharging Torpedo Mines, either on land or at sea, and in the apparatus connected therewith (Matthew Fontaine Maury), no. 3158, 8 Dec. 1865, *Patent Office Papers*.

[80] Brown, p. 580. Maury's arrangements were a new and practical application of electricity to the discharge of torpedoes. For more details see *Patent Office Papers*, 1868, no. 3158.

[81] Jefferson Davis, 2:208. The three essentials in the effective use of torpedoes were (1) a sensitive fuse primer; (2) a charge of 60 pounds of gunpowder; (3) actual contact between the torpedo and the bottom of the vessel (ibid.). Mine warfare took a heavy tool of the Union fleet, but material shortages badly hampered Confederate torpedo manufacturers. For pictures of a Confederate mine see Roscoe and Freeman, frame 658.

[82] *O.R.*, ser. 4, 2:335–6. Hitherto the price had been $500 in Confederate currency per ton, payable on arrival of the goods, whereas now it was fixed at £60 or $900 per ton, payable in advance. Heylinger thought it quite possible that some modifications of these terms could be obtained from Fraser, Trenholm & Company and John Fraser & Co.

[83] Ibid., pp. 409–10.

that they were all intended for blockade-running. Meanwhile, Huse had bought three steamers to ply between Bermuda and Confederate ports.[84]

By the middle of 1863 the agents were sorely in need of funds. On 24 May Crenshaw reported to Mason an immediate indebtedness of £19,534 and a total contingent liability on contracts in hand to the beginning of August of £115,334.[85] Of this sum it is interesting to note that £36,000 was required for preserved meats, to be provided at the rate of 175,000 pounds per week.[86]

During the summer of 1863 the importation of food became a prime necessity. Soldiers' rations were reduced, and meat became so scarce that it was placed second only to niter and lead in orders to foreign agents.[87] Ten million pounds of meat were called for, but the first purchase, probably in May 1863, was for only 2,989,944 pounds of bacon. The agents were operating before the days of efficient refrigeration and speedy transatlantic services, and their work was rendered more difficult because of a hot summer.[88]

Ordnance stores in the Confederacy also diminished alarmingly as the summer of 1863 wore on; lead was in very short supply. In September, of 200,000 pounds received at Augusta from foreign sources, only 69,604 remained in store.[89]

In June Huse wrote to Gorgas of the financial difficulties under which the agents were laboring. Huse stated that he could not complete his contracts for want of money. These difficulties heightened the clash of personalities among the agents, described in the last chapter.[90] In the same dispatch he reported a consignment of large quantities of leather and printed stationery.[91]

[84] Ibid., pp. 480–82. These were built by Dudgeon & Brothers, London. The first was ready on 6 Apr. and was guaranteed for fourteen and one-half knots per hour; the second, ready on 6 May, was guaranteed for thirteen and one-half knots per hour; and the third, ready on 30 June, guaranteed for 15 knots per hour. The fourth was ready on 15 July, guaranteed for 15 knots per hour. They all cost £14,500 each (ibid., pp. 478–79.

[85] Ibid., pp. 588–89. In addition to which there other goods bought by Major Ferguson, costing about £40,000 (ibid.).

[86] Ibid. This would amount to £4,000 per week. [87] Ibid., p. 877.

[88] Ibid. In November all of it had not yet arrived and Lucius B. Northrop, commissary general, insisted on a greater and more regular supply of meat. Between 1 Nov. 1863 and 8 Dec. 1864, 8,632,000 pounds of meat entered the ports of Charleston and Wilmington on government contract (ibid., 3:930).

[89] Vandiver, Introduction, *Blockade-Running*, pp. xxi-xxxii.

[90] *O.R.*, ser. 4, 2:645–47.

[91] Ibid. The quartermaster general relied on foreign sources for leather (ibid., p. 292; ibid., ser. 1, 33:147). The quartermaster's department was the greatest consumer of leather, which was required for baggage harness and

In May 1863 Congress passed a law establishing a seal for the Confederacy, and on 20 May Benjamin advised Mason, the commissioner in London, that he had decided to have the work executed in England. He said:

Congress has passed a law establishing a seal for the Confederate States. I have concluded to get the work executed in England, and request that you will do me the favor to supervise it. You will receive herewith a copy of the Act of Congress describing the seal, and a photographic view of the statue of Washington. The photograph represents the horse as standing on a base of a statue, but in the seal the base ought to be the earth, as the representation is to be of a horseman, and not of a statue. The size desired for the seal is the circle on the back of the photograph. The outer margin will give space for the words: "The Confederate States of America, 22D February, 1862." I do not think it necessary that the date should be expressed in words, the figures "22, 1862" being of sufficient compliance with the requirements of the law. Indeed, I know that in the drawings submitted to the Committee that devised the seal the date was in figures and not in words. There is not room for the date in words on the circumference of the seal without reducing the size of the letters so much as to injure the effect. In regard to the wreath and the motto, they must be placed as your taste and that of the artist shall suggest; but it is not deemed imperative under the words of the Act that all the agricultural products (cotton, tobacco, sugar cane, corn, wheat, and rice) should find place in the wreath. They are stated rather as examples, I am inclined to think that in so small a space as the wreath must necessarily occupy it would be impossible to include all these products with good effect; and in that event I would suggest that cotton, rice, and tobacco, being distinctive products of the Southern, Middle, and Northern States of the Confederacy, ought to be retained, while wheat and corn, being produce in equal abundance in the United States as in the Confederacy, and therefore less distinctive than the other products named, may better be omitted, if omission is found necessary. It is not desired that the work be executed by any but the best artist that can be found, and the difference of expense between a poor and a fine specimen of art in the engraving is too small a matter to be taken into consideration in a work that we fondly hope will be required for generations yet unborn. Pray give your best at-

---

shoes. The Ordnance Bureau needed leather for cavalry harness and saddles. By spring 1862 the shortage was noticed and extraordinary efforts were made to secure a supply of hides. Before two years of war had elapsed, Huse sent to the Confederacy 50 sets of Webb harness, 456 leather belts, 198 packages of leather (ibid., ser. 4, 2:383). How much leather was imported during the remainder of the war is not known. But it did enter Southern ports, and in the thirteen months from 1 Nov. 1863 to 8 Dec. 1864, 699 packages arrived in Charleston and Wilmington (ibid., 3:930).

tention to this, and let me know about what the cost will be and when I may expect the work to be finished.[92]

On 25 September 1863 Benjamin advised Mason that the drawings for the seal had been placed in the hands of Foley, R.A., "probably the most eminent sculptor in England." [93] The making was subsequently entrusted to a Mr. Wyon for the sum of 80 guineas; delivery was made to the agent Hotze during the summer of 1864.[94] The seal was a beautiful piece of work in silver and ivory, which finally reached Richmond during the autumn of 1864 in the care of a Lieutenant Chapman, C.S.N. It was packed in a lead-weighted valise that could be thrown overboard and would sink if capture seemed imminent. Although it arrived safely it was never used, for its press was sunk in another blockade-runner.[95] The seal is exhibited at the Confederate Museum, Richmond.

As the summer of 1863 wore on, Huse came in for some heavy criticism from the other agents. For example, on 3 July 1863 Crenshaw wrote to Seddon:

If reports be true Major Huse is about concluding a contract for the delivery of supplies to be paid for in cotton, which will supersede the contract with Messrs. Callie & Company and myself. Not being in the confidence of Major Huse, I do not know the terms of the proposed contract, but if it be to allow 20% profit on the goods and 10% on the cotton, as I hear it is, I look upon it simply as a swindle and ought not to be put upon our Government. I have done my duty as I understand it by telling the Hon. Mr. Mason what I have heard and expressing to him my opinion of it, but having no evidence as to the facts he says he can do nothing. He also says that all of the money arising from the Erlanger Loan has been appropriated, and that as the Quartermaster's supplies ordered through Major Ferguson are much needed they must be had even upon these terms if better cannot be done. It is exactly this that I complain of, that since this contract has for its basis exactly the same that you proposed, and for a small advance too much compensation is to be made, where if there had been a disposition to carry out your wishes on the part of Major Huse these goods might now be in the course of shipment, but unfortunately, in my opinion, for our Government this contract of mine is now not to the interest of Huse to carry out.

The fear I have is that if you desire me, in reply to my letter of 3rd May, to go on with my arrangements as they are requested, and will send me Treasury drafts, with which to work, that there will be no

92 Richardson, 2:487–88. 93 Ibid., p. 573. 94 Ibid., p. 643.

95 Henry, pp. 446–47. Although extremely rare, electro-type medals of the seal were made and sold by a Washington jeweler.

money in the Treasury. I await patiently, however, the receipt of your advice, and in the meantime will go on sending off the balance of provisions from Liverpool, as the draft of Colonel Gorgas is to be paid today, I understand.

Permit me in conclusion to call your attention to the inclosed correspondence with General McRae. To my last letter I have no reply but Mr. Schroeder informed me yesterday that Erlanger had directed him to pay the draft upon Major Huse's authority, and that he received the authority last evening and would pay the draft. Comment on such action of an officer of our Government is unnecessary, and I omit any.[96]

The following day Crenshaw wrote to Mason in similar terms:

Having heard that Major Caleb Huse is about to conclude a contract for furnishing our Government with various supplies to a very large amount, and believing, from what I can hear of the proposed contract, that if it is carried out it would result in enormous loss to our Government, but yet if he rejected it, as I believe it would be, upon the ground that Major Huse has no authority to make it, may embarrass our Government and give rise to reports that it has repudiated the action of an officer who heretofore it had endorsed, and to this extent injure the credit of our Government, I hasten to call your attention to it and protest against Major Huse entering into such contract, because it is in direct conflict with the contract made and signed in March last by Messrs. Alexander Collie & Co., and myself with you as the representative of the Hon. James A. Seddon, Secretary of War, in accordance with his letter to you. And in thus offering my protest I beg leave to add some of the reasons why such a contract should not be entered into, in my opinion, and especially why it should not be entered into at this moment, viz:

First. Major Huse is now, as I understand under charges for malfeasance in office.

Second. Major C. Huse is aware of the contract existing between Messrs. Alexander Collie & Co., and myself and the Secretary of War for furnishing Government supplies, and has orders to confer with and aid me in carrying out the said contract.

Third. Major C. Huse, instead of carrying out his orders, has, after trying to prevail upon me to cancel the contract, turn every obstacle he could in the way to prevent me from carrying it out, as is evidenced by his letters, which I have the honor to submit to you; by his action with regard to Colonel Gorgas' draft in favor of C. H. Bosher, with which you are furnished, and especially in trying to substitute the contract against which I now protest in place of it.

Fourth. I confidently advance the opinion that it is not to the interest of our Government to take such a contract as is now proposed,

[96] *O.R.*, ser. 4, 2:625–26.

because it pays the contractors 20% profit on the goods and 10% on the cotton upon the same basis of our contract—that is, exchange cotton for goods—while the contract with us stipulates only to be paid on each a commission of 2½% for the same service, except that I understand the contractors propose to make some advance till cotton comes out. This has been done already to some extent by Messrs. Alexander Collie & Co., and would have been to a much greater but for the action of Major Huse towards me. As I shall presently show, such an advance is not necessary; if it is it could have been had on much more advantageous terms than Major Huse now proposes.

Fifth. The pressing wants at the moment which are not provided for are the orders for the Quartermaster's Department placed in the hands of Major J. B. Ferguson junior and it is to meet these wants that Major Huse insists upon entering at once into this contract, involving the expenditure of many million pounds sterling, at a loss of 30% on the whole amount. Now I insist that it is very absurd to suppose the Hon. Secretary of War is going to dispose of all the funds arising from the Erlanger Loan without making any provision for these supplies, although most of them were ordered six months ago. On the contrary I have entire confidence that special drafts on the Loan will be sent forward and will be here long before the goods are ready for shipment. In the meantime Major Ferguson could go on placing his orders in course of execution at once, and there would be no more delay in obtaining these supplies than if Major Huse was to make this contract.

Sixth. According to Major Huse's own statement to me he has been obtaining heretofore very large supplies on credit from Messrs. Isaac, Campbell & Co., on which he has assured me they only charged cost and 2½% commission. Then why pay now 30%? Is the credit of our Government not quite as good as heretofore? On the contrary, does it not stand higher than it ever did before?

Seventh. Major Huse informed me, about the 25th of April last, that he had just written him fully as to the condition of Government business here and the conflict of orders, and the necessity of definite orders from the Department. I informed him that I would in a few days pursue the same course and give the Department my views fully on the subject. This I did on the 3rd May, and these letters being of such a character as to insure immediate replies, we may reasonably expect such definite advices within two or three weeks as will leave all the Government agents here without any doubt as to the wishes of the Department. It, therefore, in my opinion, betrays, to say the least of it, indecent haste in Major Huse to insist upon closing this large contract on the eve of advices from home which, in my opinion, will take from him even the show of authority which he now professes to have, but which I deny that he does possess, because it would be in direct violation of the orders from the Honorable Secretary of War.[97]

[97] Ibid., pp. 628–30.

On 10 July Crenshaw, writing to Seddon, pressed the matter still further:

I cannot expect to keep the matter open longer. If by those mails [27th July and 4th August] satisfactory letters are received, and the control is taken out of Major Huse's hands and placed in the hands of someone who will look singly to the interests of our Government, there will be no difficulty in sending forward as rapidly as need be all of the supplies that are wanting under the contract with Collie and myself at a commission of 2½% as I am assured that there remains of the Loan subject to Treasury drafts about £1,400,000 sterling, or 7,000,000 dollars, with which if properly we can meet all of our wants until cotton comes out in abundance. If on the contrary no letters are received from you by either of these mails, or they continue to retain the control in Major Huse's hands, this contract will be carried out to the loss of many millions of dollars to our people and Government. In this latter event my contract will not be needed, and I shall immediately close it up and dispose of the three steamers now building and return home.[98]

Such disputes did nothing to aid the Confederate cause, but, again, all the complaints against Huse came to nothing, and he was allowed to continue with his purchasing activities until the end of the war. He was often heavily criticized; nevertheless, he was the most resourceful and energetic of all the Confederate agents abroad.

As 1863 drew toward its close, Confederate needs were both varied and extensive. On 10 August an urgent request was sent to Huse for 10,000 pounds of strong hemp twine "for fixing field ammunition," [99] and as the winter approached, the need for woollen goods, blankets, and coal grew.[100]

Lead continued in great demand. On 9 October 1863 Mallet reported to Gorgas that a shipment of lead ordered from Europe had arrived just in time to prevent a general suspension of work on small-arms cartridges.[101] In the autumn of 1863, however, supplies of saltpeter were slightly easier, and between 1 November 1863 and 8 December 1864, 1,933,000 pounds came into Wilmington and Charleston, while during the same period 1,507,000 pounds of lead reached the Confederacy.[102]

By winter 1863, the people of the South were in desperate straits for food and clothes and almost all the necessities of life. John Beauchamp Jones, writing in his now-famous diary on 14 November

[98] Ibid., pp. 623–25.

[99] Vandiver, *Blockade-Running*, p. 41. The size of the twine was 6 to 8 inches in diameter.

[100] Ibid., p. 43. [101] Ibid., Introduction, pp. xxxi-ii.

[102] *O.R.*, ser. 4, 3:930.

1863, noted: "My family had a fine dinner today—the only one for months. As for clothes, we are as shabby as Italian lazzaronis—with no prospect whatever of replenished wardrobe, unless some European power will come and take us, as the French have done Mexico." [103] At the beginning of 1864 he wrote: "I am reminded daily of the privations I used to read of in the Revolutionary War. Then thorns were used, now we use pins, for buttons. My waistbands of pantaloons and drawers are pinned instead of buttoned." [104]

Huse and the other agents filled the secondary needs of the soldiers and civilians as best they could, but naturally they were preeminently concerned with ordnance. Nevertheless, during Huse's first twenty months of operations, he was able to import 170,724 pairs of socks. And in a lesser period of ten months from the beginning of the war, he sent 78,520 yards of cloth, 17,894 yards of flannel, 8,675 greatcoats, 8,250 pairs of trousers, 6,703 shirts, and 97 packages of trimmings.[105] By autumn 1863 he had shipped another 13,750 pairs of trousers and 14,250 more greatcoats.[106] Between 1 November 1863 and 8 December 1864, 316,000 blankets reached Confederate ports,[107] but in spite of all the agents could do, soldiers and civilians alike were very often half-starved and only half-clad.

At the end of 1863 greater supplies of meat were urgently required. Between 1 November 1863 and 8 December 1864, 8,632,000 pounds of meat entered the ports of Wilmington and Charleston on government account.[108] Yet these supplies were never sufficient,

[103] Jones, *War Diary*, 2:98. [104] Ibid., p. 125. [105] *O.R.*, ser. 4, 2:383.

[106] From 25 Oct. to 7 Dec. 1864, there arrived at the ports of Wilmington and Charleston 48 bales of cloth, 62 bales of shirts, 47 bales of flannel, 1 case of spool cloth, 7 cases of silk, 2 bales of canvas, 7 cases of woolens, 1 cask of buckles, and 9 cases of buttons (ibid., 3:955–58). The quantity bought by private merchants must have been a great deal more.

[107] An incomplete record shows that at least 380,000 blankets were shipped through the blockade, but there were probably more (ibid., 3:930, 2:383).

[108] Ibid., 3:930. Shipments of cotton to Great Britain from 1 Mar. 1864, used to pay for purchases, were as follows:

Niter and Mining Bureau	873 bales
Medical Department	328 bales
Engineer's Department	57 bales
Commissary Department	1,248 bales
Quartermaster's Dept.	1,829 bales
Ordnance Department	1,776 bales
Total for War Dept.	6,111 bales
Navy Department	4,861 bales
Treasury Department	16,327 bales
Total	27,299 bales

A bale would sell at £40 average or £1,091,960 total (ibid.).

and the need for importation continued after the end of the war.[109]

In autumn of 1863 McRae became chief purchasing agent, and as the months went by most of the friction between the agents disappeared, Confederate credit slowly improved, and large contracts were placed.[110] For example, in July 1864 McRae was able to report to Seddon that he had completed a contract with Alexander Collie and Company for the shipping of £150,000 of clothing and quartermaster's stores and £50,000 worth of medical supplies.[111] Since 19 February 1864 McRae had disbursed a total of £98,000 for supplies.[112] In August the *Times* commented, "Now is the time for those liking to run the risk of blockade-breaking, a trade which is now particularly brisk, as you will see by the late return of steamers at Wilmington." [113]

During 1864 determined efforts were made to alleviate the "secondary" shortages from which the South suffered. In September 1864 Maj. J. B. Ferguson was instructed: "Purchase woollen cloths, or flannels or felt hats in lieu of socks, as we can manufacture the latter from cotton yarn. A cheap and serviceable felt hat would be very acceptable to the army. Also wanted, best quality of blankets, and grey cloths, with a fair proportion of trimmings." On the same date another agent, Maj. R. P. Waller, was instructed to report on what terms he could import "leather of the best quality, harness,

[109] Congress was concerned over this matter and committees were investigating to determine what was to be done and how it was that Lee's army was almost without bread and fruit and without meat. Gorgas was convinced that General Northrop, the commissary general, was responsible. "He is not the man for the place, which requires plain practical sense and just the sort of sense that Northrop has not" (ibid., p. 163; *Times*, 8 Feb. 1864).

[110] Owsley, *King Cotton Diplomacy*, pp. 409–10; Thompson, pp. 126–27. McRae used to the best advantage the principles of good management. His operational techniques, unity of command, delegation of authority, and logical assignment steadily perfected Confederate finance and purchasing abroad.

[111] *O.R.*, ser. 4, 3:526.

[112] Ibid. He paid W. G. Crenshaw £40,000, Major Ferguson £35,000, and Maj. R. P. Waller, £20,000. An additional draft to Major Walker was made for £3,000 to purchase machinery for shoe manufacturing equipment. To make these payments he had to sell stock of the Erlanger loan, sometimes as low as 42. McRae did not consider the Collie contract as being favorable to the government (ibid.). On the same date McRae informed Seddon that private contracts (with Fraser, Trenholm, J. K. Gilliat, and the like) be annulled or that the government buy out the interest of the parties concerned and that for the future the government should trade on its own account (ibid., p. 528).

[113] 27 Aug. 1864; *Liverpool Mercury*, 16 Feb. 1864. For the loss of blockade-runners, see the *Shipping and Mercantile Gazette*, 17 Feb. 1864; *Times*, 16 Mar., 28 Mar. 1864.

upper and sole."[114] Shoes for the army remained an ever-present problem.

Niter was also in steady demand and in September 1864 Seddon estimated that for the first six months of 1865, the Confederates would require $12.5 million worth of niter, iron, lead, copper, and other metals to keep the armament factories supplied.[115]

Despite McRae's powers of organization, the food situation became graver toward the end of the year. In October 1864 it was reported: "With the whole Confederacy completely exhausted of supplies we have only meat rations for 300,000 men for twenty-five days. The condition of the commissariat is well described by Major French as 'alarming.' And supply must come from abroad if it is to be got at all. Meat is a bulky article and will not pay, and hence blockade-runners will not bring it."[116]

The next month the situation was even worse: "If the army is to be up to its present numbers, it will require at full rations 81,000,000 pounds of meat. Of this, a very large part must come from abroad and much of it, of necessity, and in common prudence is wanted instantly."[117]

Records of blockade-runners' cargoes are fragmentary, but a complete record of all goods received at Wilmington during the six weeks from 25 October to 6 December 1864 has been preserved and gives some idea of the rate of importation at that period. On 31 October 1864 the *Hope* arrived from Nassau with stores for the navy, including 18 cases, or casks, of steel; 8 pieces of lignum vitae; 1 case of glue; 26 cases, casks, kegs, and bags of chemicals; a bottle of quicksilver; 10 cases of hose; 64 coils of rope; 3 trusses of twine; 2 cases of belting; 2 bales of canvas; 3 bales of sole leather; 46 cases

[114] *O.R.*, ser. 4, 3:674, 675.

[115] Ibid., p. 779. The following is the breakdown of the funds:

Niter	2,500,000 dollars
Iron, cast and rolled	6,500,000 dollars
Lead	1,700,000 dollars
Copper	1,300,000 dollars
Other metals	500,000 dollars
	12,500,000 dollars

From 1 Jan. 1863 to 1 Jan. 1865, the Niter and Mining Bureau imported and received 1,909,800 pounds of lead. This was 39.8% of the total supply of the Confederacy. Up to Feb. 1863, Huse sent 10,000 pounds of sheet copper. Approximately 4% of the total supply of copper was shipped by Huse. There was a great deficiency of iron (ibid., 3:990, 2:383, 291). Iron plates and boiler iron were imported to the Confederacy throughout the war (*O.R.N.*, ser. 2, 3:552).

[116] *O.R.*, ser. 4, 3:738–39. [117] Ibid., p. 784.

and casks of tools, screws, and zinc; 5 bundles of iron; 20 barrels of oil; and 10 barrels of alcohol. The *Hope* also carried, on behalf of the Ordnance Department, 15 cases of machinery, 15 cases of castings, 200 grate bars, 6 bearers, 1 boiler, 1 cask steam chest. For the engineers the *Hope* carried a pick, for the quartermaster 23 bales of blankets and one case of samples, for the Niter and Mining Bureau 11 cases of steel as well as one or two private commissions.

On the same date the *Little Hattie* arrived at Wilmington carrying 213 sacks of saltpeter for the Niter and Mining Bureau. The *Beatrice* also docked at Wilmington on 31 October 1864. Included in her supplies were 143 grate bars for Ordnance; 10 bales of hosiery for the quartermaster, together with 3 cases of bunting; 1 bale of belting; 1 case of screws; 1 case of millpicks; 1 case of wire cloth and files; 4 cases of boots; 50 barrels of general provisions; 105 barrels of beans; and 1 lifeboat for the Navy Department.

On 8 November 1864 the *Talisman* arrived from Bermuda with 222 cases of rifles; two days earlier the *Armstrong* had arrived from Nassau with 399 barrels and 70 tierces of beef, 70 coils of wire, and 1 lifeboat for the Navy Department. The *Armstrong* also carried 8 bundles of vices, and 23 barrels, 6 cases, and 1 cask of hardware for the quartermaster.

The *Banshee* arrived from Nassau on 8 November carrying 23 cases of rifles and 1 lifeboat for the Ordnance Department. For another department, unstated, she also carried 340 boxes of soap; 904 barrels of provisions; 97 bags, 11 tierces and 32 barrels of coffee; and 14 cases of shoes.

On 5 November the *A. E. Fry* arrived with 173 boxes of bacon and 126 tierces of beef, together with some goods for a private account. The *Little Hattie* had apparently turned round quickly because, on 24 November she is again reported at Wilmington from Nassau with 15 barrels and 10 cases of hardware, 7 bundles of vices, 18 bellows, and 13 anvils on the account of the quartermaster; 43 barrels of alcohol and 50 boxes of tin plate for medical supplies; 8 cases of stationery for the Bureau of Construction; and 3 casks of copper, 4 barrels of tallow, 1 box of tools, and 1 demijohn of varnish for the navy.

On 21 November the *Old Dominion* brought 210 barrels of pork, and on 29 November the *Emma Henry* brought 130 sacks of saltpeter and 50 cases of shoes for the Niter and Mining Bureau, 58 "packages" for the navy and 18 "packages" for General Whiting. The *Vulture* arrived on 30 November 1864 with 15 cases of rifles and 15 cases of carbines. During the month several other ships had arrived with supplies for private accounts.

On 1 December 1864 the *Ella* arrived with miscellaneous supplies: 1 case of bismuth, 147 barrels of pork, 40 tierces of beef, 30 packages of horseshoe nails, 1 lifeboat, 225 sacks of coffee, 1 case of spool cotton, and 23 cases of Enfield rifles.

On the same date the *Owl* arrived from Bermuda via Nassau with 220 cases of shoes, 34 bales of cloth, 60 bales of shirts, 161 bales of blankets, 21 bales of flannel, and 2 bales of hosiery. The *Virginia*, arriving on the same date, brought 275 boxes of meat, 76 casks of bacon, 500 bundles of iron ties, and 30 bales of bagging.

On 2 December the *Wild Rover* arrived from Bermuda via Nassau with 5 cases of thread, 1 cask of buckles, 9 cases of buttons, 150 packages of lead, 2 puncheons, 1 hogshead of shoes, 117 cases of bacon, 150 barrels of port, 7 casks of bridles, and 5 cases of electrostalls.

On 4 December the *Stag* arrived from England via Bermuda with a variety of unspecified cases and drums for the navy and Quartermaster's Department, together with 75 cases of boots, 7 cases of woollens, 30 cases of rifles, 130 sacks of saltpeter, 5 tons of pig iron, and 10 cases of blankets. On 4 December the *Hansa* also arrived from England with 52 bales of blankets, 3 bales of cloth, 26 bales of flannel, 70 cases of boots, 7 cases of stationery, 9 bales of paper, 7 cases of silk, 26 cases of ammunition paper, and 9 bales of ammunition.

The *Carolina* had arrived from Bermuda two days earlier with 2 cases of general merchandise, 5 bundles of sheet iron, 18 casks of copper, 4 bundles of copper bolts, 8 casks of tin, 7 casks of pig lead, 8 casks of saltpeter, 7 cases of zinc, 6 casks of metal, 10 rolls of lead, 10 bales of blankets, and 100 bundles of iron ties.

Supplies into the port of Charleston were much lighter but included the cargo of the *Fox*, which docked on 4 November with 1 cask of rasps, 35 kegs of horseshoes, 10 kegs of horseshoe nails, 2 casks of spades, 75 cases of shoes, 100 tierces of beef, and 6 bales of baggage. On 5 November the *Julia* arrived at Charleston from Nassau with 2 bales of shirts, 25 bales of blankets, 11 bales of cloth, 2 bales of caps, 1 case of thread, 40 cases of shoes, 1 box of books, 2 packages of samples, 1 case of adhesive plaster, and 1 package of sample paper.

The next ship to arrive, on 22 November, was the *Syren* from Nassau with 30 kegs of horseshoe nails, 1 case of bismuth, 67 barrels of alcohol, 60 boxes of tin plate, 5 carboys of acid, 1 box of acid, 3 casks of copper, and 7 cases of stationery. On 29 November the *Beatrice* docked with 71 barrels of beef, 50 barrels of pork, 24 cases of steel shot, 200 bundles of iron ties, 5 barrels of alcohol, 3 casks and 4 cases of axes. The *Druid* called at Charleston on 1 December 1864 with 50 barrels of beef, and on the same date the *Kate Gregg* arrived from Nassau with 130 barrels of beef and 60 barrels of pork.[118]

On 10 December 1864 Seddon reported to the president that a total of 27,299 bales of cotton had been shipped from the Confederacy to pay for such supplies.[119] Allowing £40 per bale, these shipments represented some £1,091,960.[120] He also reported the following total importations into the Confederacy since 1 November 1863: 669 packages of leather, 12,546 pigs of lead, 54 casks of lead, 9,699 packages of saltpeter, 97 packages of revolvers, 3,172 packages of boots and shoes, 3,243 bales of blankets, 21,279 packages of meat, 3,146 cases of rifles, 2,993 packages of coffee, 43 cannon, 1,476 packages of copper, 134 cases of swords, 920 coils of rope, and 2,639 packages of medicines.[121] Seddon concluded by assuring the president that the number of vessels engaged in running the blockade was steadily increasing.[122]

A communication from Mallory to Bulloch dated 17 December 1864 is of interest because it shows the Confederacy's need for supplies for the offices of the Navy Department. After mentioning that stationery supplies previously sent by Bulloch in the *Bat* were lost when this blockade-runner was sunk, Mallory goes on to ask for 25 reams of letter paper, 10 reams of foolscap paper, 10 reams of notepaper, 25,000 official envelopes, 10,000 letter envelopes, 20 record books, 50 press copybooks, 1 dozen four-bladed penknives, 1 gross of erasers, 6 gross of best lead pencils, 20 dozen best steel pens (assorted), 1 dozen best gold pens, 1 dozen best-style inkstands, 20 gallons of best recording ink, 20 gallons of best copying ink, 1 dozen bottles of carmine, 1 gross of red tapes, and 2 dozen blue and red bolt tapes.[123]

By the end of 1864 blockade-running and the receipt of supplies at Confederate ports had probably reached their highest point. But the demands of the army in the field, now on the defensive on all fronts, and the tremendous losses of armaments and equipment meant that the needs of the Confederacy were considerably greater than they had been before McRae had taken over. However hard he and his agents labored, they could not keep up with demand.

118 *O.R.N.*, ser. 2, 3:755–58, 784–85.

119 *O.R.*, ser. 4, 3:930.

120 Or $5,296,006. Ibid., pp. 953–55.

121 Ibid., p. 930.

122 Ibid., pp. 928–29, 931–32; ibid., p. 935. The number of vessels that arrived at two ports of the Confederacy between 1 Nov. and 6 Dec. was 43, averaging more than one per day (ibid., p. 952).

123 *O.R.N.*, ser. 2, 2:782.

On 25 October 1864 Robert Kean wrote in his diary: "Our troops in Lee's army are barefooted,"[124] although Alexander R. Lawton, the quartermaster general, countered this by stating, on 27 January 1865, that "with the exception of greatcoats and flannel underwear the army had been fully provided."[125] He went on to state that toward the end of 1864, 104,199 jackets, 104,578 pairs of trousers, and 167,862 pairs of shoes had been issued for Lee's army; 45,421 jackets, 102,864 pairs of trousers, and 102,558 pairs of shoes had been supplied to the Army of Tennessee.[126]

The magnitude of blockade-running operations during the last months of the war—and the enormous needs of the Confederacy—may be judged from the following figures. Between 26 October 1864 and January 1865, 8,632,000 pounds of meat, 1,507,000 pounds of lead, 1,933,000 pounds of saltpeter, 546,000 pairs of shoes, 316,000 pairs of blankets, 500,000 pounds of coffee, and 69,000 rifles were received at Wilmington.[127]

A few weeks afterwards, Wilmington fell to the Federals. With great resource the Confederates turned their attention to the building and buying of shallow-draft vessels that could land material at inlets and creeks.[128] But it was too late. The war was lost, and McRae and his agents had no alternative but to suspend their purchases, settle matters as best they could, and decide whether to return to the United States or to remain in Europe as exiles.[129]

[124] Eaton, pp. 137–39. Jones, *War Diary*, 2:374–75.

[125] See Jones, *War Diary*, 2:280, 354.

[126] *O.R.*, ser. 4, 3:1039–41.

[127] Turner, p. 148. For an analysis of Confederate supply management, see Richard D. Goff, *Confederate Supply* (Durham, N.C.: Duke University Press, 1969).

[128] *O.R.N.*, ser. 2, 2:864–66. The draft of these vessels was not to exceed 6 feet (ibid.).

[129] The *Birkenhead and Cheshire Advertiser* (2 June 1865) claimed that merchants and manufacturers who have become used to a thriving blockade-running business "must now look for less profits and less money." For other postwar comments, see ibid., 3 June, 10 June 1865; *Liverpool Mercury*, 2 June 1863; *Liverpool Courier*, 2 June 1865.

CONCLUSION

THE PURPOSE of this work has been to sharpen the focus of the history of Confederate finance and purchasing experience in Great Britain. In retrospect, there is some evidence to support the thesis that the Confederate leaders misjudged when they decided, in 1861–62, to support the doctrine of King Cotton and to rely on its power to coerce Great Britain to support the Confederacy both economically and politically. Underlying this policy was the belief that Great Britain must have Southern cotton or face a serious economic crisis. The assumption was not unreasonable, for about a fourth of the population of Great Britain depended on cotton to provide its daily bread. The first blow to Southern interests in Great Britain came almost as soon as this policy had been determined. As Owsley and other eminent scholars of this subject have rightly concluded, surplus stocks of cotton on hand in England in 1861 postponed a shortage of cotton in Great Britain until 1862.

Nevertheless, by August 1862 England was in the grip of the cotton scarcity: two million workers and their families were on charity. At this time it looked as though the Confederate policy might succeed. Intervention was discussed in the British cabinet, but nothing came of the proposal, and when the winter of 1862 had passed without positive action, Confederate hopes for the full and open commercial support of Great Britain were doomed.

Competent economic historians have suggested—and the research for this book supports their general conclusions—that four explanations can be given for the failure of the Confederates to gain the economic and political support of Great Britain during the Civil War. The first places Britain's nonintervention on an idealistic basis: the sympathy of the common man, even when reduced to poverty, to look upon the American union as a great experiment in democracy and the North as a champion against slavery. The second, less idealistic, explanation places King Wheat above King Cotton. This school of thought has suggested that if Great Britain could not afford to be without cotton, it could afford still less to be without bread. England, so the argument ran, would starve if it did not import Union wheat.

It is probable that both these factors played some part in determining the attitude of the British government toward assisting the Confederacy. But, in themselves, these were inadequate reasons for nonintervention. Nor is there any real evidence that a wheat famine was likely to come upon Great Britain if it declared war on the United States; ample supplies were available in eastern Europe should North American supplies fail.

The third and fourth reasons advanced by historians for British nonintervention, which are more directly related to this study, are more convincing: the American Civil War was profitable for the merchants of Great Britain, and a considerable number of them looked with favor on the war as a means of impoverishing an upstart nation which, before 1860, was already threatening to become a competitor of the British Empire. It was also hoped that the war would be long and exhausting and would result in the permanent division of the United States. On the issue of profits, as this study indicates, not only were the federal and Confederate governments ready purchasers of all types of military equipment and war material, but there were many in Britain who had invested heavily in anticipation of scarcity and consequent high prices.

In effect, this work has been mainly concerned with what might be classified as secondary diplomacy—the quest, led by Confederate officials, for commercial privileges in Great Britain when the hope for direct intervention all but vanished.

The Davis administration has been frequently criticized for making a major blunder in King Cotton. It is true that in the light of later events, the Confederate government can be accused of provincialism, of a lack of knowledge of the new economic structure of Great Britain; but it is also permissible to ask what policy the Confederacy could have pursued with greater likelihood of success.

The position of the Confederacy in the war was somewhat similar to that of the American colonies during the Revolution. The Southerners, fighting for independence on home soil, could not win simply by a series of defensive actions against Northern attacks. One of the principal reasons for the American victory in the Revolutionary War was the assistance supplied by France. Similarly, to defeat the North, the Confederate States had to secure full European military and commercial support, especially that of Great Britain. This was not forthcoming.

The research for this work indicates that the Confederate government committed an error by using its available sterling exchange and coin at the outset of the war in order to support its finance and purchasing activities. As later events clearly showed, these valuable assets should have been held in reserve, and cotton should have been sent to Britain to purchase essential war supplies. As this book has attempted to point up, the weakness of Confederate finance in Great Britain was, as elsewhere, its reliance on fiat money and its futile funding operation by means of unsecured bonds. This error of policy eventually destroyed Confederate finance in Britain. Constant tinkering with Confederate financial legislation and shifts in British financial policy indicate how vital the matter was to the Confederate leadership. Yet much more still remains to be learned about Southern credit and foreign financial policy and its rationale when considered against the background of the European money market.

The importance of sea power is also evident in this work. If the Confederacy, instead of the United States, had been able to exercise command over the sea, the whole course of the war might have been altered. In this connection it is possible to argue that a really strong navy that could have broken the federal blockade, together with realistic measures to raise funds by taxation, could have saved the Confederacy. However, this work clearly illustrates the almost complete poverty of Southern resources, both natural and manufactured. Virtually everything the Confederacy required had to be imported, and it seems probable that the South was doomed from the outset by its industrial weaknesses. These could not have been entirely overcome even if the blockade had been successfully broken. The United States already possessed a navy at the beginning of the war, whereas the Confederates had to build up their sea power almost from nothing.

Thus, the Confederates were forced to attempt to purchase ships suitable for use as cruisers that could destroy the enemy's merchant marine. These ships had to be suitable in structure and general arrangement to carry the weight of a battery on deck, to berth a sufficient crew, and to be capable of long voyages. Further, as this work has attempted to point up, the Civil War stimulated the shipbuilding industry in Great Britain. All together, about 400 steamers, many of them iron, and 800 sailing vessels were sold as blockade-runners.

A key element to emerge from this study, is the fact that within the framework of British and international law of the period, it can be fairly said that the building of Confederate ships in Great Britain was a commercial venture. Able British lawyers advised Bulloch and other Confederate naval representatives that ships might be built for the South in British yards, provided that three points were observed: (1) the concealment of Confederate government ownership; (2) the concealment of destination; (3) a prohibition against the shipping of war equipment and the enlisting of a crew in British waters. Bulloch, who expertly coordinated and controlled Confederate naval activity in Britain, consistently observed these requirements. He always tried to dispatch ships as ordinary sailing vessels. The difficulties encountered by Confederate officials in Great Britain revealed that the United States consular agents had a well-organized and highly developed espionage system—an organization whose function was to prevent the shipment of goods and materials to the Confederacy. It says a great deal for the tact, integrity, and energies of Bulloch and all the other Confederate agents that so many ships got away and so much equipment and material were shipped to Southern ports. Although Confederate ships procured or constructed in Great Britain were too few to act with any effective aggressive power against the United States Navy, the commanders of the Confederate ships were able to inflict great injuries upon the merchant vessels of the North and to drive up the insurance rates to a prohibitive degree.

Although the Confederate Congress appropriated large sums for the navy (to be spent in Great Britain), the rate of exchange in the British money market always worked against the Confederates. Thus the Confederate navy was always smaller than Congress might have hoped, although Jefferson Davis was fairly consistent in his naval policy and clearly understood the need for ship construction in Great Britain. The war also provided opportunities for the British merchant fleet to make quick if hazardous profits. The lack of cotton for the Lancashire mills encouraged blockade-runners; the majority of these were English vessels.

Although this work attempts to fill in some gaps, especially as they relate to the technical aspects of the actual finance, procurement, and engineering of Confederate ships purchased in Great Britain, significant naval history on this subject remains to be written. This, unfortunately, is still largely a subject for novelists and popularizers. Further study needs to be done on naval ordnance, ship construction, and the ramifications of international law.

In the sphere of ordnance, the Confederate government was never able to equip its fighting forces adequately. The original stock of arms consisted almost wholly of smoothbore muskets, altered from flint to percussion. These disappeared almost entirely during the first two years of the war and were replaced by English rifled and percussion arms of a high quality. No official account was kept of the value of the Confederate government purchases in Great Britain, and records are discouragingly fragmentary and incomplete. This work has analyzed some statistical data in an attempt to record the quantity and value of articles that passed through the blockade, but it is difficult, in some instances, to give more than a reasoned estimate. About 1,350,000 bales of cotton were sent to Great Britain. In total, approximately 600,000 pieces of equipment were shipped to the Confederacy. These included small arms, cannon, munitions of all kinds, clothing, hospital stores, manufactured goods, and some luxuries. Goods entering the Confederate States from British ports can be valued at almost $200 million. Agents of the War Department alone spent more than $12,250,000 in Great Britain. Throughout the war munitions and supplies of all kinds poured into the North through Europe; in comparison the South was isolated and had acute difficulty in equipping and supplying its armed forces.

Several historians have expressed the belief that blockade-running hurt the Confederacy, but the research on which this book is based indicates that without it the Civil War would have been over in eighteen months. It has also been said that blockade-running prejudiced some European powers against the Confederacy. But in this work, the study of the purchasing agents and their mission in Great Britain demonstrates that they did nothing that was not justified by the rules of fair and honorable warfare, nothing contrary to British law as construed by British jurists and confirmed by the judgment of British courts.

Poorly organized and badly instructed by their superiors (especially during the first thirty months of the war), inexperienced, sometimes guilty of serious errors of judgment, prone to disputes caused by vague orders from senior officers who knew little of the circumstances under which they were working, almost always short of funds, harried by federal spies—in spite of all these handicaps, this small body of men, the purchasing agents of a government unrecogized by Great Britain, made it possible for the Confederates to sustain a war lasting over four years. Faced with so many almost crippling difficulties, it is a tribute to their initiative, skill, and energy that they accomplished so much with so little.

Appendixes
Selected Bibliography
Index

APPENDIX I

ERLANGER BANKING HISTORY

Raphael von Erlanger (Banker) Frankfurt	Before
von Erlanger & Sohne, Frankfurt	1859 (?)
Emile Erlanger & Co., founded in Paris	1859
Emile Erlanger & Co., established in London	1870
Name changed to Erlangers Ltd.	1928

Source: Interview with D. S. Ramsey, Manager, Erlangers Ltd., 10 July 1958

APPENDIX II

ERLANGER LOAN QUOTATIONS

The money market as defined by British standards is an "organisation of credit" by which capital is transferred by A, who does not want it, to B, who does want it. It is a vast borrowing machinery, composed of many links, and a vast number of persons give a surprising trust to one another.

The following are money market figures for the Erlanger loan:

Quotations			*Source*
1	Oct.	27½–26½	*Index*, 1 Oct. 1863
8	Oct.	68–70	*Index*, 8 Oct. 1863

(The last instalment of 15% having been paid, the stock was quoted at its actual money value, instead of, as before, at a discount or premium on the subscription price.)

15	Oct.	63–65	*Index*, 15 Oct. 1863
22	Oct.	66–67	*Index*, 22 Oct. 1863
29	Oct.	64–66	*Index*, 29 Oct. 1863
4	Nov.	66–67	Emile Erlanger to John Slidell, 4 Nov. 1863, Erlanger Papers
5	Nov.	65–66	*Index*, 5 Nov. 1863
12	Nov.	62–64	*Index*, 12 Nov. 1863
19	Nov.	57–59	*Index*, 19 Nov. 1863
26	Nov.	56–58	*Index*, 26 Nov. 1863
3	Dec.	50–52	*Index*, 3 Dec. 1863
10	Dec.	28–40	*Index*, 10 Dec. 1863
11	Dec.	35–40	*Adams Letters*, 2:109
17	Dec.	35–37	*Index*, 17 Dec. 1863
24	Dec.	38–40	*Index*, 24 Dec. 1863
31	Dec.	37–39	*Index*, 31 Dec. 1863
1	Jan.	37–39	*Times*, 1 Jan. 1864
7	Jan.	38–40	*Index*, 7 Jan. 1864
14	Jan.	38–40	*Times*, 14 Jan. 1864
14	Jan.	38–40	*Index*, 17 Jan. 1864
15	Jan.	44–46	*Times*, 15 Jan. 1864
21	Jan.	44–48	*Index*, 21 Jan. 1864

(The formation of several blockade-running companies to bring out cotton under the loan gave an additional impetus to dealings [*Times*, 24 Jan. 1864].)

27 Jan. 48–50 *Times*, 27 Jan. 1864
28 Jan. 49–50 *Index*, 28 Jan. 1864
4 Feb. 46–48 *Index*, 4 Feb. 1864
11 Feb. 50–51 *Index*, 11 Feb. 1864

(Up to 15 Feb. 1864 £ 150,000 in bonds had been converted into cotton [*Times*, 15 Feb. 1864].)

18 Feb. 55–56 *Index*, 18 Feb. 1864

(Emile Erlanger sends Slidell cotton prices (Emile Erlanger to John Slidell, 22 Feb. 1864 [Erlanger Papers].)

25 Feb. 52–54 *Index*, 25 Feb. 1864

(During March the market continued to rule easy at 6% [*Times*, 31 March 1864].)

3 Mar. 43–45 *Index*, 3 Mar. 1864
10 Mar. 43–45 *Index*, 10 Mar. 1864

(Benjamin declared on 15 March 1864, "Our finances are in rapid progress of improvement" [Richardson, 2:630].)

17 Mar. 50½–51½ *Index*, 17 Mar. 1864
24 Mar. 51–53 *Index*, 24 Mar. 1864
31 Mar. 54–55 *Index*, 31 Mar. 1864

(James M. Drake & Co., stock and bond brokers, 23 William Street, London, listed other Confederate stock quotations as: Tennessee, 61–62; North Carolina, 58½–59½; Missouri, 72½–72¾ [*Times* 31 Mar. 1864].)

7 Apr. 52–53 *Index*, 7 Apr. 1864
14 Apr. 53–55 *Index*, 14 Apr. 1864
21 Apr. 54½–55½ *Index*, 21 Apr. 1864
28 Apr. 57½–58½ *Index*, 28 Apr. 1864
5 May 65–67 *Index*, 5 May 1864
12 May 63–65 *Index*, 12 May 1864
19 May 66½–67½ *Index*, 19 May 1864
20 May 63–64 *Index*, 20 May 1864
2 June 64–66 *Index*, 2 June 1864
9 June 65–66 *Index*, 9 June 1864

(A quantity of forged Confederate bonds were put into circulation in England. They were sent from New York in order to depress the market [*Times*, 14 June 1864].)

16 June 64–66 *Index*, 16 June 1864
23 June 63–65 *Index*, 23 June 1864
30 June 62–64 *Index*, 30 June 1864

(Blockade-runners were intercepted on only one trip in six [*Times*, 1 July 1864].)

7 July 67–68 *Index*, 7 July 1864
14 July 73–75 *Index*, 14 July 1864
21 July 76–78 *Index*, 21 July 1864
28 July 75–77 *Index*, 28 July 1864

(The arrival at Liverpool of 1,500 bales of cotton from the Confederate States, the proceeds of which were to go toward the sinking fund for redeeming the bonds, strengthened the market [*TImes*, 28 July 1864].)

4 Aug. 75–76 *Index*, 4 Aug. 1864
5 Aug. 75–77 *Times*, 5 Aug. 1864
11 Aug. 75½–74½ *Index*, 11 Aug. 1864
18 Aug. 78½–79 *Index*, 18 Aug. 1864

(Under continued good accounts from the Confederate States, the value of the security improved [*Index*, 18 Aug. 1864].)

23 Aug. 76–78 *Times*, 23 Aug. 1864
25 Aug. 78–80 *Index*, 25 Aug. 1864

(Rumors of a probability of peace negotiations strengthened the market [*Index*, 25 Aug. 1864].)

1 Sept. 75–76 *Index*, 1 Sept. 1864

(By 2 Sept. nearly a sixth of the entire loan, £ 23,000,000, had been redeemed [*Times*, 2 Sept. 1864].)

(The total cotton sales for August were only 160,000 bales. The market for cotton was rather inactive [*Times*, 2 Sept. 1864].)

7 Sept. 79–81 *Times*, 7 Sept. 1864
8 Sept. 74–76 *Index*, 8 Sept. 1864
12 Sept. 84½–85 *Times*, 12 Sept. 1864

(The amount of cotton bonds converted by Slidell up to 31 Aug. was £ 340,800 [Richardson, 2:671].)

15 Sept. 83–84 *Index*, 15 Sept. 1864
22 Sept. 73–74 *Index*, 22 Sept. 1864
24 Sept. 68–70 *Times*, 24 Sept. 1864
29 Sept. 68–70 *Index*, 29 Sept. 1864

(The cotton loan had fallen 20% from its high estate [*Adams Letters*, 2:200].)

6 Oct. 63½–63½ *Index*, 6 Oct. 1864
13 Oct. 53–55 *Index*, 13 Oct. 1864
17 Oct. 62–64 *Times*, 17 Oct. 1864
18 Oct. 63–64 *Times*, 18 Oct. 1864
20 Oct. 64–66 *Index*, 20 Oct. 1864
27 Oct. 62–63 *Index*, 27 Oct. 1864
3 Nov. 59–60 *Index*, 3 Nov. 1864

(The annual interest of the Federal public debt was, at the end of October, $81,778,143. In London no Union money was borrowed at less than 6% [*Times*, 11 Nov. 1864; see also Ibid., 16 Nov. 1864].)

10 Nov. 60–61 *Index*, 10 Nov. 1864
17 Nov. 63–64 *Index*, 17 Nov. 1864
24 Nov. 61–63 *Index*, 24 Nov. 1864

1 Dec.	59–61	*Index*, 1 Dec. 1864
8 Dec.	57–59	*Index*, 8 Dec. 1864
15 Dec.	61–63	*Index*, 15 Dec. 1864

(Erlanger wrote to Slidell, "The Confederates are brave and I have confidence that they will win." Slidell had invested in bonds other than Confederate; in fact, he held some Northern bonds [20 Dec. 1864, Erlanger Papers].)

22 Dec.	61–63	*Index*, 22 Dec. 1864
29 Dec.	57–59	*Index*, 29 Dec. 1864
5 Jan.	54–56	*Index*, 5 Jan. 1865
12 Jan.	53–55	*Index*, 12 Jan. 1865
19 Jan.	56½–57½	*Index*, 19 Jan. 1865
26 Jan.	54–56	*Index*, 26 Jan. 1865
2 Feb.	54	Erlanger Papers, 2 Feb. 1865

(The money market was plentifully supplied and rates favored the borrower. [*Times*, 4 Feb. 1865].)

9 Feb.	54–56	*Index*, 9 Feb. 1865
10 Feb.	54½–55½	*Times*, 10 Feb. 1865
16 Feb.	57–59	*Index*, 16 Feb. 1865
21 Feb.	56–58	*Times*, 21 Feb. 1865
23 Feb.	54½–55½	*Index*, 23 Feb. 1865
2 Mar.	48–50	*Index*, 2 Mar. 1865

(The Bank of England lowered its rate of discount to 4½% [*Times*, 3 Mar. 1865].)

9 Mar.	37–39	*Index*, 9 Mar. 1865
16 Mar.	37–39	*Index*, 16 Mar. 1865
17 Mar.	36–38	*Times*, 17 Mar. 1865
23 Mar.	34½–35½	*Index*, 23 Mar. 1865
27 Mar.	35½–36½	*Times*, 27 Mar. 1865

(The Confederates still had funds in March 1865, and Fraser Trenholm & Company were paying their bills on time [*Times*, 27 Mar. 1865].)

30 Mar.	32–33	*Index*, 30 Mar. 1865

(On 31 Mar. 1865 Mason informed J. P. Benjamin that there was still hope of more English loans [*Times*, 31 Mar. 1865]. In New York money was easy and cotton was dull [*New York Commercial Intelligence*, 1 Apr. 1865]. Cotton varied from 50 to 53 cents a pound [*Times*, 1 Apr. 1865].)

6 Apr.	32–33	*Index*, 6 Apr. 1865
13 Apr.	30–31	*Index*, 13 Apr. 1865
19 Apr.	21–23	*Times*, 19 Apr. 1865
20 Apr.	18–20	*Times*, 20 Apr. 1865

(The loan was the chief event in the English market [*Times*, 20 Apr. 1865].)

20 Apr.	18–20	*Index*, 20 Apr. 1865
27 Apr.	14–16	*Index*, 27 Apr. 1865
4 May	11–13	*Index*, 4 May 1865
11 May	12½–13½	*Index*, 11 May 1865
18 May	9–11	*Index*, 18 May 1865
25 May	8–10	*Index*, 25 May 1865
1 June	7–9	*Index*, 1 June 1865
8 June	7–9	*Index*, 8 June 1865

(Holders of Confederate loan scrip can ask for no consideration at the hands of the Federal Government" [*Birkenhead and Cheshire Advertiser*, 10 June 1865].)

15 June	7–9	*Index*, 15 June 1865

APPENDIX III

MAJOR ERLANGER LOAN BONDHOLDERS

Name	Amount
Sir Henry de Houghton, Bart.	£180,000
Isaac Campbell & Co., of 71 Jermyn Street, London, army contractors	150,000
Thomas Sterling Begbie, 50 Mansion House Place, London, shipowner	140,000
The Marquis of Bath	50,000
James Spence, Liverpool	50,000
Beresford Hope	40,000
George Edward Seymour, stockbroker, Throgmorton Street, London	40,000
Messrs. Fernie	30,000
Alex. Collie & Partners	20,000
Fleetwood, Pattern, Wilson, L. Schuster, directors of Union Bank, London (together)	20,000
W. S. Lindsay	20,000
Sir Coutts Lindsay, Baronet	20,000
John Laird, M.P., Birkenhead	20,000
M. B. Sampson, city editor, *Times*	15,000
John Thaddeus Delane, editor, *Times*	10,000
Lady Georgiana Fane (sister of Lord Westmoreland)	15,000
J. S. Gilliat, director of Bank of England	10,000
D. Forbes Campbell, 45 Dover Street, Piccadilly, London	30,000
George Peacock, M.P.	5,000
Lord Wharncliffe	5,000
W. H. Gregory, M.P.	4,000
W. J. Rideout, proprietor, London *Morning Post*	4,000
Edward Akenroyd	1,500
Lord Campbell	1,000
Lord Donoughomore	1,000
Lord Richard Grosvenor	1,000
Hon. Evelyn Ashley, son of Lord Shaftesbury, and private secretary to Lord Palmerston	500
Right Hon. William Ewart Gladstone	2,000
	885,000

Source: John Brigelow, *Gladstone and the Confederate Loan of 1863* (New York: De Vinne Press, 1905), p. 8.

APPENDIX IV

THE QUEEN'S PROCLAMATION OF NEUTRALITY

By The Queen: A Proclamation whereas we, Victoria R. are happily at peace with all Sovereigns, Powers, and States:

And whereas hostilities have unhappily commenced between the Government of the United States of America and certain States styling themselves "The Confederate States of America":

And whereas we, being at peace with the Government of the United States, have declared our Royal determination to maintain a strict and impartial neutrality in the contest between the said contending parties:

We therefore have thought it fit, by and with the advice of our Privy Council to issue this, our Royal Proclamation and we do hereby strictly charge and command all our loving subjects so to observe a strict neutrality in and during the aforesaid hostilities, and so abstain from violating or contravening either the laws and statutes of the realm in this behalf, or the law of nations in relation thereto, as they will answer to the contrary at their peril.

And whereas in a certain Statute made and passed in the 59th year of His Majesty King George III, entitled "An Act to prevent the enlisting or engagement of His Majesty's Subjects to serve in a Foreign Service, and the Fitting out or equipping, in His Majesty's Dominions vessels for warlike purposes, without His Majesty's licence" it is, among other things, declared and enacted as follows:

"That if any natural-born subject of His Majesty, his heirs and successors, without the leave or licence of His Majesty, his heirs or successors, for that purpose first had obtained, under the sign manual of His Majesty, his heirs or successors or signified by order in Council, or by proclamation of His Majesty—his heirs or successors—accept any military commission or shall otherwise enter into the military service as a commissioned or non-commissioned officer or shall enlist or enter himself to enlist, or shall agree to enlist or to enter himself to serve as a soldier or to be employed or shall serve in any warlike or military operation, in the service of or for or under or in aid of any foreign Prince, State, Potentate, Colony, Province, or part of any province or people, or of any person or persons exercising power."

Given at Our Court at the White Lodge, Richmond Park this 13th day of May in the year of Our Lord 1861 and in the 24th year of Our reign.

God save the Queen.[1]

Source: Times, 15 May 1861.

[1] In the Queen's Proclamation of Neutrality an attempt was made to apply the British Foreign Enlistment Act to the American crisis. As a result, the British attitude toward the belligerents in the American Civil War was more clearly defined, and as the war progressed parliamentary discussion still further clarified the provisions of the proclamation. There were basic weaknesses in both the act and the proclamation. As an aid in detecting these weaknesses Bulloch secured the services of F. S. Hull, who was connected with a leading firm of solicitors in Liverpool, and who continued as Bulloch's legal adviser throughout the war. It was pointed out by Hull that the letter of the law might be evaded by securing the component parts of a naval expedition and having them assembled at some rendezvous beyond British dominions. English law, and the Proclamation of Neutrality, forbade the Confederate navy to contract for the construction of commerce-destroyers in British shipyards, but it was relatively easy to evade the prohibition by juggling the ownership papers, which Bulloch and others were so expert in doing. M. A. Bernard, *A Historical Account of the Neutrality of Great Britain during the American Civil War* (London: Longmans, Green, Reader & Dyer, 1870), p. 135; Edward Channing, *History of the United States* (New York: Macmillan, 1927), 6:348; Dunbar Rowland, *Jefferson Davis, Constitutionalist* (Jackson, Miss.: Mississippi Dept. of Archives and History), 5:63; Bulloch, 1:54.

APPENDIX V

DESCRIPTION OF THE *FLORIDA*

There are few descriptions of the *Florida*, and some of those which have been preserved are inaccurate, but contemporary pictures show her to be a three-masted bark-rigged vessel with 2 funnels.

She was of about 700 tons burden, built of wood by William C. Miller & Sons, and was described by acting master William P. Gibbs of the U.S. Navy as a "long, rakish vessel, long lower masts, bark-rigged which can be easily altered to a three-masted schooner by sending down the yards.[1] Bulloch described her as a "comely craft,"[2] and she certainly possessed considerable grace of line.

Her original designs were adapted from those of a British gunboat, but she was drawn out in the midship section and the floor was flattened to give her greater carrying capacity. The increased length thus admitted of finer entrance and clearance lines, which secured greater speed. Her rigging scale was also greatly increased, so as to give her a good spread of canvas, especially when close hauled or with the wind abeam.[3]

Her two engines were designed by Fawcett Preston & Co. and had a capacity of 100 h.p. each. A feature of her construction was that her propeller could be lifted clear of the water when it was intended she should proceed under sail alone.[4]

She was a speedy ship, and Gibbs stated she could steam and sail 14 knots 6 fathoms, consuming 10 tons of coal per day, with a crew of approximately 225 men, but on her maiden voyage Low reported an average steaming speed of 9½ knots, with an average sailing speed of 12 knots. In favorable conditions she could steam 10½ knots and under canvas alone, "with quartering wind, so that we could carry main topgallant studding sail, 13½ good." She drew about 13 feet of water.[5]

In March 1862 Bulloch advised Mallory that the armament intended for *Florida* would consist of one 7-inch rifled gun and one 68-pounder solid-shot gun on traversing carriages, and four 42-cwt 32-pounders in broadside. Benjamin Moran stated she had 8 rifled

[1] *O.R.N.*, ser. 1, 1:363, 3:109. [2] Bulloch, 1:155. [3] Ibid., 1:57–58.
[4] Ibid., 1:58; White, p. 48. [5] *O.R.N.*, ser. 1, 3:109, 1:757–58, 406.

cannons and 2 heavy pivot guns to rake fore and aft[6] but this information was inaccurate and premature, for on the date Moran wrote (5 March 1862) the *Florida* had not received her guns.

The exact cost of building the *Florida* is not known but Bolloch stated that the expenditure on her up to her arrival in Brest in September 1863 was £35,950.[7]

[6] Ibid., 1:753–55, 364.

[7] Bulloch, 2:275.

APPENDIX VI

DESCRIPTION OF THE *ALABAMA*

The *Alabama* was built by Laird Brothers of Birkenhead and was a three-masted bark-rigged, single-funneled vessel. The original Specification endorsed by William Laird, Jr., and James D. Bulloch shows that she was 210 ft. long with a beam of 32 ft., a depth of 17 ft. 3 ins., and a little more than 1023 tons. The rig was to be that of a bark, "long lower masts and good square sails." [1]

The building of the *Alabama* was attended by some difficulties, for by that time wood had almost gone out of use as a material for shipbuilding in Great Britain, and Lairds had considerable difficulty in obtaining suitable timber for the heavy scantling, such as the keelson and the sternpost. The building fell behind schedule because of the high standard of the Laird requirements; more than one sternpost was rejected after they had been partly fitted and bored to take the screw shaft, because of some defect.[2]

The single piece of timber finally used for the sternpost cost £100; altogether the *Alabama* was a costly vessel. Laird's diary shows her prime cost to have been estimated at £30,275, but the final costs were much greater, partly due to the overtime worked on her.[3] Strangely enough the pitchpine used in her construction probably came from Florida.

Without a doubt the *Alabama* was strongly built—her bulkheads were 3 inches thick, and she was a heavily constructed vessel for her length and beam, although she was given only three coats of paint [4] and should have had at least five.

Her sails, carried at will, were: fore; fore-topmast, staysail and jib; two large trysails; the usual square sails on fore and main masts, with the exception of the main course which was set flying; and gaff and topsails.[5]

She had two marine steam engines of 300 h.p., but this was a

[1] Specification of a Screw Steam Vessel and her Machinery, signed by William Laird Jnr. and James D. Bulloch, 1 Aug. 1861, Laird Papers.

[2] Bulloch, 1:60, 226.

[3] Laird Diary, p. 40, and Account Records of the *Alabama,* Laird Papers.

[4] Account Records of the *Alabama,* ibid.

[5] Bulloch, 1:61.

nominal rating and on her trial trip she achieved 1,000 h.p.[6] Semmes always maintained that the enemy overrated her speed and that ordinarily she was about a 10-knot ship, although at her trials she was said to have made 11½ knots and under both sail and steam Semmes once logged 13¼ knots.[7]

Her plans show her to be built on yacht lines[8]—she was a sister ship to H.M.S. *Greyhound*—and everyone who saw her testified to her grace. Bulloch thought her as fine a vessel "as could be turned out in any dockyard in the kingdom."[9] Dudley, writing to Adams, called her a splendid vessel.[10] Lieutenant Sinclair, who sailed in her for two years, describes her as "a perfect steamer and a perfect sailing vessel, each entirely independent of the other."[11] (Like the *Florida* the *Alabama*'s two-bladed screw could be hoisted into a propeller well so that when triced up it would be no impediment to her sail power.) Semmes said she was of the most perfect symmetry and that she sat on the water with the lightness and grace of a swan.[12]

The *Alabama* had 2 decks and included accommodation for a large crew, plenty of space for the ship's stores and provisions, water supplies and a considerable magazine. The engine and boiler space was surrounded by the coal bunkers. Aft of the machinery was a watertight collision-roof bulkhead and the engineers' and stewards' compartment, under which were stored the ammunition and shells. Aft again was the Captain's cabin with storage below for the ship's spirits, and next to this cabin was the gun room. On the upper deck was the sail room.[13] The inboard construction of the *Alabama* was quite usual, designed as she was for warlike purposes, to carry a large crew and plentiful supplies of coal (350 tons) and provisions. Attached to her engines was a device for condensing fresh water from sea water.[14]

She was admirably fitted out in accordance with the high quality

[6] Specification of a pair of Marine Steam Engines with Screw Propeller of 300 h.p., signed by William Laird Jnr. and James D. Bulloch, Laird Papers; Bulloch, 1:61.

[7] Semmes, pp. 402–3.

[8] Outline profile, water line including mast and spars, Birkenhead Ironworks, 4 Dec., 1861, Board of Customs and Excise Library, London.

[9] Bulloch, 1:61. [10] F.O. 5/1318, p. 281.

[11] Arthur Sinclair, *Two Years on the Alabama* (Boston: Gay & Bird Co., 1895) p. 7.

[12] Semmes, pp. 402–3.

[13] Constructional Profile of the Alabama and plan of the Lower Deck, Laird Papers.

[14] Semmes, pp. 402–3.

of her construction. She was provided with a double suit of sails and had 5 boats, including a launch, cutter, and a whaleboat, and she was also provided with ample ground tackle.[15] Bulloch planned that the *Alabama* should have a battery of one 7-inch 100-pounder rifled gun, Blakely pattern, 84-cwt; one 8-inch solid shot 68-pounder, smoothbore, 108-cwt; and six 6-inch 32-pounder guns of 55-cwt each.[16] Of the 2 pivot guns (the 7- and 8-inch guns) one was mounted on the forecastle and the other abaft the mainmast, but Semmes found that the Blakely was deficient in metal, compared with the weight of shot it threw, and it was of little use after the first few rounds.[17] Sinclair says it was intended to use all 8 guns in broadside, but in practice the battery was too heavy and in action one was omitted, being shifted from side to side as required.[18]

The final cost of the *Alabama*, including hull, spars, sails, boats, anchors, cables and all equipment was £47,028.[19] The battery cost £2,500, the magazine tanks £616, the ordnance stores £500, and the small arms £600.[20]

[15] Bulloch, 1:61. [16] *O.R.N.*, ser. 1, 2:235–39. [17] Semmes, p. 403.
[18] Sinclair, pp. 7–9. [19] Account Records of the *Alabama*, Laird Papers.
[20] *O.R.N.*, ser. 1, 1:783.

APPENDIX VII

DESCRIPTION OF THE *GEORGIA*

There are few records of the appearance of the *Georgia*, but she was built at Dumbarton, Scotland, and was originally commissioned as the *Japan*, a merchant vessel. Unlike her predecessors, the *Florida* and the *Alabama*, she was an iron screw steamer.[1]

The American Consul at Glasgow described her as a "screw-steamer—about 500 tons register, built by Denny Brothers, Dumbarton—clipper built—figure-head fiddle bow—short thick funnel—got a number of compartments forward on both sides from eight to ten feet square and stronger than a jail—strong doors to them with hinges about three inches thick and brass padlocked accordingly—a strong magazine forward in the bow." [2] In the advertisement of her sale, when the Confederates had decided to dispose of her, she was described as "a splendid screw steamer" of about 750 tons, engines of 200 h.p., with a speed of about 12-knots.[3] Scharf described her as a swift and powerful vessel for her class.[4]

The price for which the Confederates purchased the *Georgia* is unknown; however, she was sold by them for £15,000.[5] Her battery consisted of 5 Whitworth guns, two 100-pounders; two 24-pounders and one 32-pounder.[6]

[1] Bulloch, 2:261.

[2] F.O. 5/1317, p. 137. "Fiddle Bow." The same as "Clipper" and "Schooner" bows as applied to all ships of the period, sail and steam.

[3] F.O. 5/1317, *Georgia*, Copy of Advertisement.

[4] Scharf, pp. 803–4.

[5] *O.R.N.*, ser. 2, 2:663.

[6] Scharf, p. 803.

APPENDIX VIII

DESCRIPTION OF THE *RAPPAHANNOCK*

The *Rappahannock* was originally the H.M.S. *Victor*, a screw gunboat in the service of the British Navy. She was a three-masted two funneled vessel of good line and appearance.[1]

Her gross tonnage was 851 tons.[2] Built of wood at Blackwall in 1855, she did not, contrary to some reports, see service in the Crimea.[3] She was of shallow draft (about 11 feet), making her suitable for coastal work. She was originally designed as a peacetime cruiser or dispatch vessel, capable of attacking or defending herself against a small gunboat. Her length between the perpendiculars was 200 ft. and her extreme breadth was 30 ft. 2 ins. The depth in her hold was 14 ft. 6 ins.[4]

The *Rappahannock* was heavy in her timbers and had massive deck beams, giving her strength, but her lines also gave her speed.[5] Her general storage was in the forward flat, after which were the magazine and the coal bunkers on either side of the engine room. The boilers were forward of the engine room,[6] and her engines made 350 h.p.[7] A condenser for making fresh water from brine was attached to the boiler room.[8] For her size the *Rappahannock* could make a good deal of power, and she had speed—the capacity to "hit and run," rather than to carry large stores.[9] Widely deployed as were the Confederate forces, these features could be a disadvantage for long cruises. Her Captain, Lieutenant Fauntleroy, reported that she could stow only 150 tons of coal and at full speed she consumed 35 tons daily. The storage of provisions only allowed a supply of

[1] *O.R.N.* ser. 2, 2: (plate facing) 624.

[2] Office copy T 4166/55, 22 Jan. 1855, line drawing showing elevation, sheer plan, and body plan, Admiralty Papers.

[3] *The Navy List Corrected to 20 Dec. 1855* (London: John Murray, 1856), p. 174.

[4] Office copy T 4166/55, 22 Jan. 1855, line drawing showing elevation, screw plan, and body plan, Admiralty Papers.

[5] Ibid., T 4166/55, 17 July 1855, profile of the inboard works.

[6] Ibid., plan of hold. [7] F.O. 5/1052, pp. 10–12.

[8] *O.R.N.* ser. 1, 3:698.

[9] Office copy T 4166/55, 17 July 1855, plan of the Lower Deck, Admiralty Papers.

fifteen to twenty days for a complement of 125 men, and water capacity was limited to 2,100 gallons.[10]

In the lower deck she had accommodation forward for 140 seamen and aft for 6 officers. Underneath the aft section of the lower deck was storage space for shells.[11] Her large propeller aperture indicates that she could probably lift her propeller when proceeding under sail.

The *Rappahannock* was square-rigged and with a single topsail—as a dispatch vessel it was not intended she should rely on her sail-power.[12]

As the H.M.S. *Victor* she carried 6 guns, 24-pounders, 2 between the 2 funnels, 2 forward of the forward funnel, and 2 on each bow.[13]

[10] *O.R.N.* ser. 1, 3:698.

[11] Office copy T 4166/55, 17 July 1855, plan of the Lower Deck, Admiralty Papers.

[12] Ibid., plan of the Upper Deck. [13] Ibid.

APPENDIX IX

DESCRIPTION OF THE *SHENANDOAH*

The *Shenandoah* was originally the *Sea King*, a three-masted, single funneled vessel intended as a tea clipper. The first news of her comes from the *North British Daily Mail* of 18 August 1863: "Yesterday Messrs. A. Stephen & Sons launched from their new shipbuilding shed at Kelvinhaugh, another of their wood and iron combination ships. This vessel is a fine steamship of about 1,200 tons, and to class A1 thirteen years at Lloyd's. She is named the *Sea King*, and is, we understand, the first screw steamship built on the principle of iron frames and wooden planking, and also the first steamer that has been specially constructed for the China trade, having been built with a view of competing with the fastest ships in the trade direct from China to London, in bringing home the first teas of the season."

Her speed on trial was 11 knots. She was 220 ft. long between the perpendiculars by 36 ft. beam by 20 ft. 6 ins. depth of hold and 1,018 tons register. She had iron frames, floors and deck beams, being tied together with iron sheerstrake, stringer plates, and diagonal iron ties on the outside of the iron frames and on the deck beams, binding the iron framework well together. Over this framework she was planked with elm and teak wood 6 inches thick, firmly secured to the iron frames with copper bolts.[1]

She was an impressive ship both in appearance and performance, and Bulloch realised her suitability for his purpose as soon as he saw her on the Clyde.[2] She had moderate lines with a good dead rise, indicating moderate speed although her delivery and forward lines would make her a fast vessel for her displacement.[3]

The *Shenandoah* was a fully rigged ship with yards for square sails; she had 21 working sails—a large and most impressive show of canvas.[4] She had a raised forecastle, and the clipper bow stem-

[1] Mid-Ship Section and Scantlings, Alexander Stephen & Sons. The vessel also had angle dimensions, transversing steel deck beams, longitudinal tie plates (36.11/16′).

[2] Bulloch, 2:125.

[3] Lines of an Auxiliary Screw Steam Sailing Ship, Sheer Elevation, Body-Plan, Half-Breadth Plan, Alexander Stephen & Sons, Shipyard Dept., Lenthouse.

[4] Ibid., Starboard Profile and Sail Plan.

head extended from the forecastle to the forecastle bulkhead. She had a poop deck extending about 8 feet [5] which contained a dining saloon, staterooms, and captain's and officers' quarters. Under the poop was a well to receive the propeller when proceeding under sail alone. Her crew was housed in the topgallant forecastle while a large deckhouse between the fore and mainmasts contained rooms for her petty officers and the galley.[6] Her accommodation, with bathrooms and a sufficiency of toilets was up-to-date for a wooden vessel. Between the main and mizzenmast, space was provided for the auxiliary engine and boiler, which were surrounded by coal bunkers. There were 3 hatches for access to the cargo: the fore hatch, the main match, and the quarter hatch. Entrance to the main boiler and engine rooms was provided on top of the fiddley surrounding the funnel.[7]

The *Shenandoah* was sometimes called an auxiliary steamer, her smokestack being telescopic so that it could be lowered and rest only 6 feet above the rail.[8]

In view of the great spread of her canvas her engine power was not large. She usually steamed about 7½ knots an hour, but with steam and sail together she could achieve 11 knots. Her propeller had 2 flues, and her engine was of about 250 h.p.[9]

Her armament consisted of four 8-ins. 68-pounders, two 12-pounders, all smoothbore and two 32-pounders, rifled, Whitworth.[10]

The gross expenditure in the purchase and all the expenses of the *Shenandoah's* cruise was £53,715.10.9d.[11]

[5] Ibid. [6] Ibid. [7] Deck Plan, Alexander Stephen & Sons.
[8] *Times*, 19 Jan. 1865. [9] Ibid. [10] F.O. 5/1384, pp. 114–18, 93–94.
[11] Bulloch, 2:275.

APPENDIX X

BLOCKADE-RUNNERS PURCHASED, CONSTRUCTED, OR CHARTERED IN PART OR IN WHOLE BY BRITISH OWNERS

Name	Builder	Owner	Dimensions	Date of Building	Date of Purchase	Remarks
Abigail	Miller & Sons	Miller & Sons		1865	1865	Never captured
Adela	Thomson	Malcolmson	212.9′ x 22.9′ x 11.2′	1859	1861	Captured 1863
A. D. Vance	Thomson	Hutchieson	149′ x 21′ x 6′	1861	1864	Captured 1864
Alfred	Caird	Campbell & Collis	227.8′ x 26.2′ x 19.2′	1864	1864	Renamed *Sheffield* and *Old Dominion;* 2 decks, a poop and topgallant, 703 tons, oscillating engines of 160 h.p. One of the fastest of all blockade-runners–top speed 20 knots

Alliance	Tod & McGregor	Mills	140′ x 30′ x 7′	1857	1863	Captured 1864
Antona		McConnell & Laird		1860	1862	Captured 1863
Badger	Jones & Quiggin	C.S.A.	220′ x 22′ x 10′3″	1864	1864	Destroyed 1864; 532 38/94 tons
Banshee I	Jones & Quiggin		62′10″ x 14.3′ x 8′7″	1862	1863	53 tons (a steel sailing yacht); captured 1863; afterwards the N.S.S. *Banshee*
Banshee II	Jones & Quiggin		215′ x 20′ x 11′4″	1864	1864	431 86/94 tons; never captured
Bat	Jones & Quiggin	C.S.A.	230′ x 26′ x 10′9″	1864	1864	Captured 1864; 770 87/94 tons
Bay	Miller & Sons	Miller & Sons		1865	1865	Never captured
Caledonia	Smith & Rodger		132′ x 15′4″ x –	1844	1863	Captured 1864
Calypso	Denny	W. S. Lindsay	190.3.′ x 27.1′ x 13.9′	1855	1862	About 6 trips; captured 1863; renamed U.S.S. *Calypso;* geared steeple engines 140 h.p., built of iron, 1 deck, speed 12 knots, 500 tons, valued at $38416.14
Chancellor	Denny	Lochlomond Co.	167.4′ x 17.1′ x 7.1′	1853	1863	Founded on voyage 1863

Name	Builder	Owner	Dimensions	Date of Building	Date of Purchase	Remarks
City of Petersburg	Laird	C.S.A.		1863	1863	750 tons, 250 h.p.; never captured
Col. Lamb	Jones & Quiggin		281′ x 36′ x 14′	1864	1864	1788 tons, 350 h.p.
Corcovada	Thomson	C.S.A.		1865	1865	Built too late to have been used as a blockade-runner
Cornubia	Harvey & Son	Hayle & Bristol Co.	190′ x 24.7′ x 12.7′	1858	1861	23 trips; captured 1863; renamed *Lady Davis;* simple oscillating engines 230 h.p.; after capture used by U.S. Navy
Craignish Castle	Caird	Campbell, Watson & Findlay	170.3′ x 19′ x 9.3′	1844	1862	Foundered on voyage 1862; renamed *Adler*
Curlew	Jones & Quiggin		225′ x 24′ x 11′	1861	1861	645 tons, 160 h.p.; captured 1861
Dare	Alexander Stephen & Sons	C.S.A.		1863	1863	552 tons; ran ashore 1864
Deer	W. H. Potter & Son	C.S.A.		1864	1864	Captured 1865
Denbigh	Laird			1860	1865	Destroyed 1865

Diamond		Henderson			1863	Price £7,500; captured 1864
Dolphin	Napier	Burns	170.2′ x 212′ x 10.5′	1844	1862	Captured, changed owner, reentered blockade renamed *Ruby*
Dream	W. H. Potter & Son			1864	1864	Never captured; fired upon off coast of Cuba by U.S. Schooner *Annie*, 28 April 1863
Eagle	Denny	Williamson, Cook, Ferguson & Buchanan	169.9′ x 165′ x 8.5′	1852	1862	Captured 1863; 6 trips
Edith	Thomson	C.S.A.		1864	1864	Carried three rifled guns; renamed *Chichamauga;* destroyed 1865
Emma Hendry	Thomson	Hutchieson	149′ x 21′ x 6′	1864	1864	Captured 1864
Emma Henry	Thomson			1864	1864	Captured 1864
Fairy	Thomson	Hutchieson	149′ x 21′ x 6′	1861	1864	Captured 1864
Fergus	Alexander Stephen & Sons	C.S.A.	210′ x 23′ x 9′6″	1863	1863	552 tons; never captured
Fingal	Thomson	C.S.A.	185.5′ x 25.4′ x 12.9′	1861	1861	Afterwards the *C.S.S.* ram *Atlanta*
Flora	Thomson	W. S. Lindsay	215.5′ x 25.7′ x 13.5′	1858	1863	4 trips, went to Canada for repair; foundered 1863; 511 tons, valued

Appendix X (*cont.*)

Name	Builder	Owner	Dimensions	Date of Building	Date of Purchase	Remarks
						at £35,000, fastest steamer in the Bristol Channel
Fox	Caird	C.S.A.	228.6″ x 24.2″ x 13.5″	1862	1863	Destroyed 1863
Fox	Jones & Quiggin		220′ x 22′ x 10′3″	1864	1864	629 tons, 150 h.p.; captured 1864, afterwards *Fanny*
Gem	Henderson	Henderson	161′ x 15′9″ x 7.5′	1854	1863	Lost 1864 (?)
Georgia Bell	Jones & Quiggin		250′ x 28′ x 10′9″	1864	1864	972 46/94 tons, 220 h.p.; never captured
Georgiana	Laird	C.S.A.		1863	1863	Destroyed 1864
Giraffe	Thomson	Burns	270.2′ x 26.1′ x 13′	1860	1862	21 trips; renamed *Robert E. Lee;* captured 1863
Havelock	Thomson	Potter	223.2′ x 26.2′ x 14.4′	1858	1862	14 trips; destroyed 1864
Hawk	Thomson	C.S.A.	254′ x 28′ x 12½′	1863	1863	531 tons, 50 h.p.; Iron; never captured
Herald		C.S.A.		1858 (?)	1861	28 trips; captured 1863; 150 tons
Hero		Potter			1862	Steamed 16 m.p.h.

Hope	Jones & Quiggin		281′ x 35″ x 15½″	1864	1864	1697 tons, 350 h.p.; captured 1864; one of the finest and fastest steamers in the trade
Hornet	Jones & Quiggin	C.S.A.	250′ x 28′ x 10′9″	1865	1865	972 46/84 tons 220 h.p.; sunk by collision with steamer *Allison* in 1865
Iona I	Thomson	McBrayne & Paterson	225.2′ x 20.4 x 9′	1855	1862	Foundered on Clyde 1862
Iona II	Thomson	McBrayne & Paterson	249.2′ x 25′ x 9.1′	1863	1864	Foundered on Clyde 1864
Isabel	Laird			1865	1865	Captured 1865
Juno	Stothert	Denny	163.2′ x 19.7′ x 11.4′ (?)	1853	1863	1 trip; captured 1863; 247 tons, iron built, 1 deck, valued at $135,102.11, renamed *Dakotah*
Juno	Tod & McGregor	C.S.A.	188.9′ x 19.1′ x 8′	1860	1863	Captured 1863
Jupiter	Tod & McGregor	Reid & McKellar	184.9′ x 18.2′ x 8.3′	1856	1863	Captured 1864; 400 tons, paddle wheeled, equipped to carry 2 guns
Kelpie	Tod & McGregor	McGregor	191.1′ x 18.2′ x 7.6′	1857	1863 (?)	Destroyed 1863 (?)
Lady Stirling	Thomson	Potter	22.3′ x 26.2′ x 14.4′	1864	1864	Captured 1864

Appendix X (*cont.*)

Name	Builder	Owner	Dimensions	Date of Building	Date of Purchase	Remarks
Lark	Laird	C.S.A.		1865	1865	Drew 5′ of water; never captured
Lelia	Miller & Sons	Miller & Sons		1864	1864	Lost 1864
Leopard	Denny	Burns	220′ x 27′ x 14′8″	1858	1862	8 trips; destroyed 1863
Let Her B	Miller & Sons			1864	1864	740 tons; last blockade-runner to get out of Charleston
Lilian	Thomson			1864	1864	Captured 1864
Little Hattie	Thomson			1864	1864	Entered new inlet M.C. 23 November 1864
Lord Clyde	Caird	Dublin & Glasgow		1862	1863	18 trips; captured 1864
Lucy	ones & Quiggin		215′ x 20′ x 10′3″	1863	1863	Captured 1864; 431 tons, 140 h.p.
Lynx	Jones & Quiggin	Burns	220′ x 24′ x 11′3″	1864	1864	629 tons, 150 h.p.; destroyed 1864
Mail II	Tod & McGregor	Campbell	179.5′ x 18.1′ x 7.4′	1860	1863	Destroyed 1863
Mary	Laird			1864	1864	Captured 1864
Mary Anne	Connell	C.S.A.		1863	1863	7 trips; captured 1864
Night Hawk		Taylor		1864	1864	Destroyed 1864

Neptune	Napier	C.S.A.	201.7′ x 18.7′ x 8.2′	1861	1862	Captured 1863
Owl	Jones & Quiggin	C.S.A.	230′ x 26′ x 10′9″	1864	1864	770 87/94 tons; destroyed 1864; first of several steamers built for and on account of the Confederate gov't, to be run under the direction of the secretary of the Navy
Pearl	Henderson & Colobourne	C.S.A.	182.2′ x 19.5′ x 7.6′	1859	1862	Captured 1863
Penguin	Laird			1865	1865	Never captured
Phantom	Miller & Sons	C.S.A.		1863	1864	Engine of Fawcetts, speed 17 knots; destroyed 1863
Plover	Jones & Quiggin		225′ x 24′ x 11′	1865	1865	645 tons, 160 h.p.; never captured
Princess Royal	Tod & McGregor	Langlands		1861	1863	Captured 1863
Robert Todd	Laird			1864	1864	Never captured
Roe	Caird	Burns		1863	1863	Sold on stocks price £13,800
Rothesay Castle IV	Simons	Watson	191.5′ x 19′ x 8.3′	1861	1863	Price £8,500; never captured

Appendix X (*cont.*)

Name	Builder	Owner	Dimensions	Date of Building	Date of Purchase	Remarks
Rouen	Thomson	W. S. Lindsay	215.5′ x 25.7′ x 13.5′	1858	1863	Captured 1864, afterwards the *Flora*
Ruby	Henderson		172.9′ x 15.9′ x 8.2′ (?)	1854		This vessel may not have taken part
Ruby	Jones & Quiggin	C.S.A.	260′ x 33′ x 15′	1864	1864	1391 34/94 tons, 300 h.p.; never captured
Ruby III	Henderson & Colbourne	Henderson	209.2′ x 19.5′ x 8.1′	1861	1862	Never captured; 7 trips
Scotia	Tod & McGregor	Reid, Reid & Tod	141.3′ x 17.5′ x 8.7′	1845		Captured 1864; afterwards *U.S.S. Meteor*
Secret	Bowdler Chaffer			1864	1864	Never captured
Snipe	Jones & Quiggin		225′ x 24′ x 11′	1865	1865	645 tons, 160 h.p.; never captured
Sophia				1864	1864	Captured 1864
Spunkie	Tod & McGregor	McGregor	191.2′ x 18.2′ x 7.6′	1857	1863	6 trips; grounded 1864
Stag	Bowdler Chaffer	C.S.A.	202′ x 5″ x 23′1″ x 13′5″	1854	1864	Eventually went to the Australian coal trade; captured 1865
Star	Tod & McGregor	Reid & McKellar	156 x 17.9′ x 8.4′	1849	1862	Never captured

Stormy Petrel		Taylor		1864	1864	Destroyed 1864
Swan	Bowdler Chaffer	C.S.A.	202′ x 5″ x 23′1″ x 13′5″	1862	1862	Captured 1862
Swift			172.4′ x 16.1′ x 9.2′	1844		This vessel may not have taken part
Tallahassee		C.S.A.	220′ x 22′ x 14′	1864	1864	418 tons, speed 14–17 knots; never captured
Thistle P.S.		Cameron				Captured 1864
Thistle S.S.	Laurence Hill	Cameron		1859		Price £13,800; captured 1863, renamed *Cherokee*
Tubal Cain	Blackwood & Gordon	London St. Navigation Co.	151.7′ x 22′ x 12.5′	1853	1862	Captured 1863
Tuskar	Blackwood & Gordon	Clyde Shipping Co.		1860	1863	Captured first voyage 1863
Vesta	Barclay Corle	Campbell	173.8′ x 16.6′ x 7.7′	1864	1864	Destroyed 1864
Vesta	Blackwood & Gordon	Clyde Shipping Co.		1864	1864	Captured 1864
Wasp	Jones & Quiggin	C.S.A.	250′ x 28′ x 10′9″	1865	1865	972 46/94 tons, 220 h.p.; converted to torpedo boat 1865
Widgeon	Jones & Quiggin		225′ x 24′ x 11′	1865	1865	645 tons, 160 h.p.; never captured

Appendix X (*cont.*)

Name	Builder	Owner	Dimensions	Date of Building	Date of Purchase	Remarks
Wild Dayrell	Jones & Quiggin	C.S.A.	215′ x 20′ x 10′3″	1863	1863	Destroyed 1864; 431 tons, 140 h.p.
Wild Rover	Thomson			1864	1864	Formerly *Break of Day*; schooner; never captured
Will-o'-the-Wisp		Taylor		1865	1865	Destroyed 1865
Wren	Laird	C.S.A.		1864	1864	Drew 5′ of water; never captured

Sources: Compiled from accounts in *O.R.*, *O.R.N.*, and company and private papers.

APPENDIX XI

SOME FIRMS IN GREAT BRITAIN THAT DID BUSINESS WITH THE CONFEDERACY

BELFAST:
B. & E. McHugh

BIRKENHEAD:
Birkenhead Iron Works
Laird Brothers

BIRMINGHAM:
Firman & Sons
J. R. Grant & Son
Smith & Wright Ltd.

CLYDEBANK:
John Brown & Co.

DUMBARTON:
Denny Brothers

ENFIELD:
Royal Small Arms Factory

GLASGOW:
Chamberlain & Co.
Clyde Bank Foundry
Patrick Henderson & Co.
James & George Thompson

KELVINHAUGH:
Alexander Stephen & Sons

LEEDS:
Greenwood & Batley Ltd.

LIVERPOOL:
Ashbridge & Co.
Blakely Ordnance Co.
Gordon Coleman & Co.
Collie, Westhead & Co.
Curry, Killoch & Co.
Cyclops Steel & Iron Works
Fawcett, Preston & Co.
Fletcher, Hall & Stone
George Forrester & Co.
Edward Lawrence & Co.
Leech, Harrison & Forwood
Low Moor Iron Works
William C. Miller & Sons
Old Tug Co.
J. Stewart Oxley & Co.

LONDON:
Albion Trading Co.
Alexander Collie & Co.
De La Rue & Co.
Dudgeon Brothers
Emile Erlanger & Co.
Galway Co.
John K. Gilliat & Co.
W. S. Lindsay & Co.
London Armoury Co.
Zachariah C. Pearson & Co.
Railway Carriage Makers
Railway Works
Robinson & Cottum
J. Henry Schroder & Co.

Overed Guerney & Co.
T. & C. Hood
Isaac, Campbell & Co.
John Lane, Hankey & Co.
S. Straker & Sons
William & Co.
Charles William & F. Wentworth & Co.

MANCHESTER:
Lomnitz & Co.
Manchester Ordnance & Rifle Co.
Joseph Whitworth & Co.

NEWCASTLE-UPON-TYNE:
W. G. Armstrong & Co.
Elswick Ordnance Works

NORTHAMPTON:
Turner Bros. Hyde & Co.

SHEFFIELD:
William Butcher Jr. & Co.

APPENDIX XII

SELECTED BIOGRAPHICAL NOTES

Charles Francis Adams. The foreign relations of the Lincoln government during the Civil War, diplomatic, financial and commercial, were mostly concerned with Great Britain. Fortunately for the North, the U.S. ambassador to the Court of Saint James was Charles Francis Adams, son of one president and grandson of another, and a man who proved himself the equal of either in the diligence and skill with which he labored to protect the interests of his government.

The peaceful settlement of Anglo-American disputes during and immediately after the Civil War were in large measure the result of his exceptional ability. Adams knew how to be reasonable without compromising American rights as he saw them, and how to be firm without causing lasting resentment.

Edward C. Anderson. In the spring of 1861 Major Anderson was dispatched to England to investigate the work being done by Huse, the purchasing agent, to supplant him, if necessary, or to assist him in his purchasing operations. In November 1861 Anderson returned to the Confederacy after having satisfied himself that Huse was capable of supervising the purchase of munitions.

Judah Philip Benjamin. As Confederate secretary of state, Benjamin was the champion of the doctrine of King Cotton. However, later in the war he did allow some cotton to be shipped through the blockade, and he gave full support to Confederate finance and purchasing activities in Great Britain. Under his energetic leadership, the Confederate State Department did not remain idle. Throughout the war Benjamin tried, by the use of cotton and free trade, to influence Great Britain to support the Confederacy. He never forgave Great Britain for refusing to support openly the Confederate cause.

James Dunwoody Bulloch. Chief agent of the Confederate States Navy Department in Great Britain during the American Civil War, Bulloch was descended from a distinguished Georgia family of

Scots, Irish, and Huguenot origins, his great-grandfather having been the first governor of Georgia. His half sister, Martha, married Theodore Roosevelt, Sr., and was the mother of President Theodore Roosevelt.

Before the war Bulloch served in the U.S. Navy and was later a captain in the merchant service, from which he resigned at the outbreak of the Civil War. Commissioned a captain in the C.S.N., he arrived in England on 4 June 1861. Jefferson Davis wrote of him in these terms: "An officer of the old Navy, of high ability as a seaman and an integrity which stood the test under which a less stern character might have given way, was our Naval Agent in Liverpool. In his office he disbursed millions, and when there was no one to whom he could be required to render an account, paid out the last shilling in his hands and confronted poverty without prospect of other reward than which he might find in his clear conscience."

This praise was well deserved. Bulloch was the first, and remained the principal, agent of the C.S.N. in Great Britain throughout the war. He and Caleb Huse were by far the ablest agents the Confederacy sent abroad. Authorized directly by the Confederate government, he worked independently of James Mason, the Confederate commissioner to Great Britain.

After the war Bulloch did not return to the United States but settled in Liverpool, where his family joined him. His book *The Secret Service in Europe,* written after the end of hostilities, gives a graphic account of the efforts of the Confederacy to secure a navy in Great Britain.

After the war Bulloch took little interest in political affairs and mainly followed the occupation of a cotton factor. During the later years of his life, he sat on the Committee of the Liverpool Nautical College and also took an active interest in the Orphan Boys' Asylum. He assisted in the establishment of the City of Liverpool Technical School, which later developed into the City College of Technology. Together with his intimate friend, Admiral Grugh, he took a great interest in matters relating to shipping and sea affairs.

Bulloch died at the age of 77, on 7 January 1901, after some months of illness, at 76 Canning Street, Liverpool, the residence of his son-in-law, Alderman M. H. Maxwell. He was buried at Smithdow Road Cemetery, Liverpool. The net value of his personal estate was only £83.16.7., which he left to his daughter, Martha Louise Bulloch, his wife having predeceased him by some three months.

W. G. Crenshaw. Crenshaw was sent to Europe as a quasi agent for the Commissary Bureau of the War Department. His orders were very similar to those of Huse. Crenshaw disliked Huse, was jealous of him, and would have liked Huse recalled. The friction between Crenshaw and Huse did much to discredit the capable Huse.

JEFFERSON DAVIS. Davis was President of the Confederate States of America. He came from Welsh stock. A study of Confederate finance and purchasing in Great Britain during the Civil War indicates that he was a conventional thinker who was inclined to be autocratic. Naval strategy seemed to baffle him, and he took relatively little interest in the C.S.N. activities in Great Britain. An experienced artillerist, he assumed that harbor forts could prevent sea invasion. After the war he was imprisoned for a time in Fort Monroe. Following his release, he spent a considerable time in England.

Jefferson Davis was a man of mingled strength and weakness; yet, to adapt the phrase of Sir Winston Churchill, he did very much with very little. All considered, he cannot be seriously faulted for the manner in which he handled overall Confederate activity in Great Britain during the war.

EMILE ERLANGER. A German-born banker, Erlanger was a friend and supporter of the Southern cause in Europe. He was energetic and an extremely able businessman. It was generally felt that if the South had been victorious, Erlanger would represent Southern interests in Europe. During the Civil War Erlanger was centered in Paris, where he coordinated financial matters with Confederate officials.

MARGUERITE MATHILDE SLIDELL ERLANGER. The daughter of John Slidell, she married Emile Erlanger on 4 October 1864. The marriage was an immediate and lasting success. When parted, the couple corresponded daily, and many of their letters are still in existence. She strongly supported the Confederate cause. After she married Erlanger she lost her American citizenship, but an act of Congress of 4 March 1917 declared her "readmitted to the character and privileges of a citizen of the United States." Mrs. Erlanger died in 1927 and is buried in Saint Mary's Catholic Cemetery, Harrow Road, London.

JOSIAH GORGAS. Gorgas was born at Running Pumps, Pennsylvania, the son of a poor clockmaker. He graduated from West Point, sixth in his class of fifty-two. He subsequently served in the Mexican War, and while stationed at Mount Vernon Arsenal, Alabama, married Amelia Gayle, daughter of a governor of Alabama.

Throughout the Civil War Gorgas worked with tremendous energy and efficiency for the Confederate cause. An excellent administrator, he demonstrated strength of character, resourcefulness, and sagacity in pursuing the ends of his government. As chief of ordnance of the Confederate army, he did much to maintain the gray-clad soldiers in the field against the superior resources of the North. He obtained remarkable results, partly by his wise selection of subordinate officers, to whom he gave ample authority and responsibility; his support of Huse was especially successful and resulted in a tremendous amount of goods being shipped from Great Britain to the C.S.A.

Gorgas was often forthright in his criticisms of the operations of his government, and his censures extended to Jefferson Davis himself. Gorgas felt that the president selected men badly and that Christopher Memminger ruined Confederate finance both at home and abroad.

HENRY HOTZE. Born in Zurich, Switzerland, Hotze was only a child when his family emigrated to the United States. He worked with John Forsyth on the *Mobile Register* before serving with the Confederates. He was commissioned by the Confederate government as a commercial and propaganda agent in England and arrived in London on 29 January 1862, when he was only 27. Jefferson Davis considered him to be one of the ablest of the agents in England, and his dispatches from London to the Confederacy always carried weight in the highest political and commercial circles. As editor of the *Index*, a London-based Confederate publication, his special task was to win favor in Great Britain for the Confederate cause. During the war he spent most of his time in London, living near King's Cross Station. His letter books are in the manuscript division of the Library of Congress.

After the war he returned to Zurich. Nothing further is known of his life.

CALEB HUSE. Huse was a major in the Confederate army and, along with Bulloch, was perhaps the most successful of all the purchasing agents. He was born in Newburyport, Mass., on 11 February 1831. The Huses were an old Massachusetts family and traced their ancestry back to Abel Huse, who was made a freeman of that state in 1642. Caleb Huse entered the United States Military Academy in 1847 and graduated in 1851, seventh in his class. He was commissioned a brevet second lieutenant in an artillery regiment, and for a time was stationed at Key West. From 1852–59 he served at West Point as assistant professor of chemistry, mineralogy, and geology. On 4 November 1854 he was promoted to the rank of first lieutenant. During part of 1859 and 1860 he traveled abroad on leave, and on his return he accepted a private appointment as commandant of cadets at the University of Alabama.

When his leave was suddenly terminated in February 1861, he resigned his commission. His decision to serve the Confederacy, although he was a Northerner, can be explained by the friendships he had made at West Point; during his service there Robert E. Lee was the academy superintendent.

Huse entered the Confederate army as a captain and was later commissioned major. He was indefatigable in procuring supplies for the Confederacy, although, as a Northerner, he often aroused dislike and suspicion among his fellow agents and was, on several occasions, accused of misappropriating Confederate funds. These charges were never proved, and there appears to be no substantial reason for doubting this officer's integrity.

Huse had married Harriett Pinkney before the war, and at the end of hostilities he was penniless, with a large family to support. He returned to the United States about 1868 and after being concerned in a variety of business enterprises started a school at Sing Sing, N.Y., in 1876, with the object of preparing pupils for the Military Academy at West Point. In 1879 he moved the school to Highland Falls, where it prospered. Huse died at Highland Falls at the age of 74. One of his sons became an admiral in the U.S. Navy.

STEPHEN R. MALLORY. As Secretary of the Confederate navy, Mallory was at the head of an almost nonexistent naval force. However, he did better than anyone had anticipated with the scanty resources at his command. Mallory's strongest claim to distinction was the contribution he made to the development of naval warfare. With the aid of able assistants, he contributed to the development of two deadly weapons of warfare, namely, the torpedo and the submarine. Materials for these weapons were purchased in England. Perhaps Mallory was, of all the leaders of the Confederacy, the best attuned to the changes which were taking place in warfare at the time. He thought constantly in terms of machinery and metal. Pressing for the construction of ironclads and cruisers of new design in Great Britain, he strove to build a modern, mechanized navy. Severely limited resources, the conservatism of the remainder of the cabinet, and the difficulties of securing ships in Britain did much to prevent the attainment of his objectives.

C. J. McRae. As special agent for the Erlanger Loan, McRae disposed of Erlanger Bonds to liquidate Confederate debts in England and elsewhere. His great contribution to the Confederate cause was the consolidation of all purchasing and financial negotiations in Europe, especially in Great Britain. McRae was an able administrator with a talent for managing men and resources. By today's standards, he could be classified as an organization man with keen managerial abilities.

James Murry Mason. Mason was the son of General John Mason, of Revolutionary War fame, and Anna Maria Mason. In 1837 he was elected to Congress and represented his district for one term. In 1847 he was sent to the U.S. Senate from Virginia to fill the unexpired term of Senator Pennybacker. Reelected in 1849 and 1855, he was in the Senate when Virginia seceded.

Before the war, he served ten years as chairman of the Senate Foreign Relations Committee. Latter, he was appointed Confederate States commissioner to Great Britain. He shared the general conviction of the South that Great Britain would eventually recognize the Confederacy or intervene on its behalf in order to obtain cotton.

Mason acted as a central agent for the various naval and military purchasing agents of the Confederacy in Great Britain, and also cooperated with Confederate propagandists in London. To James Mason we are indebted for a most accurate definition of the great struggle: "I look upon it then, sir, as a war of sentiment and opinion by one form of society against another form of society."

Christopher G. Memminger. Confederate treasury secretary and key architect of early Confederate financial policy abroad, Memminger was born at Nayhinger, Germany, and spent part of his youth in an orphanage. As an administrator, Memminger displayed industry, devotion, and executive ability. Memminger's earlier career in South Carolina had been distinguished by an advocacy of sound money; but as chief of Confederate finance, he was forced to operate largely by the issue of tremendous quantities of paper money.

James A. Seddon. He was probably the finest secretary of war to serve in the Confederate cabinet. He was gifted with discernment and was a man of energy. Seddon was cautious in counsel and resolute in action. His annual reports to Congress show a strong grasp of the war situation. He gave good support to the Confederate purchasing agents in England and understood the importance of their work.

JOHN SLIDELL. Slidell was born in New York City and later settled in New Orleans. He was an important member of the Democratic party before the war. He was elected Senator from Louisiana, and at the outbreak of war was appointed Confederate commissioner to France. Slidell was familiar with the English money market, for prior to the war, in 1853, he accepted an agency to sell bonds of the New Orleans and Nashville railroad in London. Because of his previous experience he was accepted as a powerful influence in Confederate financial purchasing operations in both England and on the Continent.

Slidell was an astute, rather than able, person (during the Civil War he prudently invested in Northern Railway stock), and on the whole the Confederate agents in Europe distrusted him. In 1874 the Supreme Court of the United States declared him "the most guilty of the rebel chiefs." He remained unpopular in the North for many years, and he did not settle in the United States after the war. His three daughters all married noblemen and did not return to the United States. One was Baroness Erlanger of Germany, the second, the Viscomtesse Rivere de St. Roman of France, and the third, Baroness de Plyffer Hendigy of Switzerland.

John Slidell died on 26 July 1871 at Solent Lodge, West Cowes, Isle of Wight, of pneumonia brought on by pemphigus, a chronic skin disease. He was 78, his wife had predeceased him by seven months. In December 1872 his body was exhumed from Brighton Borough Cemetery and reburied in the private vault of the St. Roman's family in a small graveyard at Villejuif (Seine), France. On 28 July 1960, his remains were again exhumed, and he now lies buried in the communal graveyard of Villejuif.

JAMES SPENCE. Born in Liverpool and educated near Warrington, Spence was an active and leading member of the Liverpool iron trade and of the local Chamber of Commerce, of which he was president in 1866. In 1851 he published *The American Union: The Causes of Disruption*, a work in which he advocated the Southern cause with considerable knowledge and ability. During the war the *Times* published a series of his letters commenting on Southern strategic, political, and economic developments. These appeared under the initial "S" and did much to turn English opinion in favor of the South during the early years of the war. During the war, he organized a bazaar at Saint George's Hall to aid the Southern cause, realizing the very large sum of £22,000. After the war he interested himself in the South Wales tin-plate industry, finally retiring from commerce and settling in London, where he devoted himself to authorship. He died about the end of the century at a considerable age.

L. P. Walker. Confederate secretary of war, Walker began his term of office by haggling over prices of military hardware in England, when the Confederacy needed every gun and bullet it could obtain. He had little capacity as an administrator and found the demands of contractors, politicians, agents, and army officers intolerable. He did little to expedite the delivery of badly needed military equipment from England. Criticism in Congress convinced both Walker and Davis that the former should resign, and he was offered a foreign mission, which he declined.

SELECTED BIBLIOGRAPHY

Unpublished Private Manuscripts and Public Documents

American

Alabama Report Document. An unsigned detailed report, written by a detective employed by persons unknown to spy upon the activities of Lairds at Birkenhead during the construction of the *Alabama*. In the possession of Mrs. Helen Roosevelt Robinson, Mohawk, N.Y. Gives a day-to-day report of the building of the ship, shows the difficulties encountered, and contains descriptive information relating to construction not disclosed in *O.R.N.* or other diplomatic and official sources. Consists of 17½ foolscap pages.

American Chamber of Commerce Minute Book, Liverpool. City of Liverpool Public Library. Gives examples of the belief in England that the Confederate government had forbidden the export of cotton to neutral powers. Records discussions of the possibility of a formal cotton embargo and gives many helpful details of shipments of cotton, methods of packing, blockade-running and the shipment of war material to the South.

Bransford Papers. Manuscripts Section, Tennessee State Library and Archives. Useful for details of the Confederate branch bank system. Material relating to this subject was supplied by Mrs. Frank L. Owsley.

Dayton Papers. Manuscript Division, Princeton University Library. Give details of the sinking of the *Alabama*. Copy of letter of William Dayton, Jr., to William Dayton, Sr., sent to author by Princeton University librarian was useful for its remarks regarding the *Alabama*.

Selected Letters, Secretary of War (W.R.). The Rebel Archives, Ordnance Department, Library of Congress. Although this is a sizable collection, only W.R. 46–399 was of value to this work; it relates to Josiah Gorgas. A microfilm of these letters was most kindly supplied to the author by Professor Frank E. Vandiver. Presents the "behind the scenes" activity of the Confederate War Department in the area of arms procurement and general policy matters relating thereto.

British

Admiralty Papers (Adm.). Public Records Office, London. These papers covering the period from 1660 to 1934 consist of 8,779 volumes, only one of which (Adm. 1/5828) is relevant to this study. The papers in this volume consist of Admiralty (a) minutes; (b) special accounts / minute sheets; and (c) matters involving naval policy decisions. All papers on a given subject are grouped together and relate either directly or indirectly to Confederate naval activities. There is also a variety of miscellaneous information: reports of courts martial, letters from admirals, descriptions of dockyards at home and abroad, etc. There is a further group of Admiralty Papers (Adm.) in the National Maritime Museum, Greenwich. Included are copies of a contract specification and drawings of the Laird rams prepared by a surveyor of the Royal Navy and reports of other naval activities involving Confederate naval matters.

Alexander Stephen & Sons Ltd., Historical File. Alexander Stephen & Sons Ltd., Glasgow. Gave details of the construction of the *Shenandoah* and several blockade-runners constructed by this firm.

Board of Trade Papers. Public Records Office, London. Contain the files of dissolved companies, incorporated between 1856 and 1877 and voluntarily dissolved before 1916. These records were the source of information regarding companies and groups that traded with the Confederacy. These papers lack any real organization, and it is difficult to find needed material because many of the companies and groups that did business with the Confederates were incorporated before 1856, dissolved after 1916, are still in existence today, or have merged with other firms. Most important in identifying firms that traded with the Confederates was Affidavit Verifying Statement of Liquidation Account, Registered no. 2171, 5 Dec. 1891, Record Book no. 906h, CN.L7.

Customs and Excise Papers. H.M. Customs and Excise Library, King's Bream House, Mark Lane, London. Include a report of the customs surveyor made before the departure of the *Alabama* and a Liverpool Customs Bill of Entry (Bill A), showing details of the Blakely guns exported to the Confederacy.

Customs Papers. Public Records Office, London. Include volume 8/94, an abstract of British and Irish produce and manufactures exported to America, both North and South.

De La Rue Papers. De La Rue & Co. Ltd., Security Division, Bunhill Row, London. Gave information regarding the printing and sale of stamps, paper, and printing equipment to the Confederacy. This information is contained in the De La Rue Private Day Book of 1862. A contract for stamps and other items negotiated between Major B. F. Ficklin, C.S.A., and De La Rue has been preserved and was available for study. (S. Straker & Sons Ltd., London, have in their possession some proofs of Confederate stamps and a few supporting records, but their detailed accounts relating to major transactions with the Confederates, were destroyed during the Second World War.)

Erlanger Papers. Erlangers, London. The company ledgers for 1863–64 consist of 478 pages, a portion of which is concerned with Confederate financial transactions, and are useful because they trace the fluctuations of the Erlanger loan on the Continent as well as in Great Britain and show the activities of J. Henry Schroder, Fraser Trenholm, and Isaac Campbell. The Erlanger Papers also include some 3,000 letters and assorted papers, largely of correspondence between Emile and Mathilde Erlanger from 1862–98, but also of correspondence between Slidell and Erlanger. Of these, some forty letters mention the loan and political and military matters relating to Confederate activities in Great Britain. The later correspondence gives an interesting insight into Slidell's life after the war.

Foreign Office Records (F.O.). Public Record Office, London. Of great importance in the preparation of this book. F.O. 5/1313, August 1861—March 1863, is in two volumes and deals with the *Oreto* or *Florida.* Vol. 1 was of the greatest value, as it related directly to the financial, procurement, and legal matters concerning the *Florida.* Vol. 2 is mainly concerned with the vessel's life after the Civil War. F.O. 5/1318, June–December 1862, deals with the *Alabama.* This is in 15 volumes, and was of considerable value to this study. F.O. 5/1317, May 1864–1871 (one vol.), deals with the *Georgia.* F.O. 5/1051, 1863–65 (one vol.), is concerned with the *Canton* or *Pampero;* F.O. 5/1094, 1861–66 (one vol.), with the *Nashville, Tallahasse,* and *Bermuda;* F.O. 5/1050, 1864–65 (one vol.), *Hawk, City of Richmond, Ajax* and *Hercules;* F.O. 5/1052, 1863–65 (one vol.), *Rappahannoch;* F.O. 5/1384 Oct. 19, 1864–65 (5 vols.) *Shenandoah;* F.O. 5/1048, March 1863—February 1864 (one vol.), *Alexandra;* F.O. 5/1049, October 1864–65 (one vol.), *Alexandra* or *Mary;* F.O. 5/1000, February–September 1863, and F.O. 5/1001, September–October 1863 (4 vols.), include material on the Laird rams built at Birkenhead.

Gilliat Papers. In the possession of D. A. Gilliat, London. The material for the years 1861–65 consists of 1,764 letters in two bound volumes and shows English merchant and banking reaction toward Anglo-Confederate finance and trade generally. Gilliat and his associates give some excellent firsthand reviews of the English money market and Confederate financial and trade activities (prices, cotton stock, rates of interest etc.) including the English cotton and tobacco trade with the Confederate States and Maryland. Gilliat traded with both North and South but from a commercial viewpoint favored the Southern cause because of the possibility of unlimited and long-range trade with an agricultural section of North America.

Gladstone Papers. British Museum, London. 750 vols. Comprise the correspondence, official and private, literary papers and manuscripts of W. E. Gladstone. Of special interest were the letters exchanged between Earl Russell and Gladstone, relating to Confederate affairs. These show the workings of British policy and attitudes toward the Confederacy and are contained in box 6, vol. 509. For a consideration of belligerent right under British law, see box 72.

Greenwood & Battley Ltd., Historical File. Greenwood and Battley Ltd., Albion Works, Leeds. This file contained a ten-page detailed contract made between this company and Fraser, Trenholm & Co. for the supply of various items of machinery for the manufacture of ordnance to be shipped to the Confederacy.

Hogg Papers. In the possession of Brigadier O. F. G. Hogg, C.B.E., F.S.A., of Woolwich. Includes drawings, specifications of ordnance and ammunition, proof records from small arm ranges, extracts from War Office Papers, observations recorded at Woolwich Arsenal, extracts from British State Papers relating to Woolwich Arsenal, and general ordnance records relating to arms procured by the Confederates. The Hogg Papers cover five centuries. In all, the collection comprises some 4,000 pages of manuscript compiled by Brigadier Hogg, one of the leading British authorities on ordinance. The Hogg Papers were invaluable in preparing the ordnance chapter.

Jones and Quiggen Papers. In the possession of A. J. Quiggin of Tunstall, Blundellsands, Liverpool. These consist of two specification books and miscellaneous correspondence giving details of the building of blockade-runners for the Confederacy. The specification books are quite detailed and were very valuable in preparing the naval chapters.

Laird Papers. These important papers are in two groups. The first, in the possession of Cammell, Laird & Co. Ltd., Birkenhead, includes a detailed company report with supporting documents dealing with Confederate activities and iron shipbuilding in general and also specific details of the rams and drawings and specifications of other ships built by Laird for the Confederacy. An Account Record Book shows the price paid for every Confederate ship built by the company during this period, including the profits and detailed breakdown of costs. This correspondence and related contracts were most valuable in preparing the naval chapters. The second group of Laird Papers in the possession of Mrs. William Laird of Hereford, comprises some 2,300 documents covering the years 1834–63 and includes correspondence with Southern merchants, a complete list of vessels built at the Birkenhead Iron Works. Newspaper cuttings show Laird's connections with America long before the Civil War. Also included are John Laird's personal diaries, one of which gives details of the construction of the *Alabama*.

Palmerston Papers. Historical Manuscripts Commission, National Register of Archives, London. Useful for their reference to the activity of Confederate cruisers and British recognition of the South. Palmerston was cautious in dealing with the Confederate problem. He strongly objected to Adams's pressuring British officials over Confederate issues. The Palmerston Papers were especially useful to this study for Palmerston's contention that the *Alabama* was not actually fitted out in England and thus there was no violation of British or international law.

Schroder Papers. J. H. Schroder & Co. Ltd., 145 Leadenhall Street, London. Useful in that they evaluate the various types of bonds issued by the Confederates in Great Britain and indicate that this banking house had little faith in Confederate financial operations in Great Britain. A parcel of unissued cotton certificates are included with the papers. Good records, including accounts of practically all the bonds issued by the Confederacy are preserved. Very full details are given of the price of issue, redemption, dividend, allotment and other transactions relating to Confederate financial affairs.

Treasury Board Papers, Public Records Office, London. These papers, covering the period from 1860 to 1920, consist of 12,625 volumes, bundles, and boxes of original correspondence of the board, together with occasional minutes, reports, etc. Of special value were T 1/6445 and A/16196. These contain the correspondence between Earl Russell and the law officers of the Crown regarding steps to be taken in the trial and conviction of persons engaged in fitting out the *Alexandra*. This correspondence is of importance to this work because of the Law Officers' attitude toward the *Alexandra*, which they regarded as a test case of the Foreign Enlistment Act.

War Office Reports and Miscellaneous Papers (W.O.). Public Records Office. Includes W.O. 33, 1853–96, 56 vols. Of these, two were essential to this study, W.O. 33/6 (1858) and W.O. 33/7 (1859). This material and, in particular, the two aforementioned references, comprise printed and bound War Office reports; those on arms and armaments, clothing, experiments and tests of new weapons, and the reports of select committees and commissions of enquiry were of value in the preparation of this book.

Printed Public Documents

American

Alabama *Claims: The Case of the United States*. Washington, D.C.: Government Printing Office, 1871. This material was useful for documented testimonials relating to the purchase of Confederate war ships in Great Britain during the Civil War. The United States used the Alabama *Claims* in its quarrel with Britain over an alleged lack of neutrality.

International Law: Lectures Delivered at the Naval War College. Washington, D.C.: Government Printing Office, 1895. Useful in that it helped to better understand the principles of international jurisprudence that a lawful maritime blockade of a port requires the actual presence of the blockading force. This material is also worthy of note in that it analyzes maritime and international law of the period as it relates to the purchase and building of Confederate ships in Great Britain.

Journal of the Congress of the Confederate States of America, 1861–1865. 7 vols. Washington, D.C.: Government Printing Office, 1904–5. Are important for the "Minutes of the Confederate Congress (Senate)," giving a detailed study of the day to day proceedings of the Confederate Congress, its attitudes and policy toward finance and purchasing in Great Britain. Within this reference, the following two sources were also helpful:

1. Acts and Resolutions, 3d sess., Provisional Congress. These contain essential details of the Confederate government authorization to issue treasury notes and to impose a war tax to strengthen Confederate finance abroad.

2. Public Laws of the C.S.A., act of 18 April 1862 and act of 21 April 1862. These show that Memminger feared to sell cotton on account of the possible political effects at home and that the United States would make the blockade more effective if an attempt was made to take cotton out of Confederate ports. Memminger asserted that cotton stored by the Government in plantations was the best policy to pursue in underwriting Confederate financial policy abroad.

Richardson, James D., ed. *Compilation of Messages and Papers of the Confederacy, Including Diplomatic Correspondence, 1861–1865.* Nashville: U.S. Publishing Co., 1905. Important for its diplomatic correspondence. Biographical sketches and policy positions of key Confederate leaders are included. These volumes are compilations only, without comment, but are a valuable record of the sentiments and opinions of Jefferson Davis and other Confederate leaders toward finance and purchasing in Great Britain. The chronological arrangement of the letters and documents made it possible to synchronise Confederate correspondence with *O.R.N.*, *O.R.* and with other official exchanges. In this way the attitudes of Great Britain toward the Confederacy could be better inferred.

U.S. Congress. House of Representatives. *Confederate Property in Europe.* Document no. 304, serial no. 134, 40th Cong., 2d sess. Washington, D.C.: Government Printing Office, 1868. Contains information concerning the efforts of the U.S. government to recover Confederate property abroad.

U.S. Department of State. *Diplomatic Correspondence.* Papers Relating *to Foreign Affairs.* 12 vols. Washington, D.C.: Government Printing Office, 1861–69. This source contains reference to the published correspondence of the Department of State on the subject of Confederate activities in Great Britain and also information relating to the *Florida* and *Alabama* and the personnel connected with these vessels.

The War of the Rebellion: A Compilation of the Official Records of the Union and Confederate Armies (*O.R.*). 130 vols. Washington,

D.C.: Government Printing Office, 1880–1901. *Official Records of the Union and Confederate Navies in the War of the Rebellion* (*O.R.N.*). 31 vols. Washington, D.C.: Government Printing Office (1894–1927). These official records represent a chief source of information regarding the administration, organization, and activities of the Confederate armies and the navy. These edited sets constitute a rich mine of statistical data and other valuable information that has never been fully tapped by scholars. Specific researches are rendered easy by the use of the detailed indexes. A defect of the works is the absence of references to the present whereabouts of the original documents, but this defect is not serious since the transcripts when compared to some of the original sources, are found to be quite accurate and comprehensive. In relation to Confederate finance and purchasing in Great Britain, the Army records (*O.R.*) fall roughly into the following groups:

1. Correspondence between the Confederate secretary of the treasury with persons engaged in financial or purchasing operations abroad. These comprise "Foreign Correspondence" relating to the building of Confederate vessels in Great Britain and correspondence from Mason and Slidell and others relating to loans and the sale of cotton.

2. Financial records of the Confederate State Department including accounts of Confederate foreign finance and purchasing agents.

3. Financial records of the Confederate War Department including correspondence on the procurement of supplies and equipment for the Confederate army.

4. Records concerning the attempts of the United States government to recover Confederate property abroad and their rationale for doing so. Included are documents relating to suits generated in England against Theodore D. Wagner, James T. Welsman, Charles K. Prioleau, and William L. Trenholm, members of the firm of Messrs. Fraser, Trenholm & Co., Liverpool.

5. The War Department papers, also contained in *O.R.*, tend to be fragmentary; information on specific finance and procurement subjects is frequently incomplete, but they do contain some useful material especially dealing with ordnance, its manufacture, procurement and use.

Of the Official Records of the Navy (*O.R.N.*), the Bulloch papers, comprising some 120 documents in all, were particularly helpful in preparing this book. For purposes of this research, these papers were divided into two groups: (1) Instructions from the secretary of the Confederate States Navy, Stephen R. Mallory, to Captain Bulloch, and (2) Bulloch's reports to Mallory on his mission in Great Britain. Volumes 1 and 3, series 1, contain much of Bulloch's correspondence dealing with the *Florida* and *Alabama* and in addition contain photographs of Confederate cruisers. The naval chapters of this work could not have been written without volumes 2 and 3 of series 2. Volume 2 contains practically all of Bulloch's correspondence with the Confederate Navy Department in Richmond, letters from and to the

Confederate commissioners and orders and written advices to the numerous naval officers who served the C.S.A. in Britain. Volume 3 contains helpful correspondence between Commissioner John Slidell and Secretary of State Judah P. Benjamin relating to financial and commercial matters.

British

Foreign Enlistment Act. London: George Eyre and Andrew Strahan, Printers to the King, 1819. Laid down the principles that were the subject of so much debate during the Civil War in relation to the building and outfitting of Confederate ships in Great Britain.

Great Britain. *Parliamentary Papers. House of Commons and House of Lords.* London, 1861–65. These were most helpful in that they contained key correspondence exchanged between Adams and Russell with regard to Confederate naval activities in Great Britain. These papers also reflected British political and public opinion with regard to Confederate financial and purchasing activities in Great Britain during the great conflict.

Great Britain. *Hansard's Parliamentary Debates,* ser. 3. London: Cornelius Buck, 1830–91. Especially useful for an analysis of Huse's efforts to purchase arms and munitions in Great Britain and for an overview of Parliamentary Debates where Confederate matters were discussed. The years covering 1861–65 were the most useful.

Navy List Corrected to 20 December, 1855. London: John Murray, 1856. Gives brief history of *Rappahannoch,* formerly H.M.S. *Victor,* a screw gunboat originally in the service of the British navy.

Patent Office Papers. London: H.M. Stationery Office, Love and Malcomson, 1855–65. Include details and particulars relating to inventions and provisional specifications submitted to the Patent Office by inventors and form an excellent source of technical and mechanical information about British military equipment used by the Confederates.

Queen's Proclamation of Neutrality, 1861. Quoted from the *Times* [London], 15 May 1861. Represented an attempt to apply the Foreign Enlistment Act to the American Civil War.

General and Special Accounts

Adams, Charles Francis. *A Cycle of Adams Letters, 1861–1865.* Edited by Worthington C. Ford. 2 vols. Boston: Houghton Mifflin, 1920. Useful as a primary source of information relating to Union diplomatic activity in London throughout the war.

Adams, E. D. *Great Britain and the American Civil War.* 2 vols. New

York: Longmans Green, 1925. A well-balanced history of Anglo-American relations during the Civil War and was most important for this work. This is the first definitive American history that effectively used British primary source material.

Adams, James T. *Dictionary of American History*. New York: Scribner's, 1951. Helpful for statistics on blockade-running.

Albaugh, W. H., and Simmons, E. N. *Confederate Arms*. Harrisburg, Pa.: Stackpole Co., 1957. A most practical source of information. This is a comprehensive guide to almost every weapon the Confederate soldier fought with; ordinance manufactured in Great Britain is only touched on briefly.

Alexander, E. P. *Military Memoirs of a Confederate*. New York: Scribner's, 1907. Helpful for its comments on the administration of the Ordnance Bureau and the War Department together with critical descriptions of the quality and quantity of ordnance equipment supplied to Confederate troops.

Angle, Paul M. *The American Story*. Great Neck, N.Y.: Channel Press, 1956. Considers Confederate financial interests only briefly, but the organization of material was of value, especially in describing the economic relationship between the North and South in the mid-nineteenth century.

Ashworth, Henry. *Cotton: Its Cultivation, Manufacture and Uses*. (A paper read before the Society of Arts, London, 10 Mar. 1858) Manchester: J. Collins, 1858. Stresses the agricultural nature of the South and surveys the relationship of Britain and France with the South before the Civil War and Great Britain's need for cotton and the effect the lack of it would have on the British economy.

Bailey, Thomas A. *A Diplomatic History of the American People*. New York: Appleton-Century-Crofts, 1955. Useful for Lincoln's proclamation of the blockade and its reception in England. It proved advantageous also for background material and the bibliography provided sound suggestions for further reading.

Baxter, James P. *The Introduction of Ironclad Warships*. Cambridge: Harvard University Press, 1933. The engineering and technical features of ironclads are detailed together with the reasons for the Confederate ironclad building policy.

Beaman, C. E. *The National and Private "Alabama Claims."* Washington, D.C.: W. H. Moore, 1871. Provided sound, detailed information concerning Confederate ships, but tends to be biased in favor of the United States. In particular, it considers the case of the United States against Great Britain over the *Alabama* and Great Britain's counterclaim.

Bernard, Montague. *Neutrality of Great Britain*. London: Longmans Green, Reader & Dyer, 1870. Helpful in writing the naval chapters. Particularly helpful in that it deals with the removal of the *Victor* from Admiralty service as defective and beyond economic repair. This vessel later became the *Rappahannock*.

Bigelow, John. *Retrospections of an Active Life.* 5 vols. New York: Baber and Taylor, 1909. A pro-Northern general account of Confederate finance and purchasing in Great Britain. Useful as a Northern subjective analysis of Confederate affairs in Great Britain.

Blum, John M.; Catton, Bruce; Morgan, Edmund S.; Schlesenger, Arthur M., Jr.; Stampp, Kenneth M.; and Woodward, C. Vann. *The National Experience.* New York: Harcourt, Brace and World, 1968. An excellent survey history of the United States. Useful for its analysis of how the South's virtual monopoly of the world's cotton supply was presumed to make England a willing Confederate ally.

Bradlee, Francis. *Blockade Running during the Civil War.* Salem, Mass., The Essex Institute, 1925. Of value for its interpretation of Lincoln's proclamation of the blockade; includes the opinions of naval authorities who considered that the blockade could not be rigorously enforced and would be effective only on paper.

Bragdon, H. W., and McCutchen, S. P. *History of a Free People.* New York: Macmillan, 1954. A well-balanced general history of the United States, of value for the statistical data relating to the growth of the cotton industry in the South before the Civil War.

Bulloch, James D. *The Secret Service of the Confederate States in Europe.* 2 vols. New York: Putnam, 1883. A most important work, complementary to the *O.R.N.* The author traces the development of the Confederate navy; the greater part of his narrative is based on personal knowledge, technical correspondence, official reports, and postwar legal proceedings. Occasionally factual accounts are confused by personal disgressions. Nevertheless, Bulloch gives continuity and meaning to much of the official naval correspondence on which his work is based.

Callahan, James M. *Diplomatic History of the Southern Confederacy.* Baltimore, Johns Hopkins Press, 1901. An important work that was the first good history of Confederate activities abroad. Callahan is his strongest when dealing with diplomacy. However, some of his financial statements and accounting data are confusing and sometimes inaccurate. The struggles of the Confederate agents abroad and the difficult problems they faced received detailed treatment. Callahan is very good when emphasizing the impact the Confederates had on British foreign policy. Unfortunately, the book lacks a bibliography.

Capers, Henry D. *Life and Times of C. C. Memminger.* Richmond: Everett Waddey Co., 1893. An important work, showing how Memminger tried to balance the Confederate budget. It cannot be considered the definitive work on this statesman. Although the author justifies the Confederate loan policy, he fails to treat adequately the economics of inflation and its eventual effect on the Southern economy.

Case, Lynn. *The United States and France.* Philadelphia: University of Pennsylvania Press, 1970. Useful as a most comprehensive study of the history of the United States and France, especially as it relates to overall Confederate activity in France including the Erlanger Loan.

Channing, Edward. *History of the United States.* 6 vols. New York: Macmillan, 1927–30. Provided some useful background information relating to Confederate diplomatic activity in Great Britain.

Childs, Arney R., ed. *The Private Journal of Henry William Ravenel, 1859–1877.* Columbia: University of South Carolina Press, 1947. Discusses to what extent intervention was considered by Great Britain. Useful for its consideration of the extent of Confederate support in Britain.

Cleveland, Henry. *Alexander H. Stephens in Public and Private.* Philadelphia: National Publishing Co., 1866. Shows how Stephens favored the rights of the States and his position in relation to the Negro question. Of importance because the author shows that Stephens (the Confederate vice president), considered England jealous of the growth of the United States and thus unlikely to assist either side.

Commager, H. S. *The Blue and the Gray.* 2 vols. Indianapolis: Bobbs-Merrill, 1950. Has a good evaluation of the "This is war" letter written by Adams to Russell.

Cullop, Charles P. *Confederate Propaganda in Europe, 1861–1865.* Coral Gables, Fl.: University of Miami Press, 1969. Useful for its analysis of the *Index* and its founder, Henry Hotze, and the important role propaganda played in the overall Confederate effort in Great Britain.

Dalzell, George W. *The Flight from the Flag.* Chapel Hill: University of North Carolina Press, 1940. Contains interesting comments regarding several of the Confederate cruisers; however, this is not a well-documented book and contains little detailed information of value to this work.

Davis, Charles S. *Colin J. McRae: Confederate Financial Agent.* Tuscaloosa, Ala.: Confederate Publishing Co., 1961. Good background material in analyzing McRae's financial activities in Europe and the scope of his overall administrative and leadership responsibility, especially in regard to the management of the funds derived from Erlanger loan and the supervision of the plan of 1864.

Davis, Jefferson. *The Rise and Fall of the Confederate Government.* 2 vols. New York: D. Appleton & Co., 1881. Written with the primary purpose of showing that the Southern states had the rightful power to secede from the Union. Passion and prejudice is evident, but important material for historians is included. The author's survey of the causes, conduct, and outcome of the war is sometimes superficial, and his knowledge of Confederate naval activities is slight—he repeatedly refers to Bulloch as "Bullock." The president had confidence in Mallory as head of the Navy Department. Was useful for background material in considering naval matters.

De Leon, T. C. *Four Years in Rebel Capitals.* Mobile, Ala.: Gossip Printing Co., 1890. An interesting account of life in the Confederacy, based on original notes.

Dietz, August. *The Postal Service of the Confederate States of America.* Richmond: Dietz Printing Co., 1929. An interesting study of the Confederate postal department, the postal-stamps printed in England, and the paper and presses for producing stamps exported from Europe to the Confederacy.

Dodd, W. E. *Jefferson Davis.* Philadelphia: G. W. Jacobs & Co., 1904. Of only incidental importance to this work, but it throws some light on the types of ships that could have been manned and armed for trading purposes with Europe and how the necessary money could have been raised for such a transport navy, if the situation was properly managed by allocating the proper resources and assigning a higher priority to it.

Dupuy, R. E. and T. N. *Military Heritage of America.* New York: McGraw-Hill, 1955. A good work, though sometimes wordy; the development of ideas is sometimes confusing. It was helpful for information about the blockade and its military importance.

Durkin, Joseph T. *Stephen R. Mallory.* Chapel Hill: University of North Carolina Press, 1954. The first substantive biography of the Confederate secretary of the navy. Provided many good documentary sources and some new material, all useful in the preparation of the naval chapters.

Eaton, Clement. *A History of the Southern Confederacy.* New York: Macmillan, 1954. An excellent one-volume treatment of the would-be nation. A balanced work.

Faulkner, H. U., and Kepner, T. *America: Its History and People.* New York: McGraw-Hill, 1947. Examines the belief held by Jefferson Davis that the war was not brought about by a single cause but by a long series of irritations between two sections of a population with directly opposed economic and social systems.

Fessenden, Frances. *Life and Public Service of William Pitt Fessenden.* 2 vols. Boston: Houghton Mifflin, 1907. Helpful in that it considers an account of the Confederate debt and Southern monetary policy as viewed from Washington.

Fielder, Herbert J. *Life and Times of Joseph E. Brown.* Springfield, Mass.: Springfield Printing Co., 1883. Useful for its treatment of the extent and effect of the blockade on the people of the South and the necessity of importations from Europe.

Foster, John W. *A Century of American Diplomacy.* New York: Houghton Mifflin, 1901. Useful for its interesting discussion of Mallory's overall naval policy.

Fuller, J. F. C. *Grant and Lee.* Bloomington: Indiana University Press, 1957. Was used for information regarding the unsystematic and uncoordinated purchasing methods of the Confederate agents, especially in the first year of the war and also the attitude of Jefferson Davis toward foreign purchasing operations.

George, J. N. *English Guns and Rifles.* Plantersville, N.C.: Small Arms Technical Publishing Co., 1947. Of assistance in writing the ordnance chapter, since it includes a complete history of the evolution of both the shotgun and rifle. Also useful for its treatment of English guns and rifles shipped to the Confederacy and for its consideration of the Royal Small Arms Factory at Enfield.

Goff, Richard D. *Confederate Supply*. Durham, N.C.: Duke University Press, 1969. Another recent study of value. It considers an analysis of Confederate supply management and the problems involved in logistically supporting Confederate forces.

Gorgas, General Josiah. *The Civil War Diary of . . .* Edited by Frank E. Vandiver. University: University of Alabama Press, 1947. Was very helpful for its excellent descriptions of the shortages of war material in the Southern States during the Civil War, the importations of domestic items and the quantity, quality and manner of performance of British artillery and small arms.

Greeley, Horace. *The American Conflict*. 2 vols. Hartford, Conn.: O. D. Case, 1867. Useful for its treatment of Bermuda during the Civil War and the activity of blockade-runners in and around Bermuda.

Hamilton, Henry. *The Industrial Revolution in Scotland*. Oxford, Clarendon Press, 1932. Considers the effects of the cotton famine in Scotland, the number of operatives that were affected and to what extent.

Henderson, W. O. *The Lancashire Cotton Famine, 1861–1865*. Manchester: University of Manchester Press, 1934. A clearly written study of the cotton famine and how it affected Lancashire, dependent on a single source of supply. The text is authoritative and was most valuable. A personal interview with Professor Henderson was of considerable value.

Henry, R. S. *The Story of the Confederacy*, New York: Home Library Edition, 1943. A standard work of reference on the Civil War; mainly concerned with military and naval affairs.

Hill, James P. *Sea Dogs of the Sixties*. Minneapolis: University of Minnesota Press, 1935. Presents biographies of four Union and four Confederate naval officers. Hill reflects on the many neutrality problems that were raised by the naval activities of both Confederate and Union naval officers. *O.R.N.* has been used by the author in the preparation of his biographies. A personal interview with General Hill was most informative.

Huse, Caleb. *The Supplies for the Confederate Army: How They Were Obtained in Europe and How Paid For*. Boston: T. R. Marvin & Son, 1904. Informative as a contemporary account, but could have been more detailed. The types of supplies purchased, purchasing policies, and methods of payment are covered only very briefly.

Jones, John B. *A Rebel War Clerk's Diary*. 2 vols. Edited by Howard Swiggert. New York: Old Hickory Bookshop, 1935. A contemporary account of the Civil War; vividly presents the hopes and fears of the Confederacy as seen from Richmond. Inclined to the chatty and unfortunately not free from personal bias.

Jones, Wilbur D. *The Confederate Rams at Birkenhead*. Tuscaloosa, Ala.: Confederate Publishing Co., 1961. Another recent work. Especially useful in analyzing the British rationale in seizing the Laird rams.

Kantor, M. *Gettysburg*. New York: Random House, 1952. Gives descriptions of Whitworth cannon firing power and how these cannons acted under battle conditions.

Lefroy, General. *Hand-book for Field Service, 1866.* London: H.M. Stationery Office, 1866. Good descriptions of the barrel of the Blakely gun and technical details of its principles and manufacture.

Macartney, Clarence E. *Mr. Lincoln's Admirals.* New York: Funk and Wagnalls, 1956. An excellent history of the leadership of the federal navy. It displays considerable insight into the major personalities of the Union navy; a parallel work for the C.S.N. is needed.

McCordoch, Robert S. *The Yankee Cheese Box.* Philadelphia: Dorrance, 1938. Makes excellent use of newspaper sources in England and America and includes a good history of the technical development of ironclads.

McPherson, Edward. *The Political History of the United States of America during the Great Rebellion.* Washington, D.C.: Philip & Solomons, 1864. Constitutes a classified summary of the legislation of the 36th Congress, Executive, Judicial, Political, and Military. A similar summary of the Confederate Congress is included. Most useful as insight into the workings of Congress regarding their attitude toward the War.

Marvin, Winthrop L. *The American Merchant Marine.* New York: Scribner's, 1919. Contained a useful analysis of the damaging effect the Confederate cruisers had on the merchant vessels of the North.

Mason, Virginia. *The Public Life and Diplomatic Correspondence of James M. Mason with Some Personal History of His Daughter.* Roanoke, Va.: Stone Printing and Manufacturing Co., 1903. A detailed description of Confederate operations abroad, the correspondence between Mason and Benjamin was especially important for details of financial matters, as was similar correspondence between Spence and Mason and Slidell and Mason.

Meade, Robert D. *Judah P. Benjamin: Confederate Statesman.* New York: Oxford University Press, 1943. Was most helpful because of Benjamin's intimate association with the major personalities concerned with Confederate finance and purchasing abroad.

Merli, Frank J. *Great Britain and the Confederate Navy.* Bloomington: Indiana University Press, 1971. A recent study of Confederate naval activity in Great Britain. A good balanced treatment of the subject making adequate use of British sources.

Miller, Francis Trevelyan. *The Photographic History of the Civil War.* New York: the Review of Reviews Co., 1911. Excellent informative photographs of equipment purchased by the Confederates in Great Britain.

Millis, Walter. *Arms and Men.* London: Lowe & Brydone, 1958. Contains some good descriptions of the developments (following the Crimea), of the rifling of cannon, leading to an increase in the ranges and destructive powers of cannon. Also useful in analyzing the effect that the blockade had on the Confederacy: cut off from the outside world and all exterior sources of supply, reduced to a state of collapse, the Confederacy died a slow and painful death.

Moran, Benjamin. *The Journals of* . . . Edited by Sarah A. Wallace and Frances E. Gillespie. 2 vols. Chicago: University of Chicago Press, 1949. Gives the detailed observations of Benjamin Moran, the first secretary of the U.S. embassy in London. Useful for its consideration of Union diplomatic activity there. The material, however, is subject to considerable bias against the South.

Owsley, Frank L. *King Cotton Diplomacy*. 2d ed. rev. by Harriet Chappell Owsley. Chicago: University of Chicago Press, 1959. Uses new material and new combinations of old material to draw new conclusions. The author has given order and purpose to Confederate activities in Great Britain and the role cotton played. Owsley shows how Confederate agents sought British repudiation of the blockade and at other times sought friendly mediation. Of all the secondary works studied, this was the most helpful. Owsley was the first to use effectively the *Official Records* of both the army and navy to any extent, and his bibliographies, footnotes, and index are rich in leads for further study. An outstanding contribution to the literature of the subject.

Parkes, Oscar. *British Battleships*. London: Seeley Service & Co., 1956. Provides an outline of British armored ships from 1860–1950 and was useful for information regarding early ironclads. The scale drawings are misleading because inaccurate; the photographs are excellent.

Perry, Milton F. *Infernal Machines: The Story of Confederate Submarine and Mine Warfare*. Baton Rouge: Louisiana State University Press, 1965. A well-written, interesting, and detailed account of unusual Confederate devices, such as the torpedo. Useful in preparing material on miscellaneous purchases. Exchange of correspondence with Mr. Perry was most helpful.

Peyton, John Lewis. *The American Crisis, or Pages from the Notebook of a State Agent during the Civil War*. London: Saunders Otley & Co., 1867. Gives some lively accounts of how the war provided merchants and blockade-runners with opportunities for making quick if hazardous profits.

Rains, George W. *History of the Confederate Powder Works: Address Delivered before the Confederate Survivors Association 26 April 1882, Augusta, Georgia, 1882*. Newburgh, N.Y.: Newburgh Daily News Print, 1882. Provided a statistical analysis of the estimated amount of niter sent to the Confederate powder factories at Augusta from Europe and how niter was shipped through the blockade.

Ramsdell, Charles W. *Laws of the Last Confederate Congress*. Durham, N.C.: Duke University Press, 1941. Gives details of negotiations with respect to the issue of Confederate loans.

Reed, E. J. *Our Iron-Clad Ships*. London: John Murray, 1869. Provided useful information on early British ironclads and the Laird rams. Unfortunately Reed did not have full use of the Laird papers.

Reilly, W. E. M. *Siege of Sebastopol: An Account of the Artillery Op-*

erations. London: George Eyre and William Spottiswoode, 1859. Gives details of the rifled Lancaster gun and other British ordnance used in the Crimea. Excellent for background material in developing the ordnance chapter.

Rhodes, James F. *History of the United States from the Compromise of 1850 to 1877.* New York: Harper & Macmillan, 1893–1906; reissued with an 8th vol. on the period 1877–96 by Macmillan, 1919. Details the reasons for the seizure of the *Alexandra,* mainly from the Northern point of view. Additional information regarding the *Florida* and the *Alabama,* and the United States efforts to persuade the British government to seize these ships was helpful.

Ripley, Warren. *Artillery and Ammunition of the Civil War.* New York: Van Nostrand, 1970. An excellent recent work, it represents a detailed consideration of British artillery pieces used in the Civil War.

Rollason, E. C. *Metallurgy for Engineers.* London: Edward Arnold, 1940. Most helpful for an understanding of the principles involved in forging iron and the use of scrap iron in shipbuilding. Rollason also was helpful for an understanding of the principles involved in manufacturing plate iron and its application to shipbuilding.

Roscoe, Theodore, and Freeman, Fred. *Picture History of the United States Navy.* New York: Scribner's, 1956. Of value in the diagrammatic study of the torpedo invented by Capt. M. F. Maury.

Russell, Lord John. *The Later Correspondence of . . . , 1840–70.* Edited by G. P. Gooch. 2 vols. New York: Longmans Green, 1925. Contains key correspondence of the British foreign secretary, relative to Confederate affairs.

Russell, Sir William H. *The British Expedition to the Crimea.* London: Routledge, 1858. Provided technical details of the British guns and equipment first used in the Crimea.

———. *My Diary, North and South.* 2 vols. London: Bradbury & Evans, 1863. The value of this work to this study is its day-to-day record of events affecting Confederate activity in Great Britain and at home. The author was American correspondent for the *Times* of London during the Civil War.

Scharf, J. Thomas. *History of the Confederate States Navy from Its Organization to the Surrender of Its Last Vessel.* New York: Rogers & Sherwood 1887. Very one-sided but good—indeed the only—early comprehensive history of the Confederate navy. It includes detailed accounts of engagements fought, blockade-running, privateers, and the ironclads. The author's account of the formation of the Confederate Navy Department and the problems it faced was used in the preparation of the naval chapters.

Schwab, John C. *The Confederate States of America, 1861–65: A Financial and Industrial History of the South during the Civil War.* New York: Scribner's, 1901. This is a most important and original work, and although difficult reading and not always well organized, it is probably the finest Confederate economic history of the war, it is a comprehensive and scholarly treatment of a complex subject.

Schwab's quantitative explanations of how inflation in the Confederacy took place are not entirely consistent, but he treats personalities fairly and rightly suggests that the predominant responsibility for the financial failure of the Confederacy rested with Congress, not with Jefferson Davis personally. He was a strong critic of Erlanger and believed he milked the Confederacy. Schwab, a superb economic historian of this period, has made a most outstanding contribution to the literature of the subject.

Sellers, James L. *An Interpretation of Civil War Finance.* New York: Macmillan, 1925. Provides statistics of expenditures of the Confederacy. Good reference material for Confederate domestic fiscal policy.

Semmes, Raphael. *Memoirs of Secret Service Afloat.* Baltimore: Kelly Piet & Co., 1869. A factual account of the career of Semmes as a C.S.N. officer during the war. Useful for information concerning the cruiser *Alabama,* which he commanded.

Seward, Frederick W. *Seward at Washington, as Senator and Secretary of State.* New York: Derby & Miller, 1891. Argues that Great Britain furnished the Confederate States with most of the blockade-runners and that such action was both illegal and immoral, a subjective work of little value to this study.

Singer, C.; Holmyard, E. J.; Hall, A. R.; and Williams, T. I. *History of Technology.* Oxford: Clarendon Press, 1958. Useful for a technological understanding of Whitworth's contributions to machine tool equipment and how this equipment furthered the production of more accurate and high-powered cannon.

Smith, Ernest A. *The History of the Confederate Treasury.* Washington, D.C.: Southern History Association, 1901. Contains useful information on the shipping of cotton through the blockade the produce Loan, the Erlanger Loan and treasury management of blockade-running. The scope of the work is, however, mainly limited to domestic fiscal policy, and consideration of British financial operations is inadequate.

Soley, James R. *The Navy in the Civil War: The Blockade and the Cruisers.* New York: Scribner's, 1883. Helpful in writing the naval chapters in that it contains interesting information on the status and resources of the C.S.N. at the outbreak of war, the difficulties it had to face, and the steps required to overcome these difficulties. The author's views are somewhat controversial, but the work was especially helpful in relation to the cruisers.

Spence, James. *The American Union and the Causes of the Disruption.* London: R. Bentley, 1861. Stresses the fundamental differences between North and South, while favoring the latter. This work is also an attempt to persuade the governments of Europe, especially Great Britain, to fully support the Southern States. Very pro-Southern in its orientation.

Sprout, Harold and Margaret. *The Rise of American Naval Power.* Princeton: Princeton University Press, 1939. Shows how Lincoln loyally supported Gideon Welles in naval matters and resisted all efforts to weaken the blockading fleet. This book also includes a brief but illuminating survey of Confederate naval strategy.

Still, William N., Jr. *Confederate Shipbuilding.* Athens: University of Georgia Press, 1969. A recent study that was useful in explaining the Confederate need for ships other than cruisers and ironclads, notably blockade-runners.

———. *Iron Afloat: The Story of the Confederate Armorclads.* Nashville, Tenn.: Vanderbilt University Press, 1971. A more recent study, useful in analyzing the technical and diplomatic aspects surrounding the construction of Confederate iron ships in Great Britain.

Storey, F. S., and Jones, C. *A Text Book of the Construction and Manufacture of the Rifled Ordnance in the British Service.* London: George E. Eyre and William Spottiswoode, 1872. Most informative on the construction and manufacture of rifled ordance in Great Britain during the Civil War. Although rather technical, this is a highly useful work for studies of British ordnance used by the Confederates.

Studenski, Paul, and Krooss, Herman E. *Financial History of the United States: Fiscal, Monetary, Banking and Tariff, Including Financial Administration and State and Local Finance.* New York: McGraw-Hill, 1952. Helpful in preparing the chapter on the Erlanger loan and the plan of 1864 in that it presented a comparison of the Erlanger loan to Union issues in terms of their relative purchasing power.

Thompson, Samuel B. *Confederate Purchasing Operations Abroad.* Chapel Hill: University of North Carolina Press, 1935. An informative and critical work. Unfortunately, the author, as is the case with some earlier Confederate historians, did not go abroad, and thus many important sources were not open to him. This is the only published work entirely devoted to the imports of the Confederacy but contains very little not already covered by Owsley's *King Cotton Diplomacy,* under whose guidance Thompson's work was written as a dissertation.

Todd, Richard Cecil. *Confederate Finance,* Athens: University of Georgia Press, 1954. A key work describing how Federal specie located in the mints and customs houses was confiscated, the organization of the Treasury Department, domestic loans, treasury notes, tariffs, and taxes. The author is mostly concerned with domestic finance, and his treatment of Confederate fiscal policy in Europe is weak.

Turner, Gordon B. *A History of Military Affairs in Western Society since the Eighteenth Century.* New York: Harcourt, Brace, 1953. Is a well-organized and detailed history of military affairs, particularly useful for its study of the Civil War as the first war of its magnitude in which rifled weapons were generally used and also the first war in which breech-loading and magazine arms came into use.

Vandiver, Frank E., ed. *Confederate Blockade-Running through Bermuda, 1861–1865: Letters and Cargo Manifests.* Austin: University of Texas Press, 1947. Useful in that it stresses the early concern of the Confederate government with the problem of obtaining supplies from abroad, and Davis's awareness of the lack of Southern resources. This work includes the letter books of Bourne and Stansbury but lacks the detailed commentary necessary for their complete understanding.

Waddell, James I. *C.S.S.* Shenandoah: *The Memoirs of Lieutenant Commander James I. Waddell.* Edited by James D. Horan. New York: Crown Publishers, 1965. Useful for an analysis of Waddell and the high seas exploits of the *Shenandoah.*

Walker, James B. *The Epic of American Industry.* New York: Harper, 1949. Presents an interesting analysis of the economic causes and origins of the civil war and describes in some detail the withdrawal of Southern bank balances from Northern banks before the Civil War.

Ward, Sir A. W., and Gooch, G. P. *The Cambridge History of the British Foreign Policy, 1783–1919.* Cambridge: Cambridge University Press, 1922–23. Helpful for its discussion of belligerent's rights under British law and also the character and treatment of belligerents consistent with international law of the period. A personal interview with G. P. Gooch was most stimulating.

Wary, Colonel C. *An Historical Summary of the Breech-Loading System.* London: George E. Eyre and William Spottiswoode, 1870. Summarizes the advantages and disadvantages of the breech-loading system and was helpful in studying the methods of manufacturing Confederate cannon and the specifications for cannon procured in Great Britain.

Wender, Herbert. *Southern Commercial Conventions, 1837–59.* Baltimore: Johns Hopkins Press, 1930. Useful in describing the rationale of a proposed weekly ferry line of steamships between Chesapeake Bay and Milford Haven. Emphasizes the importance of Anglo-Southern commerce before the Civil War. It was suspected that such a scheme as this and others similar to it would form the nucleus of a future Southern navy.

West, Richard S. *Gideon Welles.* New York: Bobbs-Merrill, 1943. Useful as a study of Welles's efforts to launch a program of ironclad construction to prevent Confederate ironclads from disrupting the blockade and to attack blockade-runners.

Wharton, Francis. *A Digest of International Law.* 3 vols. Washington, D.C.: Government Printing Office, 1886. Provides details of the act passed by the Confederate Congress concerning letters of mark, prizes, and prize goods. This act led to a building program of Confederate cruisers and raiders in Great Britain.

White, Horace. *"Fossetts": A Record of Two Centuries of Engineering.* Bromborough, Cheshire: Fawcett, Preston & Co., 1958. Useful for the role played by "Fossetts" in the design and construction of the engines used in the *Florida.*

Wilson, Lt. W. *The Story of the Gun.* Woolwich: Royal Artillary Institution, 1944. Though rather brief, this was useful as a clear and readable treatment of British heavy ordnance. It describes some of the British cannon the South used during the war and details their particular features and usefulness under fire.

INDEX